The International Institute for

GW00362240

STRATEGIC SURVEY
2000/2001

Published by

OXFORD
UNIVERSITY PRESS

for
**The International Institute
for Strategic Studies**
Arundel House
13–15 Arundel Street
London WC2R 3DX
United Kingdom

Strategic Survey 2000/2001

Published by
OXFORD
UNIVERSITY PRESS

for
The International Institute for Strategic Studies

Arundel House, 13–15 Arundel Street,
London WC2R 3DX, United Kingdom

Director .... Dr John Chipman
Editor .... Sidney Bearman

Deputy Editor .... Jonathan Stevenson
Assistant Editors .... Susan Bevan,
.... Jill Dobson
Assistant Editor: Maps .... Isabelle Williams
Research Assistant .... Emma Sullivan

Project Manager,
Design and Production .... Mark Taylor

This publication has been prepared by the
Director of the Institute and his Staff, who
accept full responsibility for its contents,
which describe and analyse events up to 29
March 2001. These do not, and indeed
cannot, represent a consensus of views
among the worldwide membership of the
Institute as a whole.

First published .... May 2001

ISBN 0-19-850883-2
ISSN 0459-7230

© The International Institute
for Strategic Studies 2001

Strategic Survey (ISSN 0459-7230) is published
annually by Oxford University Press.

Payment is required with all orders and
subscriptions. Prices include air-speeded
delivery to Australia, Canada, India, Japan, New
Zealand and the USA. Delivery elsewhere is by
surface mail. Air-mail rates are available on
request. Please add sales tax to prices quoted.
Payment may be made by cheque or Eurocheque
(payable to Oxford University Press), National
Girobank (account 500 1056), credit card
(MasterCard, Visa, American Express, Diners),
direct debit (please send for details) or UNESCO
coupons. Bankers: Barclays Bank plc. PO Box
333, Oxford, UK, code 20-65-18, account
00715654.

Claims for non-receipt must be made within four
months of dispatch/order (whichever is later).

Please send subscription orders to the Journals
Subscription Department, Oxford University
Press, Great Clarendon Street, Oxford, OX2 6DP,
UK. *Tel* +44 (0)1865 267907. *Fax* +44 (0)1865
267485. *e-mail* jnl.orders@oup.co.uk

Strategic Survey is distributed by Mercury
International, 365 Blair Road, Avenel, NJ 07001,
USA. Periodical postage paid at Rahway, New
Jersey, USA, and additional entry points.

US POSTMASTER: Send address corrections to
Strategic Survey, c/o Mercury International,
365 Blair Road, Avenel, NJ 07001, USA.

Abstracted and indexed by: Reasearch Base
Online, PAIS.

PRINTED IN THE UK by Bell & Bain Ltd, Glasgow.

Contents

Perspectives 5

Strategic Policy Issues 13
    Defending the US (and Allies?)
        from Ballistic Missile Attack 13
    Military Transformation: A Report Card 23
    The Frayed Nuclear Non-Proliferation Regime 33
    The Future of Peacekeeping 44

The Americas 55
    The United States: Election Year Surrealism 58
    Latin America and the Caribbean:
        In Search of Good Government 70
    Mexico: A New and Difficult Beginning 87

Europe 95
    Widening Western Europe's Horizons, but Slowly 97
    Russia: Strengthening the State 109
    Healing the Wounds in the Balkans 124

Middle East 137
    The Crumbling Peace Effort 139
    Syria: Continuity and Change 153
    Iraq Sanctions: Towards a New Policy 160

Asia 169
    China: Struggling with Change 171
    Japan 2000: No New Dawn Yet 182
    Ebbing Tensions on the Korean Peninsula 191
    Institutional Torpor and Political Debility
        in South-east Asia 199
    South Asia: Activity Without Progress 210

Africa 223
    Congo: Less Fighting, but No Peace 227
    Sierra Leone: The Collapse of Regional Stability 235
    South Africa and Zimbabwe: Failures of Leadership 245
    Up and Down on the Horn 254

Prospectives 265

Strategic Geography 2000/2001 I
    Europe II
    Middle East V
    Asia VIII
    Central Asia XII
    Latin America XIII
    Africa XIV
    Global Trends XX

List of Tables and Maps

Map 1 The Americas 56

Map 2 Europe 96

Table 1 European Defence Spending 105

Table 2 European Spending on
Defence Equipment Procurement 106

Table 3 European Spending on Public Defence R&D 106

Map 3 Middle East 138

Map 4 Asia 170

Map 5 Africa 224

Strategic Survey Online

Members of the IISS can access *Strategic Survey 2000–2001* online at http://www.iiss.org/pub/stratsur.asp. The address for subscribers is http://www3.oup.co.uk/stsurv, where they will first need to register using their subscriber number.

Perspectives

There are times when the world seems a stable place, when most governments around the globe move from year to year little changed. There are other times, however, when the sense of approaching change is palpable. So it was in 2000. It was a year of transition, when on every continent new leaders emerged, with philosophies of government different from their predecessors. Some of the significant changes were the result of the democratic process doing its usual good work, but they contained unusual drama and created unusual discontinuities. Others resulted from deaths, either sudden – through assassination or acute illness – or the expected ending of a long and fruitful life. In many cases, the new rulers represented a generational leap, bringing some hope of flexibility where there had mainly been rigidity. A third category of governmental change was precipitated by angry people provoked by the corruption or indifference of their leaders to drive them from power through massive, but remarkably peaceful, demonstrations of discontent.

There was nothing unusual in the fact that the United States went to the polls in November 2000 to elect its forty-third president. Nor was it unusual that, as a result, the reins of government were handed from one of the major parties to the other. What was extraordinary was the surreal nature of the election, the length of time it took to declare a winning candidate and the decision of the Supreme Court to thrust itself into the partisan fray, in effect sidestepping the electorate and deciding the outcome. Even without a clear mandate, however, the new president, George W. Bush, has given clear hints in his first months in office that he intends to pursue a substantially different direction than has the last administration. He may find, however, that this is beyond his ability because of the almost even split in the Congress.

In Russia, Vladimir Putin was elected president in March 2000 amidst high expectations. As a healthy young man replaced an ill old one, there were hopes of decisive action as opposed to erratic waffle. Anticipation that economic and social problems would be tackled replaced resigned acceptance that nothing would be done. By year's end, however, there was still a lingering uncertainty about whether his efforts would be concentrated on continuing the gradual evolution to a firmer market economy and a sounder democratic state. Many of his actions seem harbingers of a return to a more autocratic model of governance.

Two other elections were triumphs of transition, leaving behind parties that had ruled since their countries took on their contemporary form, although they elevated the new leaders to the top of very shaky pinnacles. In Mexico, Vincente Fox triumphed over the candidate of the Institutional Revolutionary Party (PRI), the party that had provided the country's leader for an uninterrupted 71 years. His coat-tails were not long enough, however, to pull enough opposition candidates into the Senate to ensure that he could easily effect his radical programmes. In Taiwan, Chen Shui-bian pried power from the hands of the *Kuomintang* (KMT), which had ruled for over 50 years, but he too faced a legislature in which his supporters were a minority. In a third significant election, abrupt change at the top in Israel reflected the U-turn in the country's mood. Barely 14 months after he was overwhelmingly elected on a platform dedicated to achieving peace with Israel's Arab neighbours, Ehud Barak was thrown out of office in favour of the vehemently anti-peace leader of the *Likud*, Ariel Sharon. In each of these cases major, if still undefined, change was assured.

Death played its role in the transition process. In Jordan, a stalwart in power so long that his philosophy of government was no mystery to anyone, gave way to his untried son. Whether the son can stay in control and what difference this change in generation will make still hangs in the balance. A more unexpected transfer of power from father to son occurred in the Democratic Republic of the Congo, where the assassination of Laurent Kabila brought Joseph Kabila to power. Although another untested leader, the younger Kabila has managed to inject a welcome sense of reality into efforts to bring peace to the Congo. In Japan the sudden death of Prime Minister Keizo Obuchi from a heart attack in April 2000 left a weak government even weaker when he was replaced by Yoshiro Mori. After less than a year of ineffective, even bumbling, inaction Mori's public approval rating plunged below 10% and guaranteed that before he has been in office 12 months there will be yet another change of leader for Japan, the twelfth in 13 years.

As usual there were a number of coups during 2000 resulting in transitional governments, which are themselves under threat of change. In three instances it was the people who successfully faced down unwanted governments that refused to give up the reins. In each of these cases, as in the peaceful revolutions that overturned the governments of Eastern Europe in the early 1990s, the military or repressive secret police forces that had previously shored up the regimes made clear that they would not use force to overturn the clearly expressed public desire to be rid of an unwanted leader.

The most dramatic instance was in Serbia, where street demonstrations steadily increased in size and strength, forcing Slobodan Milosevic to accede to the almost-universal desire to see him go. In Peru, the efforts of Alberto Fujimori to retain power beyond his original constitutional term were thwarted by the clear expression of the people's dismay at evidence of his government's grasping corruption. In the Philippines, Joseph Estrada, the flamboyant actor turned politician, also lost the stand-off between his supporters in the legislature, who tried to maintain him in power, and the people. In a reprise of the earlier 'people's revolution' which toppled Ferdinand Marcos and brought Corazon Aquino, the wife of a dead hero, to office, the massive street demonstrations in February 2001, led by many of the same forces and individuals that removed Marcos, brought Gloria Macapagal-Arroyo, the daughter of an esteemed former president, to power. All three instances were welcome changes of leadership, but all three societies continue to suffer deep economic and social rifts. None of them are notably flexible. Transiting to peace and plenty will test the ability of the strongest leaders.

Regional Organisations in the Doldrums

Individual European countries, with the exception of Serbia, were spared significant changes of leadership. However, a changed mood spread over Europe as a whole. Optimism about the prospects for the European Union, whether with regard to enlargement or the introduction of the single currency, was slipping away. The euro fell steadily through 2000, recovered slightly in the early months of 2001, and then slid slowly again during March. A further blow to its prestige was struck in September 2000, when Denmark resoundingly voted down a referendum on joining the monetary union. This could prove contagious. It certainly had the short-term effect of fuelling British euro-scepticism.

One of the EU's more effective innovations, the removal of internal European border controls, came under threat. The easy flow of economic migrants and refugees through Europe as a result of the reduced controls had already raised questions. The spread of mad cow and foot and mouth diseases put paid to the scheme, at least for a time. Border controls were clamped back and long lines of frustrated traffic, a sight not seen for many years, reappeared at the borders. A downturn in the stock markets, fears about a dodgy economic outlook and deepened concern about loss of sovereign control combined to affect views of the future. This no longer looked rosy, and some of the blame landed at the feet of the EU's leaders and institutions. If there was not yet a groundswell of opposition large enough to threaten moves to a unified Europe, it did seem clear that the momentum was slowing. It was not a complete surprise when Switzerland voted in March 2001 against joining the EU, but it did indicate that the the dream of unification was not sufficient to counter strong feelings of national individualism within Europe.

Compared with other regional organisations, however, the EU was a stalwart of stability and strength. The Association of Southeast Asian Nations (ASEAN) had dwindled to a shadow of its once robust and confident self. The social and political upheavals that had accompanied the economic dislocation in Indonesia, Malaysia, Thailand and the Philippines had robbed the institution of its driving force. Although it had continued to expand, in order to take in all of the South-east Asian nations, this had failed either to provide the hoped-for coherent identity or to infuse the group with new vigour. Indeed, since the nations that had been adopted in the last intake (particularly Myanmar) were undemocratic autocracies, unacceptable as respondents by European nations and other countries that had been dealing closely with ASEAN, their membership had served mostly to interrupt a move to greater cohesion and outreach. ASEAN's budding security organisation, the ASEAN Regional Forum (ARF) was practically moribund, and another offshoot, ASEAN+3 (taking in the major North Asia countries: China, Japan, and South Korea) threatened to become the 3+ASEAN.

Other regional bodies, which had once held dreams of real viability but had hardly lifted off the ground, were in an even worse condition than ASEAN. The Southern African Development Council (SADC) was paralysed by the turmoil in Zimbabwe; Angola and Namibia's partisan involvement in the war in the Congo; and South Africa's refusal to play a significant foreign policy role. The fledgling South Asian Association for Regional Cooperation (SAARC) was rent by the ongoing rivalry between its two leading members, India and Pakistan, over Kashmir. In Latin America, *Mercado Commun del Sur* (Mercosur) is making incremental progress as a trade organisation, but shows little sign of establishing meaningful supranational political power. Previous hopes that any of these organisations, with the exception of the EU, could lift the burden of ameliorating regional rivalries from the shoulders of the UN or the world's major countries, have been accepted as a mirage.

Domestic Constraints

It is clear that most of the major countries are deeply reluctant to become physically involved in dealing with Africa's festering sore spots, or even to face the possibility of more fighting in the Albanian–Serbian–Macedonian triangle. Most of them would find it difficult to pick up the burden, even if they wanted to. Some, like the US and the EU, lack a cohesive view that would allow decisive action. Others, like Russia and Japan, are hemmed in by faltering economies. Yet others, like China, are beset by domestic concerns and political uncertainties.

The United States emerged deeply divided from an election which had been one of its ugliest, and had certainly taken the longest to determine a winner. The geographic pattern of the votes made the US look like two countries with one system. A narrow band encompassing the coastal regions and the border with Canada, plus the inner sections of the largest cities came out for Al Gore, the Democratic Party candidate. A broad swath of the centre of the country and the rural appendages of the major cities were behind George W. Bush, the Republican contender. In numerical terms it was a stand-off. Gore won the election in terms of votes cast, but Bush became the president on the basis of gathering four votes more than Gore in the Electoral College, the eighteenth-century construct that constitutionally determines the election. The Congress was finely divided: the Republicans have only a tiny ten-vote advantage in the 435-member House, and the Senate is split precisely down the middle, each party having 50 seats.

Because party discipline is not as stringent in the US Congress as it is in most parliamentary systems, this is not as dire for Bush as it sounds. The president can also take certain actions on his own account that will affect the direction of American domestic and foreign policies. Former President Ronald Reagan used his presidential powers to decree that the United States would not provide money to any organisation abroad which advocated, or gave advice on, abortion. This created financial difficulties for many international health organisations which were doing much-needed work in third world countries because of their concern with burgeoning birth-rates and their support for contraception. Within days of his inauguration in 1993, Bush's predecessor Bill Clinton issued a presidential decree that reversed Reagan's edict. And only days after his inauguration in 2001, George Bush, in turn, put the Reagan restrictions back in place.

The president also sets the tone for policy, and this can have an important international dimension. In his first months in office, Bush has made it clear that he will listen more carefully than Clinton and the Democrats did to the economic concerns of big business when those concerns collide with the need to protect the environment. Presidential action in this regard will adversely impact efforts to deal with global warming. The administration's clarity on the need for an expanded national missile defence (NMD), even though there has still been no positive proof that it would work, will establish an agenda to which other nations will need to react.

Nevertheless, the strength of the presidential position does not override the need to achieve congressional agreement on many basic issues. With little clear space between the two parties, the president will need to tread with great care, adjusting, compromising and trimming as he goes to avoid gridlock in Washington. He, of course, recognises the need. For this reason, with disarming charm, he has emphasised his intentions of maintaining 'bipartisanship'. And for the usual 'honeymoon period' of three months or so, while no outsized controversial issues were brought forward for decision, Washington basked in an atmosphere of unaccustomed comity. It could not last. The checks and balances built into the US system of governing makes it certain that the Bush administration will find it very difficult to change defence and foreign policy as much it would like.

Peace or More Fighting?

While he was president Clinton himself, and by his direction many members of his administration, devoted an unusually high proportion of their time to brokering peace around the world. There have been early signals, however, that the Bush administration intends to draw back from such efforts. It is an unfortunate time for such a decision, for 2000 was a rough year for peace processes. Much of the advance that had been made in the Middle East, Northern Ireland and on the Korean Peninsula unravelled during 2000. Many of those advances had only been possible because of the willingness of the US and Clinton to find ways around intransigent positions, to keep talking going, to offer compromise ideas (and sometimes money) that would not be advanced if the involved parties were left on their own, and to cajole the participants to accept arrangements that would otherwise be unacceptable. No one can replace the US if it withdraws from this function.

The need for it is greatest in the Middle East. The Oslo process has collapsed, and whatever confidence between Palestinians and Israelis had been created since its inception in 1993 is rapidly eroding. A more serious *intifada*, because of the increasing availability of arms on the Palestinian side, has raged since October 2000. A pall of fatalism has gripped the area, and both sides are girding for conflict. Israel has cast its vote against the Labour Party's peacemaking efforts, bringing to the head of its new *Likud* government the old warrior Ariel Sharon. On the Palestinian side a seriously weakened Yasser Arafat is being gradually nudged aside by more militant leaders. Both sides need outside encouragement and support to climb out of the hole they are busy digging ever deeper.

In Northern Ireland there has not yet been a return to active violence. The devolved government is creaking along, but both unionists and republicans are disenchanted. Although the Irish Republican Army (IRA) has made a gesture of goodwill – returning to talks with the commission charged with decommissioning arms – this will not be enough to satisfy the unionists. And the biggest deadline of all is looming: there is supposed to be meaningful, if not complete, decommissioning of arms by June 2001, and there was no indication by the end of March that the IRA was contemplating any disarmament by that date. Much of the promise that had been created through US-sponsored talks headed by former Senator George Mitchell has leached away. It will not be easy to recover.

In the last few months of his presidency Bill Clinton let loose an extraordinary flurry of diplomatic activity that included efforts to engage the North Korean government in talks about missiles, nuclear matters and relations with South Korea. These talks had made sufficient progress for then Secretary of State Madeleine Albright to visit Pyongyang in November 2000, encouraging speculation that Clinton might follow her to lend his weight to the deals being worked out. In the event, the administration decided that there was too little time left in Clinton's incumbency to warrant a trip. But many, both inside and outside of the administration, felt that a breakthrough had been made that would fortify the North–South rapprochement that was underway and that would ease US fears of possible North Korean aggression. When the new administration made a number of public statements that expressed deep suspicions about both North Korean leader Kim Jong Il and the negotiations, Kim retaliated by cancelling a carefully arranged future visit to Seoul. Not only had a potential path to better US–North Korean relations been blocked, but South Korean President Kim Dae Jung's 'sunshine policy' had clouded over.

It is possible that, as the new administration completes its ongoing reviews of various foreign policy options and becomes more comfortable with the need to be involved, it will give greater attention to the pressure that can be expected from domestic and allied interests to return to play the role in world affairs that only the US can fill. The president does not need to repeat Clinton's very personal involvement in peace negotiations, but he should not allow the US to disengage too far from its vital role as an honest broker. If he fails to recognise that necessity, it will become more difficult to contain tensions, or even to prevent a return to conflict, in a number of disputes where peace efforts had once made limited gains, but which are now fragile and tottering.

Even Weightier Threats

Although no one should be complacent about the breakdown of peace in regional conflicts, they at least do not threaten world peace and security in the way that Germany, Japan or the Soviet Union once did. There are those prepared to hoist China onto the same infamous pedestal, but it is fairly certain that China would not be capable of posing such a threat for a great many years, even if it wanted to. There are, however, two transnational developments that can easily undercut the world's present comfortable feeling of security. They have been developing for a long time, and although they will not create complete havoc for many years, there is a point of no return that is not far off. Both are well known, but because some world leaders refuse to accept that they cannot be dealt with without considerable national sacrifice, they are not being effectively addressed.

The first major threat is that of global warming. Some world leaders have managed to turn a blind eye to the mounting accumulation of scientific evidence of its reality and its deadly nature. A detailed report by the United Nations' International Panel on Climate Change released in early 2001 makes it clear that those leaders ignore the threat at their, and our, peril. The thinning of the atmospheric cover that protects the earth from deadly rays is rapidly enlarging, and the accelerated thawing of the polar ice drives home the lesson that the other predicted effects of the climate change are coming closer. Further melting of the ice caps will lead to flooding of low-lying coastal areas around the world; rising temperatures will disrupt agriculture and spread disease. Positive action is required now to halt such developments before they are unstoppable.

Instead, the new US president, putting business interests first, has reneged on a campaign promise to clamp mandatory limits on the emission from electricity generating plants of carbon dioxide, the gas that most scientists believe is deeply implicated in the global warming crisis. If this decision represents the direction in which the Bush administration plans to push the United States, which is responsible for 25% of all greenhouse-gas emissions, the effort to counter global warming will become infinitely more difficult. The president should instead resurrect his earlier promises and take the lead, as the US has so often done in the past, in opposing threats to the world's security.

The second, largely amorphous but still dangerous, threat arises out of the ceaseless flows of refugees and economic migrants from country to country. There are millions, desperate to escape poverty, famine and conflict, willing to try anything to find a niche in the more stable nations of the world. International criminal organisations have spotted this as a growth industry and, for a price, have lent their cruel talents to infiltrating large numbers of people into unwelcoming countries. Unless some means can be found to staunch the flow, or to accommodate those who can not be refused, xenophobia will be fanned. A review of mid-twentieth century history makes clear how dangerous that could be for a now vastly more overcrowded world.

Coming to grips with either of these problems would be demanding at any time; with so many nations in a transitional phase, it is a far more challenging task. Although many recent changes of government were brought about by the weakness and corruption of the previous leaderships, all too many of the replacements are equally weak and equally corrupt. Even in the United States, the taint of big money and big business will continue to affect the ability and will of the government to put probity before profit. Before President Bush decides that the absence of a military threat to global security will allow the US the luxury of adopting a parochial view, he should recognise that the new threats require as much leadership as any that came before. It is hardly a time for complacency.

Strategic Policy Issues

Defending the US (and Allies?) from Ballistic Missile Attack

Despite a muted response to the January 1999 announcement by then US Secretary of Defence William Cohen that the United States would decide during the summer of 2000 on whether to deploy a national missile defence (NMD) system, two events in late 1999 unleashed a wave of international apprehension and protest regarding NMD. First, in October that year, a test of the NMD interceptor succeeded in destroying a target ballistic missile, creating the perception that the technology was indeed reaching a sufficient state of maturity to allow deployment to proceed. Then, later in the month, the US Senate rejected ratification of the Comprehensive Test Ban Treaty (CTBT), fuelling fears that Washington was turning its back on arms control.

Notwithstanding vociferous warnings from Russia and China regarding the dire consequences of NMD deployment, as well as deep concerns expressed by some NATO allies, at the start of the new millennium the consensus in Washington was that NMD was a 'done deal'. Yet, on 1 September 2000, President Bill Clinton announced that he had decided to leave the issue of NMD deployment to his successor. An array of factors produced this 'rollback'. Several will also affect the way in which the new administration of President George W. Bush formulates its NMD policy, but the administration is nonetheless highly likely to decide to begin NMD deployment. Moreover, sometime during 2002 the US may well have either successfully negotiated a modified version of the Anti-Ballistic Missile (ABM) Treaty with Russia or have withdrawn from it.

The Clinton NMD Plan

The Clinton administration plan envisaged the initial deployment of 20 ground-based interceptors in Alaska by 2005, the earliest feasible date for an operational NMD capability. US intelligence estimates state that North Korea, Iran and Iraq all potentially '*could* test ICBMs of varying capabilities – some capable of delivering several-hundred kilogram payloads to the United States' during the 2001–2005 period. As part of its 'capability one'

(C-1) NMD architecture of 20 interceptors, the US would also upgrade five existing ballistic-missile early-warning radars, and construct a new X-band radar on Shemya Island in the Aleutians, which would take at least five years. Two of the existing early-warning radars are located outside the United States: one at Fylingdales Moor in the UK and the other at Thule, Greenland. An expanded C-1 design would involve deploying 100 interceptors at the Alaska site by 2007. A C-2 constellation for possible deployment over the following several years would add 25 more interceptors plus software upgrades and new sensor systems, including the construction of X-band radars at Fylingdales Moor and Thule. The C-3 option, envisioned for 2010 or later, would include a second site of 125 ground-based interceptors, additional early-warning as well as X-band radars, and satellite-based missile tracking and discrimination capabilities.

The Clinton NMD programme had few admirers. Many in the US arms-control community thought that it was unnecessary and de-stabilising. Some NMD sceptics argued on technical grounds that any system designed to intercept intercontinental-ballistic missiles (ICBMs) during the mid-course stage of flight, as the Clinton plan did, was condemned to operational failure because it would be unable to deal with countermeasures (decoys) to be developed along with long-range missiles. Many advocates of intensified missile defence efforts viewed the Alaska site alone as inadequate, barely able to meet the near-term threat to the US and unable to protect US allies. They have largely favoured sea-based NMD as more cost-effective and flexible, offering protection for US allies as well as the US itself. Sea-based NMD also provides a potential option to intercept attacking ballistic missiles in their boost-phase, before they can deploy countermeasures.

Apart from then Defense Secretary William Cohen, the Clinton administration itself was a relatively unenthusiastic proponent of its own plan. It had timed the deployment decision for late 2000 largely to protect Al Gore against Republican attacks during the 2000 presidential campaign. The Clinton administration was deeply committed to the continuation of the ABM Treaty. The State Department characterised it as 'a cornerstone of strategic stability', an outlook that created deep reluctance to opting for NMD deployment rather than the treaty if events forced such a choice.

Against this backdrop, four broad developments took place that helped intensify debate both within and outside the government over whether the US should take the decision to initiate NMD deployment. These included technical setbacks, Russian refusal to negotiate changes to the ABM Treaty, continued hostility towards NMD deployment on the part of NATO allies and China, and a diplomatic opening with North Korea.

NMD flight tests that took place in January and July 2000 both failed to hit the target missile. In the January test, a problem with the cooling system prevented the sensor on the exo-atmospheric kill vehicle (EKV) from working properly in the final seconds, while in July the EKV failed to separate from its final booster-rocket stage. These failures left only the October 1999 test as having achieved the desired interception of its target missile.

Even this success was questioned when it became clear that the kill vehicle had initially homed in on a decoy balloon rather than on the missile warhead. Although it subsequently switched course towards, and then destroyed, the latter, NMD critics claimed that the interceptor would not have detected the warhead if the larger decoy balloon had not first drawn it to the right area. The Department of Defense countered that the test showed the ability of 'hit-to-kill' (HTK) interception to discriminate between a warhead and a decoy. Critics in turn rejoined that the test had involved only one large decoy while a real attack would involve a large number of difficult to determine decoys.

On the arms-control front, in early 2000 the administration presented Russia with ABM Treaty 'talking points' that proposed a protocol to the treaty to allow the US to deploy only the expanded C-1 architecture. By June, it was completely clear that Russia was not prepared to accept such a protocol. Nor was Washington meeting with much success in its efforts to allay the concerns of NATO allies, which focused largely, but not exclusively, on the fate of the ABM Treaty.

Reinforcing the technical and diplomatic problems facing the Clinton NMD plan, South Korean and US diplomatic openings with North Korea – the regional proliferator deemed most likely to present a near-term ballistic missile threat to US territory – led some observers to argue that the need for NMD was becoming less urgent. North Korea suspended its missile test programme in 1999, and the widely expected launch of a *Taepo-dong* 2 missile never took place. The opening with Pyongyang, together with tentative efforts to engage with Iran and Libya, even led the US in June 2000 to characterise them as 'states of concern' rather than as 'rogue states' on the grounds that the 'rogue' label inappropriately implied a 'one policy fits all' approach.

Deferring the NMD Deployment Decision

Although the latter developments encouraged NMD opponents to step up their criticism of the Clinton plan, Clinton's NMD deferral decision stemmed fundamentally from the failure of the two NMD flight tests in 2000, coupled with other technological problems and uncertainties. In June 2000, a third report on the NMD programme issued by an independent review team under the chairmanship of retired Air Force General Larry Welch stressed that while meeting the 2005 C-1 deployment goal was feasible, it constituted a 'high-risk' endeavour. Every failed test has a knock-on effect of delaying the following test in order to provide sufficient time for evaluating what went wrong. Moreover, the development of the final NMD booster rocket that will propel the EKV into space had fallen almost one year behind schedule by the summer of 2000. This meant that the Alaska interceptor site was highly unlikely to be operational before 2006, and very possibly not before 2007, making completion of the Shemya radar for 2005 unnecessary.

At this point, international opposition to NMD became a decisive consideration in US decision-making. Indeed, some elements of the Clinton administration were reportedly hoping for a failure of the July 2000 flight test to reduce domestic pressure to take any steps towards NMD deployment without first securing an ABM Treaty modification with Russia. When that failure occurred, President Clinton felt that there was no reason to absorb the diplomatic fallout from Russia, China and the allies that would have ensued from even the limited decision regarding construction on Shemya Island, given all the uncertainties on the technology side. Deferring the decision would buy time to gain greater international acceptance of the NMD plan.

In his speech of 1 September 2000 announcing the deferral, Clinton characterised the ballistic missile threat as 'real and growing', an assertion that he repeated following the November presidential election. He termed North Korea's missile testing moratorium a 'good development', but noted that Pyongyang's missile capabilities are still 'a serious issue and its intentions remain unclear'. Broad support exists among US political and élite opinion that the deployment of some form of NMD system would be desirable if it could be made effective. The 1999 Missile Defense Act, passed by an overwhelming majority in both houses of Congress, indeed requires that the US deploy an effective NMD system 'as soon as is technologically possible'.

Bush Administration Options

George W. Bush made the need for NMD, to protect not only the US but also its allies against missile strikes from regional proliferators, one of the major defence-policy themes of his presidential campaign. After he was elected president, repeated statements on the part of Bush and his senior national security team stressing the critical importance of NMD promptly dispelled any lingering questions as to how serious this commitment would be. The appointment of Donald Rumsfeld as secretary of defense provided further confirmation of the issue's centrality: Rumsfeld had chaired a 1998 commission that greatly heightened US perceptions of the ballistic missile threat. The Bush administration largely views the ABM Treaty as an anachronism of the Cold War rather than a 'cornerstone of strategic stability'. While for international political reasons it is willing to negotiate a treaty amendment that would allow NMD deployment, rather than simply exercise the US right of withdrawal, the administration's intent to ditch the treaty if those negotiations should prove unsuccessful is not in doubt.

Nevertheless, the Bush administration has resisted calls from the most fervent NMD advocates in Congress and the US expert community to give immediate notice of withdrawal from the ABM Treaty and to start work in 2001 on the Shemya Island radar. (The latter remained an option in spite of Clinton's deferral, albeit at greater cost.) The administration's caution reflected its belief that there was no technical reason for rapid action. Moreover, such drastic moves would have sharply undermined the possibility of gaining Russian tolerance of NMD, of undertaking extensive consultations with the NATO allies in order to overcome their misgivings, and of exploring possible options for defending Europe.

Three major issues confronted the Bush team in the early weeks of its term: which system should be deployed and when; how far should NMD extend; and how can Russia and China be mollified so as to permit eventual full-scale deployment. Despite the perceived shortcomings of the Clinton plan, Bush appointees appear to agree that it constitutes the only NMD system that can achieve operational status in the current decade. For example, National Security Council Senior Director for Counter-Proliferation and Homeland Defence Robert Joseph told a June 2000 congressional hearing that, due to Clinton administration policy choices going back to 1993:

> We have now created a predicament for ourselves where we have only one choice in terms of meeting the threat in the timeframe that the intelligence community tells us that it will exist; that is, the 2005–2006 timeframe. That is the land-based system.

Sea-based NMD, whether for mid-course or boost-phase interception, requires extensive development work and could not be deployed for at least another 10–12 years. A space-based NMD capability would require even longer to develop and deploy.

The second issue derives from the stated Bush goal of protecting US allies. The key objective in deploying NMD is to preserve the US freedom to intervene in regional crises that engage major national interests. Since the US national security community considers the participation of allies to be a political precondition for US regional intervention in most instances, an NMD system that cannot protect those allies has significantly less value. Accordingly, one concept that has emerged in the Pentagon is for the second site in the C-3 architecture to be built in Europe rather than in the US. This site could protect both Europe and the US against long-range missile launches from the Middle East. Yet daunting obstacles confront the deployment of an 'Allied Missile Defence' (AMD) capability. Although the

Strategic Policy Issues

European allies in early 2001 appeared closer to grudgingly accepting US NMD deployment, it remains highly unlikely that any, except possibly the UK, would make a material contribution to the system.

The Bush administration also must formulate an approach to the ABM Treaty that allows the US to pursue a wide range of NMD technology development and deployment options while minimising harmful diplomatic repercussions. It would achieve this goal by convincing Russia that it should agree to a proposed ABM Treaty amendment more extensive than the very limited change offered to Moscow by the Clinton administration. The treaty in its current form prohibits not only deployment but also the development and testing of sea- and space-based systems or components for defending against strategic ballistic-missile attack. The Bush administration is likely to propose to Russia that a modified ABM Treaty contain no restrictions on the deployment of sensor systems or on development and testing. Affecting the prospects for modification is the Russian government's proposal to NATO Secretary-General George Robertson, tendered in his meeting with President Vladimir Putin in Moscow in February 2001, of a technically dubious 'European missile defence' plan that would include Russia. The move could be construed as an attempt to drive a wedge between the US and its NATO allies or a salutary softening of Moscow's 'just say no' approach to treaty modification. It may be a little of both. On balance, transatlantic and US–Russian political realities could require the US to agree at least to some restrictions on the development, testing and deployment of space-based systems.

The administration may want to have the latitude to deploy more than one ground-based interceptor site, and it will certainly want to remove the current prohibition on sharing strategic-defence technologies with other countries. Given that a sea-based operational capability is far in the future and therefore difficult to quantify, it may not be necessary, for now, to provide for sea-based deployment in an amended treaty. President Bush has also promised a plan for the implementation of nuclear-arms reductions within the framework of a new strategic doctrine that will seek coherently to define the roles of offensive and defensive forces.

Given that China possesses only about 20 ICBMs (versus Russia's 776, plus submarine-launched missiles), NMD is far more alarming to Beijing than to Moscow. Beijing regards NMD as materially degrading its second-strike capability against the United States and thus as giving the US greater freedom to defend Taiwan and generally to act militarily in Asia. Unlike Russia, China has no pre-existing arms-control relationship with the US, which dims prospects for a neat and formal US–China accommodation. On the other hand, the Clinton administration's rollback and the Bush administration's more ambitious NMD plans make full deployment less imminent than it was when China's concerns were initially raised. As a consequence, the parties have time to begin a strategic dialogue and work out an informal accord. Under the most likely scenario, Washington would acquiesce to a limited degree of military modernisation on China's part – possibly including the acquisition of additional ICBMs – in exchange for China's acceptance of NMD within certain broad limits.

What Next?

The Bush administration's review of NMD policy was designed to examine the potential schedule and costs of different deployment options, taking into account possible gains that sea-based systems could make in these areas if the ABM Treaty restrictions can be lifted. Unless that review unexpectedly discovers some means of greatly accelerating the initial operational date for a naval NMD capability, the Bush administration is very likely to proceed with the land-based site in Alaska, while beginning a parallel serious effort to develop sea- and space-based NMD systems.

Administration concern over the threat appears too deep to countenance postponement of an initial NMD operational capability beyond the current decade. Even if the US were able to conclude a verifiable agreement with North Korea to halt its missile development programmes and exports, which is at any rate uncertain, substantial apprehension exists regarding Iran and, to a somewhat lesser degree, Iraq. There is also a considerable body of opinion in Republican Party defence circles that NMD deployment is important to deter future proliferation of ballistic missiles. Shelving the Alaska site would give the appearance of taking a step backwards to the seemingly endless pursuit of research and development without ever having an actual deployment programme. Republican Party defence experts also think of one or more ground-based sites as a necessary 'layer' in a larger architecture that includes sea-based and eventually space-based systems.

There do not appear to be insurmountable technical or funding obstacles in the way of further development of the ground-based option. The DoD-chartered National Missile Defense Independent Review Team, known informally as the Welch panel, has arguably provided the most credible independent critiques of the NMD programme. The panel stated in its June 2000 report on the Clinton plan:

> the technical capability to develop and field the limited system to meet the defined C-1 threat is available. There has been important program progress in the past year, which includes a successful intercept, demonstrated integration of several prototype system elements, and continued development of simulations and laboratories for ground testing.

That said, the effective integration of all the NMD subsystems into a seamless system that functions with a very high degree of reliability remains a task of enormous complexity. The reasons for the Welch panel's conclusion that the technology is available to field a limited NMD capability included the system's ability to discriminate between real warheads and the kinds of decoys that the near-term ballistic-missile threat might hide behind. The report warned that the countermeasures challenge would become more severe, but added that 'there is extensive potential in the system to grow discrimination capabilities'. While there are serious and prestigious scientists who continue to disagree with this view, arguing that the decoy problem is one that the system will not be able to overcome, the Bush administration will prefer the Welch conclusion.

The Clinton administration had already allocated funding of approximately $14 billion for the expanded C-1 deployment into its future years defence programme. Bush administration pursuit of the Alaska site will therefore not require a major augmentation of NMD funding, which should provide leeway for initial spending increases on research, development and testing for sea-based NMD as well as, to a lesser extent, for space-based programmes. Funding dilemmas are likely to become acute, however, regarding what to deploy in addition to the Alaska site in order to provide more robust protection for the US and to offer potential coverage to the allies. Locating the C-3 architecture's second ground-based site in Europe would help achieve the goal of protecting US allies, but in early 2001 it still appeared unlikely that European agreement could be reached, and the US Congress would also baulk unless there was significant European cost-sharing. Moving out to sea for the following phases of NMD was expected to be viewed as a more effective, economical and politically realistic option than a second ground-based site.

Sea-based NMD, however, does not provide a panacea for the perceived threat or for the protection of US allies. Mid-course interception from the sea faces the same challenges from countermeasures as a land-based system. Unless the geographical location of potential threats allowed the US to position its ships so that they could achieve mid-course interception of missiles headed for both the US and Europe, European countries would need to acquire a sea-based capability dedicated to defending their own continent.

In theory, boost-phase interception from the sea (or from land and the air) could provide equal protection to the US and its allies without requiring any financial participation by the latter. But interceptors must be located within several hundred kilometres of the attacking missiles' launch sites, making a boost-phase intercept capability unable to counter widely dispersed regional threats. Nor can sea-, land- or air-based boost-phase interception deal with the accidental or unauthorised launch of a small number of missiles from Russia and China, a secondary goal of NMD. For these reasons, NMD advocates always characterise sea-, land- and air-based boost-phase interception as an important element in a broader NMD architecture rather than as a stand-alone capability.

From a purely technical standpoint, the ideal location for a boost-phase intercept capability is in space. Stephen Cambone, special assistant to Secretary of Defense Rumsfeld, told a Congressional hearing in June 2000 that it is critical for the US to demonstrate at a minimum a space-based intercept capability in order to discourage the development of countermeasures. While the US can hope to give a mid-course intercept system sufficient capability to discriminate between warheads and decoys, mid-course interception is helpless to counter the release early in an attacking missile's ascent phase of submunitions containing biological or chemical agents. There would simply be too many very small targets to destroy.

This threat may not matter too much in the case of chemical submunitions, which would need to deliver a large quantity of agent to achieve a meaningful level of lethality, but it is a huge concern with respect to biological weapons. A space-based boost-phase intercept capability is the only real answer to this threat, which is remote now but will probably become substantial. The Clinton administration began funding a space-based laser research programme at a level of some $75 million per year, with a first experiment planned for around 2012.

Thus, the Bush administration will need to establish investment priorities between boost-phase intercept systems, mid-course interception from the sea, land-based sites and a space-based capability. The US military has been deeply apprehensive that burgeoning NMD investment will squeeze out their favourite weapons systems. The defence acquisition budget is already too low to fund established requirements, and would need at the very least some $25bn per year in additional spending to do so. The Bush administration is conducting a far-reaching review of the US military, with the goal of accelerating its transformation into a twenty-first century, information-age force, based on systems and concepts associated with the 'revolution in military affairs'. This review will probably result in the cancellation of some major weapons programmes, which would free up money for other areas, including NMD technologies. Nonetheless, unless there is a considerable boost in defence spending, pressures on NMD funding will become increasingly severe as programmes move into more costly advanced development and testing.

Further complicating this picture, many political observers expect the Democratic Party to regain control of one or both Houses of Congress in the 2002 elections. Democratic Party control of the Congress would not spell the end of NMD, but there would almost certainly be a scaling-back of funding support, particularly on advanced systems, and a potential stretching-out of deployment. Military and industrial lobbying to rescue existing weapons programmes would probably have greater impact in a

Strategic Policy Issues

Congress under Democratic Party control, and the Bush administration will probably attempt to make as many irreversible changes as possible prior to the 2002 elections.

Resolution of the ABM Treaty issue seems likely to occur during 2002. The US will have to give notice of withdrawal from the treaty by late 2001 in order to begin Shemya Island site work in 2002. Even without the Shemya Island issue, the Bush administration will want to amend or jettison the treaty without too much delay in order to conduct unrestricted development and testing of sea- and space-based defences. Divisions may well occur within the administration over how seriously to negotiate with the Russians. Defense Secretary Rumsfeld may be unwilling to compromise on the initial US negotiating position, while Secretary of State Colin Powell could well prove more flexible. Powell's preferred approach appears to be to avoid withdrawing from the treaty until the Pentagon has demonstrated the technical effectiveness of strategic defences. However, the long lead-time for construction of the Shemya Island radar and the treaty's prohibitions on development and testing of sea-based systems argue for resolution of the treaty issue in 2002.

Russia appears to have more to lose than to gain from a US withdrawal from the ABM Treaty. While Moscow has threatened to abrogate the START II Treaty in retaliation, lack of funding suggests Russia's strategic system will inevitably decay to below START II levels. In any event, the Bush administration's commitment to unilateral nuclear reductions may help counter international fears of a new strategic arms race. The administration could also resubmit the CTBT to the US Senate for ratification as a further means of attenuating the diplomatic repercussions of an eventual ABM Treaty withdrawal. In early January 2001, former chairman of the Joint Chiefs of Staff General John Shalikashvili presented a report to President Clinton on measures the US could take to address domestic concerns over the CTBT treaty. This report could provide a basis for Senate reconsideration. Given that the CTBT is a divisive issue for the Republican Party and that the administration already has a national security agenda brimming with controversy, it is unlikely that the administration will resubmit the treaty to the current Congress. However, such action could possibly occur after the 2002 elections.

Maintaining Perspective on Strategic Defences

Two diametric, but equally unrealistic, views of strategic defences have gained popular currency. One is that the US NMD programme's technical problems indicate that strategic defences will never be deployed. The other, stemming from the Bush administration's strong commitment to ballistic missile defence, is that AMD and even 'GMD', or global missile defence, are readily at hand.

At a very basic level, the US has already demonstrated that HTK technology can succeed in destroying long-range ballistic missiles. Given the depth of concern over the threat, this technical progress is a sufficient condition to allow Washington to commit to a ground-based NMD site, although the final decision to build and deploy the interceptors will not take place before 2004. The countermeasures debate is highly unlikely to halt deployment of a mid-course intercept NMD capability. Once an NMD system achieves operational status, efforts will continue to make it more reliable and effective.

Yet, the Bush administration does not seem prepared to throw endless amounts of money at strategic defences, and even if it were, Congress might well baulk. In his speech at the February 2001 Munich Conference on European Security, Secretary of Defense Rumsfeld carefully stated that the US is prepared 'to assist' friends and allies to deploy ballistic missile defences, not actually to pay for them. A wholehearted European political and financial commitment to deploy defences for defending national territory against ballistic missile attack now appears unlikely. Without this commitment, the emergence of an initial AMD capability is a decade or more away, when US boost-phase and mid-course intercept systems based at sea potentially become operational. GMD is even further away. While it is a virtual certainty that the US will deploy a strategic defence capability, that capability's eventual shape and ultimate effectiveness remain very much open to question.

Military Transformation: A Report Card

Over the past decade, the nature of war has been affected most profoundly by cathartic political changes. A growing number of defence experts and military officers, however, have predicted that the development and diffusion of information technology will alter the character of future wars more radically still. They frequently compare the current era to the 1920s and 1930s, a period that witnessed the development of a variety of new weapon systems, including the tank, aircraft and aircraft carrier. But while many armies acquired tanks, only Germany adopted the doctrine and created the structures necessary to allow it to wage a *Blitzkrieg*.

Now as then, although military organisations are attempting to transform their armed forces to exploit the opportunities offered by the information revolution, they are finding it difficult to accommodate technological innovation through doctrinal and organisational change. The US armed forces have most directly embraced the need for fundamental changes to meet the opportunities and challenges of the information age. Even there, however, attempts to innovate have met with institutional resistance. Furthermore, mismatches have been revealed between the revolutionary way of war emblemised by 'smart' technologies and the like, and the kinds of battles – to deter ethnic cleansing, contain an *intifada* or thwart asymmetric threats – that need to be fought.

Similar circumstances hold for most of the world's militaries. Both Russia and China have expressed considerable interest in transforming their armed forces, but face substantial constraints. Other large militaries in Europe and Asia have chosen to pursue more incremental approaches, but most are still organised and trained in much the same way as they were a decade ago. By contrast, smaller militaries have proved more willing to experiment with new technology, doctrine and organisations.

Still Leading, but Hobbled

The US armed forces have taken the lead in speculating on and experimenting with new ways of war and the Bush administration has promised to skip a generation of technology in an effort to exploit the information revolution. Yet, while each service has explored innovative approaches to combat, attempts at innovation have faced opposition from service traditionalists. For example, regional commanders-in-chief (CinCs) have noted the need for presenting a common electronic picture of a given battlespace to coalition forces to facilitate 'network-centric' joint operations. The technology exists to accomplish this, but much of the military bureaucracy has remained wedded to rigid Cold War-era procurement practices that make developing and installing the appropriate software unnecessarily difficult. To facilitate an information revolution, the military would have to adopt faster development cycles and more fluid procurement practices – no small feat for an organisation that has been doing things the same way for decades. In a similar vein, the Bush administration's radical plans for carrying forward the technological revolution may require cutbacks on systems such as the US Air Force (USAF)'s F-22 fighter, the army's heavy tanks and the navy's aircraft carriers. These systems are near and dear not only to the individual services, but also to legislators whose constituents build them.

Nevertheless, the US Army has made great progress in transforming itself. *Operation Allied Force*, NATO's war in Yugoslavia, highlighted the US Army's lack of units light enough to move quickly, yet heavy enough to strike hard. The experience prodded the Army Chief of Staff, General Eric Shinseki, into launching an effort to transform the army into a more mobile yet equally capable force. In October 1999, he announced a goal of reconfiguring it into a medium-weight force capable of deploying a 5,000-strong brigade anywhere in the world within 96 hours. Two brigades have traded their tracked M-1A1 *Abrams* tanks and M-2 *Bradley* fighting vehicles for LAV III armoured vehicles on loan from Canada.

In November, the army awarded a $4 billion contract to build a new generation of light wheeled vehicles to equip these medium-weight units. In 2012, it will begin fielding the Future Combat System (FCS), a network of vehicles – possibly unmanned – to replace tanks and self-propelled artillery. The system will weigh no more than 20 tonnes (compared to 70 tonnes for the M1 *Abrams*) to allow it to be transported aboard the C-130, the air force's most numerous transport aircraft. Because medium-weight forces will lack the armour to slug it out with enemy tanks, they will need the capability to identify and engage enemy forces before the enemy can engage them.

The army's modernisation plans threaten its traditional emphasis upon armour as the centrepiece of ground combat, a notion it has nourished for the past six decades. Indeed, they challenge the very definition and purpose of armoured units. On the face of it, trading heavily armoured tanks for more vulnerable, but also more mobile wheeled vehicles constitutes a significant risk. Some would argue that ultimately enemy armoured forces will have to be engaged directly by better-protected units, and at the very least, systems to degrade enemy armour before engaging in close-quarter battle will have to be developed before a lighter and more vulnerable vehicle can work.

The US Navy faces the challenge of transforming itself from a fleet designed to fight in the open ocean to one that can dominate the littorals and project power ashore. To carry this out, the navy has sought the capability to wage network-centric warfare by linking weapon, sensor and command-and-control systems. It has begun conducting Fleet Battle Experiments to explore concepts for implementing network-centric warfare. The US Marine Corps, for its part, is exploring new methods of power projection as well as ways to come to grips with the challenges associated with military operations in urban terrain.

While the navy's acquisition programmes are dominated by incremental improvements to current surface ship and aircraft designs, the service is also exploring concepts to replace large platforms with a network of smaller and less vulnerable systems. The Naval War College, for example, has examined the *Streetfighter* – a family of small platforms designed to gain and sustain access to the littoral region in the face of a robust access-denial capability, as well as the *Corsair*, a small aircraft carrier. Inspired by the performance of HMAS *Jervis Bay* in East Timor, it is

Strategic Policy Issues

also exploring the use of fast catamarans to deploy and sustain amphibious forces. Other navy innovators have proposed converting four *Ohio*-class nuclear-fuelled ballistic-missile submarines (SSBNs) to platforms carrying large numbers of land-attack cruise missiles and special operations forces. Such ideas have predictably drawn fire from those who see them as a threat to existing surface-ship programmes.

The US Air Force, a service defined by the technology of manned aircraft, faces the challenge of adapting to unmanned aerial vehicles (UAVs) as well as to military operations in space and cyberspace. The hurdles it has faced in integrating UAVs into its force posture are illustrative. The air force currently operates two squadrons of RQ-1A *Predator* medium-altitude and endurance UAVs. Controlled by ground-based operators, these aircraft transmit electro-optical, infrared and synthetic-aperture radar imagery via satellite to ground stations in the United States or to the theatre of operations. The air force is also evaluating the *Global Hawk* high-altitude, long-endurance UAV, an aircraft designed to fly 12,500 nautical miles at an altitude of up to 20 kilometres and remain aloft for 38–42 hours. Advocates of the system argue that it can replace the venerable U-2 reconnaissance aircraft, and do its job better.

The army, navy and marine corps also use UAVs for reconnaissance and surveillance. They are also developing more advanced designs, including man-portable micro-UAVs for tactical reconnaissance, and vertical-takeoff systems. Indeed, one survey estimates that some 50 US companies are developing more than 150 UAV designs.

In autumn 2000, the air force rolled out the first prototype uninhabited combat aerial vehicle (UCAV), the X-45A. The aircraft is designed to fly as high as 12km, have a 1,600km range, and carry 12 miniature bombs. Controlled by a ground-based operator, its primary mission will be to attack enemy air-defence sites, paving the way for manned aircraft. The air force also plans to test the *Predator* as a UCAV. Support for unmanned vehicles within the air force has been lukewarm. While it plans to spend nearly $70bn on the F-22 fighter aircraft, and the air force, navy and marine corps $200bn or more on the Joint Strike Fighter, the UCAV budget stands at a mere $126 million. Indeed, one of the chief advantages of UCAVs is that they are relatively cheap. Over the next 15 years, the most sensible option appears to be some mix of manned and unmanned aircraft in the air-defence suppression role. On this score, the US is both technologically and conceptually far ahead of any other country. At the same time, the US Congress' general requirement that by 2010 one-third of all military aircraft designed to strike enemy territory be unmanned is too rigid to accommodate the uncertainties of operational need with respect to a developing technology.

The US armed forces increasingly rely upon space assets for reconnaissance, surveillance, communications and navigation. US space capabilities have proved to be a crucial force multiplier for the past 15–20 years. While America's military use of space represents a great strength, many also see it as a growing vulnerability. Potential adversaries that could obstruct US access to space assets – by interfering with reconnaissance satellites and jamming communications links and navigation signals – would put US forces at a grave disadvantage. It is therefore hardly surprising that Secretary of Defense Donald Rumsfeld has identified defending US space assets as one of his top priorities.

No Lack of Ideas, Only Money

Soviet military theorists were the first to predict that the development of information technology would spawn a 'revolution in military affairs'. Russian military analysts have continued this trend, speculating extensively about how the information revolution may transform the character and conduct of war. In addition, the Russian defence industry continues to produce innovative weapons, such as the SS-NX-27 *Novator Alfa* anti-ship cruise missile (ASCM) and the *Shkval* high-speed underwater rocket. Still, a weak economy has prevented the Russian armed forces from exploiting the information revolution. Russia's continuing war in Chechnya and a broader focus on counter-insurgency have also been distracting. With 70% of the Russian defence budget spent on maintaining current forces, there is little left for modernisation. In November, however, Moscow announced plans to reduce the size of the Russian armed forces by 600,000 men, and President Vladimir Putin has made clear his intention to make deep cuts in nuclear forces to finance conventional modernisation. Although elements of the Russian military resist such moves, Putin appears to have won the argument.

China: Scrambling to Catch Up

China's ongoing dispute with Taiwan, coupled with the prospect of US intervention in a Taiwan Strait conflict, serves as a strategic focus for Beijing's modernisation efforts. In March 2000, Beijing announced an increase of 17.7% in the Chinese defence budget. The publicly announced budget itself is substantially lower than the actual one, so Chinese claims should be taken with a grain of salt. Nevertheless, the announcement itself indicates genuine anxiety about the Bush administration's harder line with respect to China and prospective arms sales to Taiwan.

Chinese analysts have paid particular attention to information warfare as a revolutionary influence on the military in general and as a relatively cheap way of countering the technological superiority of the United States in particular. They have also outlined concepts to counter US power-projection forces, particularly carrier-battle groups. Despite extensive

Strategic Policy Issues

discussion of emerging warfare areas, however, the People's Liberation Army remains opaque to outside observers, and it is unclear how much it has begun to experiment with, or to adopt, innovative approaches to combat.

In its efforts to harness science and technology to improve its armed forces, China is known to be developing doctrine and concepts for information warfare (IW). It is studying the offensive employment of IW against foreign economic, logistics and Command, Control, Communications, Computers and Intelligence (C⁴I) systems and appears interested in researching methods to insert computer viruses into foreign computer networks. Chinese authors have discussed forming a 'net force' dedicated to conducting information operations. Moreover, although they are substantially behind major Western powers, the Chinese armed forces have begun incorporating information warfare into their exercises.

China has also begun fielding a new generation of precise ballistic missiles guided by signals from the Global Positioning System (GPS) satellite constellation. These missiles give Beijing the capability to target air-defence installations, airfields, naval bases, C⁴I nodes and logistics facilities. China has deployed the CSS-6 (DF-15 or M-9) short-range ballistic missile (SRBM), a road-mobile missile that can deliver a 500-kilogram payload to a range of 600 km. It has developed the CSS-X-7 (M-11) SRBM, which has an estimated range of 300 km, and it is also developing an improved version of the CSS-7, the CSS-7 Mod 2, with greater range. This missile will reportedly be able to carry conventional, fuel-air explosive (FAE), cluster and electro-magnetic pulse (EMP) warheads. By 2005, the PRC may have as many as 650 such missiles. In addition, Beijing is developing a land-attack cruise missile.

There can be little doubt that China is working hard to develop a range of advanced technologies. It is improving its space capability, including intelligence-gathering, communication and navigation satellites, and it is also believed to be developing a ground-based laser anti-satellite system. But Chinese modernisation efforts face a series of constraints, including an ageing capital stock, widespread corruption and weak defence industries. China still has far to go.

Japan

China's growing power, the prospect of a conflict across the Taiwan Strait, the potential for instability on the Korean Peninsula and uncertainty over the future role of the United States in Asia have all prodded Tokyo into a re-examination of its security requirements. Following North Korea's 1998 *Taepo-dong* 1 missile test, Tokyo decided to develop its own reconnaissance satellite constellation. It has also begun to cooperate more closely with the

United States on theatre missile defence. Moreover, a number of Japanese security experts have begun to discuss openly the need for Tokyo to acquire a counter-force capability, something that would have been taboo a few years ago.

Japan has also expressed interest in a more radical transformation of its defence posture. In December, the Japan Defense Agency (JDA) released a study paper examining the implications of the information revolution for Japan. The paper argued that a transformation of the Japan Self-Defense Forces (SDF) would boost their effectiveness and reduce casualties in a future conflict. It would also improve combined operations with the United States. The JDA also raised the possibility of creating experimental units within the SDF to explore new ways of war.

Despite growing interest in transformation in Japan, any such efforts will face substantial political, legal and social barriers. For example, Japan's constitution prevents it from acquiring offensive weapons, and the Japanese public is extremely wary of proposals to send military forces abroad. And while Tokyo is a world leader in producing information technology, it is less adept at major innovation. Japanese weapon development has at times been glacially slow. Any attempt at transformation will thus face daunting challenges.

Slowly, Slowly in Europe

NATO's European members have been less eager than the United States to embrace the notion that the information revolution will transform the conduct of war. While many are investing in advanced technology, including stealth, precision-guided munitions and space assets, they have generally taken an incremental approach to force modernisation. Most are configuring their forces to handle peacekeeping and low-intensity conflict, missions that do not place a premium on advanced technology. NATO's European members have good reasons to explore new ways of war, insofar as they would promote interoperability with the United States as it transforms its forces. Unfortunately, however, they appear under-motivated and are certainly not prepared to raise defence budgets sufficiently to make major advances.

The air war over Kosovo revealed a marked disparity in the capabilities of NATO members, particularly in precision strike, command-and-control and intelligence. In the wake of the conflict, NATO members have been attempting to augment their forces in several areas, including the ability to launch precision strikes from a distance. France will field the stealthy *Apache* air-launched cruise missile, while Britain and France will both deploy the stealthy *Storm Shadow*, an extended-range version of the *Apache*. France and Greece are acquiring the *Scalp* strategic land-attack cruise missile. These developments will boost significantly the coalition's long-range precision-strike capability.

European states are attempting to augment their reconnaissance and surveillance capabilities as well. France is currently the only European NATO member that operates a reconnaissance satellite, and its capabilities are limited compared to American platforms. However, France and Germany have agreed to coordinate development of a new generation of reconnaissance satellites with a resolution of less than a metre. France plans to loft the first of its *Helios* II electro-optical satellites in 2004, and Germany plans to inaugurate the *SAR-Lupe* constellation of radar satellites the same year. Cooperation may expand to include Italy, which is currently developing the *SkyMed-Cosmo* constellation of radar and optical satellites. In addition, Turkey is interested in purchasing a high-resolution surveillance satellite.

While European states are acquiring some high-technology weapons, most feel compelled to devote increased attention to crisis-response and peacekeeping missions. In November, European Union defence ministers pledged troops and equipment to create a 60,000-strong crisis-response force by 2003. This force is composed of units that already exist, are already trained and equipped, and, in large part, are already committed to NATO. The change is mainly organisational and the units would require upgrading whether or not they were configured into a new EU force. Nevertheless, the political and institutional upheaval accompanying the inception of the force may crowd out modernisation efforts, or at least put them on hold. Resource constraints form another barrier to transformation. No European state has shown a willingness to increase its defence expenditures to pay for these undertakings. Indeed, some are still cutting their budgets.

Swifter Sweden

While NATO's European members are incrementally improving their ability to conduct peacekeeping and small-scale operations, the Swedish armed forces have undertaken a more radical transformation. Having cut its officer corps from 15,000 to 9,400 and reorganised its armed forces into three joint commands, Sweden spends more money on research and development as a proportion of gross domestic product than any other nation in the world. It is therefore hardly surprising that its armed forces are actively pursuing a range of advanced weapon systems. They are leveraging Sweden's expertise in information technology to develop a unified battlespace-information network. They are also interested in employing UAVs for reconnaissance, surveillance and attack missions. Saab, for example, is reportedly studying a low-observable UCAV, dubbed the Swedish Highly Advanced Research Configuration, or SHARC, for strike missions. It is also examining electromagnetic pulse and non-lethal warheads for the RBS-15 Mark 3 cruise missile.

The Swedish Navy has been actively involved in exploring new ways of war. During the early 1990s, it used the *Smyge* surface-effect ship to evaluate stealth techniques as well as new weapons, sensors and communication systems. In June 2000, it launched the first of six stealthy *Visby* class corvettes. The ships, which displace 600 tonnes and have a crew of 43, are designed for anti-surface warfare, anti-submarine warfare, mine countermeasures, and mine-laying missions. Despite innovative instincts, however, even Sweden appears ambivalent about making the full transition from the old system to a smaller and more mobile regular military.

Australia Tries to Move Ahead

Australia is another regional power that has devoted considerable attention to the prospect that the information revolution may transform warfare. The Australian government has followed closely US speculation and experimentation regarding emerging warfare areas and has established an Office of the Revolution in Military Affairs within the Department of Defence to review the development of advanced technology and to develop a strategy for exploiting it. The Australian Defence Force (ADF) believes that force projection, protection and sustainability, together with information warfare, represent crucial areas for Australia, and that pursuing them will greatly enhance the ADF's ability to undertake joint and combined operations. They have given the highest priority to the so-called 'knowledge edge': the exploitation of information technology to maximise the effectiveness of Australia's small armed forces.

Australia recently shifted its defence strategy from homeland defence to force projection in Australia's immediate neighbourhood. In December, it announced an $A23.5bn increase (roughly 3% annually) in defence spending over the next decade. It has also increased funds allocated to research and development. The ADF has emphasised advanced intelligence, surveillance and reconnaissance capabilities. The Defence Science and Technology Organisation has established the *Takari* programme to ensure that the ADF has an integrated Command, Control, Communications and Intelligence (C^3I) and information-operations capability. The ADF is acquiring over-the-horizon radars and airborne early-warning and control aircraft, and is interested in purchasing long-range UAVs.

On balance, however, Australia's revolutionary inclinations are constrained by ground-level realities. Its continuing commitment to peacekeeping in East Timor will drain funds from military modernisation. Moreover, between 2007 and 2010, it will face block obsolescence in a

Strategic Policy Issues

number of its major weapon systems, including the F/A-18, F-111 and P-3C aircraft and FFG-7 frigates. Australia will face some painful choices in replacing these systems and must be selective in its acquisition of emerging capabilities.

Whither the Transformation?

It is clear that recent attempts to exploit the information revolution have varied considerably in scope and pace. While a large number of states are acquiring stealth, precision and information technology, efforts to develop the doctrine and organisations needed to realise radical improvements in military effectiveness have lagged. Armed forces today, like their counterparts in the 1920s and 1930s, have to come to grips with new technology and work out how best to harness it in the service of national goals. To date, however, no military has yet unlocked the full potential of information technology.

The United States has distinct advantages in information technology and is far ahead of the curve. The history of innovation, however, shows that early leaders in emerging warfare areas often fail to sustain their lead. Britain took an early lead in tank technology and doctrine in the 1920s, only to have Germany overtake it. While innovators within the US armed forces are experimenting with new ways of war, service traditionalists have strenuously opposed their efforts. On top of that, NATO's European allies and Japan have yet to embrace the information-age warfare methods. The reluctance or inability of some of the United States' closest allies to transform themselves may, in turn, limit US efforts. Particularly with respect to NATO members, interoperability and closing the capability gap are important American priorities. Insofar as accelerating modernisation would decrease interoperability and widen the gap, Washington may decide that modernisation must remain merely gradual.

Regional powers – particularly those focused on a concrete strategic or operational problem – have historically proven quite adept at innovating. Sweden under Gustavus Adolphus, Prussia in the nineteenth century and Japan in the twentieth century all mastered new ways of war before their adversaries. More recently, Sweden and Australia have proven willing to experiment with new technology, doctrine and organisations. Other regional powers may follow. But all such efforts are likely to be inhibited not only by institutional malaise and caution, but also by the fact that most contingencies call for proven capabilities rather than untested ones.

It should not be surprising that a revolution in military affairs has yet to be realised. Militaries, like all large bureaucracies, are exceedingly difficult to change. Past innovations have taken decades to implement. Success ultimately requires vision and a willingness to take risks –

qualities that most militaries lack. Perhaps at this stage of complacency, incremental advances that eventually add up to major change are more to be expected than any leaping revolution in military affairs.

The Frayed Nuclear Non-Proliferation Regime

Is the treaty-based nuclear non-proliferation regime eroding? The evidence is ambiguous but worrying. Not all of the news in recent years has been bad. The Nuclear Non-proliferation Treaty (NPT) was indefinitely extended in 1995. Ukraine, Kazakstan and Belarus relinquished the nuclear weapons left on their territories after the demise of the Soviet Union. South Africa dismantled its small nuclear arsenal and joined the NPT as a non-weapon state. Brazil and Argentina abandoned their nuclear weapon aspirations and similarly joined the NPT. Moreover, the formally recognised nuclear weapon states have reduced their arsenals by thousands of warheads. Those who wish to paint a positive picture can highlight this side of the ledger.

Nevertheless, it is at the same time clear that the international non-proliferation regime has been subjected to severe stresses over the past decade that have exposed its weaknesses and limitations. The ongoing and unresolved crisis over Iraq's nuclear programme and its apparently unabated nuclear appetite has starkly revealed the regime's inability to cope effectively with a determined cheater. Similarly, the outcome of the lingering confrontation over North Korea's nuclear programme remains in doubt, despite more than a decade of arduous deliberations and diplomacy. Acrimonious debate over Iran's nuclear ambitions raises questions about whether emerging non-proliferation challenges can be addressed early and effectively.

In addition, more than a decade after the dissolution of the Soviet Union, concern persists about the possibility of serious nuclear leakage from Russia. While extra-treaty and bilateral factors, like the US Nunn-Lugar Cooperative Threat Reduction (CTR) programme and the Moscow-based International Science and Technology Centre's efforts, have made some impact, a substantial and coordinated effort to prevent this potential disaster has yet to materialise. A regime that cannot handle the most significant challenges is susceptible to being undermined eventually. On the other hand, it appears politically impossible to develop a regime that can deal with determined cheaters. To address this problem, tough decisions on economic, political and possibly military action are essential.

Exploding Nuclear Myths in South Asia

The most recent setback to the treaty regime occurred in May 1998, when India conducted a series of nuclear weapon tests and Pakistan followed suit almost immediately. In one sense, the tests represented only a minor change of status for the two South Asian states. Neither was a member of the NPT, so no international legal obligations were violated. Indeed, both had explicitly preserved the legal right to exercise the nuclear option. Moreover, the nuclear weapon programmes of India and Pakistan have long been open secrets. The tests dispelled the opaqueness of the programmes, but the reality of the two countries' nuclear capabilities was certainly not a great surprise. A sanguine interpretation of the events of May 1998 would suggest that what had long been assumed about India's and Pakistan's nuclear efforts had been explicitly confirmed, but otherwise the world was not much changed.

However, the sanguine interpretation did not carry the day. Rather, the May 1998 tests provoked dismay, criticism and alarm. Though India and Pakistan were merely exercising their legal right to possess nuclear weapons, many states denounced their actions and some, including the United States, imposed sanctions in response. The international non-proliferation community was particularly disturbed and disappointed by the tests. It reacted with anger, condemnation, and countless calls for India and Pakistan to 'roll back' their nuclear programmes, to join the NPT as non-weapon states, or otherwise to exercise forms of restraint far greater than the older nuclear powers had been seen to exercise. Though arguably a lawful and minor alteration of the nuclear status of India and Pakistan, the tests are widely regarded as marking a hugely detrimental watershed for the non-proliferation regime.

The explanation for this reaction is several-fold. First, many believed that the norm of nuclear non-proliferation had become almost universally accepted. No state had openly joined the nuclear club in several decades. Almost every state in the international system had become a member of the NPT. Total nuclear disarmament is very widely supported within the United Nations. Denunciations of nuclear weapons as immoral and useless are commonplace around the world, even in official diplomacy. The South Asian tests, however, shattered the comforting presumption that nuclear weapon programmes were in retreat.

Second, India and Pakistan are relatively reputable states: Pakistan has long been an ally of the United States; India, the world's largest democracy, had for many years positioned itself as a leader of the international campaign for nuclear disarmament. These are not 'rogues', outlaws, obvious cheaters, or 'states of concern'. They do not belong to any category that makes them easily dismissible exceptions to the rule of non-proliferation. The very fact that their tests were lawful acts by reputable states makes the violation of the perceived norm of non-proliferation seem all the more alarming.

Third, the open acquisition of nuclear weapons by India and Pakistan, and their repeated assertions that these weapons will be integrated into their military doctrines, undercuts the argument that nuclear weapons are useless – an argument often advanced by advocates of non-proliferation. Whatever choices were made in past decades, this argument has run, the irrelevance of nuclear weapons to genuine security concerns is now more widely understood. India and Pakistan have rejected such arguments, suggesting that their interests are served, their security enhanced and their status elevated by the acquisition of nuclear capabilities. Though appealing, the notion that nuclear weapons are expensive and militarily useless is, in any event, subject to serious challenge. For a country facing a threat to its very survival – for example, Israel or Pakistan – nuclear weapons and other weapons of mass destruction (WMD) have obvious utility. Indeed, to argue otherwise would diminish the case for a treaty-based non-proliferation regime.

Fourth, some of the dismay over the advance of the nuclear weapon programmes in South Asia derives from the tense and occasionally violent relations between India and Pakistan. The Soviet Union and the United States, though unquestionably hostile during the Cold War, were widely separated geographically and lacked any tradition of fighting one another. India and Pakistan share a disputed border and have fought a series of wars and skirmishes along it. As many see it, one of the world's most dangerous and war-prone rivalries now has a nuclear dimension. Fear that nuclear weapons might be used in this dispute naturally arises.

Finally, many of the factors giving rise to nuclear stability in the strategic relationship between the Soviet Union and the United States are lacking in South Asia. The internal political stability that characterised both countries for most of the Cold War can not be relied on in South Asia, especially in troubled Pakistan. This raises the spectre of nuclear weapons becoming involved in domestic turbulence. The complex and enormous arsenals that underpinned mutual deterrence in the Soviet–American context will not exist in South Asia for many years, if ever. In addition, serious command-and-control vulnerabilities are likely to exist for years to come, raising fears and risks of so-called nuclear decapitation. South Asia presents a classic case of strategic instability, which is particularly worrying because of the likelihood of conflict in the region.

In short, coming on top of the lingering non-proliferation crises of the 1990s, the open nuclearisation of South Asia was a serious shock and contributed to unease about the health and long-term effectiveness of the existing NPT regime. That regime remains valuable, but it may be insufficient to stem the slow spread of nuclear weapons. The question immediately arises as to what steps the existing nuclear powers (especially the United States and Russia, as the world's largest nuclear powers) might take to reinforce the NPT. If avoiding the spread of nuclear weapons is an important objective for these powers, as they often state, they should be willing to attach priority to actions that would, or might, promote non-proliferation. What might they do and what are they doing?

Dramatically Trim Their Own Nuclear Arsenals

Non-proliferation might be promoted by large reductions in existing nuclear arsenals, especially by Russia and the United States. If, at the end of the Cold War, they had made vigorous and purposeful efforts to divest themselves of their enormous inventories, putting themselves – and the world – on a trajectory heading rapidly and certainly towards much smaller nuclear holdings, this might have conveyed – and might still convey – the message that Cold War nuclear excesses were being eliminated and that nuclear weapons would play a much smaller part in world affairs in the new era. This would have increased the credibility of US and Russian claims to be fulfilling their obligations under Article VI of the NPT (calling for genuine movement towards nuclear disarmament) and of their declared support for nuclear disarmament. This would in turn have lent credence to their claims that nuclear weapons are of limited value. Steady shrinkage of the world's largest arsenals might have addressed the widespread international complaint about the discriminatory nature of the NPT regime. In sum, non-proliferation is more likely to be achieved in a world that is steadily being rid of large numbers of nuclear weapons.

Substantial reductions have in fact taken place, and some weapons have been dismantled. Further reductions in deployed intercontinental systems may yet take place. But both Moscow and Washington still retain huge nuclear arsenals and their combined holdings still number in the tens of thousands. More than a decade after the end of the Cold War, their strategic forces are still legally governed only by the Strategic Arms Reduction Treaty (START) I, which originated in the first term of US President Ronald Reagan. Even if, by agreement or through unilateral action, numbers of deployed strategic weapons are noticeably reduced, little has been done to address the large inventories of tactical and reserve warheads held by both Russia and the United States.

It is often suggested that the US and Russian arsenals provide aspiring proliferators with an excuse, but not with their real motivation. It follows that significant reductions in weaponry by Moscow and Washington would not loom large in the proliferators' calculations. This is a plausible argument. It may nevertheless be worthwhile to eliminate the excuse. And while deep retrenchment by the major nuclear powers may not be a certain path to successful avoidance of proliferation, their maintenance of huge nuclear arsenals surely undercuts the case against nuclear acquisition by other states. If Moscow and Washington continue to justify their own possession of many thousands of nuclear weapons, how can they effectively argue against very small holdings by others?

Devalue Nuclear Weapons

In parallel with dramatic reductions in their arsenals, Moscow and Washington might have done much to devalue nuclear weapons by downgrading the role in their own security policies that such weapons play. They might have concluded, as have many past officials of their governments, that nuclear weapons are no longer necessary or important for US or Russian security. Such a posture could help foster the idea that a nuclear armoury has limited utility and lacks legitimacy, though the argument is unlikely to be endorsed in Baghdad, Pyongyang or even Tel Aviv.

The American and Russian positions are complicated. Until 2000, Moscow had embraced nuclear weapons in its military doctrine to compensate for the seriously weakened state of its conventional forces. It had adopted a nuclear doctrine resembling that of the Cold War period, calling for early first use of nuclear weapons if necessary in response to conventional attack. President Vladimir Putin, however, has reversed both doctrinal and budgetary priorities and called for modernisation of conventional forces and reduction of the Strategic Rocket Forces. While the US focus is now on intense conventional military modernisation, it has also expanded the rationale of its nuclear posture, suggesting that it might employ nuclear reprisals in response to attacks with chemical or biological weapons. In addition, it has refused to accept suggestions that it adopt a no-first-use policy.

NATO's new strategic concept, announced at its fiftieth anniversary summit in 1999, asserts unambiguously that the alliance views nuclear weapons as necessary for the indefinite future. Nuclear weapons are said in this document to be the absolute bedrock, the ultimate guarantor, of alliance security. From a non-proliferation point of view, this claim is problematic. Given NATO's unrivalled conventional military capacity and the absence of any substantial direct threat to its security, if the alliance requires nuclear weapons to guarantee its security, then what state or coalition should feel secure without them? The arguments supporting NATO's nuclear policy apply with even greater force to weaker powers. Yet the counter-argument is also compelling: if NATO were to divest itself of nuclear weapons, smaller potential adversaries would have a greater incentive to acquire WMD to gain asymmetrical advantages.

In May 2000, as part of a long-term global agenda reached at a month-long conference review of the NPT at the UN, the five Permanent Members of the Security Council (P-5) issued a pledge asserting their 'unequivocal undertaking … to accomplish the total elimination of their nuclear arsenals, leading to nuclear disarmament to which all parties are committed'. While this is a salutary aim, no definite timetable was cited for achieving it, rendering the pledge largely symbolic. Thus, for the time being, some states should be expected occasionally to seek the benefits of nuclear possession for themselves.

The Importance of Security Commitments

States that are confident in their security are less likely to seek nuclear weapons. Powerful states can help others to feel safe by offering security guarantees (as does the United States via its alliances in Europe and Asia) or entering into other relationships that enhance the security of other states (as the US has done with Israel and Taiwan). It is sometimes said that the US alliance system is one of the most important barriers to proliferation – a fact that should not be forgotten in the ongoing and inconclusive debate about what America's role should be in the post-Cold War era. Many of America's friends and allies are fully capable of becoming nuclear-weapon states and some have been tempted in the past (for example, South Korea and Taiwan). US retrenchment could well result in the emergence of new nuclear powers, especially among those friendly states that are in dangerous and/or heavily nuclear regions (such as Turkey, South Korea, Taiwan and Japan).

Moscow's declining power and the interruption of some of its security relationships provide a salutary illustration of the point. Several of the world's proliferation trouble spots – Iraq, North Korea and India – are states that had longstanding security relationships with the Soviet Union. For these states, the collapse of the USSR represented a significant and adverse shift in the international balance of power: they lost a friend, a patron, a reliable source of weapons and spare parts, and a counterweight to American and Chinese power. In these less favourable circumstances, their pursuit of nuclear weapons gained greater momentum and importance. These cases illustrate the proposition that increased insecurity can breed nuclear proliferation.

Employ Threats Carefully to Avoid Provoking Proliferation

Adversarial confrontations between strong and weak countries may provoke the latter to acquire nuclear weapons. This means that the diplomacy of force must be handled skilfully to avoid undercutting the non-proliferation regime. If reassuring states about their security reduces the likelihood of their seeking nuclear weapons, threats may have the opposite effect. This can pose complex policy dilemmas, because Washington or NATO may often perceive a need to deter or coerce hostile powers. Threats are an unavoidable component of the diplomacy of force. But they should not be employed without considering their possibly counterproductive effects from a non-proliferation perspective.

Thus, any state that is or feels seriously threatened by the overwhelming power of the United States may be tempted to acquire nuclear weapons as the only conceivable way to counteract America's vast conventional military supremacy. It should be no surprise that several states that have been particular subjects of American ire have apparently judged that pursuit of nuclear weapons is in their security interest. These include Iran and North Korea. The state most directly engaged in military confrontation with the United States, Iraq, is also thought to have persisted with unwavering determination in its efforts to acquire WMD, despite enormous difficulties and obstacles. Ironically, Baghdad first developed WMD in 1986–90, when the Washington was one of its strongest allies. Iraq's goal then was to secure a strong military deterrent, particularly *vis-à-vis* Iran, to compensate for having a relatively small population, and to further its aspirations to regional hegemony. While these concerns undoubtedly continue to figure in President Saddam Hussein's thinking, since the Gulf War his primary aim in maintaining a WMD capability has almost certainly been to counter the overwhelming American threat.

Accommodate Multilateral Arms Control

For much of the world, or at least that portion of it involved in non-proliferation issues, there are a suite of multilateral arms-control agreements that are viewed as desirable or necessary supplements to the NPT. The most important of these is the Comprehensive Test Ban Treaty (CTBT), but the Fissile Material Cut-off Treaty (FMCT) is also on the list. For many non-nuclear parties to the NPT, these concordats appear to have particular symbolic or political value. But they also represent efforts to curtail, on a non-discriminatory global basis, certain kinds of weapons-related activity.

By further restricting the ability of signatories to engage in such activity, these multilateral agreements would buttress the NPT. Moreover, in connection with the NPT extension conference of 1995, many states believed that the nuclear weapon countries had provided assurances of progress in these areas.

Instead, multilateral nuclear-arms control appears to be faltering. The CTBT suffered a major blow when the US Senate voted against ratification in 1999. Without ratification by one of the necessary signatories, the conditions for the treaty's entry into force seem unlikely to be met soon. Similarly, efforts to launch negotiations on the FMCT have foundered. These failures have provoked ill will and accusations of bad faith from states that had regarded progress on these agreements as part of the bargain made in 1995. More fundamentally, the failure to fashion acceptable multilateral nuclear arms-control arrangements leads to the perception that at least some among the nuclear powers are reluctant to accept meaningful constraints on their own weapon programmes even as they continue to insist that others should engage in complete nuclear abstinence. Nuclear contraction and nuclear restraint, then, do not appear to be priorities. Nevertheless, US and Russian stockpiles of strategic weapons could well diminish without further treaty negotiations, as informal confidence-building measures grow in their place.

Strengthen Controls on Weapons-Usable Fissile Material

In its essence, the NPT is a denial regime built around the difficulty of producing or obtaining the fissile material necessary to manufacture nuclear weapons. It follows that any strengthening of controls on the manufacture, storage and transfer of fissile material promotes the regime's effectiveness. Obviously, the regime itself restricts manufacture and transfer of fissile material, and some international standards for storage are in place. But a systematic assessment of how these might be augmented and comprehensively applied to all facilities and holdings would be desirable.

Similarly, any development that threatens to undermine the denial system poses a serious threat to the regime and demands urgent attention and priority. The problem of 'loose nukes' in the former Soviet Union (especially Russia) falls into this category. Russia possesses huge quantities of both weapons and fissile material. Over the past decade, these holdings have coexisted with high levels of political instability, economic distress and social dislocation. Many nuclear facilities were unable to establish meaningful levels of safety and security for their inventories. Any large-scale rupture of the Russian custodial system for nuclear weapons would pose a massive, potentially mortal, threat to the non-proliferation regime.

A treaty system built around denial cannot survive if the materials being denied become widely available on an international black market.

Substantial risks of leakage from Russia persist and a non-proliferation disaster cannot be ruled out. Despite this worrying reality, mounting a large and coordinated international effort to reduce these risks rapidly and dramatically has thus far proved impossible. But the United States, in particular, has made a sustained and substantial, if still insufficient, effort to work with Russia on safety and security upgrades under the CTR programme. As a consequence, the problem is less acute than it was a few years ago. In addition to financing technical assistance for weapons deactivation, fissile-materials disposal and similar matters, CTR funds have been used to neutralise the proliferating effect of the 'brain drain' by employing Russian scientists in the West, thus diverting them from peddling their knowledge to states (such as Iran, Iraq or North Korea) interested in acquiring a nuclear capability.

In late March 2001, the administration of new US President George W. Bush began a careful six-week review of the CTR and related programmes, with an eye towards ensuring that funds used to assist Russia in dismantling its nuclear arsenal – budgeted at $458 million for fiscal 2001 – were being well spent. The administration appeared disposed to endorse the continuation of the programme. Given the limitations of treaty-based solutions, the sustenance and reinforcement of such informal bilateral programmes is essential to stemming proliferation. More formal non-treaty mechanisms are also useful. One example is the Korean Peninsula Energy Development Organisation, a consortium led by the United States, Japan, South Korea and the European Atomic Energy Community that is building two light-water nuclear reactors for North Korea in exchange for Pyongyang's halting its nuclear weapon programme.

Harmonise Enforcement of the NPT

What should be done about cheaters? It is apparent from the experience of the last decade that the world has no clear answer to this question. Should violators be rewarded for coming back into compliance or punished for transgressing their international obligations? Should they be isolated and ostracised or drawn back into normal diplomatic intercourse? Should their NPT transgression affect the full range of their international interactions or should some aspects of international engagement – for example, trade, travel and diplomacy – remain unaffected? How long can and should enforcement efforts persist?

The unseemly disputes among the P-5 over what to do about Iraq and, to a lesser extent, about North Korea, make it evident that among the nuclear powers (as well as among other states), there are no consistent answers to these questions – despite the fact that both countries have presented clear-cut and disturbing instances of cheating. There have been disagreements over the imposition and protraction of sanctions on Iraq, over travel to that country, over its role in the international petroleum market, over trade and military sales to Baghdad, and many other matters. There has been criticism among the P-5 of overly harsh treatment of Iraq. On the other hand the agreed framework with North Korea was criticised for excessively rewarding a cheater.

It is naïve to think that the nuclear powers will be able to take fully concerted action against non-compliance. Their interests, their perceptions and their relations with the guilty party, will never be identical. But some greater harmonisation of approaches is necessary if the regime is to cope with cheating in any meaningful way. Perhaps there needs to be some general consultation among the nuclear powers about how to react to non-compliance, apart from the particulars of any given case, so that in future they can at least proceed from common premises. Certainly the cause of non-proliferation is not advanced by the remarkable spectacle of Russia and France siding with Iraq against the United States. If a determined cheater needs only to outlast a fragile consensus among the P-5, the regime will be unable to address the most serious cases. Thus, better coalition management is a necessary step towards a more effective non-proliferation policy.

Improve and Strengthen the IAEA

The International Atomic Energy Agency (IAEA) has become a favourite whipping boy, commonly subject to attack for any and all failings of the non-proliferation regime. In many circles, it is neither respected nor supported. It is often condemned as just another dysfunctional UN agency. There is little impulse to treat it generously in budgetary terms. It lacks the confidence and strong support of many major states.

No doubt some of the criticism is deserved. But the fact remains that the IAEA is the primary international implementing agency associated with the NPT regime. It is not, and was never intended to be, the whole answer to the problem of nuclear proliferation. The IAEA is a fissile-materials accounting organisation and is not, by itself, capable of uncovering weapon programmes. The organisation probably will never be able to handle hard cases like Iraq. But it does have responsibility for important pieces of the puzzle, and it is hard to see how any non-proliferation regime could function effectively without something like the agency in place. When it is forced to operate with weak political support and inadequate funding in an atmosphere of derisive criticism, its inadequacy may be a self-fulfilling prophecy.

The marginal improvements of the IAEA's 93+2 safeguards system – aimed at facilitating the discovery of undeclared nuclear activities – will not be in widespread operation for some years. But if the IAEA – or something like it – is a necessary element of an international non-proliferation regime, then it behoves the nuclear powers to work to reform and strengthen it now. Indeed, if mounting concerns about global warming produce growth in civilian nuclear-power programmes over the next two decades, the IAEA's role in overseeing and inspecting civilian nuclear activities may be even larger and more important in the future. At the same time, its inherent limits need to be recognised: casting the IAEA as a panacea will yield only false confidence.

Accept More Transparency

The NPT regime cannot function reliably and effectively in the absence of some minimum level of transparency. Covert weapon programmes are the curse of the regime. The more transparent the world's nuclear infrastructure and nuclear commerce, the more reliable assurance the NPT system will be able to provide that the treaty is being respected. There is a good case for trying to maximise the transparency measures associated with the treaty in order to strengthen and boost confidence in the regime

However, while the nuclear powers insist that all other signatories to the NPT must be subjected to intrusive international inspection of their (presumably civil) nuclear activities, their own nuclear programmes are exempt from such scrutiny. This is another of those NPT-related double standards that attracts international criticism and has irritated even friendly states. No doubt there are multiple barriers to the acceptance of greater transparency, but presumably this would be easier to accomplish if the system were to be augmented in a non-discriminatory manner. But Russia and the United States have been unable to achieve high levels of transparency even in their own cooperative nuclear programmes. In fact, the transparency negotiations between Moscow and Washington were an almost complete failure throughout the 1990s. If the United States and Russia are unwilling to accept transparent arrangements in connection with their own nuclear activities – even on a bilateral basis – it is hard to condemn or persuade other states that resist the expansion of transparency measures in the context of the NPT regime.

Treaty Regimes Are Not Enough

While imperfect, the non-proliferation regime has functioned surprisingly well over several decades, despite unfavourable realities and conditions. There are fewer states with nuclear weapon programmes now than there

Strategic Policy Issues

were ten years ago. But the world conditions that would most favour international non-proliferation and that would most strongly support the arguments against more widespread nuclear acquisition do not exist and may never exist. And while there is much that might be done by the existing nuclear powers to create an international context more conducive to successful non-proliferation efforts, the measures outlined above have largely been unacceptable to one or more of the nuclear powers. By contrast, those powers – the United States and Russia in particular – have been fairly receptive to informal bilateral arrangements, such as the CTR programme. Such programmes are indispensable complements to any non-proliferation regime for controlling the supply of nuclear material and know-how. But whatever the nuclear powers may do in the context of the NPT and the CTBT, and in terms of CTR, this will have only a marginal impact on the demand side of the equation. Thus, treaty-based and cooperative activities need to be complemented by sustained attempts to resolve conflicts – in the Middle East, the Persian Gulf, South Asia and the Korean Peninsula – that give rise to the demand for WMD.

The Future of Peacekeeping

The publication in August 2000 of the Report of the Panel on United Nations Peace Operations – known as the Brahimi Report after the panel's chairman, former Algerian foreign minister Lakhdar Brahimi – was the focal point of the international community's efforts that year to improve peacekeeping operations. The report's recommendations are based on a review and analysis of past experiences. While they are salutary, and the proposals are sensible and constitute a useful stocktaking, there is little in the Brahimi Report that has not been said before. Moreover, there remain immense practical barriers to serious improvement in the practice of peacekeeping.

The Brahimi Report and the Real World

The Brahimi Report is intended to guide the strategic direction of the UN, as well as to address practical issues such as decision-making, rapid deployment, and planning and support. An important operational conclusion is that disarmament, demobilisation and reintegration of combatants must be integral parts of a peacekeeping operation. Although the importance of such schemes in the abstract has been recognised for some years, the UN's approach in practice has been erratic. For instance, while programmes in El Salvador and Mozambique in the early 1990s seemed better than the UN's inconsistent approach in Somalia in 1992–93, the under-funded and poorly thought-out policy applied in Sierra Leone in 1999–2000 indicated that little real progress had been made over the course of nearly a decade.

Other key recommendations include:

- Increasing emphasis on strengthening 'rule-of-law' institutions in post-conflict situations;

- Higher budget allocations for headquarters' support for peace-keeping operations so that they can retain qualified personnel instead of relying on short-term contracts;

- Strengthening the UN's permanent capacity to develop and implement peacebuilding strategies;

- Ensuring that peacekeeping mandates afford UN soldiers robust rules of engagement and other recourse against 'spoilers';

- Endeavouring to make cease-fire and peace agreements that are, to the extent practicable, consonant with human-rights standards;

- Exploring the feasibility of developing a criminal code – open to customisation – which could be applied pending the re-estab-lishment of local rule-of-law institutions and law-enforcement capacity;

- Encouraging member states to enter into partnerships to form brigade-sized forces together with logistical support, deployable within 30 days of the adoption of a Security Council resolution, or within 90 days for complex peacekeeping operations; and

- Sending advance teams to confirm that troops committed to a given peacekeeping deployment meet minimal training, equip-ment and force-protection requirements.

These recommendations seek to reduce the present haphazard, *ad hoc* character of UN peacekeeping operations and to bring some coherence to them. Some critics have argued that the report provides no useful suggestions about how to address the difficult political issues that hamper peace operations. But there would seem to be no general prescription for solving problems that involve sovereign priorities and philosophical differences about the use of force in peacekeeping. The most sobering realities relevant to UN peace operations remain existential. Wealthier Western countries are increasingly reluctant to engage in peacekeeping

Strategic Policy Issues

out-of-area and developing countries fear that the West is abandoning them.

East Timor and Kosovo

Despite these constraining influences, two of the largest UN peace operations in 2000 – in East Timor and Kosovo – were comprehensive peacebuilding endeavours. Both operations follow the post-Cold War tendency of UN peace missions to be authorised for humanitarian and political, as opposed to more narrowly military, purposes. Thus, in 2000 the UN recognised the need to accommodate civilian problems and to increase its own civilian personnel. Although the number of UN 'blue helmets' deployed has decreased to 30,000 in 2001 from an all-time high of 76,000 in 1994, the number of civilian-affairs personnel has risen to roughly 15,000 in 2001 from about 4,000 in 1994. Such personnel include staff in the major UN agencies, such as the UN Development Programme and the UN High Commissioner for Refugees, UN civilian police and other civilian administrators.

In short, the UN's role has changed rather than diminished, perhaps reflecting the common observation that soldiers are not diplomats, administrators, police or social workers. The shift towards civilian peacekeeping is also reflected in the UN's increased cooperation with non-governmental organisations (NGOs). *Ad hoc* mechanisms have struggled to keep pace with the mushrooming organisations involved in peacekeeping. All this guarantees that coordination will continue to be a key challenge in the future.

Implicitly or explicitly, current peacekeeping operations usually entail some degree of nation-building or democratisation. Kosovo is a protectorate, East Timor a trusteeship. In both operations, the UN has faced the acute problem of effectively containing deprivation and political disarray on the one hand, while developing local political and administrative capacity on the other. When the UN moves into a conflict area with a massive civilian apparatus and a robust mandate, it is difficult – at least in the short term – not to deprive the local population of responsibility for and control over the peace process. The UN Transitional Administration in East Timor (UNTAET) has been called, tellingly if facetiously, 'The UN's Kingdom of East Timor'.

The UN tries to cope with this problem by creating participatory structures and nurturing them. The working presumption is that indigenous ethnic and political groups should be treated impartially. In practical terms, that is a tall order, particularly as state-building requires the UN to address power relations that may have been at the root of conflict. In addition, there may be institutional reluctance on the part of the

UN to cede control to local authorities, particularly where, as in East Timor, indigenous leaders are inexperienced at self-government.

Given that the commitment of local players, however fickle, to a peace process is essential to its success, the UN risks the legitimacy of the operation if it discriminates between local parties, however much this may be justified. For example, efforts by the civilian administration in Kosovo to involve locals in reconstruction and political development have run into significant setbacks. Because of the bombing campaign that preceded it, the NATO Kosovo Force (KFOR) and the UN Mission in Kosovo (UNMIK) were initially biased in favour of the Kosovo Albanians. It proved exceedingly difficult to make the transition from intervening forcefully on behalf of one party to being an even-handed third-party ensuring security for all. UNMIK has been especially reluctant to deal decisively with the remnants of the Kosovo Liberation Army, their hidden arms caches and their continuing provocations.

The maintenance of law and order has emerged as a pivotal element in state building and democratisation. In both Kosovo and East Timor, full responsibility for law and order has overextended the capacity of the civilian police and the civil administration of the United Nations. The operational shortfalls of the international civilian police were exacerbated by the lack of coordination between them and military peacekeepers. Still, the missions represented qualified progress in that they chose a more holistic approach to security-sector reform. They were the first missions to embrace from the outset the training and appointment of police and judges, prison oversight and related tasks as part of peacebuilding.

In 2000–01, direct attacks on representatives of UN missions have increased and, in and around Kosovo, the activity of dissident rebels has intensified. While there are no magic formulas, it is clear that to attenuate these problems the UN will have to improve law enforcement and make inroads on political reconciliation. It appears that the UN's track-record in Kosovo and East Timor is adequate to encourage future endeavours of the same kind. In the short term, however, it is highly unlikely that the UN has the capacity to stage a third operation on the same scale, given that neither UNMIK nor UNTAET nor the ongoing mission in Bosnia-Herzegovina will be able to complete their tasks in the near future.

Sierra Leone and Congo

Expectations of successful peacekeeping are lower in Africa than elsewhere. Nevertheless, the breakdown of the Lomé accord in Sierra Leone probably posed the biggest challenge for the United Nations in 2000. The experience of the United Nations Mission in Sierra Leone (UNAMSIL) has already showcased several important facets of peacekeeping. These include: the regional dimensions of some internal conflicts; the difficulty of devising and implementing enforcement mandates; the need to define clear mission objectives; the reluctance of Western contributors to put their forces at risk in 'non-strategic' locales; and the role of unilateral action in connection with a peacekeeping operation.

To a significant extent, the conflict in Sierra Leone is driven by profitable but generally illicit business relationships in the region, centring around Sierra Leone's brutal rebel group, the Revolutionary United Front (RUF). The key business is diamonds. Although there has been some progress with the establishment of a sanctions regime aimed at under-cutting the profits from illegal diamond transactions, the effective management of the economic incentives to conflict remains elusive. As yet, there are no mechanisms to deal effectively with unconventional alliances that have arisen between private security firms, corrupt governments and rebel factions, private businesses and organised crime. All these groups stand to profit from continued instability and conflict.

When the situation in Sierra Leone began to deteriorate in May 2000, there was no agreement in the Security Council as to the substance of the UN mandate or on whether the Lomé accord remained viable or even valid. There was no agreement on the use of force, nor on the ends to which force might be used. The increasing involvement in atrocities of the democratically elected Sierra Leone government also challenged the legitimacy of UNAMSIL insofar as the UN force was deployed not only to oversee the implementation of a peace agreement but also to support the government. When the Security Council and the contributors finally did reach an agreement, it was to continue on the basis of a Chapter VI, non-enforcement mandate and to increase the force from 6,000 in October 1999 to 13,000 in May 2000.

Among Western governments, only Britain was willing to send soldiers. London would not place them under UN command owing to doubts about the UN force commander's competence, the force's weak mandate and unwillingness to engage the RUF aggressively, as well as to Britain's own reluctance to undertake a long-term commitment. A cease-fire has been maintained since November 2000, but the deployed force dwindled to under 10,500 in February 2001, when two of its largest and most qualified contingents, from India and Jordan, became disenchanted and departed. This left the force too small for effective peacekeeping in RUF-held areas, which cover at least a quarter of the country. The UN's inability to mobilise the necessary political will among contributors in Sierra Leone has led some observers to ask the more fundamental question of whether the UN can or should be counted on to mount effective peace-enforcement operations.

The war in the Democratic Republic of Congo (DROC) involves 11 nations and several rebel militias, and has claimed upward of 20,000 lives since 1998. The UN Organisation Mission in the DROC (MONUC) has been struggling to implement a cease-fire since December 1999, but its efforts have been curtailed by some of the same economic forces and member-mobilisation problems that are at play in Sierra Leone. Zimbabwe, Kinshasa's chief supporter, was drawn into the war in significant part by the promise of mineral concessions. To attempt to keep the peace in an area nearly as large as the United States east of the Mississippi River, the authorised strength of the UN troop contingent was initially only 5,537 and was subsequently reduced. A mere 10% of that number – approximately 550 military and civilian personnel – had been contributed through February 2001, and deployed in-theatre. The partisan involvement in Congo's war of five neighbouring countries, including four of Central and Southern Africa's strongest armies, has diminished potential regional sources of UN peacekeepers.

By default, during the first year of MONUC's existence, the United Nations has been limited to trying to secure improved conditions for the peace operation and to persuade the parties to the Lusaka accord to abide by its terms. The replacement of Congolese President Laurent Kabila, who was assassinated in January 2001, by his less-obstructionist son Joseph has serendipitously facilitated this objective. In February 2001, pursuant to UN Security Council Resolution 1341, warring armies began to pull back and the establishment of a 30-km buffer zone was contemplated. The UN force – whose authorised strength was reduced to 3,000 – may be sufficient to monitor a cease-fire, which further political progress could help keep intact. Nevertheless, the operation clearly illustrates the limitations on what the UN can achieve in conditions of minimal political cooperation and the absence of international backing.

The Politics of Peacekeeping

The UN's first involvement in an interstate war since the 1991 deployment of the UN Iraq–Kuwait Observation Mission (UNIKOM), began when it authorised a 4,200-strong peacekeeping force to patrol a buffer zone along the Ethiopian–Eritrean border in September 2000. A cease-fire had already been brokered by the Organisation of African Unity and bilateral sovereign mediators. The UN Mission in Ethiopia and Eritrea (UNMEE) is, in essence, an old-fashioned inter-positioning force, akin to those used in 'sleepy' missions in Cyprus, Southern Lebanon, Georgia and Western Sahara. Twenty-two countries – including seven Western European nations, Canada and the United States – made at least a nominal contribution to UNMEE. Compared with the low level of commitments to MONUC, despite its high level of force requirements, this enthusiasm appears to reflect contributing countries' wish to take up a token share of the burden of peacekeeping in Africa where there is relatively low risk.

Strategic Policy Issues

Yet one salient lesson has emerged from past peacekeeping operations: the commitment of at least one major power to support and participate in an operation through strategic leadership and contributions on the ground is generally a condition for success. Recent experience in Kosovo and Sierra Leone tends to reinforce this lesson. Clearly, then, the attitudes of the United States, Russia, China and the European states profoundly influence the ability of the United Nations to conduct peace operations effectively.

For over a decade, the United States' relationship with the UN has been coloured by the country's $1.3 billion non-payment of membership dues, mainly because of the Republican Congressional consensus that the UN was wasteful and relied too heavily on the US for peacekeeping funds. The General Assembly finally responded to American concerns in December 2000, when it agreed to redistribute members' funding obligations. The United States now has to provide 22% of the operating budget and 27% of the peacekeeping budget – both 3% reductions. In February 2001, the US Senate voted without dissent to release $582 million to the UN. The funds will go directly towards arrears to contributing countries and will at least ease the UN's financial strains. The revised mechanism for calculating dues should lead to a more reliable and predictable flow of income that will provide a more secure basis for peacekeeping. A secondary hope is that US policy towards the UN will now be more pragmatic and consistent.

Although the advent of a Republican government in the US in 2001 and the appointment of Colin Powell as Secretary of State point to a more limited direct role for the US in peacekeeping, this is likely to be a long-term shift rather than a sudden withdrawal. In February 2001, for example, Washington announced that it would not immediately withdraw a large portion of its 11,000 troops in the Balkans, despite Republican campaign rhetoric to the contrary. While the administration of President George W. Bush will continue to encourage European burden-sharing and to admonish the European Union to subordinate any EU rapid-reaction force to NATO, it is not likely to risk a more serious transatlantic rift by pulling out abruptly from the Balkans.

For the United States, however, the Balkans are something of a special case in that they implicate its core strategic interests in European security. With respect to substantial engagement in peacekeeping in non-strategic areas, such as sub-Saharan Africa, US officials and the American public probably will remain reluctant to place troops at risk. Washington's preferred approach is to encourage the regionalisation of peacekeeping in such areas through train-and-equip programmes. Rather than send troops to Sierra Leone, in August 2000 the US committed $50m and sent 200 military advisers to train five Nigerian battalions, one Ghanaian battalion and one Senegalese battalion to be used in peacekeeping operations under the aegis of the Economic Community of West African States Cease-fire Monitoring Group (ECOMOG). Beyond that, the US has done little. In the wake of the Rwandan genocide, the Clinton administration created the Africa Crisis Response Initiative to help regional military forces prepare for complex emergencies. Since its inception in 1995, however, it has received only $20m annually and trained only 6,500 soldiers. Thus, it seems doubtful that the Bush administration – given its pronounced disinclination toward peacekeeping interventions – would allocate substantial additional sums for training and equipping African peacekeepers.

The United Kingdom, though it critically sent a small contingent of combat troops to Sierra Leone in May 2000 and stabilised a dangerous situation, is also more likely to settle for train-and-equip programmes than a larger out-of-area deployment as a means of contributing to peacekeeping there. In November 2000, the UK dispatched 600 soldiers to Sierra Leone, mainly to train and rehabilitate the Sierra Leone Army. Training and equipping troops, of course, takes time. It is not a short-term solution to the problems of UN peacekeeping illuminated by Sierra Leone and Congo. But robust Western-supported programmes could provide medium-term alternatives to wholesale UN responsibility for peace-keeping.

In the shorter term, there are some, though not enough, sources of regional help. A conspicuous bright spot in 1999–2000 was Australia's effective leadership under UN auspices of the military intervention in East Timor. Australia is anticipating regional insecurity (particularly in Indonesia, Papua New Guinea, the Solomon Islands and Fiji) and reconfiguring its armed forces to allow for more effective regional deployments. There are also signs in Japan's long-term defence plan that it too sees the need for greater hands-on participation in regional peacekeeping, despite the substantial Japanese anti-military sentiment and legal impediments that would have to be overcome. The fledgling EU rapid-reaction force, which has received commitments of 60,000 troops, is not yet operational, appears unsupportable by current European defence budgets, and has no clear mandate. There is a reasonable chance, however, that it will eventually evolve into primarily a peacekeeping arm with authority for some out-of-area deployments.

In Africa, though somewhat fatigued by 2000, Nigeria has shown some commitment to taming regional conflicts, notably those in Liberia and Sierra Leone. A similar sovereign assertion of regional responsibility on the part of South Africa, though far less likely, is possible. ECOMOG, West Africa's principal regional military organ, authorised a 1,676-strong force drawn from the armies of Nigeria, Mali, Niger and Senegal to provide security for refugees trapped on the Liberia–Guinea–Sierra Leone border. While the UN continues to frown on private armies, they are still a potential source of peacekeeping assistance.

Both Russia and China will continue to add an element of unpredictability to peacekeeping discussions in the Security Council. The spirit of cooperation among the permanent members of the Security Council that had emerged since the late 1980s has been compromised by reservations on the parts of Russia, China and France about sanctions against Iraq, and on Russia and China's part over the air war in Kosovo.

The Limits of UN Peacekeeping

Following the publication of the Brahimi Report, expectations of the UN's ability to secure peace in areas threatened by conflict have risen. The report is perhaps a small step forward, but experience in all the operations of the past year has underlined how inherently fraught with difficulty peacekeeping is – both practically and politically.

The UN remains especially frustrated by conflicts in Africa, where many combatants simply may not be ready for peace and are therefore unreceptive to peacekeeping. Most of the world's conflicts are taking place on the African continent and Africa's wars claimed 60% of the world's war casualties in 1999–2000. For the United Nations, this means that Africa will continue to require significant attention. To date, UNAMSIL has not been particularly successful and the deployment of MONUC troops has been stalled by political paralysis. A number of other African conflicts – in Angola, Burundi, Sudan and potentially Guinea – remain largely unaddressed by the UN. Substantial peacekeeping commitments in the near future are highly improbable. It is more likely that the UN will adopt a limited approach involving political officers and aid-agency officials rather than a military force. Such a programme for Somalia was tentatively approved by the Security Council in January 2001.

The evolving acceptance of the legitimacy of humanitarian intervention has lowered the political and perhaps the legal threshold for international interventions in internal conflicts. Further, UN Secretary-General Kofi Annan has become more rather than less enthusiastic about intervention, reinforcing the UN's continuing determination to take on complex and ambitious operations on the scale of those in Kosovo, East Timor and Sierra Leone. Thus, the UN is likely to authorise at least as many interventions in the near future as it has so far. Yet the UN's recent peacekeeping experiences reveal the absence of – and need for – strategic thinking, lasting commitment and unity of approach among contributors to an operation. As the levels of force required for a given operation become higher and its political challenges become more complex, these requirements become more difficult to meet.

That said, the UN's limited resources dictate that each crisis must still be assessed individually, in a unique context of potential contributors' national interests and public opinion. While the prescriptions that the

Brahimi Report offers are eminently rational, international politics limit the degree to which they can be implemented. A mission will be initiated and sustained only if there is a group of states that have a particular interest in managing a conflict and that are willing to pay a considerable financial and political price. Thus, the tasks actually undertaken by a given UN peacekeeping mission are regulated by the level of commitment of national actors, and for that reason are often incongruent or incommensurate with the circumstances of the conflict they are meant to redress. Institutional reforms at the UN are not likely to change this state of affairs.

Strategic Policy Issues

The Americas

It was election year in much of the Americas. Results included a turn to the right in the United States; a new level of democracy in Mexico; the flight of an erratic president from Peru; and, in Chile, the reassuringly uneventful defeat of a moderate conservative by a moderate socialist.

In the United States, it was hardly a time of quiescence for the out-going incumbent. Having survived the impeachment battle, President Bill Clinton seemed determined to close out his time in office with a spectacular final act of peacemaking – and nothing would have been more spectacular, or more challenging, than a conclusive deal between Israel and the Palestinians. In pursuit of this goal, Clinton bulldozed the Palestinian leader Yasser Arafat into attending the July 2000 meeting at Camp David, encouraged the politically teetering Israeli Prime Minister Ehud Barak to offer unprecedented concessions, and generated subsequent meetings and negotiations literally to the last days of his presidency. When the US mediation effort failed, it was accompanied by worrying reminders of America's exposed position in the Middle East: the 12 October terrorist attack against the poorly guarded *USS Cole* on a port visit to Aden; and unnerving signs that Iraqi President Saddam Hussein's credibility in the Arab world, as a champion against the 'US–Zionist conspiracy,' was rising again.

While foreign policy rated fairly low on the scale of concern for US voters, the campaign season certainly impinged on the discussion, if not always the content, of American foreign policy. The election also shaped the decision-making process for developing a national missile defence (NMD). Although partly persuaded by an undeniable threat of missile proliferation, the Clinton administration was never particularly enthusiastic about deploying NMD, and certainly not eager to abrogate the Anti-Ballistic Missile (ABM) Treaty. Campaign pressures – the determination to shelter Democratic candidate Al Gore from Republican attack – were part of what dictated a decision deadline of summer 2000. But technical realities – the failure of two out of three missile-interceptor tests – gave Clinton the opportunity to defer the decision to the new administration. The deferral was welcome to just about everyone. It gave even the most vehement NMD hawks in the Republican Party greater scope to plan a more ambitious system than the one Clinton supported, while avoiding immediate crisis with NATO allies or the Russians.

The sense of urgency driving the NMD decision was also undercut by what looked like a real potential for detente on the Korean Peninsula.

Map 1 The Americas

Following a June 2000 summit between the leaders of North and South Korea, US and North Korean officials seemed to make considerable progress in negotiating an end to Pyongyang's long-range missile programme. But the talks, and a possible Clinton visit to Pyongyang, were suspended pending the US election dispute, and the victorious team of George W. Bush expressed more scepticism about the scope for a deal.

At the turn of the millennium, the Americas as a whole looked like a laboratory for political and economic globalisation – with results that were largely, though not entirely, positive. Most heartening was the change in Mexico: for the first time in 71 years, an opposition candidate for president, employing modern media techniques, was able to dislodge the ruling Institutional Revolutionary Party. In Peru the populist President Alberto Fujimori may have been surprised to discover a wall of public intolerance for his extra-constitutional attempt to grab a third term in office. The public's reaction, echoed in a condemnation by the Organisation of American States, suggested how much times have changed in Latin America.

Latin America overall enjoyed something approaching 4% growth over the year, in part a happy spillover of the US boom. Economic advancement through globalisation, however, does not solve all national problems. One huge country that did well economically, Brazil, also suffers from an AIDS epidemic. Yet Brazil in 2000 showed other developing, AIDS-ravaged countries how to be the master of one's own fate by defying multinational drugs companies and using 'compulsory patents' to produce its own cheap, generic anti-AIDS drugs. Another malign engine of pan-American interconnectedness – the illegal drug trade – continued to wreak havoc in Colombia. President Pastrana's *Plan Columbia*, with some stepped-up US military aid, stirred fears among Colombia's Andean neighbours that guerrilla war would spread.

Two sides of globalisation were evident in the United States. President Clinton toured Vietnam – a cathartic breakthrough a quarter-century after the war – and brought a message of market prosperity and creeping democratisation. But it was the same year that an anti-globalisation backlash in the United States, though moderate enough, handed enough votes to environmentalist and consumerist Ralph Nader to cost Clinton's vice-president the election. Structural economic changes during Clinton's presidency included a vast expansion of stock-market shares in the hands of ordinary Americans. This helped propel the longest economic expansion in US history. Yet, when the expansion slowed, the unprecedented reality that close to one in two Americans held stocks created an unsettling overhang of psychological uncertainty. How much poorer would they feel as the stock-market fell, how much less would they spend on the real economy and how much in the way of American economic contraction could the rest of the world bear?

The United States: Election Year Surrealism

It was never likely that the Clinton presidency would fade away quietly. But few were prepared for what the 2000 election – a close-run contest, though not particularly exciting until the day Americans voted – delivered as its bizarre finale. The five weeks after election day seemed like an unending flashback into the fierce partisanship and impeachment bitterness of the previous eight years. When the court battles were over, George W. Bush became the second son of an American president to become president himself, and just the third candidate in US history to win the presidency while losing the popular vote. The new chief executive offered his divided nation a more quiet, CEO-style presidency than had his predecessor: calmer conservatism at home and a somewhat lower profile abroad. But his first weeks in office were drowned out by more noise from Bill Clinton, whose administration – phenomenally successful in objective political and economic terms – ended with the bang of yet another scandal, this time setting some of his hitherto most ardent defenders into a competition to denounce him.

American allies, who had been unsettled by indications that the Bush campaign planned more 'unilateralist' policies and at least a partial retrenchment from Europe, were reassured by the administration's early moves. The largest uncertainty for everyone was what would happen to the amazing growth machine of the US economy, which seemed to falter in December 2000. Although impossible to predict whether it would come to a soft or a hard landing, the joyride was evidently over – bad news for the rest of the world as well as the United States.

A Nation as Divided as Washington?

In one sense, it was not even a particularly close election. Vice-President Al Gore won the popular vote by some half-million ballots: four times the size of John F. Kennedy's 1960 victory over Richard Nixon; a bit more than Nixon's 1968 margin over Hubert Humphrey. But the electoral college – an eighteenth-century institution which serves to protect regional interests by awarding a state's 'electoral votes' on a winner-take-all basis – was almost evenly divided: 271 votes for Bush; 267 for Gore. The possibility that the popular-vote loser might win the presidency can never be discounted. It happened in 1876, a contest that still carried the heavy burden of the US civil war; President Ulysses S. Grant had to send federal troops back into several southern states in order to ensure Rutherford B. Hayes disputed entry into the White House. It happened again in 1888, when Grover

Cleveland won the popular vote but lost the election. Ironically, while the possibility of it happening again in 2000 had been much discussed, it was widely assumed that it was Gore who might squeak in through electoral-college anomaly, in part because so many of Bush's popular votes were 'wasted' in his home state of Texas.

But in a scenario that no self-respecting screenwriter would pitch with a straight face, Bush edged ahead on the basis of 25 electoral votes from Florida, the state where his brother Jeb was governor. Most incredibly, the Florida vote itself was, in effect, a statistical tie: the first count gave Bush a margin of under 1,800 votes out of six million cast. After a legally man-dated machine recount narrowed the margin to less than 400, Democrats demanded a hand recount of ballots in four counties where Gore had done particularly well. The argument was carried through various levels of the Florida courts. It was finally ended on 12 December , when the United States Supreme Court ruled that the recounts mandated by the Florida Supreme Court applied such different standards as to violate the equal protection clause of the fourteenth amendment to the US constitution. That judgement was endorsed by seven of the court's nine justices, but it was accompanied by a far more controversial 5–4 ruling that the electoral-college calendar did not allow enough time for a fairer recount to be organised. As far as Democrats were concerned, the Bush team had managed – with help from the high court's conservative majority – to run down the clock.

The anger on both sides was somewhat softened by Gore's self-effacing concession speech and Bush's own message of reconciliation, reprising his campaign theme that America needed a 'uniter, not a divider'. In the months that followed, independent audits by two consortia of news organisations cast surprising light on the controversy. On the one hand, it appeared that the ballots rejected by machines in the counties targeted by Democratic lawyers did not yield enough uncounted Gore votes to hand him the election. On the other hand, an investigation by the *Orlando Sentinel* of several counties where Bush had won decisively showed that visual examination of machine-rejected 'over-votes' – that is, ballots which seemed to be marked with more than one presidential choice – actually revealed a significant number of extra Gore votes. Thus, Gore's decision to target specific counties rather than the entire state of Florida for recounts was not just a political and legal blunder; it also may have ruined his best chance of catching up. In any event, it became harder for Democrats to argue that five Republican-appointed Supreme Court Justices had cost Gore the election.

A more important question, in the longer term, is what the election bitterness says about the divisions in American politics and society that were already on such angry display in the Clinton impeachment battle. A serious examination of this question uncovers more complexity than certainty. At first blush, the fierce divisions in Washington do not seem to be replicated in the country at large. Americans grew considerably richer in the 1990s, and opinion polls have shown a corresponding satisfaction with the country's direction. The candidates' election-year differences, though significant, were not huge. Gore ran slightly to the left of his own history and Clinton's 'Third Way': he stressed populist themes in attacking corporate interests, arguing for a gradual move in the direction of universal health care, including free prescription drugs for the elderly. On the basis of projections of continuing federal budget surpluses, he offered modest spending increases, a fairly sizeable tax cut, and continued progress on paying down the national debt.

Bush also ran slightly to the left of his party base, in tone if not in substance. He shunned the unpopular Congressional right, avoided any mention of the impeachment battle (except for coded references to bringing 'integrity' back to the White House) and he concentrated in many of his speeches on improving education, his signature issue as governor of Texas. To be sure, the Bush campaign theme that figured even more prominently than education was the promise of lower taxes, a Republican battle-cry in every election since 1980 and the single most important ideological litmus test for the Republican right. Bush proposed to cut federal taxes by $1.6 trillion over 10 years. His package of cuts went across the board, with the practical consequence that the benefits would go disproportionately to the very wealthy, whereas Gore's more modest cuts were targeted on lower- and middle-income taxpayers. Bush also vowed to eliminate entirely the estate or so-called 'death' tax.

Polling data indicates that the popular tax revolt of the 1970s and 1980s has crested; voters were more attracted to the Gore argument that the priorities should be to pay off the national debt, secure the future of the social security (public pensions) system, and modestly increase spending on other public services. Indeed, on most of the issues raised by pollsters, a majority agreed more with Gore than with Bush. Yet they were more attracted to Bush as a person, viewing Gore as stiff and unnatural. And they were largely unmoved by the suggestions that Bush lacked sufficient experience or knowledge to be a successful president.

The voters' equanimity and the relative narrowness of the candidates' ideological differences tend to obscure, however, some deeper social and cultural divides. Most glaring was the racial divide: blacks in Florida came out in record numbers to vote, almost uniformly, for Gore. They were disproportionately frustrated, however, in having their votes counted – whether because of antiquated voting machines in poorer precincts, or due to the inexperience of many first-time voters among them. There was no evidence of a systematic effort to deny their voting rights; nonetheless, memories of the segregationist South hung heavy over the political and legal battlefield.

The racial divide was one component of broader geographic and cultural fault-lines. The nearly even tallies in the electoral college reflected a strikingly clear electoral map. Bush won solidly in the old Confederate South, including, of course, Texas and Florida, plus the sparsely populated western mountain states and most of the mid-western farm belt. Despite his hopes of replicating his experience in Texas and attracting large numbers of Hispanics, most Spanish-speakers stayed with the Democratic Party. With their help, Gore took the entire west coast, including California. He won the Great Lakes states of Michigan, Illinois, Wisconsin and Minnesota, together with almost the entire eastern seaboard north of Virginia. If America's divisions have one symbol, it might be the pick-up truck that fills the roads of the states that Bush won (including Clinton's home state of Arkansas and Gore's of Tennessee): states that are rural and imbued with Protestant fundamentalism and passionate opposition to abortion and gun control.

Whether these divisions and symbols are superficial or fundamental may largely determine how effectively President Bush can govern. The assumption that he lacks a clear mandate is undermined by the fact that his party controls the presidency and both houses of Congress for the first time since 1954, and also that he enjoys the high approval ratings that first-term presidents almost always receive in their early months. But during the first months of his presidency he also had an unusually high disapproval rating, apparently an effect of the election controversy among disgruntled Democrats. And the Republican control of Congress could be fleeting. It is razor-thin in the House of Representatives, while the Senate is evenly divided, 50 Democrats versus 50 Republicans, with Vice-President Richard Cheney casting the deciding vote. One death in the Senate could tip the balance; moreover, the party that controls the White House almost always loses Congressional seats two years on in the first mid-term elections. In fact, Republicans have been losing seats steadily since 1996.

As a matter of political strategy, the administration obviously decided that there was no profit in behaving as though it had any doubts about its mandate. Its nomination of John Ashcroft, a hard-line conservative, to be attorney general was a red flag in front of the opposition bull. And although his Senate confirmation was never in doubt (rejection of cabinet nominees is extremely rare), the 42 Democrats who voted against him sent a signal that President Bush could find himself in trouble if he chooses a strongly conservative jurist to fill a Supreme Court vacancy. The more uncertain battle was over tax cuts: in pushing for the entire $1.6 trillion package (some analysts estimated its real price tag at over $2 trillion), Bush suggested that his definition of 'bipartisan' was to pick up a few Democrat votes for Republican policies. In March 2001, the package passed the House essentially on a party-line vote, with a handful of conservative, mainly southern Democrats, also voting in favour. Its fate in the Senate

The Americas

was considered the most important early test of whether Bush's first term would be a political success or failure.

There were two other big tests, both highly unpredictable in their dynamics and political effects. One was campaign-finance reform. Republican Senator John McCain, a Vietnam war hero with an independent streak that made him a favourite of journalists and a bane to his own party, pushed a proposal for tight restrictions on so-called 'soft money' as the centre-piece of his own presidential bid. In the spring of 2000, it looked as though McCain might derail Bush's quest for the nomination, and there was no evident love lost between the two men. Although the fundraising scandals of the Clinton administration, and the proof that Democrats could raise large campaign contributions from business, were part of what propelled the issue, Bush insisted that the reform bill, co-sponsored by McCain and Democratic Senator Russell Feingold, would hurt the Republican party. But McCain returned to the Senate promising to push the bill forward.

The second test was the economy. In the later Clinton years, as the US economy and stock market continued to defy gravity, there was much talk of a 'new economic paradigm' in which information technology delivered something close to the kind of perfect market information that would abolish business cycles. Such talk did not survive the general decline in stock prices as the stock-market was pulled down by a near-collapse in technology stocks. This fall did not, in and of itself, mean anything particularly bad, since it had long been obvious that technology companies were hugely overvalued. But it coincided, in late 2000, with an old-fashioned manufacturing slump brought on by excess inventories, which suggested that the simultaneous troubles in the stock-market and in the real economy were having damaging knock-on effects on consumer confidence.

Foreign and Defence policies

Bush's foreign and defence policies will be formulated against the background of two debates. The first is explicit: the Bush and Gore campaign teams presented voters with some surprisingly clear foreign-policy choices. The second debate is mainly implicit, the product of early divisions in the first Bush administration, of the clash between competing schools of Republican foreign-policy thinking during the Clinton interregnum, and of the widely anticipated (though so far only latent) turf battles between Secretary of State Colin Powell and Secretary of Defence Donald Rumsfeld.

The Bush–Gore debate was surprising because, as with every US election since the end of the Cold War, foreign-policy questions played no discernible role in the outcome. Whether or not anyone was listening, however, the two candidates conducted a serious discussion of the purposes of American power. Bush and his foreign-policy advisors accused the Clinton–Gore administration of damaging military 'readiness' through inadequate defence spending, too many overseas deployments, and misguided and ultimately futile attempts at 'nation-building'. Bush adviser Condoleezza Rice put it succinctly: 'We don't need to have the 82nd Airborne escorting kids to kindergarten'. She said that a Bush administration would start talks with the NATO allies about a phased withdrawal of US troops from the Balkans and a complete hand-over of Balkan peacekeeping responsibilities on the ground. Gore called this 'isolationism' and responded with an unapologetic defence of US involvement in humanitarian interventions, adding that 'nation-building' was precisely the task that the US had taken on in post-war Germany and Japan.

Victorious presidential candidates are invariably constrained, once they take office, by political realities and their predecessor's legacies. George W. Bush appears to be no exception. His administration has shown every sign of recognising that a precipitous US withdrawal from Bosnia and Kosovo could provoke a NATO crisis – something the new administration will make every effort to avoid. After a few weeks of hedged comments from members of his foreign-policy team and from Bush himself, Powell took an unambiguous message of reassurance to a NATO meeting in Brussels in February 2001. The United States 'is committed to the success of peacekeeping forces in the Balkans', said Powell. 'The simple proposition is that we went in together, we will come out together'. Since European governments expect to keep troops in the region for upwards of 20 years, this repudiation of a campaign position seemed almost complete.

But it is not clear that the administration speaks with one voice on such matters, or how Powell's Brussels statement fits with other administration priorities and commitments. Early in his term, President Bush toured US military bases. He promised uniformed personnel that he was listening to their complaints that excessive overseas deployments – for Balkan peacekeeping, Iraq air patrols and short-term responses to natural disasters – have raised 'operational tempo' to a pitch that strains family life. He also suggested that the increasing use of National Guard and reserve troops for such missions has overstepped the implicit bargain with civilian employers about how much military duty should be required of their employees in peacetime. Promising to return the armed services to being 'trained and prepared to fight and win war', Bush again suggested that the threshold for US military interventions will be higher than it was under Clinton. (As in the campaign, however, he offered few specifics on what kinds of missions can be avoided.)

The future missions that the United States undertakes could depend, in significant measure, on how its armed forces are funded, structured and

The Americas

equipped. Bush had actually promised a smaller increase in defence spending than his Democratic rival. Senior military commanders were nonetheless startled when the new President announced that he would submit the Clinton administration's fiscal 2002 defence budget to Congress unchanged, except for a modest pay increase and some new money for military housing. Although some proponents of higher military spending suspected that the freeze was tied to the push for major tax cuts, administration officials intimated that, following a 'comprehensive review' of military strategy and procurement, the Pentagon would get roughly the increases it wanted. The review was delegated to Andrew Marshall, a veteran defence intellectual who runs the Pentagon's in-house think-tank. Marshall has irritated top brass over the years with his criticisms of some of the services' favourite platforms. But he has had a decades-long relationship with Defence Secretary Donald Rumsfeld, and some of his ideas were picked up by the Bush campaign.

Administration spokesman have vowed that, unlike past reviews, this one will not be sidelined by Pentagon inertia or hostility. The armed services would be pushed 'into the twenty-first century whether they like it or not', said one Republican defence expert during the campaign. If Marshall's ideas are adopted, it could mean the phasing out of heavy tanks and aircraft carriers because of their vulnerability to powerful precision-guided missiles, and cancelling the F-22 fighter because its range is too short. He has argued for a move away from ponderous divisions designed for armoured warfare in Europe and towards mobile units capable of rapid lift over large distances, with or without overseas bases. This redirection would mean a greater focus on Asian threats, the development of new missiles and long-range bombers, and a transition from the current surface fleet to more submarines and 'arsenal ships' – basically coastal platforms for missiles to be launched deep into enemy territory.

Republican Discord

During the campaign Democrats tried, without evident success, to get political mileage out of Bush's relative inexperience: he had been Texas governor for one term and part of a second, and before that owned a share of a baseball team. Bush said he would compensate by choosing the right advisers. He certainly assembled one of the most experienced senior teams of any recent administration, the members of which demonstrated impressive skill and speed in taking over the levers of government. Many served in the administration of the president's father; a surprising number held senior posts in the Gerald Ford administration of the mid-1970s.

Cheney, who was the elder Bush's defence secretary, has assumed the most distinct role. By many accounts, Gore was the most influential vice-president in history, but Cheney looks likely to surpass him. To be sure, he failed in a bid to take the chair of the National Security Council 'Principals' meetings away from National Security Adviser Rice. But Cheney emerged quickly as the president's point man in presenting administration policy to the public.

The power balance carrying the greatest implications for foreign policy is that between Secretary of State Powell and Secretary of Defense Rumsfeld. Together with Rice, Powell was featured prominently at Bush's nominating convention by a Republican Party eager to improve on its dismal record of attracting minority voters. A political moderate, and well to the left of prevailing Republican ideology on such issues as abortion rights and affirmative action, General Powell retired in 1993 from the chairmanship of the military joint chiefs amidst speculation that the presidential nomination of the Republican party could be his for the asking. (As with General Eisenhower before him, there had also been some scenarios of his running as a Democrat.) Thus, Bush might have to pay a heavy political price if he ever felt compelled to ask Powell for his resignation. Rumsfeld may lack Powell's political prestige, but he arguably makes up for it in bureaucratic savvy and experience. He has already served as defence secretary, a quarter-century ago under Ford, when he used his Congressional ties to out-manoeuvre Secretary of State Henry Kissinger in opposing the Strategic Arms Limitation Treaty (SALT) II. More recently, in chairing the Congressionally mandated commission that bears his name, Rumsfeld helped set the US on the course of developing and deploying national missile defences.

On the most critical foreign issues facing the administration, Powell quickly emerged as a relatively doveish voice in some discord with harsher tones from Rumsfeld, Cheney and, in at least one instance, the president himself. In March, for example, Powell suggested that the administration would pick up where the Clinton administration left off in negotiating with North Korea to end the country's long-range missile programmes. The next day Bush contradicted him. On Iraq policy, Powell toured the Middle East in a bid to shore up the sanctions regime – in effect, by relaxing it, through so-called 'smart' sanctions that would continue to target weapon programmes while allowing in more civilian goods. Powell's position is consistent with some of his earlier views: as chairman of the joint chiefs on the eve of the Gulf war, he argued directly to the elder President Bush that, before resort to war, sanctions should be given more time. The new Bush administration may well decide that there is no politically viable alternative to more sustainable long-term sanctions. However, at the head of the Pentagon are two men – Rumsfeld and his deputy, Paul Wolfowitz – who argued passionately in the late 1990s for direct action to overthrow Saddam Hussein. They meant, in the first instance, organising opposition groups to do it, but their strategy also implied recognition that US military force could be needed.

The Americas

The Pentagon and State Department chiefs have also expressed different attitudes towards arms control. While publicly supporting the deployment of an NMD system, Powell has tried to send reassuring signals that the US would be 'looking at the diplomatic ramifications', and would try to coax the Russians to 'move beyond' the Anti-Ballistic Missile (ABM) Treaty. Rumsfeld has dismissed the treaty as 'ancient history'. Even on the question of America's long-term military commitment to the Balkans, Powell's reassuring words to the European allies cannot yet be taken to express an unambiguous administration policy. When asked whether he backed Powell's promise, Rumsfeld was pointedly non-committal. The Comprehensive Test Ban Treaty (CTBT), which the Clinton administration signed but failed to get through the Senate, is considered anathema by most of the Republican Party, Rumsfeld included. Whereas before joining the administration Powell was a prominent backer of the treaty, he stated in his January 2001 confirmation hearings that the CTBT was a 'flawed treaty' and echoed the incoming administration's position against ratification. But it remains uncertain to what extent Powell will continue to be willing to go with the administration's flow or to defer to Rumsfeld.

Bureaucratic battle lines were drawn differently when it came to international financial problems. Bush was criticised, as he started to assemble an economics team, for failing to include anyone with high-level experience or an academic reputation in global financial markets. His advisers did have a financial-markets philosophy, however. Treasury Secretary Paul O'Neill and White House economics adviser Lawrence Lindsey had joined Congressional Republicans attacking the Clinton administration's 1995 financial bail-out for Mexico, and its support for International Monetary Fund (IMF) rescue packages in general. The Republicans said they were concerned about the 'moral hazard' of rescuing governments and investors from the consequences of bad economic decisions. A currency and stock-market crisis in Turkey, however, put this philosophy to the test of strategic realities. Both the State and Defense Departments argued that the country's security importance, especially as a base for enforcing the no-fly zone in northern Iraq, militated in favour of IMF generosity.

End of an Era

The second Bush presidency was also, of course, the end of the astonishing political paradox that was the Clinton administration. The paradox continued to the bitter end. Clinton enjoyed the highest approval ratings of any out-going president in the 50 years since such polling began. (His 65% job-approval score was just ahead of Ronald Reagan's 63%.) He had survived impeachment and bested the Republican Congress in their most important political battles. Political analysts speculated that if the US constitution had allowed him to run for a third term, he could have won it easily.

And yet, the president who had weathered so many controversies, who was said to be determined to leave a legacy more inspiring than a sex-and-perjury scandal, seemed wilfully incapable of leaving office without generating another big scandal. In his last night in office, Clinton issued a batch of pardons, including one for Marc Rich, a fugitive financier wanted for tax fraud and other offences including illegal oil trade with Iran. Whatever the president's real motives for granting the pardon, it certainly showed how great wealth could buy useful access. Rich's ex-wife had donated money to the Democratic Party, to Hillary Clinton's successful Senate campaign, and to the Clinton Presidential Library. And Rich's charitable contributions had produced many friends in high places, including Israel's then prime minister, Ehud Barak, who lobbied for the pardon. For Clinton's many critics, the affair was just gratuitous evidence of a glaring deficit of integrity. For his many supporters, it was bitterly incomprehensible.

The Rich pardon had to be added to a substantial list of ethical failures. Aside from the most dramatic – Clinton's lying in a civil suit about his relationship with Monica Lewinsky – there was an air of impropriety in the use of the White House for his prodigiously successful political fundraising. There were also significant policy failures. Clinton's first term was much coloured by the collapse of his complicated plan to add the United States to the list of countries offering universal health care. In foreign policy, the bad hand that he inherited in Somalia was not played brilliantly. Moreover, after attacking both the Bush administration and European governments for doing too little to stop ethnic cleansing in Bosnia, it took Clinton the better part of two years to engage American power and diplomacy there effectively. Most egregiously, the Clinton administration failed to intervene – and even stymied a UN response – against the 1994 genocide in Rwanda. It is only partly extenuating to observe that it is difficult to imagine any other US president sending troops under such conditions into a faraway African country about which Americans know very little.

But Clinton's achievements were formidable. Most impressive was the longest economic boom in US history. This success had many ancestors, including a determined fight against inflation under Presidents Carter and Reagan, and a regulatory climate conducive to entrepreneurial verve, technological innovation and new-economy synergies. However, it was President Clinton's focus on deficit reduction, through tax increases and spending restraint, that helped create a virtuous cycle of low interest rates, low inflation, record low unemployment and high growth. At the heart of this success was Clinton's ability to convince holders of long-term government bonds that he was serious about debt and deficit reduction; as a consequence they were willing to accept lower interest rates, which helped bring the deficit and debt down further still. And Federal Reserve Chairman Alan Greenspan, also impressed by the anti-inflationary impact of debt reduction, collaborated in keeping short-term interest rates low as well.

On the international level, notwithstanding the Republican criticisms of IMF bail-outs, many economists and market analysts believe that Clinton's economics team, through judicious interventions and deft financial-market diplomacy, helped to avert global financial panic after the Asian financial crisis and Russian market meltdown of 1997 and 1998. Clinton also made substantial progress in expanding trade. He pushed, against considerable opposition in his own party, for Senate ratification of the North American Free Trade Area (NAFTA), and helped negotiate China's entry into the World Trade Organisation (WTO).

In the Balkans, after its fitful start, the Clinton administration did conclude that serious American interests were at stake, and acted accordingly. Through the measured use of NATO force in support of Muslims and Croats on the ground, wedded to a mainly American-driven diplomacy, an uneasy peace came to Bosnia. And the peace has endured, not least because of an American determination to keep troops there, as long as its European allies do. In Kosovo, faced with Bosnia-style atrocities, the Clinton administration joined its allies in using military force – not instantly but relatively quickly, and with nothing like the transatlantic recriminations that Bosnia had inspired. On the basis of this Balkans engagement, together with the policy of NATO enlargement, the Clinton administration could make a plausible claim to having strengthened European security and America's transatlantic role. It was far less successful in nurturing Russian democracy and market capitalism, and NATO enlargement was perhaps not very helpful in this regard; but Russia's fate is of course largely its own. The 1990s even saw progress in resolving the intractable conflict in Northern Ireland, and here too Clinton can take some measure of credit, not least for dispatching the highly competent George Mitchell to mediate.

On the whole, the Clinton administration leaves its successor not a bad legacy, but much unfinished business. On trade, despite some progress, Bush will have to court Congress assiduously for the 'fast-track' negotiating authority that it never granted Clinton. The new administration's trade negotiators also will have to confront the confusion and resentment that Clinton inspired in much of the developing world when he raised issues of environmental and labour standards at the December 1999 Seattle trade talks. On other issues of global governance – the establishment of an International Criminal Court; or international cooperation against global warming – Clinton was unable to get past the opposition of a hostile and often insular Congress. The world may find the new administration to be a more reliable international partner insofar as it will be politically better able to make and keep agreements. But whether it will actively seek such agreements is perhaps more doubtful. Despite new evidence that the problem is even worse than scientists had feared, Bush has been hostile to the Kyoto Convention on Global Warming. And after he took office, the president abandoned a campaign pledge to regulate power plants' emissions of carbon dioxide.

Thus, the Bush promise to present a more 'humble' American face to the world obviously does not mean that the US will be more forthcoming in areas of perceived national interest. But it could imply a less crusading tone. It could also mean less hyperactive diplomacy. The Republicans were highly critical of President Clinton's deep personal involvement in the Camp David peace talks; they felt vindicated by its spectacular failure and have suggested that their initial approach to the Arab–Israeli peace process will be one of benign neglect.

Bush's Critical Challenges

As a matter of style, Bush himself is unlikely to bring the same high-level focus to foreign affairs as did Clinton. If his cabinet can speak with a single voice, this need not be a problem. Indeed, in its early days the new administration showed an inclination to send clear signals to competitors and allies alike, which Clinton did not always do. There remain some critical policy challenges, however. First, continued American scepticism with respect to European Security and Defence Policy would make Washington's relations with NATO/EU partners especially fraught. Particularly *vis-à-vis* France, Washington will find it awkward both to question the need for an operationally strong EU rapid-reaction force, on the one hand, and, on the other, to seek to minimise NATO's burden in the Balkans. Bush may have to choose between acquiescing to a regional peacekeeping role for NATO – which is likely to entail leaving American troops in the Balkan indefinitely – or allowing the EU force a degree of autonomy previously ruled out.

Second, while the new administration has decried the ambiguity of Chinese foreign policy, its own China policy remains unformed. Though avowedly focusing on Asia, the Bush team has not yet formulated an Asia strategy that at once constrains China, preserves serviceable Sino-US relations and satisfies allies such as Japan, South Korea and Taiwan. Japan, in particular, faces difficult choices about how to re-orient its regional security profile, and will require clear and considered guidance from the US. Finally, it will be extremely difficult for Washington to re-energise the coalition to contain Iraq without assuming a more proactive role in the Arab–Israeli peace process in order to attract moderate Arab

The Americas

backing. A more measured line with respect to sanctions and under-mining the Baghdad regime will also be required to win the support of European capitals. The Bush team, then, will probably find that a politically viable plan for reinvigorating containment requires more give-and-take than some in the administration might have hoped. Thus, the new administration will almost certainly have to make substantial practical adjustments to a somewhat inflexible, if elegant, foreign-policy blueprint.

Latin America and the Caribbean: In Search of Good Government

For many Latin Americans in 2000, hopes of economic development, political stability, and government institutions able to provide justice, security and basic human requirements remained unfulfilled. The region's two-decade-long struggle to reform state institutions, so that they promote economic growth and provide capable civilian leadership focused on public welfare rather than personal convenience or gain, continued to yield mixed results.

Economic development has been more readily realisable in Latin America than political objectives, perhaps because of the strong consensus shared by the region's finance ministers and economists on the goals to be pursued. Latin American countries have generally undertaken market reforms. The deficit in governance – the shortage of effective institutions for determining and implementing policies and representing all levels of citizen policy-preferences – remains. The region's political institutions are, by and large, still not up to the enormous challenges that they face. Political parties and public bureaucracies work more often in their own interests than for the people who elected them. Politicians in general are held in low esteem. This is changing slowly, with the prognosis especially good in the Southern Cone countries. Much of the turmoil related in the media over the past year was a reflection of different countries' struggles to manage serious social, economic and political problems through political institutions that are fragile, dysfunctional and ill-prepared to meet the challenge.

While the region overall posted substantial economic growth in 2000 – 4% according to the Economic Commission for Latin America – Colombia, Ecuador, Bolivia and Venezuela saw little growth, and Argentina, Uruguay and Costa Rica suffered sharp downturns. On the political front, important advances occurred in democratic governance, despite near tragicomic events in Peru, Venezuela and Ecuador and the on-going political turmoil in Colombia. Economic and political success is more closely connected than ever before as the economic reform process increasingly points up areas where political activity is necessary or institutional reinforcement is required. Despite all the difficulties, the overall results at the year-end were encouraging. Economic forecasts for 2001 were positive and most countries in the region were doggedly, but democratically, managing their political problems. These, however, were increasingly complex.

Recovery and Return to Growth

Economic growth is critical to Latin America both because of the support it provides to domestic institutions and because of the positive signals it sends to the global financial markets and external investors. For this reason, Latin America and the Caribbean's 4% growth rate in 2000 was a significant improvement over 1999's 0.3% expansion. It was a continuation of the recovery begun at the end of 1998 from the impact of the Asian and Russian financial crises of 1997–98 that had disastrously interrupted a decade of uninterrupted Latin American growth. Mexico – whose fortunes are tied most closely to the booming US economy – outpaced all other major Latin American economies with 7% expansion in 2000. The Central American and Caribbean countries also benefited from the US buoyancy. The Dominican Republic and Nicaragua posted 8.5% and 7% growth respectively. Chile's economy grew by some 5.5% despite concerns in some circles that its export-oriented model was losing steam. Brazil followed with slower expansion – around 3.8% – but this was still an improvement over 1999.

Growth in all cases was led by exports and these were mostly driven by the US boom. Exports improved dramatically for a few countries, notably Mexico, and inflation remained in single digits for all but Jamaica and Haiti in the Caribbean and Ecuador in South America. Amidst the generally positive economic news, however, employment did not improve – a reflection of the nature of the new marketplace – and under-employment remained high.

Capital investment in the region improved in 2000 – reaching $52 billion as compared to $40bn in the previous year – but did not return to the headier levels of 1997 and 1998, when investment was $85bn and

The Americas

$70bn respectively. Results might have been better had the US economy not begun to slacken in the final quarter of the year.

Intra-regional trade improved in all the regional free-trade areas – the Andean Community, *Mercado Commun del Sur* (Mercosur) and the Central American Common Market. This lays a solid foundation for further trade-integration talks, both at the regional level or with the United States in the context of the Free Trade Area of the Americas (FTAA). US–Mexico trade grew dramatically and the bilateral trade, at roughly $250bn, exceeded the comparable sum for US trade with the whole of the rest of Latin America.

Southern Cone – Democracy Has Taken Root

Of the Southern Cone countries (Argentina, Brazil, Chile, Paraguay and Uruguay), all but Paraguay are making solid progress in institutionalising both market reforms and functioning democratic practice. In January, Chile's ruling coalition, the *Concertación*, won a tough second-round presidential election run-off against a moderate candidate of the right-wing Alliance for Chile (the margin was less than 200,000 votes). Ricardo Lagos, Socialist Party head of the coalition, took office on 11 March, just a week after former president, General Augusto Pinochet returned to Chile following 17 months under house arrest in the UK. British courts had been determining whether to extradite him to Spain for trial on charges of human-rights abuse. Pinochet received a warm welcome from his family and the heads of the armed forces, but promptly retired, first to a military hospital and then to his private residence.

The Chilean public wants to leave the authoritarian past behind and Chilean democracy proved up to the task over the year. President Lagos maintained throughout that the General's fate should be handled by the judiciary. Prosecuting Judge Juan Guzman accumulated charges and in August, Chile's Supreme Court confirmed by a 16–4 vote an Appeals Court decision stripping Pinochet of immunity from prosecution, thus opening-up the possibility of a trial. In December, Guzman issued an indictment and order for the general's house arrest, but this was struck down on a technicality – Pinochet had not been interviewed as required under Chilean law.

The indictment raised alarm among the military leaders who demanded that the president call a meeting of the national security council (COSENA), which is dominated by the military chiefs. While Lagos yielded on that point, he won on the more important matter: that the courts could proceed with the investigation of Pinochet. Earlier in the year, both the government coalition and the right-wing opposition parties agreed to constitutional amendments to eliminate unelected senators, and to reinstate presidential powers to name and dismiss military chiefs and to modify the composition of the COSENA so that civilian leaders would control it.

In June, the government also reached agreement with the armed forces to create a commission that would receive information from officers on the whereabouts of bodies of 'the disappeared'. The agreement was the result of over a year's negotiations between government, human-rights lawyers and military officers and represented a tacit acknowledgement that the armed forces had some role in the dictatorship's atrocities. The agreement also reflects the current and future military leadership's desire to put the past behind and establish better relations with the population. Lagos' moderate coalition government remained committed to Chile's open-market economic policies while focusing on social issues. The president informed the armed forces that they would have to accomplish ambitious modernisation plans paid for solely out of their constitutionally guaranteed share of state copper sales. While this puts a constraint on military procurement, it is consistent with Chile's slow but steady progress towards civilian control over defence policy issues.

Next door, the new government of Argentine President Fernando de la Rua seemed unable to get off the ground. Plagued by persistently poor performance and overly vulnerable to external influences, the Argentinian economy showed zero growth in 2000 and de la Rua's team was not able to spark the confidence and enthusiasm needed to move the country out of its current despair. Argentine industrialists continued to complain that their costs (labour, phones, credit and energy) are too high for global competitiveness and want the government to do something about it. Critics blame the government's exchange-rate policy – the peso is rigidly pegged to the US dollar – but the public is happy with the stability it brings.

The president's campaign had been based on a promise to fight the corruption that had flourished in the government of his predecessor, Carlos Menem. De la Rua was already seen as moving too slowly in this area when his governing coalition fell apart in the wake of a bribery scandal allegedly involving De la Rua's party and close friends. De la Rua shuffled his cabinet in October but appeared to stand by tainted officials while letting stronger allies go, and in the process narrowed the base of his coalition. Vice-president and coalition partner Carlos 'Chacho' Alvarez resigned in response and took his party out of the governing alliance. The press spent most of the latter half of the year speculating about whether Argentina would reach agreement with the International Monetary Fund (IMF) on a bail-out to redress a financial crisis, and about further cabinet changes. The fund's agreement to extend emergency assistance of nearly $40bn came in December 2000, calming financial markets. Cabinet changes eventually occurred in March 2001.

The Americas

Brazil made few headlines in the international press in 2000, while enjoying economic stability and steady expansion following a 1999 devaluation that was widely predicted to fail, and that certainly wreaked havoc on the economy. International investment returned to Brazil with the good news about inflation control. By far the largest economy in the region, it was the second most preferred site for global foreign direct investment (FDI) after China – a position it had not enjoyed since the early 1980s. So attractive is the Brazilian market that Spain's Banco Santander Central Hispano paid $3.7bn or four times the government's minimum asking price for the São Paulo State Bank, Banespa, which only three years earlier was the subject of Brazil's largest bank bail-out. At the same time, Brazil enjoys the dubious reputation of having the least equitable distribution of wealth in the hemisphere. Over a third of its population lives in poverty and slow domestic job growth did not help that situation. Moreover, blacks and mulattos, who account for 45% of the population, earn about half the wages of whites.

The economic good news failed to boost the popularity of President Fernando Henrique Cardoso. He is well liked in developed country capitals and at the IMF, and has stuck to his guns on economic and political reforms at home. This has not endeared him to the electorate; at one time his approval rate was as low as 12%, and nearly 60% of the population disapproved of him, according to one report. Brazil's activist press uncovered a series of high-level corruption scandals over the year. In December 2000, the Congress issued a report of an 18-month investigation into organised crime and cited 827 individuals across the country as targets for criminal prosecution. The list included federal and state deputies, mayors, governors, police, bankers and businessmen. For the first time in its history, the Brazilian Senate expelled one of its own members for 'misconduct' (read corruption).

The slow domestic economic growth, continuing scandals, tight money and low job creation all gave a boost to opposition political forces. In October 2000 municipal elections, the *Partido dos Trabalhadores* (Workers Party), headed by former autoworker Luis Ignacio da Silva (Lula), made big gains in major cities across the country. The media and the government both attributed the opposition's success to its focus on local issues, not to the Cardoso government's programme, and the president's coalition remained strong in small and medium municipalities across the country.

Paraguay had a bad year all round. With the economy flat, unemployment rising and investment falling, President Luis Gonzalez Macchi was unable to get Congress to act on key legislation needed to privatise bloated state enterprises. Macchi, the former Senate leader whose elevation in March 1999 followed the 'double vacancy' caused by the ousting of elected President Raúl Cubas Grau (a stand-in for exiled General Lino Oviedo) and the assassination of Vice-President Luis Argaña, was also frustrated in his efforts to change the political system. Efforts to deal with government corruption were brushed aside; early in the year, 18 charges of corrupt practices were raised against the Comptroller-General Daniel Fretes Ventre, but although he resigned in August 2000, the lower chamber turned down a request for his impeachment. The opposition Liberals stonewalled government initiatives and insisted on raising questions about Gonzalez Macchi's 'legitimacy' since he had not been elected to office. They put their bets on electing a new vice-president in mid-year elections. The president insisted he would not leave office until the presidential term was over, however, and the Supreme Court backed him up.

When Macchi's Colorado Party barely lost the vice-presidential vote in August 2000, the exiled Oviedo seemed to be behind the Liberal winner who won by a 0.8% margin. The government also maintains that the general and his supporters promoted a poorly supported military uprising in May. Oviedo is now in jail in Brazil, whose Congress produced evidence suggesting that the general was involved in massive drug trafficking. This should ensure that he will not be freed soon.

Paraguay has had a great deal of assistance from the World Bank, IMF, European Union and assorted aid agencies, but has not been able to muster the collective resolve to cut government spending or the government bureaucracy. Both the economy and the political system continued to be fragile in 2000, with little to encourage much optimism in the short term. The country's neighbours, especially Brazil and Argentina, monitor Paraguay's democratic mood closely, and democracy is a prerequisite to the country remaining within *Mercosur*, the Southern Cone's common market.

Struggling with Mercosur

Southern Cone countries continued to labour with the integration of their unevenly matched economies within the *Mercosur* framework. Intra-*Mercosur* trade, which was sharply down in 1998 and 1999, grew by 20% during 2000. In March, Argentina and Brazil signed a new automotive-products agreement (a framework accord on such products launched the regional free-trade effort in the mid-1980s) intended to integrate further the two countries' economies and to 'revitalise' *Mercosur*. Plenty of other bilateral and regional inequalities remain in agriculture, footwear, textiles and steel. Both Paraguay and Uruguay complained of the lack of benefits targeted for them. Uruguay's new President Jorge Batlle made the 'institutionalisation' of the organisation – the creation of a permanent bureaucracy to manage issues – a top priority for his government. Talks continued with Chile and Bolivia, both observer countries. Chile continued to insist it was fully committed to join *Mercosur* 'in the future'.

Tariffs remain a principal stumbling block. Chile's common external tariff (CET) is 9% and scheduled to fall to 6% in 2003. The *Mercosur* CET is 14% and Brazil has resisted any substantial cut. Chile announced its intention to open tariff negotiations with the US separately, a move that irritated Brazil and it required considerable diplomacy to paper over the rift at the final *Mercosur* summit in mid-December. That meeting did yield a commitment to firm up macroeconomic coordination and common fiscal targets to further align the economies. Mercosur is currently negotiating free-trade arrangements with the European Union, the Andean Community and South Africa, and the region remains committed to negotiating as a bloc with the US in an FTAA.

Slippery Andean Slope

While the Southern Cone countries are slowly but successfully progressing with political and economic reforms, the five Andean countries – Bolivia, Peru, Ecuador, Colombia and Venezuela – are far behind them. International media attention focused on political shenanigans in Peru, Ecuador and Venezuela, and on Colombia's continuing struggle with drugs and thugs. None of the countries did well economically, and only high oil prices saved Venezuela from repeating its negative growth of 1999. Politically, it would be difficult to chart any progress in improving institutional performance, except, perhaps incredibly, in Peru, where the Congress acted responsibly following the departure of President Alberto Fujimori in November 2000.

This followed a degree of election fraud in Peru that had challenged the government's credibility. First, Alberto Fujimori insisted on running for a third presidential term despite poor support and questionable constitutional grounds. The spring 2000 elections then provided a series of cliffhangers. In the first round, which outside observers concluded was 'fraught with irregularities', the government elections commission declared that Fujimori had not won outright and that a run-off would be needed. When the Organisation of American States (OAS) observer mission announced that it would be impossible to hold a credible run-off as scheduled on 28 May, opposition candidates called for a postponement. Fujimori rejected this offer, and in response, the leading opposition candidate, Alejandro Toledo, withdrew, calling on his supporters to split their votes. In Fujimori's favour, a majority of public opinion disagreed with Toledo's withdrawal; they wished that he had stayed in the running although they expected Fujimori to be a legitimate winner in the run-off. Fujimori decided to go for the election, sweetening the pill by promising to withdraw from politics in 2005 at the end of his term.

The OAS moved slowly, but with increasing confidence, to address the 'problem of democracy' in Peru. Latin American presidents do not like to criticise their peers openly, but at the June 2000 Rio Group meeting, Colombia, Mexico and Brazil issued a statement that 'democratic solidarity means that Latin America cannot accept or coexist with retreats from or the capture of democratic institutionalism. Sovereignty cannot be an instrument to halt the perfecting of democracy'. The Peruvian Congress, in its turn, took cognisance of the conclusions of a commission investigating election corruption. The committee's report charged that ten departmental-elections chiefs, the head of computer operations and a large number of administrative employees were guilty of vote tampering, failing to count opposition ballots and fabricating votes for Fujimori's party. And all this before the inauguration.

Fujimori's third-term inauguration was marred by riots and police brutality. The opposition did not help itself as support for Alejandro Toledo's 'Peru Possible' party defected one by one. The beginning of the end came in mid-September. With Fujimori barely ensconced in office, Peruvian television showed a videotape of his spy chief Vladimiro Montesinos, offering a bribe to a congressman in return for support for the pro-government party. Demands for Montesinos' removal were imme-diate. Obviously shaken by the turn of events, Fujimori announced 'new elections' in which he would not run; but he did not resign. After a week-long stand-off, Montesinos was spirited to Panama briefly before returning to Peru, where he quickly vanished. Hoping to improve his bad press, Fujimori undertook personally to lead troops in the search for the spy – a reminder to voters of his personal involvement in the 1997 hostage-rescue operation at the Japanese Embassy in Lima.

The carnival ended when, following the November Asia-Pacific Economic Cooperation (APEC) meetings in Brunei, Fujimori stopped off in Japan and announced first, his resignation from the presidency and second, his decision to remain for a time in Japan, where he claimed citizenship. Had he made that claim earlier, he would not have been able to run for the Peruvian presidency. Fujimori was forced to show his hand, for he had already lost control of the Congress as a result of defections from his party. Moreover, Montesinos had begun to speak about their 'shared complicity'.

The Peruvian Congress named respected congressman Valentin Paniagua, head of the *Accion Popular* Party, as interim president, and set an April timetable for new elections. The legislature then 'dismissed' Fujimori from the presidency for 'permanent moral incapacity'. Paniagua chose as his vice-president former UN Secretary-General Javier Perez de Cuellar, named a respectable cabinet and began to purge the military- and security-forces leaderships of Fujimori/Montesinos allies. As 2000 ended, the congressional leaders seemed to be making calculated and correct decisions across the board that will help put Peruvian democracy back on track.

The Americas

In Ecuador, the political scene was not much quieter. On 21 January 2000, members of Ecuador's indigenous movement, the Federation of Indigenous Nations of Ecuador (CONAIE), joined by a group of dissident army colonels, occupied the legislature and declared a 'peoples' parliament'. The group's demand was for the ousting of President Jamil Mahuad, who was at the time presiding over a corrupt and failing economy and feckless political system, and was threatening to tie the economy to the dollar in the hope of stopping inflation. A triumvirate government was sworn in, consisting of the CONAIE president, Antonio Vargas, a former Supreme Court president, Carlos Solorzano, and the commander of the armed forces, General Carlos Mendoza. In turn, Mendoza joined in an attempted countercoup by military officers and then, under pressure from international governments, resigned and backed the solution put forward by the opposition parties: the elevation of Vice-President Jaime Noboa to the presidency.

Ecuador's turmoil reflected the whole country's profound frustration with a succession of governments that have not been able to curb corruption or inflation, or to stimulate the economy. In its annual rankings of the corrupt systems of the world, the respected international watchdog group Transparency International put Ecuador near the top. One government study counted two-thirds of Ecuador's 12 million people as poor – twice the figure of five years ago. The leader of the colonels' movement was an admirer of Venezuela's President Hugo Chavez, an acknowledged spokesman for the poor majority in his country. Though the immediate catalyst of the Indian rebellion was President Mahuad's determination to tie the economy to the dollar, Noboa took this step anyway. It contributed to an immediate sharp rise in prices, but did appear to begin dampening inflation later in the year. Despite this improvement, the inflation rate still stood at 90% as 2000 ended.

Venezuela began 2000 under a plague of torrential rain, floods and mudslides that destroyed more than 150,000 homes and wreaked massive damage along the country's Caribbean coast where 80% of the population lives. President Chavez' dramatic first response – leading the military airlift of supplies and assistance – gave way to a long and slow reconstruction. Many residents vowed not to return to Vargas State and migrated to Caracas, where urban violence boomed. The capital was already notorious for crime – one international report noted that more than 30% of the population reported suffering from its effects

Venezuela's environmental disaster struck in the midst of the country's worst recession in memory. The slowdown was in part the result of uncertainty among foreign firms about the policies that might be adopted by Chavez, who claimed Alberto Fujimori and Fidel Castro as his political models. His approval ratings among Venezuela's poor – more than 80% of the population – wavered in the aftermath of the floods and in the face of high levels of unemployment, but only once fell below 50%. His promises to revolutionise the political system, clean up government and end social inequities was highly appealing to voters who had never benefited from Venezuela's 40 years of democracy and who regarded the traditional political parties and their leaders as hopelessly corrupt and self-serving.

In December 1999, voters approved a new constitution that called for fresh elections for all government offices to 'relegitimise' the political system. More than 14 political parties and at least 36,000 candidates ran for 6,251 posts in town councils, state governments, a new national legislature and the presidency itself. Chavez himself faced a handful of rivals, including several former allies from his failed 1992 'colonels' coup' attempt and former ministers from his own government. Despite defections, Chavez' Patriotic Front (PP) party and its allies won 93 and six respectively of the 165 seats in the legislature, enough to pass legislation but below the two-thirds majority needed to amend the constitution. The traditional ruling parties, *Acción Democrática* (AD) and the Social Christian Party (COPEI) won 32 and five seats respectively. *Proyecto Venezuela*, a splinter from COPEI and the party of Chavez' rival Fernando Arias, took only eight seats, leaving a tiny base from which to organise future opposition. The traditional parties were clearly devastated, but older opposition groupings like the Movement toward Socialism (MAS) and *La Causa R* (Revolutionary Cause) did little better. Venezuela's traditional party system shows few signs of recovering from its drubbing at the hands of Chavez.

The president celebrated his victory in the national elections that were finally held in July with a trip to the capitals of the Organisation of Petroleum-Exporting Countries (OPEC), meeting with Saddam Hussein in Iraq and being photographed embracing Libya's Moamar Gadaffi. He praised Peru's Fujimori at the August Latin American summit in Brazil, renewed a preferential oil arrangement with Cuba and other Caribbean countries, and spoke out in support of the Colombian guerrillas *Fuerzas Armadas Revolucionarias de Colombia* (FARC). These moves were all perceived in Washington as efforts to flaunt his independence. Some see the unpredictable and energetic Chavez as presaging the future of politics in the politically fragile and troubled Andean region. But the Venezuelan turn of events may instead provide just the alarm needed to wake political leaders throughout the region to the need to address their low standing in public opinion and their failure to provide the leadership and legislation needed to reform the way politics is conducted in their countries.

The Immediate Threat

Colombia has continued to be both the key drug source in the region and home to its most serious unrest. Little or no progress was made during

2000 in the Bogotá government's two-year effort to pacify the main rebel groups, FARC and the *Ejército de Liberacion Naciónal de Colombia* (ELN). It is a country where violence begets violence. The government's own analysis of the insurgency describes the Marxist rebels and the right-wing paramilitaries who claim to be acting in self-defence as rivals in a high-stakes battle for control of productive land. The roots of this competition can be traced back to the 1950s *violencia* between rival political factions. Both the left and the right run a high-priced protection racket, vying with each other for the business of the hapless populace. Those suspected of working with the rival gang or refusing to pay the protection price are summarily murdered. The Colombian government has never had the manpower or administrative ability to provide government services in remote villages, so the law of the gun prevails. The army, the guerrillas and the paramilitaries all dress in 'military' camouflage, further blurring the differences between the various forces. The rewards from controlling coca production have only raised the stakes, and both the left and the right finance their armies with the proceeds of the cocaine trade.

The government's patience in the face of the rising violence and persistent stonewalling by the insurgents has been beyond reproach. FARC has made no concessions to the peace process; instead its leadership has toured European capitals and invited international diplomats – along with the head of the New York Stock Exchange and a senior AOL official – to meetings in its 42,000 square kilometre demilitarised safe haven in the Meta Department. FARC has little interest in negotiation, as they have no following in Colombia that would secure them a piece of the political action were they to compete on a level playing field.

In the face of this intransigence, the government has developed the three-year *Plan Colombia*, which took shape following President Andrés Pastrana's first visit to the US after his election in 1998. The plan's emphasis is first on eradicating the commercial coca plantations controlled by FARC and ELN and then on long-term alternative crop development, strengthening local government, the justice system and civil society. Its objectives are ambitious: to halve drug production within six years and revive Colombia's economy. Reinforcement of the police and military (support for three counter-narcotics battalions are in the plans) is necessary to accomplish the first goal and then to provide the long-term security needed for economic and political change. But the plan has not been presented effectively, and international and media attention has focused on the first tranche of US assistance, particularly its military component.

Although *Plan Colombia* was a Bogotá initiative, the US government is the driving force behind the programme. Colombia is the source or transit zone for roughly 80% of the cocaine used in the US, leading former President Bill Clinton to cite in 1998 'a compelling national interest' in supporting the plan. Under Clinton, Congress voted $1.3bn for anti-drug efforts in Colombia, Peru and Bolivia, with almost $900m of it earmarked for Colombia. Of that, $519m is for military assistance (including, controversially, 60 *Blackhawk* and 42 *Huey* helicopters for the army battalions and for the Colombian National Police), $123m for police support, and the remainder for social, legal and development programmes, training and support for the Colombian Army and the National Police, and for drug interdiction in general. Thanks to the plan, in 1999 Colombia became the third-largest recipient of US grant security assistance (after Israel and Egypt).

Colombia itself is responsible for contributing $4bn to the plan, but its investment so far is unclear. The EU and international lending institutions (the World Bank and the Inter-American Development Bank) were counted on for just under $2.5bn, but so far only Spain among the EU states has agreed to provide support. Loans from the international financial institutions have been caught up in Colombia's on-going negotiations with the IMF. New President George W. Bush has underlined the US commitment, but American officials believe that broader international support is needed for plan's social and economic aspects to succeed.

Plan Colombia has not yet had a decisive military or political, let alone social, impact. By mid-2000 President Pastrana had begun discussing a safe haven in the north of the country for the smaller ELN guerrilla group. Killings, kidnappings and blackouts caused by ELN attacks on the energy grid produced an environment of fear in the north, where public sentiment was almost unanimously opposed to the safe haven. This was, perhaps, partly because the right-wing paramilitaries launched a campaign of terror against anyone suspected of tolerating the guerrillas. The government estimates that in the ELN- and paramilitary-controlled north some 400–600,000 peasants have been evicted from their land – mostly by the 'self-defence' groups.

Kidnappings and extortion have replaced out-and-out murder as the threat-of-choice by both the guerrillas and the paramilitary organisations. Colombian government statistics show a decline – from 28 to 23 murders per thousand over the past decade. However, this is still ten times the US murder rate. As a consequence of the continuing violence, more than 1% of Colombia's population has emigrated in the past year and the continuing battle between guerrillas, paramilitaries and the security forces has created an equally large, if not larger, number of internally displaced persons

Pastrana extended his self-imposed 31 December 2000 deadline for the FARC to agree to negotiating terms for an additional month. If he fails to start a process leading towards resolution of the 50-year conflict in 2001, he will have had his last chance. By December, under Colombia's election timetable, he will be a lame duck. Candidates are already developing their stump speeches for the upcoming campaign. Few believed that the guerrillas would suddenly become disposed to negotiate, but when FARC

The Americas

agreed to continue talks in January 2001, Pastrana travelled to the demilitarised zone to launch them. The shadow-boxing thus continues.

The Contagion Effect

The rising and spreading violence in Colombia rightfully concerns the country's neighbours, who fear being infected by the criminal activities that accompany drug production and trafficking. Colombia's own problems are perhaps exacerbated by the success of Bolivia and Peru in halting cocaine production within their borders. In Bolivia, the government of President Hugo Banzer Suárez succeeded in uprooting the last illegal coca plant in the rich Chapare region despite prolonged violent protests by coca producers and traffickers. Infused with millions of dollars of US aid, Bolivia has managed to implement a programme in that region to encourage farmers to substitute other crops for coca. In Peru, Fujimori managed to constrain, if not completely eliminate, the drug-running *Sendero Luminoso* (Shining Path) guerrillas and to cut off the supply chain for coca production. This allowed peasants to move into other crops. To complete the job, the Peruvian Air Force took to shooting down drug runners' light aircraft. The end result was to chase the narcotics business further north to Colombia.

Leaders throughout the Americas now admit that drugs flow through their countries and most admit to a growing drug-abuse problem at home – South America consumes about 100 tonnes of cocaine a year. South American leaders gave grudging support to *Plan Colombia* at the regional summit called by Brazil in September 2000 to discuss trade integration. They also talked about cooperating against narco-trafficking at the fourth Defence Ministerial of the Americas, held in Manaus in October. At the same time, they expressed their concern over *Plan Colombia's* military content, the very high US profile in its implementation, and their fears that excessive militarisation of the drug-interdiction effort would spread guerrilla activity and increase refugee pressures. In addition, Ecuador and Venezuela have expressed worries that Colombia's acquisition of US hardware could spark a regional arms race.

The dilemma for the region's leaders is that they are already being forced to deal with the spillover from the Colombia conflict. Ecuador's border region with Colombia is a 'Wild West' region that serves as a safe-haven for Colombian traffickers and combatants. Many believe that the region has been spared an influx of coca production because the guerrillas and drug traffickers want to 'keep it clean' for their families and themselves. At the same time, the money generated by the coca trade heavily influences the region's economy and the armed forces have seized coca processing plants inside Ecuador.

Similarly, drug traffickers, guerrillas and paramilitary seeking a safe haven have infiltrated Venezuela's poorly guarded border. Colombian peasants have taken refuge from the fighting and set up semi-permanent villages in Venezuela. The complex jungle-river network that integrates Colombia, Ecuador, Peru, Venezuela and Brazil is an open highway for smuggling drugs and small arms. No country has the resources or manpower to patrol the vast, unpopulated tropical forest of the interior region where contraband moves with ease. In early 2001, Brazil took steps to triple its Federal Police presence along the Colombia–Brazil border and to increase army presence and mobility along its borders with Peru, Venezuela and Guyana. When its air-surveillance radar network (SIVAM) becomes operative in 2002, permitting identification of the true level of illegal flights in the region, Brazil will become the focal point of illegal-trafficking information in the Amazon. Brazil has already organised a monthly meeting of intelligence chiefs in the region to promote information sharing.

Recognising their common dilemma, law-enforcement officials across the region are cooperating more closely than ever with each other, with the US, and with international law-enforcement agencies to prevent trafficking in drugs and in small (and not so small) arms. In March 2000, a US Drug Enforcement Agency (DEA)-coordinated multinational operation in the Caribbean Basin led to the arrest of more than 2,000 suspected drug traffickers (half from the Dominican Republic and a quarter of them from Colombia) and the seizure of 5,000 kilograms of cocaine, 56kg of heroin, 14kg of morphine base, 362 tonnes of marijuana, 73 kg of hashish oil and a vast array of precursor chemicals. The operation was the first effort by 28 Caribbean Basin countries sharing information via the Unified Caribbean On-Line Regional Network (UNICORN), a DEA-sponsored information-sharing network. In August 2000, Colombian, Venezuelan and US law enforcement authorities seized more than 25 tonnes of cocaine in the Venezuelan jungle, seized storage facilities and a freighter and arrested 43 people, including one Colombian drug baron. Most of the neatly bagged drugs were earmarked for shipment to Europe where street prices are becoming higher than in the United States.

Evidence is mounting of widespread arms-trafficking in support of the FARC and other insurgents. One of the scandals discrediting the Fujimori government in Peru was the discovery in August 2000 of 10,000 rifles intended for the FARC that had been air-dropped inside Peru's border. The weapons originated from Jordan, which maintains that they were sold to the Peruvian military. Flights carrying arms have repeatedly been observed from Paraguay and several of the planes have crashed in Brazil. Intelligence sources claim that up to two illegal flights a week provide continuing arms supplies to FARC. Small arms have been captured moving from Panama to Colombia. Collusion between international criminal and drug-trafficking elements is clear. Mexico recently confirmed a link between the FARC and Mexico's Tijuana drug and crime cartel.

The Americas

Security, the Police and the Armed Forces

Across Latin America and the Caribbean, the institutional incapacity of governments, legislatures, judiciaries and law-enforcement agencies contributes to high levels of personal insecurity. In a study, the Inter-American Development Bank (IDB) noted that 'levels of criminal violence in Latin America are astonishing, with violent and property crimes at least six times as prevalent in Latin America as they are in the rest of the world'. The bank observed that violence against goods and people is equivalent to the destruction or transfer of resources equal to nearly 14.2% of Latin America's entire gross domestic product. The human capital lost through crime is equivalent to the whole continent's expenditure on primary education, while the financial capital losses amount to more than half of all private investment in the region. The transfer of resources from victims to thieves is greater than the sum total distributive effect of all public-finance policies.

Urban vandalism, organised criminality, youth mobs, high levels of unemployment, poor policing – whether through incompetence or inadequacy in the face of the volume of criminal activity – all affect the climate of personal security in Latin America and the Caribbean, and contribute to the low opinion that Latin Americans hold of government institutions, whether police, municipal leaders, or politicians in general. The IDB study noted that when citizens do not have confidence in the police or in the judicial system, they are more likely to take justice into their own hands. Personal-security concerns receive priority ranking in most countries of the region and are particularly acute in Colombia, El Salvador and Brazil.

The New Military

Despite their generally poor press, both at home and abroad, the armed forces continue to enjoy the confidence of large segments of the population in most Latin American countries. In many cases, although not all, they have been more successful in incorporating reforms than other government bureaucracies. Over the 1990s, most of the region's armed forces absorbed significant budget cuts. Many, especially the smaller navies and air forces, have used the cuts to introduce management reforms and streamline their hierarchies. Collaboration among forces is widespread in the Southern Cone, where the navies of Brazil and Argentina have engaged in combined exercises for many years. Brazil's new naval-air wing trained under Argentine instructors. Brazilian and Argentine air forces are collaborating in monitoring their common border – long an open sky for drug-trafficking aircraft. Argentina is building its new frigate in Chile's Talcahuano shipyard. Despite lingering grudges over the outcome of the Peru–Ecuador border conflict, which was settled after brief fighting in 1995, Ecuador's ships are being serviced in a Peruvian shipyard, as are Colombia's.

Argentina has had successful experience with an all-volunteer military service. Peru and Chile are about to embark on a move to professionalism and other countries are discussing it. Declining recruitment at military academies has led leaders to look for more ways to encourage bright individuals to join the officer corps. Argentina, Brazil, Chile and others now require military-academy graduates to earn university degrees and several have converted their schools into degree-granting institutions, sanctioned by the same authorities that govern public and private universities. Officers are encouraged to earn advanced degrees – generally at civilian universities – to gain promotion, and most recognise that a degree is their insurance of employability in a post-service career. The services are eager to participate in peacekeeping missions that place them alongside their US, British, French and Canadian counterparts, from whom they can learn new ideas and attitudes to take home.

The brigadiers, admirals, captains and colonels who are products of this new system have a far different mind set than the stereotype authoritarian *caudillos* of the recent past. They understand the concept of professionalism and recognise that civilians have the right and responsibility to control the military. While a few dinosaurs remain – Uruguay's President Jorge Batlle sacked his army chief of staff when the latter opined in public that the war against subversives was not over – the majority of the new generation of Latin American officers is committed to a professional military under democratic civilian control. However, many also worry about the commitment and competence of the political establishment.

The gap between the higher quality training and greater discipline that the military provides its forces and the haphazard and ineffective training provided to police and other elements of federal forces explains in part the continuing reliance of many governments on the military to accomplish tasks outside their mission areas. Sorting out policy priorities to focus on judicial and law-enforcement reform is one of the biggest challenges confronting Latin American governments and one these governments have only begun to respond to, often at the insistence of international lending authorities.

Challenges to Democracy

The events of 2000, especially the continuing political crises in the Andean countries, fuel an ongoing debate over the fragility of democracy and democratic institutions in Latin America. Indeed, opinion polls seem to confirm such scepticism. Perceptions about the economic future figure importantly in citizens' feelings about government. Half of those responding to one opinion poll viewed the economic situation as bad. Similarly, confidence in public institutions – the legal system, the political leadership, the legislature, political parties and the police – is low. On average, 76% of respondents lacked confidence in political parties and 67% lack confidence in the legislature. The Church and the armed forces continue to enjoy the greatest public trust across the region. Corruption is increasingly recognised as a critical public problem. A handful of Latin American countries fell into the bottom half of Transparency International's annual corruption index (which reflects domestic and international perceptions of corruption). These included Brazil and Argentina (barely), Mexico, Colombia, Bolivia and Venezuela, in addition to Ecuador.

Frustration with corruption is only the tip of an iceberg of concerns about the stability and functionality of political institutions. While most countries have successfully adjusted to market-oriented economic reforms, market opening has unveiled the weaknesses of the broader government apparatus. Whether it is primary education, social security, bank regulation, judicial due process, basic health and sanitation, or urban law and order, the government seems unable to provide efficient or effective service. Frustration with poor government service, and the perception that a few were enriching themselves at the expense of the many, contributed importantly to Ecuador's January 2000 coup attempt and to Hugo Chavez' overwhelming popularity in Venezuela. It is to be hoped that the examples of those and other failing systems are not lost on Latin American leaders. Consciousness is rising, but the challenge of good governance is still very great and the realisation of good governance is somewhere in the distant future for most, particularly in the Andean region.

The role of the US will be crucial to the direction taken by Latin America. The Bush administration has explicitly made the Western hemisphere a priority in both economic and geopolitical terms. Latin America is looking to the US to bring it out of the economic doldrums. US–Latin America trade liberalisation would contribute to that objective. Against considerable domestic pressures, Bush has cast himself as a champion of free trade, and his commitment is likely be tested at the April 2001 Summit of the Americas in Quebec City, intended to produce a Western-hemisphere trade agreement and make progress towards an FTAA. Facilitating north–south trade in the Western hemisphere would increase US leverage to encourage better political norms. But in the short term, Washington's popularity among South American leaders may to a greater extent turn on how effectively *Plan Colombia* can contain threats of regional instability.

Mexico: A New and Difficult Beginning

Mexico faced a more promising but also more uncertain future as a result of developments in 2000. The country's first truly democratic election on 2 July 2000 was a political watershed. Charismatic opposition candidate Vicente Fox Quesada of the National Action Party (PAN) was chosen as president for a six-year term, dislodging the Institutional Revolutionary Party (PRI) from power for the first time in 71 years. Fox, a former president of Mexico's Coca-Cola bottling company and governor of the state of Guanajuato, shed the PAN's reputation as an élitist centre-right party by sending a pluralistic message: he championed a professional, non-cronyistic approach to governance and extolled economic modernisation as a means of improving the lot of all Mexicans – including, in particular, its impoverished rural population. But while his election had a cathartic effect on Mexico's political culture, it also provided something of a shock to the system.

The PRI had been in power since 1929. Carlos Salinas de Gortari, president from 1988–94, plunged the peso into a crisis that required a massive US bail-out in 1995 and was shadowed by hints of corruption after leaving office. But his successor, Ernesto Zedillo Ponce de Léon, brought into the PRI a group of modernising 'technocrats' in lieu of the old guard of corrupt, populist 'dinosaurs' and launched Mexico onto a path of unprecedented economic strength. Nevertheless, its history of corruption and patronage hung over the party and opened up political space for change. Assuming office in December 2000, however, Fox was an unknown quantity as a national political leader. He immediately faced serious challenges: reversing decades of popular mistrust of corrupt government, a contracting economy, a rebel movement in the Chiapas, and massive income disparities and poverty. Still, the first 100 days of Fox's presidency justify some, albeit highly cautious, optimism.

The Historic Election

Several developments set the 2000 election apart from previous ones. First, the swashbuckling, outspoken Fox started campaigning some three years before the election. Recognising that the centre-right PAN – pro-business and strongly Catholic – probably could not carry the traditionally centre-left electorate, he formed 'Friends of Fox', an organisation built around himself alone and designed to attract grassroots support. Second, Zedillo gracefully declined to exercise the *dedazo*, or 'big finger' customarily used by the PRI incumbent to handpick its next presidential candidate. He opted instead for a national primary in November 1999. This afforded the PRI – as well as the winner, Francisco Labastida Ochoa – democratic legitimacy. Zedillo also gave the Federal Electoral Institute, which regulates voting, full independence. These departures from tradition produced a presidential election in which a far larger portion of the people could claim ownership of the result. Voter turnout was a record-high 64%.

The PRI had been widely seen as an insular corporatist élite of big business, labour unions and the military that provided stability in exchange for government favours. Endemic corruption at all government levels, at the expense of those outside the PRI's tutelage, was an accepted fact. According to a 2000 opinion poll, 59% of Mexicans believe that while the population is generally honest, the government system is corrupt. Fox offered a fresh alternative. His broad appeal was based on a US-style media-heavy campaign that emphasised both his ability, as a savvy businessman, to continue to attract foreign investment, and his conviction, as an ordinary man of the people, that Mexico's impressive economic growth should trickle down to the poor. With this hybrid executive-populist approach, Fox won 43% of the vote, against 36% for Labastida. Fox appointed a 'rainbow' cabinet – including a former telephone company executive, a left-wing academic and an ex-World Bank economist – covering a wide range of the political–economic spectrum. Only one member of his frontline team belongs to the PAN.

Although the PAN's strong showing makes the political stripe of Mexico's bicameral federal legislature marginally centre-right, the composition of Congress does not reflect a clear mandate for Fox. In the 500-member lower house, the Chamber of Deputies, the PAN holds 45% of the seats while the PRI holds 42%. In the 128-member Senate, however, the PRI holds a 46% to 42% edge over the PAN. The Party of Democratic Revolution (PRD) suffered heavy losses in the 2000 election, does not share Fox's economic agenda and is likely to oppose PAN reforms favouring market liberalisation. To further complicate the exercise of presidential power, the PRI still holds sway in 19 of Mexico's 31 states. To govern effectively in Mexico's fledgling modern democracy, Fox will have to forge complex and undoubtedly fragile alliances.

A Testing Domestic Scene

Despite an auspicious election, Fox has tough problems at home. He dramatically promised '100 actions in the first 100 days' of his adminis-tration, and to an extent has delivered, with health care and education initiatives, an environmental awareness campaign, credit schemes for small businesses and an employment hotline. As Fox has had so little time to act, these are largely symbolic first steps rather than comprehensive solutions. The two key reforms he promised – a new tax structure and the privatisation of the energy sector of the economy – were due to be presented to the national legislature at the end of March 2001. But in practice the wholesale overhaul of systems that have enabled corrupt officials to enrich themselves for years will be difficult to achieve. One of the major problems facing Fox is inefficiency and large-scale corruption in the civil police. The military has had to put its own senior officers into the police force to try and clean it up, with only mixed success.

Fox's relationship with opposition parties also deteriorated during his first three months in office due to electoral squabbles. In Mexico City, he became embroiled in an eccentric dispute about daylight-savings time, with the mayor construing the imposition of the standard as bowing to Wall Street's schedule. The first solid evidence that the diffusion of political power throughout Mexico could hinder Fox's reform efforts came in February 2001 in the state of Yucatan. The federal electoral authority, at the prompting of local opposition parties, had declared the PRI over-represented on the electoral council charged with running the state gubernatorial elections. Supported by rambunctious PRI backers, the governor, Victor Cervera, defied federal attempts to replace the original councillors. Fox threatened to send in federal police, but relented.

The Chiapas Challenge

The rebels of the *Ejército Zapatista de Liberation Nacional* (EZLN, or Zapatista National Liberation Army) – called *Zapatistas* – in the south-eastern state of Chiapas pose a more formidable problem. Over a seven-year period armed conflict between the rebels and the security forces has resulted in about 5,000 deaths. In 1996, the *Zapatistas* and the previous government struck a peace deal, known as the San Andrés Accord, but it was never implemented. Fox, for his part, declared during his campaign that he would bring peace to the Chiapas 'in 15 minutes'.

It will not be that easy. The *Zapatistas*, who are Mayan Indians, want greater autonomy for Chiapas, prisoner releases and federal military withdrawal from the state, and they oppose economic modernisation and globalisation, which they say crowds out the already impoverished Indians. Their argument is not completely without substance. Almost a third of Mexico's population still lives in poverty, while the country now boasts more billionaires than any country apart from the US.

In March 2001, the reclusive *Zapatista* leader 'Subcomandante Marcos' emerged from the bush with an entourage of fellow rebels. For 16 days they toured by bus through 12 states, from the *Zapatista* stronghold of San Cristobal de las Casas to Mexico City, following the route of Indian guerrilla folk-hero Emiliano Zapata in 1912. Covering his face with a balaclava, through which he smoked a pipe, Marcos spread a socialist, anti-globalisation message in a series of roadside speeches to mesmerised crowds, and upstaged a meeting held by the World Economic Forum in the upmarket resort of Cancún. Although the nominal purpose of the tour

The Americas

was to persuade the Mexican Congress to pass an Indian rights bill, shelved by the previous government and revived by Fox, its deeper aim was to inspire populist support for the *Zapatista* cause and to test Fox's broader willingness to accommodate the rebels.

In the first two months of 2001, the president released more than 50 prisoners and closed four army bases in Chiapas. During Marcos' public appearances, Fox expressed his willingness to sit down with the *Zapatista* leader and talk face to face. While this may appease the rebels, it will upset most congressmen – including many from Fox's PAN – who believe that the bill confers too much *de jure* autonomy and will put Indians completely outside federal law. The EZLN is not an isolated problem. The insurgency *Ejército Popular Revolucionario* (EPR, or People's Revolutionary Army), though smaller and less active than the EZLN, has similar aims and operates in Guerrero and Oaxaca. Immediately after Fox ad-libbed a pledge to help 'the poor and marginalised' of the country as he took the oath of office in December 2000, the Chamber of Deputies passed a resolution formally criticising him for breaching constitutional protocol.

More Rural Discord

About ten million Mexicans, or one-tenth of the population, are Indians. Most believe that globalisation – the North American Free Trade Agreement (NAFTA) in particular – has accelerated rural poverty. This attitude has made Indians spurn the federal authorities; many localities are so physically isolated that they already have achieved effective autonomy. Some local authorities, for example, are able to coerce girls into arranged marriages with little fear of federal action. Others customarily allow polygamy, which federal and some state laws prohibit. To stave off a Chiapas-style revolt, the state of Oaxaca changed its constitution in 1998 to permit formally what had been done before by most of its 16 Indian groups: choosing mayors by traditional assemblies rather than secret ballot.

An especially telling instance of local assertiveness has occurred in the state of Guerrero. When the state police failed to suppress crime in 1995, a grassroots coalition of 42 villages set up a 450-strong unpaid vigilante force and meted out 'hard labour' sentences to those deemed offenders. Implicitly conceding the Guerrero force's effectiveness, the state government reluctantly distributed 20 one-shot rifles to the community force. By 2001, however, the force's demands had escalated. It now wanted the government to allocate vehicles and more sophisticated weapons, while at the same time recognising its independent authority.

Perhaps the biggest domestic challenge President Fox faces is devolving authority to remote rural authorities without completely sacrificing federal control and the rule of law. Even if the Indian-rights bill is passed, additional problems could arise in Indian communities that may be inspired by the *Zapatistas'* success in using pressure tactics short of violence. Moreover, the bill calls only for political autonomy and the recognition of cultural and judicial rights. The *Zapatistas* and other indigenous groups are also seeking land and agrarian reforms that run counter to economic modernisation.

Commanding Bush's Attention

Foreign affairs present a sunnier outlook. Mexico's most important bilateral relationship is with the United States. More than 85% of Mexico's exports are sold in the US, and American capital, along with money sent home by the 350,000 Mexicans who migrate to America annually, has fuelled Mexico's economic growth. Fortunately, whereas the Bush administration's relations with other Latin American countries have become tense owing to *Plan Colombia*, Washington's rapport with Mexico City remains warm. Bush had extensive and agreeable contacts with Mexico while governor of Texas, and his predecessor, Bill Clinton set the scene for sustained good relations with the 1994 implemenation of the North Atlantic Free Trade Agreement (NAFTA), which eliminated substantial barriers to economic interaction. During his campaign, Bush pledged to maintain a 'special relationship' with Mexico. On 16 February 2001, he made his first foreign trip as president to visit Fox at his ranch in Mexico.

There are good reasons for such favour from Bush's point of view. He and Vice-President Dick Cheney view Mexico, with its substantial oil reserves, as a key element in a hemispheric energy policy. More broadly, Mexico is now the United States' second-largest trading partner, with bilateral trade at roughly $250 billion in 2000 putting it ahead of Japan, the United Kingdom and Germany, and behind only Canada. Humbled by the peso debacle, in 1999 and 2000 Mexico luxuriated in its highest economic growth in 20 years, and kept much better control of inflation, which dropped to 8.1% in 2000 from 16.6% in 1999. Although trade is still a potentially volatile bilateral issue, NAFTA has provided institutional mechanisms for handling disputes. Fox's election has also relaxed US concerns about the integrity of Mexico's political process and, more tentatively, concerns about alleged human-rights abuses, mainly against the indigenous Indian population.

There are, however, other potential sources of US–Mexican friction. Drugs and immigration are foremost. Both countries ostensibly want to stop drug trafficking, but Mexico remains the primary trans-shipment country for cocaine bound for the US from South America. In March 2001, the US Coast Guard seized nine tonnes of cocaine – the fourth-largest haul in American maritime history – from a ship heading for California from

The Americas

Mexico. Poppies and cannabis are also indigenously cultivated, and Mexico is a major supplier of heroin and marijuana to the US market. In 2000, drug-related violence in Mexico increased, and major drug syndicates grew more powerful. A number of high-ranking public officials have been implicated in drug trafficking. Using a police chief as a 'bag man', Mario Ruiz Massieu, Mexico's former top anti-narcotics official, is believed to have laundered $9m in profits for drug dealers. American prosecutors believed he could tie other high-ranking Mexican officials to drug trafficking, but he apparently committed suicide in September 1999 while under house-arrest in New Jersey.

These facts make US law-enforcement authorities sometimes doubt the Mexican government's commitment to stanching the flow of cocaine and other narcotics into the US. Mexico, for its part, chafes over what it sees as an American tendency to shift blame for an essentially home-grown demand-side problem. Pressure on Bush to deliver on the war against drugs – particularly in view of *Plan Colombia*'s controversial nature – could bring differences over drug enforcement to a head. Nevertheless, in March 2001 the US certified Mexico as having 'cooperated fully' in drug-enforcement efforts. The Bush administration has also shown interest in ending the punitive certification process in respect to Mexican drug-enforcement cooperation, which Mexico City considers hypocritical and insulting.

On immigration, the United States and Mexico's public agendas diverge. Mexico wants relatively uninhibited cross-border movement, whereas the US closely monitors the border in an effort to keep out illegal aliens. A US recession will increase American sensitivities to illegal cheap labour streaming in from Mexico, but Fox may be open to accommodation. In August 2000, while voicing his advocacy of open borders, Fox offered to cooperate actively with the US in monitoring the flow of migrants. This offer was unprecedented in US–Mexican relations and, if Bush capitalises on it, could provide a springboard for better cooperation in other areas. After Fox took office, illegal migration (based on number of arrests) appeared to diminish. Both Bush and Fox tend to view expanded bilateral commerce as the long-term solution to the immigration problem. Overall, the US–Mexico relationship should stay reasonably amicable.

The Honeymoon is Over

During its first 100 days, the Fox government could bask in its landmark victory. Subsequently, however, it will be called upon to do the tougher, grittier business of day-to-day governance in a factionalised country faced with serious inequalities in a declining economy. Owing to the slowdown in the US economy and the stabilisation of oil prices, in 2001 Mexico's economic growth is expected to slow to 3.5% from 6.9% in 2000. The trade deficit is widening, the government deficit was 1.1% of gross domestic product (GDP) in 2000, consumer credit is tight and investment flows have slowed. Thus, there is reason to anticipate currency, inflationary and recessionary pressures.

For Fox to ensure the viability of the multiparty democracy that his triumph established, he will need to handle these economic threats effectively. Success requires deft management of Mexico's diplomatic and trade relations with the United States, and control over government spending, which Fox has promised to cut to 0.5% of GDP in 2001. Fox's leadership is likely to draw firm support from the Bush administration, given its inclination to accord the Western hemisphere prominence in its foreign-policy agenda and Mexico's generally pro-American, pro-democracy cast against opposite trends in the rest of Latin America.

Yet *Zapatista* leader Marcos has accused Fox of planning 'to convert [Indian] history into a marketing exercise'. Other indigenous groups share this view. Mexico as a whole cannot afford to reverse its ambitious and modern economic programme. Thus, the hardest task Fox faces is one with which the United States can offer only attenuated help: he must sell globalisation to the substantial portion of the country's population that has not yet reaped its benefits, and somehow ensure that those benefits soon reach them. This is likely to require earnest but politically controversial negotiations with rural Indian groups, some inventive devolution policies, and possibly a degree of land redistribution. Fox has plainly indicated his willingness to try to reach accommodations with the rural indigenous population. For the latter half of 2001, on this and most other pressing matters, the question is how far a sharply divided Congress will let him go.

Europe

In many ways, 2000 was an uneasy year for Europe. The European Union (EU)'s ambitions to broaden and deepen the institution continued to exceed its capacity for consensus. The Nice summit in December revealed a split between key members over the EU's shape and role, with France and the United Kingdom more wary of a European 'superstate' than Germany and Italy. The summit's advances in terms of integration were modest at best. The Nice summit did pave the way for EU enlargement by some 13 countries. This development, however, also uncovered latent problems. Greece, for example, implicitly threatened to block the accession of all candidates unless Cyprus was among those in the first wave, to the consternation of Turkey and the Turkish Cypriots. Within the existing membership, in the wake of the mad-cow scare, an epidemic of foot-and-mouth disease (also centred in the United Kingdom) promised to test Brussels' wisdom and authority in the fundamental area of agriculture.

Europe's external relations were also animated by potential rifts. The new US administration of President George W. Bush bemoaned EU reservations about national missile defence (NMD) and registered concerns about the planned European rapid-reaction force's relationship to NATO. The shrill transatlantic newspaper rhetoric may have belied the magnitude of the problems: given the technological complexity of NMD and the failure of European defence budgets to match the EU's defence aspirations, there is time for accommodations to be reached. On the other hand, the advent of a more conservative US administration and the EU's centre-left tilt mean that the US–EU gulf on trade and environmental issues as well as defence and security matters has the potential to widen. The premium in the near term is on close and earnest transatlantic consultation.

In the meantime, Europe still has to deal with the Balkans – politically, economically and militarily. There was a momentous and salutary regime change in the Federal Republic of Yugoslavia in 2000, as Vojislav Kostunica beat Slobodan Milosevic in the October 2000 elections. A newly stable and well-intentioned Yugoslavia constitutes a potential core of political stability. Whether wider and more durable regional stability blossoms may depend on the progress of the EU's Balkan reconstruction programme under the auspices of the Stability Pact, and on NATO expansion. In the realm of security, irredentist Albanian terrorism in the Presevo Valley near Kosovo and in Macedonia constituted a retrograde

Map 2 Europe

step. It appears to be containable, but the degree of NATO's active involvement remains a delicate issue.

Further east, Russia is still hobbled by a structurally dysfunctional economy that is hostage to oil price fluctuations and by a persistent insurgency in Chechnya. President Vladimir Putin's programme for military reform and modernisation – which apparently favours conventional capabilities over nuclear forces – remains classified and ambiguous, casting some doubt on the degree of his commitment. Putin has moved to centralise government authority with an eye to curtailing corruption and crime, normalising the economy and rehabilitating Russia's status in international affairs, but the reforms have yet to produce concrete results. In foreign affairs, he has looked to Europe to engage a new US administration that considers Russia a secondary power to be contained more than engaged. On NMD in particular, Russia has decried any American abrogation of the Anti-Ballistic Missile Treaty but also mooted the notion of a European theatre missile defence using Russian and European technology. This proposal may reflect receptivity to civil three-way dialogue.

The dynamic situation in the Balkans, Russia's transitional phase, the new American administration, the ongoing NMD debate and looming NATO and EU enlargement place relationships among the United States, Europe and Russia in a state of substantial flux. At the same time, the problems on all these fronts appear to be ripening towards greater resolution in the near and medium term.

Widening Western Europe's Horizons, but Slowly

The European Union and its member countries, which together account for 28% of global gross national product, faced a crucial year in 2000. The EU's overburdened agenda, from the intricacies of admitting new members to the delicacies of taking away a slice of NATO's military role, forced them to muster determination and resources to substantiate their claim to international political power and respect. The December 2000 summit meeting in Nice had to remove the most immediate obstacles to the EU's intended east- and southward expansion by reforming the community's decision-making rules. In addition, the first practical steps needed to be taken towards implementing the defence ambitions announced at the Helsinki summit a year earlier. The EU aims to have a fully operational European crisis-reaction rapid deployment capability by 2003, but this looks an increasingly unrealistic deadline. Meeting it while maintaining healthy links with NATO will be even more difficult. It has become clear that lagging European defence budgets need to be adjusted upwards, and that intensive diplomacy is needed to ensure that the EU force is not anti-NATO in form or substance.

The Nice Summit

The task facing the Nice summit on 7–9 December 2000 was to conclude the fourth Inter-Governmental Conference (IGC) since 1986 to amend the European Union treaties, thus enabling the EU to take on new members without collapsing under its own weight. The French EU presidency appeared preoccupied with domestic rivalries between President Jacques Chirac and Prime Minister Lionel Jospin in the run-up to their expected contest in the spring 2000 French presidential elections. But despite France's lacklustre performance, the summit made enough progress on the most pressing issues to be considered a success.

One of the outstanding problems was to find a way to streamline decision-making in the EU Council. The EU could no longer afford to have its operational policies paralysed by a single large member's veto, or by the votes of a group of smaller countries. The most important achievement at Nice was the agreement to extend the range of issues subject to qualified majority voting (QMV), replacing each member's veto with a weighted voting system. This new scheme for the 15 existing and 12 prospective members will be applied from 2005. In a community of 27 members, the votes of at least four countries, or of up to 14 of the small and medium-sized states, will be needed to block QMV decisions. At the insistence of the more populous members, it was also agreed that decisions must be agreed by countries representing 62% of the EU's overall population. In effect, then, it will still not be possible for the EU Council to take binding decisions against the combined vote of Germany and two of the other big EU countries – France, the UK or Italy.

Some Enlargement Around the Corner

This success in adjusting the relative voting power of member-states – a sticking point for a decade – enabled EU leaders to project that the next batch of membership applicants would become full members within three years. Negotiations are underway with 12 aspirant countries, ranging in size from Malta to Poland, on the terms of accession and the adoption of the EU's rules and regulations, or *acquis communitaire*. Most leaders of the applicant countries feel that the EU Commission has not pursued negotiations with any intensity. This perception was aggravated by European Commissioner for Enlargement Günter Verheugen when he suggested in summer 2000 that expansion might be subject to a referendum in existing member countries – a notion quickly dismissed by Germany and the UK among others.

The remarkable progress achieved by Spain, Portugal and Greece since their accession remains the most potent argument of those who maintain that well-targeted, determined EU enlargement is, above all, a strategic imperative to stabilise regions that are otherwise likely to become a burden for the rest of the continent. The EU, however, was now unwilling to admit new members that would require a decade or more to adjust to its economic standards, as it had done during its earlier expansion to the south. In the Zagreb summit declaration of 24 November 2000, EU leaders promised the five countries of the western Balkans that had been left out of the last expansion round that eventually they too would be considered for membership. However, few observers believed that these countries would be able to meet the accession criteria soon, if ever.

How Much Enhanced Cooperation?

European citizens, along with their leaders, are concerned that the EU seems to lack a sense of direction, and that, as a result, its practical operations are not always smooth or effective. At the same time, the notion that most major problems can only be tackled by institutionalised cooperation beyond the framework of the individual nation-state is today more widely accepted than ever before. The more fundamental question of whether power should ultimately remain with the member nations or be passed to a European political entity, while increasingly less academic, seems of waning relevance. For the time being, at any rate, national governments are fully in control of European policies, hardly challenged by a European Commission and a European Parliament that both lack popular appeal.

Clearly, European nations are coalescing. With few exceptions, they are content with this and see it as in their interest. Changing the EU's constitution to enable it to deliver more effectively what member governments and their electorates expect is thus a sensible idea. The diplomatic sanctions against Austria – imposed by fellow members individually (but not by the EU as an institution) after the right-wing, populist Austrian Freedom Party (FPÖ) joined the centre-right Austrian People's Party in the governing coalition in February 2000 – demonstrated some of the dilemmas caused by the EU's ongoing political integration.

Europe

Facing the spectre of xenophobic attitudes and parties in their own countries, EU governments felt they had to make a strong statement about Austria's lurch to the right, well aware that ideas and trends, like disease and economic problems, cannot be stopped at national borders. On the other hand, the common values on which the EU rests include the primacy of democratic national elections, and it was hard to see why all Austrian voters should be penalised because some had cast their votes for the FPÖ.

The unfriendly treatment accorded Austrian government officials by the EU for most of the year helped to establish the convention that domestic political events in one country are no longer off-limits for consideration and action by other EU countries. It also sent a sobering message to some aspirant member-states where parties and politicians with views akin to FPÖ leader Jörg Haider's are in the political mainstream. However, in the end, an EU panel discovered the obvious: that while sanctions initially reminded Austrians that Haider's views were inconsonant with EU membership, they also fuelled Austrian nationalism and were perceived to be directed against Austrian citizens in general, and therefore became counterproductive. They were lifted in mid-September. Reflecting the Austrian case, EU countries added a paragraph to their new Treaty of Nice, establishing a procedure for confronting member-states that are about to violate fundamental norms.

The EU leaders in Nice referred constitutional issues that did not need to be resolved before admitting new members to a 'process'. This will lead to another IGC scheduled for 2004, which is expected also to address a more precise delimitation of competencies between the EU and its members and the role of national parliaments. In May 2000, German Foreign Minister Joschka Fischer triggered an agitated debate on the final status of European integration, carefully left undefined since the 1950s. An enlarged EU, he argued, risked becoming unworkable and losing its relevance; it needed clear democratic legitimacy and transparent lines of decision-making.

The novelty of Fischer's vision, although fuzzy on details, was his suggestion that these aims could be achieved not through new supranational institutions but through engaging national political élites while clearly limiting EU authority over member-states. The problem with this vision – otherwise shared even by UK Prime Minister Tony Blair in his July 2000 Warsaw speech – was the underlying notion that only an advanced subgroup of member-states would opt for such a degree of political integration. There are many who fear that this would result in a two-tier EU, with founding members pushing for a 'hard-core' approach that would marginalise others. Given the need for immediate answers on big issues – such as on world trade, eastern enlargement and Balkans stability – these constitutional debates are unlikely to lead anywhere soon.

On a more practical level, the Nice summit agreed on a flexible approach to those member-states that wish to move ahead with enhanced cooperation. Removing the veto power of non-participating member-states, the new treaty language confirms that groups of at least eight member-states may adopt integrative measures that reach beyond what the EU as a whole is prepared to do, without having to establish a separate institutional framework. One such measure already adopted is, of course, the common monetary policy, which forms a part of the EU even if some member-states may not yet qualify economically or prefer to opt out. The common currency established in 1999 – the euro – is scheduled to enter circulation at the beginning of 2002. As at March 2001, 12 of the EU's 15 members had adopted the currency.

The euro area has enjoyed marginally higher growth than the other major industrialised areas, North America and Japan. Businesses saw considerable potential in Europe despite its reluctance to pursue liberalisation and deregulation speedily. Indeed, when they auctioned third-generation mobile telecommunications licenses (UMTS), major European countries managed to achieve spectacular, eleven-digit dollar sums in windfall revenues from the flagging bull run of 'new economy' stocks. Yet the euro slid substantially against the dollar and other major currencies in 2000. At launch it was worth $1.17; by October 2000 it had fallen to 84 cents before climbing slowly back to about 90 cents, where it has since hovered. The European Central Bank kept interest-rate levels too high to stimulate consumption and investment in core countries like France and Germany, yet too low to stop small, dynamic economies, such as Ireland's, from overheating. Inflation rates vary widely, from 1.4% in France to 4.9% in Portugal and the Netherlands, highlighting the manifold imperfections of the European single market.

The euro's popular appeal has dwindled with the exchange rate. In a September 2000 referendum, the Danes rejected their government's proposal to join the common monetary policy. UK Prime Minister Blair said in October 2000 in Korea that at that moment he himself would vote against Britain's entry because the economic conditions were not favourable. While he remained committed to a referendum on Britain's eventual entry into the euro zone, his statement made it practically necessary for him to identify the significant economic change that would justify the UK's adoption of the euro, which 62% of the British oppose, according to a January 2001 Harris poll. Greece grasped the opportunity to become the twelfth member to join the euro, from January 2001, after a remarkable effort to get crucial economic indicators into shape. But the Harris poll, published simultaneously in *The Guardian*, *Le Monde* and *El Pais*, indicated that only 41% of the people in eight euro-zone countries surveyed were happy with the new currency. In France, only 50% were satisfied with the euro, in Germany a mere 29%. Of the eight countries examined, only Luxembourg showed strong support, at 72%.

European Security and Defence Policy

After having failed for decades to establish a common European policy on security and defence, the EU has made astonishingly rapid progress since 1998, indicating the broad consensus this initiative now enjoys. The tragic embarrassments in the Balkans have forced the EU and member governments to recognise that they must acquire the ability to act coherently and effectively in crisis situations. A coherent defence policy is seen as vital if the EU is to make the best use of its considerable international weight, and particularly if it hopes to 'project stability' into crisis areas.

The declared ambitions are quite modest. The interpretation of the 'Petersburg tasks' – humanitarian and rescue missions, peacekeeping efforts and the use of combat forces in crisis management, including peacemaking – is far from clear. There is still no clear answer on whether these tasks might include contingencies outside the geographic confines of Europe and its immediate neighbourhood, or embrace full-scale war as opposed to only crisis management.

NATO Still Comes First

European governments, including France, have said many times that European Security and Defence Policy (ESDP) is not about creating a European army. As a result of British pressure, they are reluctant to refer to the planned vehicle for military action (devised at Helsinki in 1999) as a European rapid-deployment 'force', preferring to refer to it as just a set of capabilities. Among EU countries, motivations for engaging in ESDP differ, as do views on what is desirable and possible. All agree, however, that it is NATO, not ESDP, that provides both the main reference point and the operational framework for European defence.

The UK and France, disturbed by European insufficiencies in the preparations for the Kosovo contingency, launched the ESDP initiative in 1998 at St Malo. Britain continues to be the key country behind the concept, which serves its interests well. ESDP affords the UK a leading role in Europe, reinforces its preferred intergovernmental approach within the EU, and allows London to play a stronger hand in relations with the US by deepening defence and defence-industrial cooperation both across the Atlantic and within Europe. The decision in May 2000 to give the $1.3 billion contract for the *Eurofighter*'s radar-guided beyond-visual-range air-to-air missile to the British–French *Meteor* and not to Raytheon's AIM-120 medium-range air-to-air missile (AMRAAM) was an important manifestation of the latter policy.

A number of NATO members outside the EU, including Canada, are concerned that ESDP could undermine their interests. After the EU's Feira meeting in June 2000, the six European but non-EU NATO members called for concrete mechanisms for regular political consultation and practical cooperation on ESDP matters. The EU in turn offered a set of measures, ranging from semi-annual ministerial meetings and routine involvement in the preparation of the Political and Security Committee (PSC) meetings to permanent liaison with the EU military staff and intensified consultation at all levels before decisions are taken on EU-led operations. The EU accession candidates and Norway have supported the EU's initiative by pledging force contributions of their own to the putative rapid-reaction force.

France and Turkey, however, have impeded the process of EU–NATO harmonisation. Paris has prevented the EU from consulting NATO on operational analysis, and has generally tried to ensure that the defence links between the two organisations remain weak. Conversely, Ankara has blocked arrangements between the EU and NATO that would make pre-identified NATO assets and capabilities available for EU-led operations, insisting on first having decision-making input. If Nice's 'headline goals' for establishing EU operational capabilities are to be met by the end of 2001, as scheduled, France needs to become less anti-NATO, and Turkey less anti-EU.

The EU Starts Thinking About Defence

Unsurprisingly, a security and defence culture that would facilitate responsible decision-making on defence matters and on the conduct of operations does not yet exist within the EU. The tangible shift towards a Brussels-based common security and defence policy, however, has already produced a remarkably open mindset and removed previous psychological barriers between a 'civilian' EU and the world of defence. Since March 2000, the EU's interim military staff has been providing in-house expertise to the Council General Secretariat, headed by former NATO Secretary-General Javier Solana, and has established liaisons with NATO, the Western European Union, national delegations and other parts of the EU. But the EU military staff is a secretariat, not a command staff. It does not conduct any operational-level military planning. For the time being, the EU's new military structures still lack the secure information technology, including access to intelligence systems, they would need to provide effective military support to EU crisis management.

From the beginning, the new EU institutions cooperated closely with NATO. A high-level task force (HTF) that also met regularly with NATO experts (as 'HTF +') developed the catalogue of military assets required for the rapid-deployment scenarios (evacuation, humanitarian assistance, disaster relief, conflict-prevention missions and forced separation of belligerent parties) envisaged at Helsinki. On 5 February 2001, the EU PSC had its first regular meeting with the North Atlantic Council at the ambassadorial level. Under the new arrangements, six such joint meetings – involving all 23 member-states of the EU and/or NATO – will take place every year. In addition, two at foreign-minister level are planned.

After a public row between the French and British at Nice, it has been made clearer that there is not to be a separate European military planning capability outside NATO's established planning structures. Separate planning would be duplicative, and thereby could jeopardise the coherence of joint military efforts in NATO, given the difference in focus and mandate between NATO and the EU. NATO is expected to grant the EU permanent, guaranteed access to NATO's planning structures. But France, as noted, remains skittish about how close EU and NATO consultation should be.

Rounding Up the Capabilities

From the US viewpoint, ESDP's virtue is that it could lead to increased defence budgets and thus stronger European defence capabilities. For Europeans, too, it is clear that the expectations raised must be fulfilled with real capabilities if there is to be a credible and sustainable ability to act. The criterion of progress is whether additional capabilities are created, or existing ones better applied. In this regard, the goal set in Helsinki overlaps somewhat with NATO's 1999 Defence Capabilities Initiative (DCI). This aims to prepare the allies for multinational operations across the full spectrum of NATO missions through their having interoperable, mobile, readily deployable, well-protected and well-equipped forces. Yet, the Pentagon review under new US Secretary of Defense Donald Rumsfeld – with its focus on China and the Pacific, and reduced dependence on forward bases – highlights the fundamental strategic significance of Europe's own capabilities in underpinning European defence and NATO if US forces in Europe drop far below current levels.

Based on the catalogue of requirements identified in cooperation with NATO, the 15 EU nations in November 2000 pledged military assets and capabilities to the EU crisis-management capacity. They committed a total of 80,000 land personnel, sustainable for at least a year, with each of the four large member-states accounting for 15% or more of this total. Assets include 23 brigades and a variety of national and multinational head-quarters elements up to the corps level. In addition, over 600 aircraft and nearly 100 ships were committed to the rapid-deployment capability goal.

Impressive as these commitments may be, they merely underscore the remaining need to upgrade and augment European capabilities in many crucial areas, including strategic air and sealift, air-to-air refuelling, helicopters, precision-guided munitions (PGMs), command, control and communications, and reconnaissance and strategic intelligence. There have been a number of moves demonstrating that this challenge has been understood, and that the EU is thinking of how best to cope with it. They include the decision to procure Airbus A400M air-lifters and tankers multinationally, and eventually to operate them jointly, and the Dutch-led initiative by five European countries with F-16 aircraft to purchase PGMs multinationally.

Defence Budget Restructuring: Myth or Reality?

In principle, the fact that the EU nations combined spend roughly 60% as much as the US on defence should mean that the existing level of defence spending is sufficient, even if they get much less value for it in terms of fighting power. Unfortunately, however, their forces are still in many respects configured for the Cold War era. Rising personnel costs and a wave of systems acquisitions initiated some time ago, as well as the costs of ongoing operations, leave little room for investment to satisfy newly identified requirements. The continued desire for a 'peace dividend' (in spite of the wars in the Balkans), the low priority accorded to defence in the absence of a perceived military threat, and the macroeconomic preference for reduced public spending mean that new pounds, marks and euros for increases in defence spending are slow in coming. NATO Secretary-General George Robertson's claim that most European defence budgets are no longer being cut, and that some are at last rising, is not yet supported by the figures, at least in constant-dollar terms. The US is sure to apply just this standard when judging allied efforts, and European planners – whose expenditures on equipment, ammunition and operations are to a substantial extent dollar-based – should do the same. In fact, European defence spending in real terms continues to fall at a rate of nearly 5% each year.

Table 1 **European Defence Spending**

(Constant 1999 US$m)	**1997**	**1998**	**1999**	**2000**	**e2001**
France	43,342	41,189	37,811	34,292	32,547
Germany	34,639	33,796	31,174	28,229	26,303
UK	36,585	38,050	36,302	33,894	n.a.
EU-15	178,240	176,948	165,215	152,695	147,568

A more precise indicator of the generation of new capabilities is spending on equipment and research and development. R&D spending is falling by 2% a year, marginally less than overall defence spending, but equipment procurement by European NATO members is at its lowest level in decades, having fallen 6.9% since 1996 compared with a rise of 4.7% in US spending over the same period.

Table 2 **European Spending on Defence Equipment Procurement**

(Constant 1999 US$m)	1997	1998	1999	2000	e2001
France	6,634	7,312	5,690	4,780	4,594
Germany	3,082	3,716	3,679	3,200	n.a.
UK	8,733	10,380	9,707	8,737	n.a.
EU-15	28,129	29,743	28,076	27,435	26,851

Table 3 **European Spending on Public Defence R&D**

(Constant 1999 US$m)	1997	1998	1999	2000	e2001
France	3,920	3,185	2,886	2,833	2,719
Germany	1,550	1,406	1,143	1,117	n.a.
UK	4,191	3,839	3,349	3,579	n.a.
EU-15	10,508	9,875	9,114	9,105	8,923

A handful of European countries did manage to increase their defence budgets for 2001 in real terms, if only marginally. Others, such as the Netherlands and Belgium, at least began to redirect spending from personnel to equipment. Germany is sadly behind with its much-advertised reforms. Even the independent Weizsäcker Commission, in its May 2000 report, shied away from recommending full professionalisation of the forces and ending the draft. To be realistic, the German government's attempt to preserve a total force strength of 285,000, and at the same time to more than double available, well-equipped and well-trained operation forces (*Einsatzkräfte*) to 150,000, clearly requires additional funding.

German efforts to free up funds through rationalisation, privatisation and property sales have been anaemic and unavailing. Defence Minister Rudolf Scharping had to admit in March 2001 that he needed $180 million to meet obligations, with no hope of extracting additional appropriations from the treasury or parliament. The Bundeswehr's General Harald Kujat announced publicly that, as a consequence, German forces were no longer fully operational and were stretched to the limit in Balkans deployments. Unless defence is again given top-level attention in Germany, and is provided with adequate funds, the refusal to honour multinational commitments is bound seriously to damage Europe's security and defence aspirations, as well as NATO's European pillar.

Defence Industries and Procurement

In a remarkable though indecisive development in May 2000, the US launched its Defence Trade Security Initiative (DTSI). The programme is founded on a number of legal and administrative improvements designed to remove some of the 'Fortress America' obstacles that hinder US arms exports to allies and defence-industrial cooperation with them. The US offered a select group of allies the option to become exempt from the US International Traffic in Arms Regulations (ITAR) licensing requirements by accepting US export controls. The UK and Australia were willing to sign up, which would offer them a status like Canada's and open up the possibility of eventual full access to the US defence market. Implementation, however, requires congressional approval and this was not forthcoming while Bill Clinton was president.

Meanwhile, the repositioning of Europe's old national defence contractors, driven much more by business requirements than by governments, continues at breathtaking speed. The European Aeronautic, Defence and Space Company (EADS), comprising Daimler–Chrysler Aerospace (DASA), Aerospatiale, Matra and Construcciones Aeronauticas (CASA), legally came into being in July 2000. Its space operations are merged with those of BAe Systems in the new company Astrium. Both EADS and BAe Systems are now comparable in size to US contractors such as Lockheed Martin or Raytheon, though still far behind Boeing. British-based BAe Systems continued its transformation into a truly transatlantic company in 2000. Its takeover of Lockheed Martin's Aerospace Electronics Systems won the Pentagon's approval and was completed in November. The company is now doing almost a quarter of its business in the US.

On the government side, the entry into force in 2000 of the OCCAR (Joint Body for Cooperation on Armaments Matters) agreement between Britain, France, Germany and Italy in 2000 meant that for the first time there existed a permanent framework for multinational arms procurement that did not require a case-by-case balancing of national industrial work-shares. This should allow a new level of efficiency and help to establish a European marketplace for defence equipment. In July 2000, another agreement was signed by Europe's six leading arms producing countries (the four OCCAR members plus Spain and Sweden) based on the so-called 'letter-of-intent process' launched in July 1998. It is meant to facilitate cross-border industry consolidation through harmonising procedures and policies in fields such as defence acquisition, security clearances and export licensing.

Practical Challenges of a Different Kind

The EU has clearly been making progress. In defence and other areas, however, successful outcomes remain subject to doubt. Often it is even uncertain what 'success' might mean. It is unlikely that defence will become one of the major forces driving further European integration. Much closer to the heart of European concerns are the currency union with its economic implications and internal security issues, above all illegal immigration. Here, improved control of external borders – especially the coastlines of Italy and Spain – might provide an emerging shared challenge that overlaps, to some degree, with ESDP.

For some time, the EU is likely to be overshadowed by the huge agricultural crisis caused by foot-and-mouth disease, on top of the widespread loss of consumer confidence caused by the spread of bovine spongiform encephalitis (BSE). Eventually, however, a drastic shake-up of the EU's agricultural sector could make it easier to find solutions for the unresolved problems of European agricultural policy. These may include adjustment to world agricultural trade liberalisation within a decade and reform of the costly, interventionist and distorting Common Agricultural Policy inherited from the early days of Western European integration. Often overlooked, agriculture still tends to be of existential importance to rural regions in Europe. The ability of political leaders to provide effective and sustainable redress to the international farming crisis that seems to be evolving throughout Europe and, more generally, the perceived ability of political systems to solve problems and cope with crises, will be decisive in making and breaking governments and institutions.

Depending on the new US administration's actions, a similar challenge may arise from a general atmospheric crisis in transatlantic relations. It is doubtful whether the EU is prepared for the kind of forceful free-trade agenda that it may soon face from the US. At the same time, there seems to be a mood in Europe in favour of challenging the US on a broad front of issues, some of which involve fundamental values and arouse strong emotions, and thus are hard to control. These issues range from how to handle global warming, subsidies, taxation of e-commerce and regulations for biotechnology to improving food safety, protecting non-English media industries and abolishing the death penalty. The debate about missile defence, occasional transatlantic differences over security issues in regions such as Russia, the Persian Gulf and the Balkans, Brussels' diplomatic intervention in the Korean Peninsula and uncertainty over the thrust of Europe's independent defence structures add up to a formidable mix of factors that will require careful leadership on both sides of the Atlantic. In particular, the UK government, having co-sponsored the European Security and Defence Initiative and made public pledges to Washington of the rapid-reaction force's compatibility with NATO, must now make good on those pledges if it is to maintain its standing as a leading European power and transatlantic bridge. Doing so will require more confident and assertive inter-European diplomacy than London has shown to date.

Russia: Strengthening the State

Vladimir Putin's overwhelming victory in the April 2000 presidential elections raised many concerns among the liberal Russian intelligentsia and Russia watchers in the West about the re-emergence of authoritarian trends in Russia. These concerns were prompted in the first instance by Putin's background as a KGB bureaucrat with a correspondingly low public profile and an uncertain political agenda. They were reinforced by Putin's *blitzkrieg* presidential campaign, which was built almost exclusively around four promises: to strengthen the Russian state; to introduce a 'dictatorship of the law'; to fight terrorists in Chechnya to the end and at any cost; and to revive Russia's status in world affairs. None of these aims suggested strong support for democratic reforms.

Putin has taken actions in the year since his inauguration in early May 2000 that have made it clear that the concerns about Russia's new authoritarianism were exaggerated. Instead, the main challenge to Russia comes not from the Kremlin's attempts to consolidate its power throughout the country, but from its inability to use any power it has clearly to articulate and consistently to implement the difficult policy choices needed to pull Russia out of its domestic crisis.

Putin: Year One

The first year of Putin's presidency was predominantly dedicated to one goal: to consolidate the power of central state structures and, by definition, the president's own powers under the super-presidential constitutional system. A number of measures were undertaken to curtail the power of regional governors and oligarchs, to develop and maintain a pro-presidential majority in the State Duma, to reassert state control over the media, to increase tax revenues for the federal budget, and to preserve Russia's territorial integrity through an uncompromising military campaign in Chechnya.

These policies were built on three pillars: a strong budgetary surplus from increased oil and gas export revenues; Putin's high public-approval rating, which at times reached 70%; and increasingly intense activities by various security and bureaucratic structures in support of presidential policies. The latter were exercised through alternative power centres, such as businessmen and their media assets, and regional autocracies with criminal and business interests. These policies, and the publicity which surrounded them, created an image of a more active, confident and strong Russian state and central government. The long-term benefits of these policies for Russia's domestic reforms, however, have been very limited, particularly in the context of the favourable political and economic

Europe

environment that Russia enjoyed during 2000 for the first time in its post-Soviet history.

The strengthened and more active Russian state developed by Putin did not require the construction of a new authoritarian system. Indeed, the profound systemic changes that have occurred in Russia over the past decade have imposed an unacceptably high price for making state control more centralised. The state has neither the economic resources nor the human or institutional capital to back up its ambitions. This was clearly demonstrated during winter 2000–01, when the country went through numerous emergencies involving electricity blackouts in many regions and no state structures were capable of an effective response. At the same time, the Russian people, as demonstrated when the submarine *Kursk* sank in an accident in August 2000, were no longer prepared to accept old-style secrecy, demanding instead the accountability of the government and the president for their actions. Another constraint was made plain when the international community insisted that Russia fully comply with its debt repayment obligations, thus indicating its determination to see Russia play by internationally accepted rules. At the same time, despite Russia's strong economic growth during 2000, foreign investors would not increase their commitments without seeing practical results from the anti-corruption campaign and judicial and corporate governance reforms.

Indeed, the main challenge to Russia and the international community arising from Putin's presidency comes not from an increasingly strong and authoritarian state, but from the absence of a clear government strategy for overcoming continuing, and in some areas escalating, domestic crises. Despite being blessed with a favourable economic and political environment and a newly empowered bureaucracy, the Putin government has failed to develop, clearly articulate or present for legislative approval medium- and long-term priorities for economic, judicial, federal and military reforms, or for Russia's foreign and security policies. Putin's lack of strategic vision and demonstrated inability to take difficult political decisions can be explained both by his limited personal experience in economic and political affairs, and, more importantly, by his failure to assemble a strong team of like-minded professionals in the presidential administration and in the government.

The credibility of government policies has been destroyed by an ineffective public information policy that combined attempts at media censorship with a lack of regular and consistent official statements on government policies. There has been ongoing open disagreement among government ministers and presidential advisers on all key reform issues. The most notorious case involved conflict between the then defence minister, Igor Sergeyev and the chief of general staff, Anatoly Kvashnin about the priorities for military reform; a disagreement which continued throughout the year without a presidential decision on the reform priorities. Similarly, in the area of economic reform, Putin's economic adviser, Andrei Illarionov openly criticised government policy without any clear policy statement from the president.

As a result, during 2000, economic and political resources were spent on short-term measures with high political impact but of uncertain direction. These included continuing the military operation in Chechnya without a long-term political strategy; raising salaries and pensions without implementing structural reform of *de facto* bankrupt state institutions and a multiplicity of Russian banks; addressing electricity crises in various regions on an *ad hoc* basis without restructuring and attracting new investment into the major state monopolies (United Energy Systems and Gazprom); and pursuing criminal investigations against a few notorious tycoons while failing to stop illegal capital flight from Russia. These short-term measures laid no foundations for sustaining Russia's economic growth, or even for sustaining public support for Putin and his policies. Despite its initial promise, 2000 has become another year of lost opportunities for Russia's reforms.

Unsustainable Economic Growth

A key factor behind the strong public support for President Putin during his first year in office was Russia's economic good fortune. It was driven by the rapid increase in world oil and gas prices. Oil and gas remain Russia's main exports, accounting for over 25% of all budget revenues. In 2000, Russia earned over $11.3 billion from the export of oil and gas, 2.4 times more than in the previous year. Although many oil companies are now in private hands, oil revenues – both direct and through increased tax payments – produced over 20% of the surplus in the 2000 state budget. Overall state revenues in 2000 exceeded budgetary levels by 38.4%, the first surplus registered in more than a decade. Russia's gross domestic product (GDP) increased by 7.5%, with about one-third of the growth estimated to come from the increase in oil and gas prices, while real *per capita* income increased by almost 9%. Russia had a positive foreign trade balance of over $50bn and Russia's gold reserves increased from $12bn to over $28bn.

These trends provided an unprecedented opportunity for the government to pursue long-overdue structural reforms. What is needed is to close down numerous failing state enterprises, ease the tax burden, speed up deregulation and improve corporate governance laws and practices, undertake a sweeping Central Bank and general banking reform, move decisively to curtail illegal capital flight, and restructure Gazprom and United Energy Systems. Instead, Putin's government chose to move

Europe

slowly. Although it can report some achievements on the economic front, the government failed to initiate serious structural reforms.

Among the achievements are the adoption of a new tax code and the opening of investigations into illegal money laundering schemes and tax evasion by some of Russia's most infamous tycoons. These measures, however, were not enough to convince foreign investors, despite positive macroeconomic indicators. Their reluctance to plunge back into the Russian market was not only due to the government's failure to communicate its short- to medium-term economic programme effectively, but also to the more damaging public display by the Putin economic team of profound disagreements on economic strategy. This simply confused foreign and Russian investors further.

Nevertheless, there was some increase in foreign direct investment. According to the Russian State Statistics Committee, foreign investment into Russia in 2000 amounted to $11bn, up nearly 15% from 1999. Unfortunately, outflows from Russia totalled $15bn, a near-90% increase from the year before. Foreign-source lending accounted for about 58% of foreign investment inflows; foreign direct investments of $4.4bn accounted for 40%; and portfolio investments represented about 1% of the total.

An increasing share of foreign investment is coming from the re-investment of Russian money previously taken out of the country and now returning through foreign-registered companies. Many large foreign companies that previously invested in Russia, such as BP-Amoco, have reduced their interest because of Russian companies' refusal to guarantee minority shareholder rights. At the same time, Russian capital flight was up 30% in 2000, thus denying badly needed investment that could underpin sustainable economic growth.

Instead of using the government surplus to promote sustainable economic growth, the government chose to use it for social programmes, increasing pensions and minimum wages, financing the war in Chechnya and other military programmes. It also increased Russia's gold reserves while at the same time keeping a stable exchange rate for the rouble (the nominal dollar rate increased by only 4% during 2000). These measures paid short-term political dividends in terms of assuring Putin's popularity. But they came at a price. By early 2001, signs started to emerge that Russia would be unable to keep up this rate of economic growth. According to some experts, every $1 fall in the price of a barrel of oil means a $1bn fall in Russian budget revenues; since late 2000, Russian revenues from oil had already diminished by over $12bn by March 2001.

The fall in energy prices and state revenues will coincide with a dramatic increase in Russia's foreign-debt repayment obligations, which totalled $144bn as of January 2001. By 2003, Russia will have to pay $18bn on Soviet Union-incurred foreign debt obligations to the Paris Club of creditors; Germany alone holds over 30% of this debt. The obligation is projected to represent about 5.57% of Russia's GDP, or more than one-third of the annual state budget. At the meeting of G-7 finance and central bank chairmen in Palermo in February 2001, Russia attempted to raise the issue of further debt rescheduling, or even forgiveness. In the past, Russia has faced a strongly negative reaction from its creditors, who have refused to consider debt rescheduling or relief because of Russia's budget surplus and high revenues from oil and gas exports. After a poorly handled information campaign – which further damaged the credibility of Putin's economic programme – Russia agreed to cover all its current interest payment obligations ($3.5bn) in full in 2001 and to continue negotiations on possible debt rescheduling. The question is to be raised again in the G-8 meeting scheduled for June 2001. In order to make the promised full payment in 2001, the government had to introduce changes in the federal budget which had been passed by the Duma in December 2000, since it did not include adequate funding to cover all foreign-debt obligations.

Such problems are not new for Russia. According to the World Bank, in 1995–99 Russia paid on average $10bn a year, 3.77% of GDP, to service its debts. During that period, however, Russia was mainly using new credits from the International Monetary Fund (IMF) to cover its old debt obligations. Since the financial collapse of August 1998, Russia has not received any new IMF credit. It is generally accepted that high debt service, which must now come from Russia's own funds, will significantly slow future economic and social reforms, as well as other reforms that are closely tied to them, such as military restructuring and modernisation. The resulting shortage of funds available to Putin's government will significantly challenge his political ambitions.

Reasserting Control over the Regions

A decade of former President Boris Yeltsin's attempted reforms resulted in deep economic, demographic and social crisis while transferring unlimited political and economic power to a small group of oligarchs, corrupt bureaucrats and regional governors who ruled their regions as absolute monarchs rather than as elected officials. As a result, Moscow faced uncontrolled devolution of state power to new political actors in the regions – often groups combining the region's political élite with local business and, sometimes, criminal organisations – which had no incentive to support economic, political and social reforms and in fact deliberately blocked them. The central government lost revenues from unpaid corporate taxes, illegal privatisation deals, corruption and irregular regional payments to the federal budget. Ironically, this situation meant Russia never had to face disintegration: these virtually independent regional oligarchies thrived precisely because of their access to federal funds and other resources. It was clear that no serious reforms would be possible while these groups were neither controlled nor accountable.

Perforce, federal reforms became Putin's priority. The strategy for implementing these reforms, however, was chosen more to strengthen central authority over regional governors than to increase accountability at the regional level. These reforms did not offer significant rewards for economic achievements, or incentives to pursue such reforms. As a result, Putin's federal overhaul was primarily administrative and institutional; it has yet to strengthen the Russian state beyond increasing federal and regional bureaucracy. The real indicator of these reforms' success will be the regions' future economic performance, reduced corruption, development of an independent judiciary, improved social conditions for their residents and ability to attract foreign and domestic investment. Thus far, the reforms have not succeeded in curtailing the power of the most notorious and powerful governors, who received seats on the new State Council and permission to run for a third term in office.

Putin's federal reforms had three main components. First, there were changes to the Federation Council, the upper chamber of the Russian Parliament, composed of governors and other regional representatives who had been appointed after local elections, rather than separately elected as senators. Previously, governors themselves adopted federal laws and controlled their implementation. Putin replaced this system with one which requires senators to be directly elected. This could potentially create a healthy system of checks and balances on the regional level. But having taken two steps forward, Putin took one back. He agreed to form the State Council, a new consultative body not mentioned in the Russian Constitution, and to appoint to it some of the most powerful governors, giving them responsibility for advising the president on federal policies. This is another indication that Putin needs the support of the governors, particularly with economic problems looming. He is unlikely, therefore, to mount a strong challenge to their political and economic power in their respective regions.

The second element of Putin's federal reform was to increase central oversight of the activities of the governors. In July, a new law was adopted by the Federation Council under pressure from the State Duma and the administration, giving the president power to remove a governor for violating the constitution or for professional incompetence. In the first case in which Putin might have enforced this measure – against the Primorsky Krai Governor Yevgeny Nazdratenko, who had failed to deal with an energy crisis that left thousands in his region without heat at a time of record low temperatures – presidential action was pre-empted when Nazdratenko submitted his resignation. The press has speculated that his resignation was triggered by the threat of removal.

In addition to the new law enhancing presidential power, Putin's policy has been actively to influence the outcome of gubernatorial elections. In some regions, his agents supported the opposition candidate; in others they pressed local courts to disqualify the incumbents by providing compromising materials. In the Kaliningrad, Voronezh and Ulyanovsk regions, the Kremlin successfully assisted former military commanders or security forces officers to be elected governor, while in Kursk *oblast*, it prevented Governor Alexander Rutskoi from running for re-election. The Kremlin's interference, however, has not always brought about the desired result. In St Petersburg and Moscow *oblasts*, for example, efforts to install a governor more loyal to Putin failed. Similarly, the centre could not prevent some powerful businessmen from running for office. Under considerable pressure from 69 governors, Putin had to agree to their election for a third term – previously banned by their constitutions – by stipulating that two terms should be calculated as one. And even some carefully chosen and newly elected governors turned out to be less than compliant. Kaliningrad Governor Admiral Vladimir Yegorov, the former commander of the Baltic Fleet, for example, challenged the central government immediately after his election by refusing to implement the federal law which abolished the special tax-free status of the region.

The third component of Putin's federal reforms included the creation of seven special federal districts (see map, *Strategic Geography* pp. VIII–IX). Seven presidential representatives were appointed to represent federal authority in each of the districts; five are former military and security forces officers. The role of these representatives, or 'super-governors', is to ensure that the legislatures in each district are in full compliance with Russian federal laws. They also are charged with oversight of legal reform at the regional level – under Yeltsin, governors appointed all judges – and with coordinating the activities of various law-enforcement and security agencies in order to prevent the development of separatist trends. These 'super-governors' are also responsible for advising the president on a strategy to ensure Russia's cohesion. Since only one of them – ex-Premier Sergei Kiriyenko – has a background in economics, these proposals are likely to be limited to administrative, law-enforcement and security measures.

Thus far, the super-governors have not had much success, apart from helping to implement the Kremlin's strategy of promoting amenable candidates in regional elections, and bringing regional laws in line with federal legislation: between 43% and 78% of identified discrepancies between regional and federal legislation were eliminated in the first eight months of the super-governors' appointment. Because the super-governors do not control financial flows between the centre and the regions, their ability to influence regional governors is limited. Their main impact has been on local security structures, courts and law-enforcement agencies.

Europe

Yet, unless all the officials in these agencies are replaced, there are likely to be many who support the governors who originally appointed them, and with whom they shared common interests prior to Putin's reforms. Nor do the super-governors have much power over regional and Russia-wide oligarchs who control important resources, including utilities and major industrial enterprises. Thus, the super-governors are unable effectively to address real crises in their regions, such as electricity and fuel shortages in the Siberian and Far Eastern federal districts.

Putin's regional reforms have created an institutional foundation for reinforcing central control over the activities of the governors. But the lack of economic leverage, the shortage of uncorrupted professionals, the reliance on military and security services cadres without economic and business knowledge, and the need for the governors' support in the face of anticipated economic problems represent significant challenges to the success of these reforms. Ultimately, the strength and cohesion of the state will depend on the federal government's ability to achieve sustainable economic growth and obtain reliable economic leverage over regional policies. Without such leverage, new institutions and personalities will seek other means to guarantee stability in their regions. Just as happened during the 1998 economic crisis, a new economic decline will expose the ineffectiveness of a purely administrative approach to state reform.

Military Victory Without Political Solution in Chechnya

It is common knowledge that Putin's presidential victory was closely linked to public support for his electoral promise to guarantee Russia's territorial integrity, to stop all terrorist activities in Chechnya, to destroy or capture and prosecute Chechen leaders and to break their ties with international terrorist organisations. This was to be achieved through decisive military action. Less noted, however, is that after the elections, the war increasingly became a liability for the president. Not only is the cost of the campaign high in financial terms, it also adversely affects Russia's relations with European states and institutions. In the future, Russia will have to invest substantial resources in a programme of reconstruction for Chechnya.

By summer 2000, Russian forces had captured virtually the entire territory of the Chechen republic. Then Defence Minister Sergeyev optimistically announced the end of large-scale military operations and the gradual withdrawal of Russian troops. Yet, it soon became clear that Russia's military presence does not mean actual control over the territory. Large-scale military offensives, with excessive use of artillery and air power, had enabled the Russian military to destroy large groups of Chechen guerrillas. But the Chechens then changed tactics: instead of attempting to preserve control over specific territorial strongholds in the face of massive Russian attack, they reverted to traditional methods of small-scale guerrilla warfare. They fragmented into small groups of well-trained fighters, targeting Russian installations deep in territory officially declared under Russian military control. The main targets included Russian bases or military convoys; in some cases, suicide bombers were used. Local officials who had joined pro-Moscow government bodies were the targets of assassination.

Despite their declaration of victory, Russian forces have failed either to eliminate the small- and medium-sized Chechen armed groups and their leaders, or effectively to seal the region against an infusion of military supplies and financial resources to support guerrilla activities. The initial euphoria of victory was quickly replaced by concerns about Russia's open-ended military commitment in Chechnya. Nevertheless, the Russian military started to withdraw from Chechnya, planning eventually to leave only one brigade, while the Interior Troops will have two brigades and additional special forces units. In January 2001, Russian forces in Chechnya stood at 40,000, a significant reduction from the peak of an estimated 100,000 in April–May 2000.

In early February 2001, Putin signed the decree transferring responsibility for the joint operation from the General Staff to the Federal Security Service (the successor to the KGB). This underscored the fact that major military operations were finished, and that in the future the Russian forces would primarily undertake special operations to eliminate or arrest key warlords, and reconnaissance missions to discover and destroy Chechen weapon stockpiles and bases inside Chechen territory. Despite government claims that the military and the Interior Troops control Chechnya in its entirety, none of the most notorious rebel commanders have been captured. This has had a strong negative impact on the morale of Russian forces: in the 1994–96 war, many Chechen commanders had close links to Russian officials and businessmen who earned large sums of money from the conflict.

The Russian military strongly opposed any suggestions that a political solution be negotiated with those Chechen leaders who had participated in the fighting, including previously elected Chechen President Aslan Maskhadov, who had allegedly supported decisive military actions against Russian troops. The majority of the Russian political élite, including Putin, agree with the military's position and sought as negotiating partners Chechen leaders who did not take part in the war and who are capable of consolidating Chechen society. At the least, they looked for leaders who represented those parts of the population who were tired of the war and actively sought an end to military activities. On 21 June 2000, Putin appointed former Mufti Akhmed-hadji Kadyrov to head a transitional administration in Chechnya, and in January 2001 he appointed Stanislav Iliyasov to head the Chechen government. Iliyasov was charged with the

Europe

implementation of a reconstruction programme expected to cost over 14bn roubles ($500 million) in 2001 alone.

Any effective reconstruction that might rebuild Chechen public support for cooperation with the Russian authorities depended upon the end of fighting and full Russian control over the territory where this money will be spent. More then a year after capturing Grozny, and 10 months after the end of large-scale operations, Russian forces are still engaged in low-intensity war with the Chechen guerrillas. Continuing casualties further weaken the morale of Russian forces and turn Russian public opinion against military operations. The Russian military command has promoted the view that the tactics they used from August 1999 to May 2000 were designed to minimise losses among Russian forces: indeed, the 2,585 killed and 8,050 wounded between August 1999 and April 2000 are relatively low figures compared to previous Russian operations in Afghanistan and in Chechnya in 1994–96, when the Russians lost over 1,500 troops during the first attack on Grozny. Since the end of large-scale campaigning, however, Russian casualties have continued, though at an even lower level. These, and wider reporting of high civilian casualties and human rights violations in Chechnya (despite heavy censorship on their coverage in the state-controlled media), have started to erode public support for the campaign. By the end of 2000, the Russian public supported the military campaign by only a small majority; a much larger number anticipated that the conflict was likely to continue for more than ten years.

The Future of Military Reform

The military believes in Putin's priority commitment to its reform and modernisation. Over 90% of the military voted for Putin, anticipating that his military background and campaign rhetoric would be translated into greater attention to, and thus financial investment in, defence. The Chechen campaign put this belief to the test. While the operation itself received much greater financial support than the first Chechen campaign of 1994–96, the government failed to fulfil many of its commitments, including the payment of special salaries to civilians who joined as contract soldiers and non-commissioned officers to fight in Chechnya. These salaries were set at about $1,000 a month (the salary of a mid-ranking officer in the Russian armed forces is about $200 a month), attracting many ex-conscripts to join. Many of them are still awaiting payment – in some case, their sole income – more than a year after signing the contract.

The military is also concerned about Putin's indecisiveness on the future direction of military reform. Despite his electoral promises to increase funding for military modernisation and to improve the readiness of the armed forces, the programme of reform eventually signed by the president on 16 January 2001 focuses instead on further reductions and organisational restructuring. Unlike any previous programme, this one remains classified, despite Putin's statement that military reform is a task for all Russian society. According to apparently reliable reports, the armed forces' personnel will be reduced from 1.2m to 800,000 over the next five years, with the major reductions coming in 2001. At the same time, the programme envisages that the share of defence budget outlays for salaries and other personnel expenses will fall from 80% (as it stands now) to 50%. The larger share will be spent on research and development, and modernisation. These reductions will be achieved by the liquidation of entire units, particularly in the Siberian and Far Eastern military districts, as well as by major reductions in the numbers of servicemen in Moldova and Georgia. The long-bruited merger of the Volga and Urals military districts will finally occur by the end of 2001. Such reductions will require substantial funding for social programmes for retiring officers and their families. Money for this purpose are not included in the budget and their absence is certain to produce further social tension.

The Strategic Rocket Forces (SRF) are expected to be downgraded from the status of a separate service to that of a branch of the armed forces and to be eventually incorporated into the air force. The Missile Defence Forces (MDF) and Space Forces (SF) will be separated from the SRF into a separate Space Forces branch. The MDF and the SF were incorporated into the SRF in 1997; their separation only five years later is symptomatic of Russian military reform in general, which emphasises institutional reorganisations, all too often to the detriment of readiness and morale. In addition to structural changes, the SRF will face reductions in the procurement of the *Topol*-M (SS-27) strategic weapons system. In the past, Russia produced around ten SS-27s a year, but this year produced only four. It is expected that future procurement will be maintained at six per year. Any reorganisation of Russia's strategic forces is likely to be influenced by the US plans to deploy a national missile defence (NMD) system. Another significant factor is the ability of the US and Russian governments to reach agreement on the future of the Anti-Ballistic Missile (ABM) Treaty, one of Putin's many foreign policy challenges.

Notwithstanding Putin's ambitious plans to readjust national security priorities, there remain serious differences over those plans within the government. Putin's superficially significant changes to his national security team are unlikely to resolve these disputes. In March 2001, he replaced the leadership of virtually all of the national security and defence agencies, including the Minister of Defence and his two deputies, the Minister of the Interior and the Head and Deputy Heads of the Security Council. The reshuffle was in part inspired by disagreements over procurement priorities between outgoing Defence Minister Sergeyev, who favours upgrading nuclear forces, and Chief of General Staff Kvashnin, who favours modernising conventional forces.

Europe

The new Minister of Defence, Sergei Ivanov, and new Minister of the Interior, Boris Gryzlov, are close personal friends and political allies of Putin. These cosy ties reflect Putin's intention to maintain control over security policy. But the appointments stand little chance of improving civil-military relations: all of the new appointees are civilians, and none have demonstrated commitment to military and security-sector reforms. In particular, Ivanov, like Putin, had a long career in the KGB, which the military hierarchy tends to regard with suspicion. His appointment and the declining influence of the Security Council, whose brief is now more focused on domestic and information security, tend to reinforce the primacy of the military in defining military reforms. On the other hand, Putin retained Sergeyev as his adviser on strategic issues. The former defence minister is likely to enjoy greater access to Putin than will Kvashnin, which will perpetuate rather than resolve the central procurement dispute.

Putin's new appointments, then, portend more friction than consensus in civil-military relations and a degree of gridlock in military reform. In the long run, prospects for substantial military reform will depend not only on personalities at the top of the hierarchy, but also on their ability and willingness to find professionals to fill mid-level gaps in Moscow and the military districts.

Russia's Pragmatic Foreign Policy

Russia has sought to reassert its international profile on several fronts: undertaking bilateral dialogue with European states and the EU; reviving relations with Soviet-era allies to address Russia's economic interests and debt issues; promoting Russian arms exports; and abandoning the idea of integration with the Commonwealth of Indepedent States (CIS) in favour of bilateral relations with its neighbours. Unlike his predecessor Yeltsin, Putin conducted an active foreign policy in 2000 with regular state visits around the globe. The importance of foreign policy in Putin's agenda was highlighted by a June 2000 directive that outlined, although in rather general terms, key foreign policy principles. Its pragmatic orientation was made clear through its emphasis on economic relations; but it did not define any priorities. As a result, Russia continues to view itself as a global power with worldwide interests.

The geography of Putin's foreign visits only reaffirmed this global commitment. In less than a year after taking office, Putin met with almost all of the key European leaders, visited China and India, took part in the Central Asia Group of Five meetings that took place in Shanghai, paid a special visit to some old Soviet allies in Asia (Vietnam and North Korea) and the Americas (Cuba), as well as to new partners such as Canada and South Korea, attended G-8 meetings in Okinawa and the EU–Russia summit in Paris, met twice with NATO Secretary-General George Robertson, hosted a meeting with Iranian President Mohammed Khatami and held meetings with the leaders of the CIS states. His visit to Azerbaijan was the first by a Russian leader.

Such an itinerary is very impressive for any leader, particularly during his first year in office and with many unresolved domestic problems requiring constant presidential attention. Traditionally, however, a Russian leader's popularity is closely linked to his ability to project an image of a powerful international leader. Thus, despite looming domestic problems, Putin's popularity at home received a major boost from his active foreign policy, which also helped transform his image abroad, particularly in the West. After initial concerns about his KGB past and his authoritarian rhetoric, Putin's visits earned him a reputation as a man with whom the West 'can do business', as former UK Prime Minister Margaret Thatcher famously said of Mikhail Gorbachev. In contrast to Yeltsin, Putin is a leader of the new generation, who speaks a foreign language and is more interested in discussing practical issues – from economy to security – than in receiving symbolic gestures and rhetorical acknowledgements of Russia's great-power role.

In terms of practical results, Putin's foreign policy scored some points for both his domestic and geopolitical agendas. His trips to China and India resulted in major new arms export agreements, as did his meetings with the Iranian president. On visits to Cuba and Vietnam, he sought creative ways to recover their debts to Russia by converting them into barter arrangements or preferential conditions for Russian businesses. Putin's trip to South Korea and China, as well as his meetings with German Chancellor Gerhard Schröder and then with EU leaders in Paris, resulted in agreements to increase exports of Russia's energy resources to both Europe and Asia in the next decade and to develop new infrastructure projects. At the same time, Putin put pressure on the Paris Club to reschedule or even forgive some of the Soviet Union debts inherited by Russia.

In geopolitical terms, Putin's efforts signal the end of the post-Soviet phase in favour of a new strategy which will better reflect Russia's present position in the world and its domestic interests. This was particularly clear in Russia's relations with CIS states. President Yeltsin was personally committed to preserving the CIS in the hope of reintegrating some parts of the Soviet Union back into Russia. Putin has no attachment to the CIS and considers it more as a burden for Russia, which has been supporting its partners by discounting energy prices and forgiving debts in order to maintain the pretence of integration. Thousands of agreements were adopted under CIS auspices but very few were implemented. Putin's policy, on the other hand, has been to conduct bilateral relations with CIS states so as to defend aggressively Russia's economic and security

Europe

interests. This approach has put many of Russia's neighbours in a difficult position, arousing anti-Russian feelings among their political élites and potentially among their publics.

This phenomenon was particularly striking in relations with Georgia. When Georgia refused to allow Russian troops to enter the Pankisi Gorge on the border with Chechnya, Russia retaliated by introducing visas for Georgian citizens and by halting gas supplies until past energy debts were repaid. Similar pressure was put on Ukraine and Moldova, which were pressed to settle their debts to Russia or to face possible cessation of supplies. The Putin administration also expressed greater caution about a putative Russian–Belorusian union than had Yeltsin, primarily on economic grounds.

Another sign of Putin's shift from a post-Soviet to a Russian phase in his foreign policy agenda is the declining importance he attaches to US–Russian relations. Putin seeks to build closer ties to Western European states and institutions and to use these to influence US policy. By mid-March 2001, Russia–US relations were at their lowest ebb since the end of the Cold War. Conversely, Russia's relations with Europe were developing steadily and had even begun to expand into new areas, such as the EU–Russia Paris summit decision to cooperate more closely in the areas of security and defence policy. Russia's interests *vis-à-vis* Europe are diverse and substantial. The EU now accounts for over 40% of Russia's foreign trade. (Russia's trade with the US remains small and US investment in Russia has not increased significantly since the 1998 economic crisis.) As EU enlargement progresses, the EU share is expected to grow to over 60%. The European states also have made a clear commitment to continue a policy of engagement with Russia. Because of its geographic proximity, Europe sees a further weakened and unstable Russia as a potential major source of insecurity.

In contrast, the new US administration views Russia as a secondary power with policies (such as selling arms to Iran) that threaten US interests. It is therefore more interested in containing than engaging Russia. This attitude could be clearly seen in the US NMD debate. The overwhelming consensus among the US political élite is that while it would be desirable to obtain Russia's agreement to ABM Treaty modification, if that is not possible, the US is prepared to withdraw unilaterally from the treaty. Russia, in turn, has sought to mobilise European political and public opinion to convey its concerns to the US administration, suggesting that unless the ABM Treaty is preserved, Russia will have no choice but to abandon other arms-control agreements such as START and the Intermediate-Range Nuclear Forces (INF) treaty to preserve the credibility of its nuclear deterrent.

As part of its effort to gain European support for its position on NMD, Moscow proposed the joint development of a European theatre missile defence system, using Russian and European technology, and an early-warning data exchange, as well as a joint study on missile proliferation threats and non-military means to address them. By the beginning of 2001, however, it was increasingly clear that European governments would not actively oppose a US decision to go ahead with NMD deployment. There also appears to be a growing, if grudging, acceptance in Moscow that NMD will proceed. If US–Russian relations remain reasonably congenial, there is a possibility that some form of deal – possibly including informal unilateral reductions in strategic nuclear weapons – could be struck over the ABM Treaty. Nevertheless, the prospect of NMD deployment, and the pending decision (to be taken during the 2002 NATO summit) on a second round of NATO enlargement that may include at least one of the Baltic states, will undoubtedly strain Russia's relations with Europe. Russia's economic interests in Europe are so important, however, that it can no longer afford to take uncompromising foreign policy positions.

Still a Disquieting Future

After a year of economic growth, but lost opportunities, Russia is entering a period that will be characterised by a tight budget with declining commodity prices, negative trends in Russian public confidence and the prospect of worsening conditions for the most vulnerable social groups as subsidies for utilities and housing are cut. As a result of the ten-year hiatus in domestic investment for maintaining basic economic infrastructure, new domestic disasters can be expected. Russia's access to resources on international financial markets will be limited due to fears of global recession; and EU and NATO enlargement and US NMD plans will pose difficult foreign policy choices. Putin has demonstrated over his past year in office that, in the face of serious domestic problems, it is difficult for him to make and to implement the necessary clear and definitive decisions. Given the taxing circumstances ahead, it will be increasingly challenging for him to make and to implement vital strategic ones.

Europe

Healing the Wounds in the Balkans

During the years of communism, the people of Eastern Europe used to joke that it did not matter how they voted, what mattered was who did the counting. Yet, as the collapse of the Milosevic regime in Yugoslavia last year indicates, election results ultimately do matter, regardless of how rigged the tallies are. Astute observers had noted that Milosevic's days were numbered and predicted that, when change ultimately came, it would be as a result of a messy combination of 'people's power' and a military coup, similar to the events that toppled Nicolae Ceausescu's dictatorship in neighbouring Romania. And so it proved to be.

Milosevic is down, but certainly not completely out of the political landscape. Yugoslavia is a democracy, but one in which many of Milosevic's former henchmen have been recycled into today's 'moderate' politicians. The new regime in Belgrade means well and wishes to create a civilised, stable and responsible European state. Yet the wounds of the lengthy dictatorship run deep, and the country's corrupt bureaucracy is unlikely to heal them. Slobodan Milosevic's departure is therefore only a first step in Yugoslavia's return to Europe. Nevertheless, the political change in Belgrade has altered the situation throughout the region. Although terrorist incidents and localised violence will continue, the Balkan wars, which repeated themselves with terrifying monotony during the last century, are now over. For the first time since the end of the Ottoman Empire, the entire region is now controlled by democratic governments, however faulty and fragile these may be. The challenge for the Balkans is not how to prevent another mass bloodshed, but rather how to transform these hesitant positive steps into a long-term and sustained economic and political reconstruction. Whether the Balkans can be integrated into a stable European continent still awaits an answer.

The Strongman Stumbles

In calling for early presidential elections last autumn, Milosevic characteristically pursued three aims simultaneously. He wanted to gain a new legitimacy inside Yugoslavia, a year after his military defeat in Kosovo. He sought to tell the West that, regardless of the economic sanctions and NATO's military presence along his country's borders, he was likely to remain in power forever. And he planned to use his re-election as a justification for crushing the growing independence movement in Montenegro, still a component but restless part of Yugoslavia.

The elections proved to be Milosevic's crucial and fatal error. He did not believe that Yugoslavia's opposition movement would be able to agree on a unified candidate. Nor did he believe that the West had much influence inside his country. He was wrong on both counts. The strong performance of Vojislav Kostunica, the opposition candidate, made ballot rigging much more difficult. And the rush of Western governments to recognise Kostunica as the country's rightful president immediately after the first round of elections prevented Milosevic from using his other traditional trick: that of eliminating a strong opposition challenge by bureaucratic procedures immediately after an election. This was the first clear example of Western governments beating Milosevic at his own game.

Images of crowds storming the Yugoslav parliament or burning the television station in protest against Milosevic's refusal to accept the electoral results in October 2000 may have been exhilarating, but they were ultimately a deception: the real battle in Belgrade took place behind the scenes and was over the loyalty of the Yugoslav security services and the military. The Milosevic dictatorship, one of the most powerful repression machines in Europe, did not break down because of popular pressure, but because of internal disputes and the ultimate refusal of the regime's most important pillars – the military and the police – to confront Yugoslavia's enraged people. While the siege of the Yugoslav parliament was still in progress, on 6 October Milosevic negotiated his departure from power with president-elect Kostunica and the army commanders. Yugoslavia was spared prolonged bloodshed like that which swept Romania during the previous decade. But the price was the survival of the Milosevic repression apparatus and a guarantee of personal safety for the dictator himself. The seeds of Yugoslavia's future troubles were sown at the same moment that the world media reported that democracy had triumphed on Belgrade's streets.

Nevertheless, Kostunica started his administration well. Mindful of his country's wounded national pride, he eschewed an immediate normalisation of Yugoslavia's relations with NATO, but quickly re-established diplomatic relations with individual Western countries. Kostunica also avoided any recriminations, although some of the key murderers of the Milosevic era were quietly retired. Above everything else, the new president concentrated on consolidating the opposition's triumph by holding fresh parliamentary elections. The tactic worked: Milosevic's acolytes were routed. Theoretically, the triumph of democracy was complete. But Yugoslavia's new government is a brittle collection of parties, united more by hatred of Milosevic than any common ideology or any clear idea of what they seek to accomplish.

In the coming years, the country's main problem will be the rising confrontation between two factions within the ruling Democratic Opposition of Serbia (DOS). One faction is led by Kostunica; the other by Serbian Premier Zoran Djindjic. The two leaders are already barely on speaking terms. The ambitious Djindjic has been trying to keep his pledge to fight crime and corruption, but thus far with little success. The security services,

Europe

still unreformed and hardly under government control, will continue resisting such efforts by playing on the differences between premier and president. Apart from the supposed fight against corruption, the government does not seem to have a single coherent economic programme and for good reasons: many of the supporters of the opposition, the miners and the industrial workers who poured on to the streets last year in order to topple Milosevic, will also be the first to suffer from any serious economic reform. The task of economic reconstruction is so huge and so urgent that the government, swamped by various problems, has been reduced to vague appeals for international financial help and little else.

The current opposition, Milosevic's Socialist Party of Serbia and the Yugoslav Left (JUL) controlled by Milosevic's wife, Mira Markovic, are not in a position to threaten the government. But economic decay remains a serious threat to the authorities in Belgrade. The population is becoming impatient and expects salaries to be increased substantially in line with the rise in the cost of living caused by curtailment of state subsdies and price controls. Yet the authorities can hardly satisfy such demands without fuelling a new round of inflation, similar to the one engineered by Milosevic during the mid 1990s.

Demands that Milosevic and other indictees be extradited to the International Criminal Tribunal for the Former Yugoslavia [ICTY] are another painful issue for the authorities. President Kostunica believes that extradition can be avoided. Those close to him think that the escalation of terrorism in southern Serbia and Macedonia will sideline these demands, as the West focuses on maintaining regional stability, rather than extracting justice for past wrongs. They may be right, but so long as Milosevic remains free, and even if he is put on trial in Belgrade, the authorities will not be able to regain full international respectability.

Overall, the new Yugoslav government may only have until the end of 2001 before it starts encountering more serious opposition at home. This opposition will be aimless and very often related to sectional interests (such as farmers or industrial workers). But the result will be the same: the honeymoon for the Yugoslav authorities will be over. And as Prime Minister Djinjic becomes less popular, the confrontation between him and the president, who is determined to stay above the fray and not take political responsibility for the economic pain, will intensify. Ultimately, however, the biggest test for Belgrade remains the same as it has been for a decade: maintaining a semblance of regional security and the rump Yugoslav state's unity.

Cracks in the Kosovo Facade

Nearly 40,000 international peacekeepers remain in Kosovo. But Kosovo Albanians are clearly discontented, as are the remaining Serbs. Serb representatives keep drawing public attention to the difficult position of their compatriots, and Albanians are dissatisfied with the foot-dragging in resolving the final status of the province. The international administration has sought to overcome some of the problems, but there is no sign that it will soon find a formula to reconcile the views of the two ethnic communities.

There are hopes that the departure of the former UN Interim Administration Mission in Kosovo (UNMIK) chief, Bernard Kouchner, and the arrival of his successor, Hans Haekkerup, will bring a different approach to the province. Haekkerup, a former Danish defence minister, has the tenacity needed to tackle Kosovo's critical questions, such as the return of the Serb refugees and the establishment of a legal framework for parliamentary elections. In a bid to improve relations with the authorities in Serbia and Yugoslavia, the new UN administrator has moved quickly to establish an UNMIK office in Belgrade. It is a step of reconciliation, but hardly one large enough to answer Kosovo's larger problems.

Kouchner failed to resolve the problem of the divided city of Kosovska Mitrovica in the north of the province, which will also be a very serious obstacle for his successor. He failed to carry out a plan for the symbolic return of some 1,000 Serb families, which he had approved prior to his departure from Pristina, essentially because he was unable to persuade local Albanian leaders to consent to any return of expellees; UNMIK will discover that the same ethnic hatred will continue. On the positive side, during Kouchner's 18 months in Kosovo, the Kosovo Liberation Army (KLA) was demilitarised and its members grouped into the Kosovo Protection Corps, a vaguely conceived but nevertheless functioning paramilitary force. Meanwhile, part of the KLA joined the Kosovo Police Force, founded under the auspices of the Organisation for Security and Cooperation in Europe. Nevertheless, despite many attempts, Kouchner failed to convince Kosovo Serb representatives to join the Kosovo Protection Corps, and only a few former Serbian policemen, mainly in the northern municipality of Leposavic, agreed to put on the new Kosovo police uniforms.

The delay in establishing functioning administrative structures in the province carried a heavy price tag. The Transitional Administrative Council and the Interim Kosovo Council were meant to be multi-ethnic bodies replacing the parallel authority formed by the KLA and political parties close to this organisation (primarily Redhxep Qosja's United Democratic Movement) in the wake of the NATO air strikes against Yugoslavia. But the interim institutions of Kosovo were formed in December 1999 without Kosovo Serb representatives, which heralded the subsequent lack of cooperation of the Serb population with the international missions in the province. After 18 months of Kouchner's administration, just over 75,000 Serbs remain in the province, according to

KFOR's statistics. The 'silent exodus' of Serbs and Roma people shows no signs of abating and, despite all the promises to the contrary, it will be very difficult to reverse.

Kouchner's major success in Kosovo was undoubtedly the organisation of local elections in October 2000, when, as expected, the relatively moderate wing, headed by the leader of the Democratic Alliance of Kosovo, Ibrahim Rugova, won. For a while, it appeared that the crushing electoral defeat of the political parties that had their roots in the former KLA was a sign that the Serbian–Albanian clashes would eventually die down and that moderation would prevail. But one bitter struggle was replaced by a more significant confrontation among ethnic Albanians, which is now being played through proxies on the territory of Serbia itself and among the ethnic Albanians of Macedonia. Theoretically, these bouts of violence are unrelated. The Presevo Valley in southern Serbia, where much of the fighting has taken place, is an acknowledged part of Yugoslavia; Macedonia is an independent state, which has done much to integrate its sizeable Albanian ethnic minority. In practice, however, the two developments are the product of the same sense of frustration among ethnic Albanians about their nebulous legal status, coupled with their growing fear that, for the third time in a century, the West is about to sacrifice their interests in order to appease the Serbs.

NATO's military action in Kosovo was and remains contradictory. The alliance repeatedly claimed that it was not fighting on behalf of the Albanians, despite the fact that the only beneficiaries of the 1999 operation were the Albanians. NATO loudly condemned Albanian terrorism, but somehow managed to bomb only Yugoslav military targets. The war was also supposed to protect the multi-ethnic character of Kosovo, but NATO was ultimately unable to prevent the exodus of hundreds of thousands of ethnic Serbs and Roma from the province. Finally, the alliance remains committed to the maintenance of Yugoslav sovereignty over Kosovo, although no Western leader has ever specified how the province could ever be returned to Belgrade's rule. The ethnic Albanians of the province were initially unperturbed by such contradictions. They guessed correctly that NATO would not be able to stop their acts of intimidation against ethnic Serbs in the province and that, sooner or later, Kosovo would be a pure Albanian territory regardless of the West's support for the concept of 'multi-ethnicity'. Nor were the Albanians perturbed by the fact that Kosovo was denied independence, because they knew that this was a pure formality: to all intents and purposes the province was torn away from Yugoslavia and was likely to remain so.

The ethnic Albanians, however, did not reckon on two surprises: a political change in Belgrade, accompanied by one in Washington, hitherto their chief ally. And, ironically, both happened at more or less the same time. The overthrow of Slobodan Milosevic's regime in Yugoslavia allowed the West to normalise relations with the country; the return of Kosovo to Yugoslav sovereignty, until recently a theoretical question, suddenly looked perfectly possible. And the election of a new US administration, ostensibly committed to a withdrawal of US troops from Kosovo, merely added to the Albanians' sense of unease.

As is often the case in the Balkans, perceptions are more important than realities. Despite the Western rush to re-establish relations with Yugoslavia, the idea that Kosovo will be forced to return to Yugoslav control remains far-fetched. And statements by President George W. Bush's close advisers, suggesting the imminent withdrawal of US troops from the province, should not be taken too seriously either: a draw-down of US troops in Bosnia is on the cards, but no major rearrangement of the composition of the troops in Kosovo itself is contemplated, if only because this will raise again the thorny issue of creating a Russian sector in the province and ring alarm bells in European capitals about the US commitment to transatlantic relations. Nevertheless, the Albanians concluded that they were about to face their worst nightmare: being abandoned just when they seemed so close to achieving their dream of liberation.

This was the political background to the wave of violence in February and March 2001. The Albanians fighting in the Presevo Valley and in Macedonia were few in number and knew full well that no government would support their demands for a territorial change; they were fighting to put pressure on NATO to resolve Kosovo's final status by according the province independence. This renewed wave of violence has placed NATO in a bind. As long as bloodshed continues in Yugoslavia, the question of Kosovo cannot be addressed. Furthermore, even if Western governments were willing to grant Kosovo independence, this would require a change in the terms of the United Nations mandate, something which both the Russians and the Chinese are sure to veto. Nor can NATO contemplate withdrawal from the region, and the alliance remains reluctant to be drawn even deeper into a new conflict in Macedonia.

As always, it is easy to paint a bleak scenario for the entire region. Fighting in the Presevo Valley could escalate, provoking new atrocities from the Yugoslav forces which, in turn, would tarnish the image of the new government in Belgrade and bring pressures for Western intervention, perhaps in the shape of creating an autonomous Albanian region in southern Serbia. The creation of such a region would be a disaster: it would destroy Kostunica's nationalist credentials at home, increase pressures from Vojvodina (another ethnically-mixed area of Serbia) for its own autonomy and bring the spectre of a 'greater Kosovo' that much closer. The clashes between guerrillas and the Macedonian authorities could spread from the border region of Tetovo to Skopje, the Macedonian capital, thereby provoking a backlash from the Slav majority in the republic. The country's multi-ethnic government, which includes one ethnic Albanian political party, could collapse, leading to the *de facto* division of the state and prompting an intervention from neighbouring Greece and Bulgaria. But there are good reasons to believe that none of these terrible scenarios will come to pass.

NATO has accepted the return of Yugoslav forces to the buffer zone created at the end of the Kosovo war between the border of the province and Serbia. The return of Yugoslav troops is gradual and conditioned on their good behaviour. The aim of the operation was to make it clear that Western governments are not likely to support the creation of a new autonomous region within Serbia and that they remain determined to prevent further terrorist cross-border infiltration. The balance that NATO seeks to strike is delicate: just enough Yugoslav troops to ensure that the border is sealed, but not so many as to threaten new massacres. For the moment this appears to be working: the Yugoslav military, highly restricted in the equipment it can bring into the buffer zone, has just enough capabilities to reimpose control but is unable to implement a 'scorched earth' strategy even if it wanted to. The retention of the concept of a buffer zone can also reassure the ethnic Albanians in the Presevo Valley that, although they are unlikely to obtain full autonomy, they will be treated differently from the rest of Serbia's residents and are entitled to some residual NATO protection. Overall, this informal and sometimes messy arrangement has every chance of reducing violence without humiliating the authorities in Belgrade or giving the Albanians false hopes. And it has already resulted in a high level of cooperation between the Yugoslav military command and NATO, a huge achievement, given the resentment that NATO stoked up throughout the region during the Kosovo war.

Moving into Macedonia

A partly reassuring conclusion can also be reached about Macedonia, despite some ominous signs. The fact that a small group of troublemakers has managed to instigate demonstrations in the city of Tetovo and provoke weeks of fighting is clearly worrying. Nor can NATO seal the borders of Macedonia completely. Quite apart from the fact that many weapons have already been smuggled in (and much more military equipment has been in the hands of extremists in the republic for years), the border between Albania and Macedonia will always remain porous. The Albanian government has never been able to eliminate paramilitary formations inside the country and is unlikely to succeed now.

Nor can Western governments contemplate another military deployment in Macedonia with equanimity. The Bush administration has no intention of becoming embroiled in another Balkan state, although

Washington is likely to support any European effort to deploy troops in Macedonia. Politically, a European show of force would make sense. It would be the first real test for the continent's new security arrangements calling for the Combined Joint Task Force arrangements discussed between the European Union and NATO. Such an operation could also involve both EU countries which are members of NATO (Greece, for instance) and NATO countries which are not in the EU, such as Turkey. Furthermore, a Macedonian deployment could also involve countries which are in neither organisation but have a direct stake in regional security, such as Romania or Bulgaria.

In many respects, therefore, a Macedonian operation would represent a text-book example of the arrangements for a new European security structure: one that is undertaken by a coalition of willing states, regardless of formal membership in existing institutions; one in which Europeans bear the burden of their own security; and one which complements NATO in a conflict where the alliance as a whole does not wish to be involved. But if the political advantages are tempting, the military dangers remain very great. A military deployment in Macedonia may be precisely what the hardline Albanian elements expect. Once on the ground, a European force would be embroiled in arbitrating between Albanians and Slav-Macedonians. If the European force were to crack down on Albanian extremists, it would provoke a backlash in Kosovo and KFOR troops would be instantly regarded as the Albanians' enemy. If, on the other hand, a European force tried to maintain its neutrality, Albanian extremists would intensify their attacks in the hope that an international presence would lead to the *de facto* division of Macedonia into cantons: a Bosnian solution without a formal Dayton accord. It is therefore easy to see why most Western governments in late March 2001 were still resisting the temptation to commit their forces.

But this reluctance should not, and probably will not, amount to total inaction. Although some terrorist activity will continue, resources can be provided for the training of Macedonia's own armed forces. Assistance could also be given with intelligence and joint patrols along the Kosovo–Macedonian border. Political pressure should be applied to the moderate Albanian political leadership in the republic to retain its coalition agreement within the Macedonian government.

Crucially, the troubles in Macedonia have literally redrawn the pattern of alliances in the Balkans. For a variety of historic and emotional reasons, both Bulgaria and Greece harboured reservations about an independent Macedonian state. These reservations have disappeared: Greece and Bulgaria have become Macedonia's closest allies. Turkey can be expected to have some sympathy for the Albanians, but Ankara will have no truck at all with their new separatist demands. And Romania and Serbia, the two other major regional actors, also have a stake in maintaining the current

Europe

status quo. Overall, therefore, extremist Albanians have no chance of generating a new Balkan war: they are too weak to sustain such a confrontation, bereft of international sympathy and confronted by a steadfast Balkan alliance. Sporadic violence will probably continue, but the Macedonian state can be expected to hold.

This will not make the West's task any easier. NATO remains stuck in an unwinnable position, seeking to defend the Albanians' entitlement to govern themselves in Kosovo, but denying them the right to be completely self-governing there, or to enjoy a similar status in the rest of Serbia or Macedonia. It is possible to envisage a compromise which might lead to Kosovo's formal independence. The Yugoslav authorities, who know that they will never regain sovereignty over the province, may be persuaded to grant Kosovo its independence in return for safeguards for other ethnic minorities there and access to some Serb religious and historic sites. If Belgrade wishes to grant Kosovo independence, neither the Russians nor the Chinese are likely to object to an amendment of the current United Nations mandate. But this outcome is dependent on negotiations between Yugoslavia and the Kosovo Albanians, and these cannot take place as long as violence continues in the region. Furthermore, as long as Macedonia's territorial integrity is challenged, no regional government would welcome an independent Kosovo. The 'Albanian Question' will nag the Balkans for years to come, theoretically solvable but in practice intractable.

Good News in the Wider Balkans

Elsewhere in the Balkans, the picture is more optimistic. Montenegro, still part of Yugoslavia, may well decide in spring 2001 to opt for independence. As long as the Milosevic regime remained in power in Belgrade, the Western powers looked on Montenegrin President Milo Djukanovic with favour. They were always divided over the merits of Montenegrin independence, but governments could not resist the temptation of playing the 'Montenegrin card' in order to tighten the noose around Milosevic. The result was a curious game of mutual and usually unspoken threats. Milosevic knew that he could not move to crush the Montenegrin government, because he could not predict NATO's military reaction. For exactly the same reason, Djukanovic did not know whether he could move towards an outright declaration of independence.

Milosevic's fall from power has made all these games redundant. The usefulness of Montenegro to the rest of Europe has largely disappeared; the West now expects the Montenegrins to support Yugoslavia's President Kostunica, or at least not to create trouble for the new federal authorities. Djukanovic's irritation at his fading international importance has become palpable. As a result, the prospects for a smooth dialogue between the Montenegrins and the federal authorities in Belgrade do not look good.

Kostunica has offered his Montenegrin counterpart many concessions, including the restoration of Montenegro's equal status under a new Yugoslav constitution and greater autonomy in the management of the local economy. But the offers were refused by Djukanovic, who is clearly treating these negotiations as little more than routine haggling in an oriental bazaar. In reality, the two negotiating sides have very little room for manoeuvre. Djukanovic will not settle for a deal as long as he does not know what Belgrade's final offer will be and this is unlikely to happen for quite some time, partly because the new Yugoslav government is still fragile, and partly because a new constitution cannot be written unless the question of Kosovo is settled. At the same time, Kostunica cannot afford to alienate the Yugoslav military and the Serb nationalists in Belgrade by making too many concessions; the Yugoslav president has ruled out Montenegro's proposal for a 'loose' Yugoslav federation as a 'meaningless concept'. So, for the moment, both sides hope to gain time by wasting time in irrelevant negotiations. The Montenegrins' independence referendum is part of this time-wasting technique.

There is a strong possibility that the Montenegrins will opt for independence. Yet this does not necessarily mean that the republic will immediately secede from Yugoslavia. Poor, defenceless and with a potentially militant Muslim minority in its midst, Montenegro will be careful about severing its ties with Belgrade too quickly. In all probability, if Serbia were to agree to independence, this would be used by Djukanovic as justification for new negotiations with Kostunica. Nobody in Yugoslavia is contemplating the use of force and negotiations will be protracted. Nor are Western governments likely to rush to recognise this state. About the only significant outcome of the Montenegrin episode would be a delay in the implementation of meaningful reform throughout Yugoslavia, as time is wasted on petty disputes about the division of assets and the military. Reason is not always the guiding principle in the Balkans, and Montenegro may secede. The chief casualties are guaranteed to be the Montenegrins themselves, but wider Balkan security structures are unlikely to be affected.

Further afield, the Bulgarian government is likely to be re-elected in this year's general elections. The composition of the future government is not clear, and the possible entry into the political fray of King Simeon, the country's wartime ruler, may add a further complication. But it is clear that the Socialists, responsible for much of the economic disaster in Bulgaria during the 1990s, are unlikely to return to power. The country has made great strides in economic reform and has eliminated inflation. It needs to do much more, but already has the admiration of many Western governments. Bulgaria's problem with its Muslim Turks has disappeared; indeed, many of these ethnic Turks, driven away from the country during the latter years of the communist dictatorship, are now returning to

Europe

Bulgaria in the expectation that the country will one day join the European Union.

The Romanians, however, are beginning the third millennium with the same leftist leadership that wasted much of the 1990s by failing to undertake economic reform. The return of President Ion Iliescu to power in the November 2000 elections and the rise of an extremist nationalist party have raised worries in many European capitals that Romania will follow Belarus and Moldova into oblivion. But Romania's new government, although including many old faces, is still committed to economic reform. During 2000, the Romanian economy grew slightly after three years of nose-diving. The country's currency reserves have increased in one year from $900 million to over $2 billion. Inflation, although still the highest in this part of Europe, shows signs of dropping. Moreover, the current account deficit has diminished, while exports have, for the first time, exceeded $10bn. Many of the reforms started by previous governments will have to be continued, willy-nilly, by the new government because they are included in the medium-term economic development strategy submitted in 2000 to the EU and represent the sole route to European Union membership, Romania's only meaningful political option.

Looking Ahead

The key question for the entire Balkan region in 2001 will therefore not relate to war, but rather to integrating into existing European economic and security structures. The EU is running the biggest economic reconstruction package in its history in the Balkans. As always, efforts have been hesitant, often contradictory and sometimes inefficient. Yet, after more than a year of regional conferences and feasibility studies, EU money is finally starting to pour into the region. The problem is that these funds are insufficient to kick-start local economies and cannot act as a substitute for genuine political integration.

The EU's immediate economic dilemma is partially alleviated by the anticipated growth in Balkan cooperation. The Danube, blocked since the Kosovo war, is being cleared for navigation, thereby allowing Romania and Bulgaria access to central European markets at cheaper transport costs. Trade will flourish between Balkan countries, this time not solely on the basis of the smuggling mafias that were so much a by-product of the sanctions against Yugoslavia during the last decade. Greek companies involved in infrastructure development, such as cement producers and telecommunications, are well-positioned to benefit from regional aid projects. And the movement of people in the region, hitherto subjected to impossible bureaucratic hurdles and corrupt officialdom, is already improving. But even here, the gains, although real, will not be sufficient. All Balkan countries suffer from similar problems. They all compete for scarce Western investment; they all have a decrepit industrial base which needs to be dismantled; they all have a large but poor agricultural sector starved of financial credits; and they all seek to join the same European institutions. Most of the products that the Balkan countries export compete with those of their immediate neighbours; it is therefore difficult for any single country to realise economies of scale, even if the political climate allows for regional cooperation.

Furthermore, each Balkan country has a different status with the European Union. Bulgaria, Romania and Slovenia are candidates for fully-fledged membership, even though the time-span required for their full integration differs widely. The other former republics of Yugoslavia and Albania enjoy no such advantages. This division presents the EU with a further, inherently insoluble dilemma. If it extends the status of candidate membership to all the region's states, it will be accused of diluting the whole concept of union enlargement, since it is hardly likely that all of them can be accommodated into the union, even in the next 15 years. However, if Brussels maintains the distinction between those which are fully-fledged membership candidates and those which are not, it would condemn the poorer Balkan states to semi-permanent neglect. President Kostunica of Yugoslavia is already discovering that, although he has been welcomed as a regional partner, he is still expected to compete with his neighbours from a position of inferiority. And Macedonia has already found that expressions of political support are not translated into any beneficial relationship with the EU.

NATO will face a similar dilemma in the coming year. When the alliance decided to admit three new member countries in 1997, it turned down the application of Slovenia and Romania. As a sweetener, these two Balkan states were offered 'sympathetic' consideration of their candidature when the next round of NATO enlargement came. They chose to interpret this bland statement as an undertaking that they would be among the most prominent future candidate countries, only to discover during NATO's Washington summit in April 1999 that their supposed exalted status amounted to nothing much.

The alliance will hold its next major summit in the second half of 2002 in Prague, and the question of enlargement will have to be faced yet again. Romania and Slovenia are still pushing hard, but events have overtaken them. Quite apart from the fact that there is no great enthusiasm for another round of enlargement, other countries may have a better claim. Bulgaria has performed better than Romania in economic and political terms; Slovakia needs to be rewarded for its political transformation and countries such as Croatia, Macedonia and even Yugoslavia have a more urgent claim for NATO's attention. If NATO decides to postpone its enlargement yet again the disappointment in the Balkans will be palpable. No amount of new offers of enhanced Partnerships for Peace (PfP) arrangements will persuade the countries of the region that they are still in the running; the resentment against the West as a whole and the US in particular will grow, to the benefit of all the extremist elements, which are currently still kept in check.

Salvation for the Balkans has to start in the region itself: chief responsibility for economic and political reform remains in the hands of its leaders. But consolidating regional stability will need years of hard work and large amounts of cash. In short, the region will require constant engagement at all levels; precisely what Western governments have invariably failed to achieve in the Balkans for all too long.

Middle East

Prospects for the Middle East and the Gulf looked reasonable at the start of 2000, but the year finished very poorly. Although the Syrian–Israeli peace process collapsed in April in Geneva, Israel unilaterally withdrew its forces from Lebanon in May, depriving Syria of a credible pretext for drawing Israeli blood with the help of its proxy, *Hizbollah*, or for maintaining a military presence in Lebanon. After a devastating civil war, Lebanon held parliamentary elections in August and September to open up the possibility of rebuilding the country. And Bashar al-Assad, who succeeded his late father as president of Syria in July 2000, showed signs of politically liberalising what has been an intolerant martial state and modernising a struggling, inefficient economy hobbled by a bloated public sector. Positive political momentum in the region thus preceded the July 2000 Camp David Summit.

But during US-mediated peace talks at Camp David between Israeli Prime Minister Ehud Barak and Palestinian Administration Chairman Yasser Arafat, the Middle East's atmosphere changed decisively for the worse. While Barak offered unexpectedly and unprecedentedly generous concessions to the Palestinians – including the return of over 90% of the West Bank and Gaza, 'functional sovereignty' over the Muslim and Christian quarters of the Walled City in Jerusalem and the repatriation of a large number of Palestinian refugees – Arafat rejected the offer.

In the wake of Barak's failed gamble, hawks gained the upper hand in Israel, while Palestinians grew increasingly frustrated. Subsequent efforts by President Bill Clinton to save the peace process came to naught. A visit by *Likud* party leader Ariel Sharon – a hate-figure among Palestinians – to the Temple Mount in late September sparked a new *intifada*. Sharon was elected prime minister in February 2001. Both Israel and the new American administration stepped back from negotiation, insisting that an end to Palestinian fighting was required first.

Washington's inability to forge peace between the Palestinians and Israelis has made its security interests in the Gulf more difficult to manage. The bombing of the *USS Cole* in Yemen in October 2000, killing 17 American sailors, appeared to be inspired by Palestinian strife. The attack cast a pall over the diplomatic dimension of the US military presence in the Gulf, heightening US perceptions of 'asymmetrical' threats. The unrest in the West Bank and Gaza also made an already fragile containment policy

Map 3 Middle East

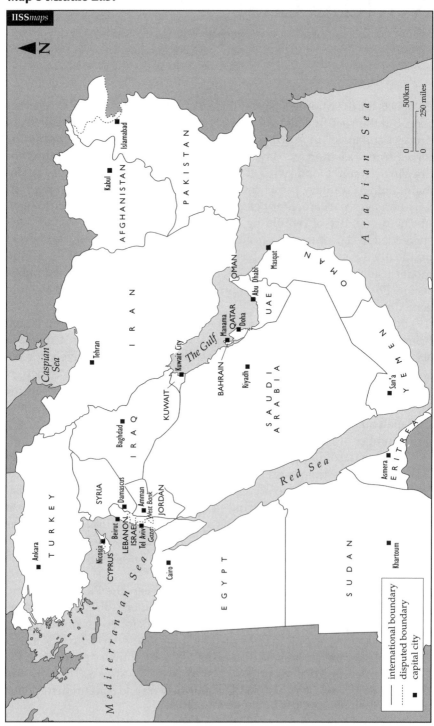

against Iraq politically harder for the US and the United Kingdom to enforce. US strikes against upgraded air-defence systems near Baghdad in February 2001 drew heavy criticism from important coalition partners, notably France and Turkey. The Bush administration has inherited a volatile region in dire need of re-energised policies and broad engagement on two fronts.

The Crumbling Peace Effort

Almost anything that could go wrong for the Middle East Peace Process did go wrong in 2000. The Syrian track collapsed. A far-reaching framework accord on final-status issues between the Israelis and the Palestinians disintegrated, and the two sides fought a vicious war as a result. The Palestinian Authority (PA) also became increasingly plagued by corruption, pauperisation and internecine violence; its leadership was overcome by strategic paralysis and was perhaps on the brink of losing control over the Palestinian street.

Amid the darkness, however, were a few shards of light. In the course of the year, Israel ended its occupation of southern Lebanon and put sovereignty over Jerusalem and the right of return of Palestinian refugees, key issues of Palestinian identity, up for negotiation. More generally, Israelis began to question the mesh of their national narrative with the grittier realities of history. And the Palestinians made clear that they would accept what the late Egyptian President Anwar Sadat and the late Syrian President Hafiz al-Assad rejected: less than full return of conquered land, the presence of Israelis within their territory, and *de jure* demilitarisation. Implicit in these concessions was the recognition that co-existence with Israel was unavoidable. If the Madrid Conference of 1991 and the Oslo Accord of 1993 were milestones in Palestinian–Israeli relations, the 2000 Camp David Summit and the exploration of its results at Taba in January 2001 were no less.

Be Careful What You Wish For

In early 2000, Israeli Prime Minister Ehud Barak vowed to fulfil his campaign pledge to redeploy Israeli military forces from southern Lebanon, which they had entered nearly 20 years before. Although

Middle East

domestic political pressure from lobbying groups (such as Mothers Against the War) to withdraw had become intense, there was significant countervailing pressure from communities arrayed along the border, which would once again be vulnerable to attack from Lebanon.

There were strategic considerations, too. Some believed that Israel's military presence in Lebanon generated attacks against Israel, secured broad Lebanese political support for insurgent groups, such as *Hizbollah*, and justified Syrian control. They argued that Israel's withdrawal would undermine the pretext for attacks, accelerate the transformation of guerrilla fighters into ward politicians, and undermine the rationale for Syria's military presence. Whether Barak was this optimistic is doubtful. But he did judge that – with a peace agreement in place that would motivate Damascus to rein in rejectionists and cut off Iranian support for *Hizbollah* – a combination of defensive measures and a credible Israeli deterrent would obviate the need for an Israeli presence in Lebanon. This objective dictated a 'Syria first' negotiating strategy.

The prospect of withdrawal had the added virtue, it was thought, of threatening the viability of Assad's sole presumed leverage over Israel – the ability to bleed the Israeli Defence Force (IDF) in southern Lebanon and pose a threat to towns in the upper Galilee. Even when the chances for an agreement over the Golan evaporated, Barak saw little reason not to neutralise Assad's Lebanon card, and withdrew in May 2000. His instinct was to rely on international pressure, backed by broad hints of Israel's willingness to take the war to Syria, to temper Assad's pique. Nevertheless, the northern border did not remain completely quiet. *Hizbollah* was divided about its new identity as a political party, with some believing that its *raison d'être* still lay in the fight to liberate Jerusalem.

The *Hizbollah* rejected the UN demarcation of the border with Israel and disputed the UN Secretary-General's certification that the Israelis had fully withdrawn from Lebanese territory. They focused on a sliver of Syrian land in Israeli hands pending a peace agreement – the Shebaa farms – and asserted it was actually Lebanese; Israel, therefore, had not in fact withdrawn completely from Lebanese territory. The Lebanese government, which could be no less zealous, joined in the challenge to the UN report. The UN disputed these allegations, but they sufficed as a pretext for resuming *Hizbollah* provocations in October 2000, including the kidnapping of IDF soldiers and roadside bomb blasts within the area. Since then, two IDF soldiers have died in *Hizbollah* attacks. Desultory attempts to penetrate northern Israel were subsequently made by an allied group, Palestine Islamic Jihad. Israel avoided responding militarily, not wanting to complicate its diplomatic and security agenda by opening up a second front while relations with Palestinians closer to home were brittle, and then dominated by violence. Instead it enlisted

Paris, London and Washington to impress upon Assad's son and successor, Bashar al-Assad, who is said to speak of Israel as a 'paper tiger', that Israel is willing to use force if further provoked. US Secretary of State Colin Powell is reported to have underscored this point during his March 2001 visit to Damascus.

Israel's withdrawal from Lebanon and the 'Syria first' strategy it required had important implications for what was to follow on the so-called Palestinian track. The Israeli–Syrian initiative affirmed Arafat's realisation that he was subordinate to Assad in Israeli strategy. A deal between Barak and Assad would consign Arafat to the weakest possible negotiating position, a long wait until a deal between Israel and Syria was finalised before his turn came, and the need to manage the increasing restiveness of his constituency in the interim. Perhaps worst of all, in Arafat's estimation, was the likelihood that Assad would get back all of Syrian territory, an end-state Arafat knew he could not possibly achieve for his own people. Arafat's bitterness grew in the coming months as Barak's political cautiousness delayed the transfer to the Palestinian Authority of key Palestinian towns, including Abu Dis, near Jerusalem, and postponed the final redeployment of Israeli military forces, required by the Oslo Accord, from large sections of the West Bank.

In addition, the withdrawal from Lebanon led many Palestinians to believe – with the radio-broadcast encouragement of Sheikh Hassan Nasrallah, the leader of Lebanese *Hizbollah* – that *Hizbollah*'s perceived success in driving Israel from Lebanon through asymmetric military confrontation could be replicated at home. Powerful rhetoric emanating from Lebanon, vivid images of the IDF in retreat, the failure to see the crucial differences between Israel's interests in southern Lebanon and in the West Bank, and accumulating resentment of Israeli occupation galvanised West Bank and Gazan youth. *Hamas* studied *Hizbollah* tactics methodically and began to experiment with roadside bombs and car bombs. The stage was set for a year of sharply higher violence.

Tremors

The initial Palestinian civil uprisings of 2000 took place in the West Bank and Gaza in May, a week before the last Israeli soldier left Lebanon. The occasion was *al-Nakba* Day, the commemoration of the great catastrophe (*al-Nakba*) of Israel's war of independence in 1948. The catastrophe lay in the establishment of a Jewish state and the consequent displacement of some 60% of the Palestinian Arab population. In 2000, the confrontation swept the West Bank and Gaza and lasted for four 'days of rage'. It was the first time since the 'tunnel riots' of 1996, when Binyamin Netanyahu was prime minister, that Palestinian police exchanged fire with Israeli forces.

Middle East

The violence was ultimately brought under control in part because Palestinian security forces resumed cooperation with Israel authorities. Nevertheless, the apparent complicity of Palestinian authorities in encouraging the violence and raising its intensity by permitting police to use their weapons against Israelis had its own implications for the way in which the rest of the year would unfold.

First, it reinforced the view of Israeli military planners, a view which had emerged in the wake of Oslo and was held more firmly after the 1996 tunnel riots, that if and when the big confrontation came, it would be fought against a Palestinian army equipped with Kalashnikovs (provided through Oslo mechanisms) and heavy weapons it managed to smuggle in or obtain illegally from IDF stocks. So the IDF trained, equipped and planned not for a few gunmen interspersed in rock-throwing crowds, but for a more conventional conflict. Second, the violence had a profound effect on thinking in Washington about how to advance the flagging peace process. A sense of urgency was now injected into the realisation that the Oslo process had undercut mutual confidence and was draining the impetus for agreement on final-status arrangements.

Indeed, Oslo appeared to have run its course, with each side believing that it merely provided cover for the other side to advance its unilateral objectives. Israelis believed that in return for two redeployments, they had received little real security cooperation. Palestinian security forces had proliferated far beyond the limits agreed upon in the Oslo Accord and the Palestinian leadership had done nothing to prepare the ground for peace by enforcing the Oslo ban on incitement. Conversely, Palestinians viewed their territorial gains as meagre and as having taken far too long to achieve, giving Israel time to occupy more land by enlarging settlements or establishing new ones.

Nevertheless, throughout this period, leaders of both sides saw it in their interest to participate in the Oslo process. For Arafat, it facilitated the flow of relatively significant funds from outside donors, maintained *Fatah* in a position of primacy within the PA, kept relations with the US on an even keel, ensured assistance from the Central Intelligence Agency (CIA), and enabled him to create a large paramilitary force. For Israel, too, it was convenient. Oslo sustained the illusion that the conflict with Palestinians was coming to an end, but without real territorial sacrifice or the civil strife anticipated upon the evacuation of Israeli settlements deep inside the West Bank. Oslo also buoyed Israel's diplomatic initiatives, which led to official representation in Morocco and Qatar and trade relations with a range of countries that had long been out-of-bounds, boosting Israel's surging economy.

Ordinary Palestinians, however, did not benefit much from Oslo. Poor economic performance, exacerbated by the corruption of the West Bank and Gazan élites and the abusive unregulated activities of uniformed PA organisations, made the lot of those in Zones A and B – as the Palestinian Territories are known – as bad as ever. Palestinians also still had to submit to the offensive day-to-day realities of military occupation: roadblocks, identity checks, arbitrary detention, long queues at transit points, and, from time-to-time, complete closures which made day-to-day planning for families difficult.

Against this background, Washington peace planners saw the May *Nakba* riots not as a cathartic event, but as a harbinger of more intensive and sustained violence that would push the sides farther apart. From Washington's perspective, the only way to save the peace process was to move forward to negotiations on a final-status agreement.

Prime Minister Barak, in his conversations with then US President Bill Clinton and Secretary of State Madeleine Albright, insisted that rapid progress on a package deal was vital to his political survival. When he established his government in May 1999 he had opted for a wide coalition so he could negotiate agreements with the Syrians and Palestinians that would be painful for many Israelis to accept. The very breadth of the coalition, however, made it unstable, since it united secular, modernising parties with traditionalist, particularistic and ethnic parties whose interests, outside the realm of the peace process, were incompatible. In some cases, their views about territorial compromise in return for peace were fluid or untested. The American assessment of the Israeli political landscape suggested that Barak was probably right, and the White House accepted his argument that an agreement would enable him to call elections with confidence that he would win and that his victory would ratify the agreement.

Arafat, on the other hand, fought the developing momentum towards a summit for powerful reasons. Barak had stated the conditions by which he would be bound at a summit, including the indivisibility of Jerusalem and the impossibility of an implicit acceptance of responsibility for the Palestinian diaspora that would underpin serious concessions on refugees. Israel would come to the table with a comprehensive proposal backed by the US, which would place Arafat under unacceptable pressure in an isolated environment. Finally, Palestinians were unprepared to compromise on refugees or Jerusalem, and would reject the finality of claims, which the US and Israel were known to be seeking.

Timing was dictated primarily by Arafat's stated intention to declare a Palestinian state on 13 September 2000. It was feared that a unilateral declaration would spark a crisis, whereby Israel might annex major settlement areas, reassert full administrative authority in Zone B, and impose a closure on the rest of the new Palestinian state, possibly triggering large-scale fighting.

Middle East

Failure

The summit at Camp David began on 5 July 2000, preceded by the detonation of Barak's coalition. His foreign minister, David Levy, refused to join the delegation. The Sephardic religious party, an Ashkenazic ultra-orthodox party, and the largest Russian immigrant party bolted, leaving him with a minority government of 42 members, barely a third of the 120-seat legislature. A no-confidence vote fell only seven votes short of a full parliamentary majority of 61. While Barak's purported lack of concern was either disingenuous or naïve, polling data showed that a narrow majority of Israelis was willing to make substantial compromises for a peace agreement with the Palestinians.

The summit meeting lasted 15 days at the Camp David presidential retreat. Barak disregarded his earlier stated conditions and put forth unprecedentedly generous proposals. Israel would return 90% of the West Bank and Gaza, including the strategic Jordan Valley; put the Walled City's Muslim and Christian quarters and the surface of the Haram al-Sharif, on which the two holy mosques are situated, under Palestinian control (described by some summit participants as 'functional sovereignty'); hand over the Arab neighbourhoods of East Jerusalem outside the walled city to Palestinian control; and accede to the repatriation of Palestinian refugees under the guise of family reunification. On the other hand, the Israeli position still encompassed *de jure* Israeli sovereignty over Jerusalem; practical control over parts of the Temple Mount (the Jewish term for Haram al-Sharif) that surround and underlie the surface platform and the mosques upon it; and refused to consider a 'right of return' for 1948 Palestinian refugees analogous to the right of return to which the Jewish diaspora is entitled under Israeli domestic law.

Despite the extraordinary advance that this offer represented in Israel's position in relative terms, it was insufficient in absolute terms. The Americans hoped that Arafat would acknowledge the audacity of the proposal and respond with a counter-offer, or at least a positive assessment and a pledge to return to the table with his own proposal in the coming weeks. But Arafat rejected Barak's terms. Despite the summit's failure to yield an agreement, it did touch upon subjects that had been taboo and thus transformed the basis for Palestinian–Israeli negotiations. Members of the Palestinian delegation accepted the notion of annexation of settlement blocs and suggested a percentage, offering 2% 'free' (that is, not swapped for land) and a further 2% in exchange for Israeli land. They also discussed formulas short of exclusive Palestinian sovereignty in Jerusalem's old city. In addition, there was some progress on security issues, including an agreement in principle that Israel could get early warning stations in the West Bank (subject to agreement on number). The

Palestinian side also put forward proposals that would have limited refugees' right-of-return to a symbolic number.

The political atmosphere, however, was envenomed by the recriminations over responsibility for the summit's failure. Clinton stated publicly that Barak had shown 'more creativity' and that 'the ball was in Arafat's court' to shore up Barak's rapidly eroding credibility in Israel. Clinton also spoke on Israeli television to reassure viewers that Barak had done nothing to jeopardise Israeli security and that in light of 'recent events', Washington would review the possibility of moving the US Embassy from Tel Aviv to Jerusalem. This failed, however, to help Barak, while stirring anti-American resentment among Palestinians.

Arafat countered with his determination 'to put our friends and brothers, the Arabs and Europeans, far away from Israeli propaganda and big lies that they are trying to put out about what happened at Camp David'. He succeeded insofar as most Palestinians, let alone the general public in the wider Middle East region, were not to learn of the specifics of Barak's offer. Public commentary dwelt instead on the supposedly fraudulent Jewish claim to an historical connection with Jerusalem, the presumed intention of Israel to raze the mosques on the Haram al-Sharif, and Clinton's perceived attempt to force Arafat to a accept an Israeli offer that the US president knew was far short of Barak's actual bottom line. This rhetoric – combined with religious passions stirred by the debate over Jerusalem, rising Palestinian frustration with continuing occupation and expanding settlement activity, and Arafat's 16 August decision not to declare statehood – increased tensions in the West Bank and Gaza. In August 2000, Arafat spent three weeks on a 20-country tour to convince friendly governments that the offer presented to him at the summit was in fact a *diktat*, which would have required him unilaterally to surrender the natural sovereignty exercised by the world's Muslims over Jerusalem. He pressed instead for Israel to return all the territory taken in the 1967 war, including the Jewish quarter of the Walled City. American attempts to cast Arafat's claims – and popular perceptions of the summit – in a different light, and to urge Egypt, Jordan and Saudi Arabia to encourage Arafat to respond in some positive way to Barak's offer, were unavailing. Arafat also did not receive the vocal support from these Arab states that he would have needed to compromise on Jerusalem.

On 21 August, Barak attempted to seize the domestic political high ground in Israel by shifting the focus of his administration from the peace process, which appeared to be going nowhere, to constitutional reform under the banner of 'secular revolution'. His motley coalition had been assembled only for the purpose of pursuing a peace agreement, so there was no point in maintaining it. Barak told his party leaders that he intended to form a coalition that would eliminate the Religious Affairs

Middle East

Ministry, authorise civil marriage, draft ultra-orthodox youth into the army or other voluntary service, and give Israel a written constitution. To achieve these goals, he said he would consider a unity government with *Likud*, a secular party. Barak's initiative struck most Israelis as bizarrely out of touch with reality and his approval rating shrank rapidly in national polls.

Washington, in the meantime, struggled to resuscitate dialogue on peace issues. Clinton announced that he would see Egyptian President Hosni Mubarak in Cairo towards the end of August, then Barak and Arafat in New York at the Millennium Summit at the United Nations in early September 2000. The hour-long meeting with Mubarak smoothed ruffled feathers over the US administration's failure to consult more intensively with Cairo before the Camp David Summit, but produced no undertaking to work with Arafat to produce a negotiable response to a proposal that Barak himself already appeared to be walking away from. Clinton's subsequent meeting with Arafat elicited only the Palestinian leader's proposal that sovereignty reside with the Jerusalem Committee of the Organisation of the Islamic Conference, a multinational grouping of countries including Iraq and Iran. This left nothing to raise with Barak in the meeting that followed. Yet, the picture was not all black. Barak invited Arafat to his home in Kochav Yair for what turned out to be an amiable, if non-substantive encounter in the third week of September. Negotiators for the two sides met repeatedly, although without significant progress on key issues. Security cooperation was also proceeding. There was little evidence of unrest until the ominous explosion of two roadside bombs in Gaza that killed an Israeli soldier on the night of 27 September 2000.

Things Fall Apart

On that same day, Binyamin Netanyahu, the former Israeli prime minister and presumed successor to caretaker *Likud* Party leader Ariel Sharon, had just been cleared of corruption charges and was prepared to retake the party leadership. Sharon, a war hero whose career was derailed by his responsibility as Defence Minister for the massacre of hundreds of Palestinians in Lebanese refugee camps by Phalangist militiamen in 1982, had worked hard to isolate Netanyahu's allies within the party, but was still vulnerable to his challenge. To deflect attention from Netanyahu's return and to reinforce his public image as a defender of Israeli territorial prerogatives, he decided to visit the Temple Mount, or Haram al-Sharif, on 28 September.

Hamas, alerted by the publicity surrounding Sharon's plans, issued a communiqué the day before the visit urging Palestinians to gather at the site to confront Sharon's 'aggression'; *Fatah* issued a similar statement. The visitor, amid a phalanx of bodyguards, legislators, and reporters attracted the protests – and projectiles – of Palestinian worshipers and others who congregated around the mosques. Given Sharon's reputation as a mortal enemy of Palestinians, this was not surprising. Rioting spread outside of the Walled City, but was contained without fatalities. The next day, the mood at the Haram was still feverish as the Friday sermon called for Muslims to resist Jewish efforts to desecrate the al-Aqsa mosque. Youths atop the Western Wall rained rocks and chunks of cinder block on the Jews gathered below for holiday prayers. When the Israeli police commander on the scene was felled by a stone, troops opened fire and killed as many as seven Palestinians on the Haram. It was this confrontation that triggered the *al-Aqsa intifada*. Early in the uprising, Israeli riot police killed 13 unarmed Arab-Israeli protesters. The débâcle was emblematic of the inferior status of Israeli Arabs, insofar as most observers agreed that Israeli police would not have used force on this scale against Jewish Israeli rioters. The rioting also revealed the burgeoning radicalisation of the Arab community that this status had engendered.

The fighting has gone through a number of overlapping phases. Rioting in which armed Palestinians intermingled with unarmed, rock-throwing protesters attracted rifle fire and riot-control agents from the IDF strong-points under attack. This was followed by IDF use (after warning) of helicopter gunships, naval assets and armour against PA installations; Palestinian use of roadside bombs against Israeli vehicles in Gaza; diminishing street rioting and increased firing from Palestinian towns into Israeli settlements; Palestinian sniper fire at Israeli vehicles and the killing of vulnerable individuals. Increased Israeli reliance on assassination of Palestinians suspected of directing anti-Israeli attacks elicited an upsurge in *Hamas*-style suicide bombings, use of mortars and heavy machine guns, and apparently spontaneous attacks against targets of opportunity. Palestinian casualties have outnumbered Israeli losses (military and civilian) by about 5 to 1. The greatest proportion of Palestinian deaths occurred in the early stages of the *intifada*, when crowds assailed exposed Israeli outposts and drew fire. Despite relatively restricted rules of engagement, the particular dynamics of the encounters, the ambiguity of the threat to Israeli soldiers, the diverse and rapidly moving crowds confronting them, and variable skill and discipline within the IDF units involved led to high Palestinian fatalities, including many children under the age of 17. As the *intifada* evolved, however, the rate of Palestinian deaths slowed and Israeli casualties accelerated. As of late-March 2001, 360 Palestinians, 69 Israelis and 13 Israeli Arabs had been killed.

Arafat's role in directing the fighting remains a matter of controversy, revolving around the extent of the control he actually exercises over those using firearms and explosives. There is evidence that many of the attacks are carried out by groups under Arafat's control, such as the *Fatah Tanzim*. Palestinian action has evidently been calibrated: violence dropped

Middle East

dramatically in the immediate aftermath of the lynching in Ramallah of two Israeli soldiers, to which Israel replied with attacks against PA offices, during the October 2000 Sharm el Sheikh conference, and while Arafat was meeting with German Chancellor Gerhard Schröder on November 1. Moreover, with the exception of several suicide attacks that do not fit the broader *intifada* pattern, there has been no concerted attempt to carry the confrontation over the green line. The violence seemed to serve Arafat's purposes: to transform the image of Palestinians from obstacles to peace, as they were portrayed after Camp David, to victims of Israel's military machine; to internationalise the dispute; to compel Barak to enhance his offers regarding Jerusalem, territory and refugees; and, according to some observers, to offer a more fitting path to independence than negotiated compromise.

Two weeks of violence was enough to propel a Clinton administration effort to achieve a cease-fire at a tripartite meeting at Sharm el Sheikh in mid-October 2000, attended by UN and EU representatives as well as Arafat, Barak and the US president. The EU and the UN declined further involvement in the peace process, dashing Arafat's hope for a wider international dimension. Neither Barak nor Arafat would join Clinton in the closing statement, which described the two sides as agreeing to take measures to reduce the level of violence and to set up a commission of inquiry into its causes and ways to prevent its recurrence. The agreement was broken the day after the meeting. Whether Arafat instructed Palestinians to cease fire, as required by the agreement, is not clear since Arafat made no public statement (although Clinton made one on his behalf); he appears to have demanded quiet on the part of selected units, if in only some areas. In November 2000, a five-member international fact-finding committee was established, under the chairmanship of former US senator George Mitchell, to investigate the Palestinian–Israeli violence. The committee visited the West Bank and Gaza the following January and March, and was expected to issue a full report in May 2001.

As Sharon was concentrating on his political future, Barak began to focus on his own. When the Knesset reconvened from its autumn holiday recess on 29 October 2000, his government's ability to survive was widely seen to be limited. Spiralling violence coupled with the popular perception that Barak was doing precisely what he had forsworn – making concessions to Arafat under fire – continued to erode public support. His cabinet began to disintegrate as aides departed and challenges emerged from within the Labour Party itself. He was denounced by Haim Ramon and Ben Eliezer from the right, and Yossi Sarid from the *Meretz* Party on the left. His Arab constituency had abandoned him after the 13 Arab Israelis were killed. Shimon Peres, sidelined by Barak early in his administration and assigned to the junior role of minister for regional cooperation, swept past him in opinion polls to run neck-and-neck with

Sharon. Many in the party began to see Peres as a steadier hand and a more credible candidate in a general election. Barak, besieged in the Knesset and facing an insurgency in his own party, resigned on 9 December 2000 with the intention of running again for prime minister. His objective was to reach a new equilibrium with Arafat, obtain a cease-fire, and return to negotiations. Barak's stratagem exploited a provision of election law that limited candidates in the election to sitting members of Knesset, a category that did not include Netanyahu, whom he presumed to be his most potent rival.

Clinton's Last Try

While this baroque manoeuvring contorted Israeli politics, Clinton was developing a proposal that might serve as the basis of one last round of negotiations before he left the White House and Barak had to face Sharon at the polls. On 23 December, Clinton shared his ideas verbally with both sides:

Territory
Israel should annex 4–6% of the West Bank, compensating the Palestinian Authority through a 'land swap' of 1–3%. He suggested that the parties consider an exchange of leased land. The final map should place 80% of Israeli settlers in annexed blocs, while promoting territorial contiguity, minimising annexed area and minimising the number of Palestinians who would be affected. On Jerusalem, Clinton is reported to have said, 'Arab areas are Palestinian and Jewish areas are Israeli' with maximum contiguity for both. Each state would have sovereignty over and rights to the Haram al-Sharif, or Temple Mount. Palestinians would have sovereignty over the top, Israel over the Western Wall. Neither could excavate beneath the Haram or behind the Wall.

Refugees
Clinton proposed that refugees should have a right to return to historic Palestine or 'their homeland', but no specific right to return to what is now the state of Israel. All refugees should have the right of return to the State of Palestine, but resettlement elsewhere would depend on the policies of the countries concerned.

Security
Clinton suggested an international presence to guarantee implementation of the agreement. Israel would withdraw gradually over three years, with the international force phased in over that period. Israel would maintain a presence for another three years in the Jordan Valley under the authority of the international force. Israel would maintain three early warning

stations for at least ten years and be permitted to deploy its forces to Palestinian territory during a state of national emergency. Palestine itself would be a 'non-militarised state'. Palestine would have sovereignty over its airspace, but would negotiate arrangements with Israel for military overflight for training and operational needs.

Israeli concessions which Barak had agreed by the end of his tenure tracked with some of these stipulations: Palestinians would control the Muslim and Christian quarters and three-quarters of the Armenian quarter within the Walled City, have full control over the outer Arab villages and the neighbourhoods of east Jerusalem, and, according to the outgoing foreign minister, Shlomo ben Ami, sovereignty over the Haram. Taking into account a small 'land swap,' Israel would return 97% of the West Bank and Gaza. Together, these concessions constituted a major advance on his offer at Camp David.

There was one more round of negotiation between Israelis and Palestinians at Taba in January 2001. The two sides were motivated by the impending elections on 6 February and, on the Palestinian side, the somewhat-belated recognition that significant progress was the only hope for a Barak victory. Despite the extensive work that had already been done and the clear-cut, if insufficiently detailed Clinton proposals, there was not enough time to develop anything resembling a framework accord. There was some progress on territory and security, and an interesting discussion on options for dealing with refugees, but no advance on the matter of Jerusalem. In sum, nothing emerged from Taba to suggest that the parties were on the verge of a final agreement.

Clinton's extraordinary hands-on involvement in the peace process from Camp David until the end of his presidency was criticised by many Palestinians, who believed he merely conveyed Israeli proposals. Some US analysts also maintained that he squandered the prestige of the presidency through his personal intercession and violated a basic rule of conflict resolution by mediating before the sides were ripe for American intervention. The alternative view is that Clinton's influence was key to Barak's willingness to consider positions that had been outside the parameters of Israeli political discourse, and that an aggressive assertion of US prestige was necessary to exploit a brittle peace between Israel and the Palestinian Authority that was about to shatter.

Palestinians who felt manipulated by Clinton, and recalled his predecessor, the elder George Bush's empathy for Arabs and (occasional) firm handling of Prime Minister Yitzhak Shamir, have greeted the new US administration with a cautious optimism. Secretary of State Powell's March 2001 visit, following a US statement that the Clinton proposals are 'off the table', did not seem to justify this optimism. His calculated praise for Sharon was not matched by corresponding rhetoric about Arafat. He endorsed Sharon's insistence that Palestinian attacks end before funds are released by Israel to the PA and negotiations begin again, while criticising the Israeli closure of Palestinian areas. Nor would US domestic public opinion support an approach that downplayed Israeli concerns. A recent Gallup poll shows that 63% of Americans have a favourable view of Israel, versus 22% with respect to the Palestinian Authority. The favourable view of Israel has increased during the *intifada*. As much as the Bush administration may want to stand clear of the conflict until ideas for negotiation emerge from the parties, the same Gallup poll indicates that 83% of Americans believe that a settlement of the Arab–Israeli conflict should be a top US foreign-policy priority.

What Next?

However much was achieved, it was not enough to spare Barak a crushing defeat – 62.38% to 37.62% – by Ariel Sharon on 6 February 2001. The low 62% turnout reflected dissatisfaction with the choice of candidates; the lopsided result stemmed more for disgust with Barak, perceived as having conceded key issues without stopping the violence, than enthusiasm for Sharon. Significantly, only 18% of the 500,000 Arab Israelis voted (compared to 75% in 1999), indicating that they would no longer align themselves with the Labour Party. Sharon formed a unity coalition quickly, bringing in Labourites Shimon Peres as foreign minister and Binyamin ben Eliezer as defence minister. One of the government's first acts was to revise the election law so as to unify the prime ministerial and parliamentary elections.

Sharon's victory over Barak need not mean the end of the peace process, even though the *intifada* signals the end, for the time being, of most of the 'solutionist' phase of the conflict. The issues, rather, are when the Palestinians and Israelis are likely to return to the negotiating table and with what agenda. There is no question that the Israeli economy can withstand a prolonged confrontation. Although the Israeli economy has declined by almost 10% during the *intifada*, much of the decline was due to the downturn in the NASDAQ; the effects have been confined to specific industries, such as tourism and construction, and have yet to be felt in other sectors. The economy overall registered 5.9% growth for the year. While Sharon would like an interim agreement, he can afford to wait.

The ability of the Palestinian economy to withstand the stress of the *intifada* for very long, however, is doubtful. The UN, drawing on multiple sources, estimates that Palestinian workers lost $243.4 million in labour income from October 2000 through January 2001. The *intifada* has deprived some 100,000 Palestinians of work. Some of the jobs will be lost permanently as Israel replaces Palestinian labour with South-east Asian and Eastern European workers. Gross domestic income is estimated to

Middle East

have dropped $907.3m, due to decreased exports. The UN calculates that the loss amounts to some $1,850 per family over the course of the *intifada*. While the Arab states have deposited the bulk of their $1 billion pledge to the PA in the Islamic Development Bank , as of March 2001 only $23m had been released to the PA. In general, disbursements from this fund have been chronically delayed by concerns about corruption, and in any case are tied to specific aid and development projects. The EU has subsidised PA operations to the amount of roughly $65m, but this does not cover all the personnel and programme costs the PA continues to incur, and Brussels has imposed strict transparency and austerity conditions on future aid. Thus, many PA employees have not been paid regularly during the *intifada*, although the security services continue to get their salaries. While humanitarian aid has offset some of this calamitous decrease in income, unemployment is over 30% and one million Palestinians are now believed to have fallen below the poverty level.

Arafat's capacity to absorb pain is well-established and his senior officials, though many are corrupt, are tough, committed nationalists prepared to share the pain. Still, Arafat may eventually see it as in his interest to begin talking to Sharon about meeting the Israeli leader's conditions for the transfer of $75m in tax funds to the PA. The conditions include a public statement by Arafat calling for the end of violence, a halt to incitement and renewal of security cooperation between the two sides. At some point, this money will be needed to pay the security forces, which are the ultimate guarantor of PA authority. A unity government might, in turn, redeploy forces to reduce points of friction, halt settlement activity and perhaps return certain areas that would give PA-administered territory greater contiguity. These steps would have to be carried out in parallel and carefully coordinated. Painfully aware of how their withdrawal from Lebanon was perceived by Palestinians, Israelis have little appetite for another unilateral withdrawal. Arafat, on the other hand, will have to produce a tangible gain for Palestinians if he is to justify a clampdown on violence and real limits on incitement.

Whenever the two leaders decide to talk, the US is likely to return to play a key role. While the new administration is somewhat more focused than the last on the adverse impact of Israeli–Palestinian strife on American objectives elsewhere in the region, it does not necessarily follow that the Bush team will act to rein in an Israeli unity government faced with uncontrolled, or uncontrollable, violence. Further, Powell himself is said to have privately told Israelis – despite Washington's public pronouncement that Clinton's proposals were 'off the table' – that Israel and the Palestinians cannot start again 'from zero'. Thus, it seems likely that domestic politics and regional dynamics will lead to a more energetic American involvement, especially if violence escalates sharply. Should a deeper US role materialise, the fact that the core issues were the subject of detailed negotiation at Camp David and after may make a renewed accommodation easier to negotiate.

Syria: Continuity and Change

The first father-to-son succession in an Arab republic took place on 25 July 2000 when Bashar al-Assad formally became President of Syria after the death of Hafiz al-Assad on 10 June. The new president faced the same basic problem confronting the young rulers who have succeeded long-serving parents over the last three years in Arab monarchies like Jordan and Morocco: how to consolidate a grip on power while at the same time introducing necessary reforms. The younger al-Assad seems to have chosen a path of continuity and change, a middle course between the vested interests of the old guard and the expectations of the new generation. This has so far involved limited economic reform and some political freedom in Syria, coupled with continuity in policy with respect to Israel and some change in the relationship with Lebanon. This cautious mix appears to have been effective.

Grasping the Reins

There were concerns at first that the new president was not up to the job. His older brother Basil, killed in a car crash in 1994, had been portrayed as a dashing military man and was said to have had the required ruthlessness to be president of Syria. In contrast, Bashar, an ophthalmologist and cerebral type, was seen to be inexperienced and weak. He seems, however, to have grown into the job. A six-year apprenticeship under his father helped him to learn the tricks of the trade. By June 2000, he had used anti-corruption drives to place loyalists in positions of power in important institutions like the army and the security services, as well as to curry favour with the people.

Given control of the crucial Lebanese portfolio several months before his father's death, Bashar al-Assad had some success in building his own power-base there as well, thus undermining the position of General Ghazi Kanaan, the formerly all-powerful head of Syrian military intelligence in

Middle East

Lebanon. However, his father may have died a bit too early for Bashar to have completed the job in Lebanon and Syria. This may account for the interruption in the anti-corruption drive when the younger Assad took over the presidency. The resumption of the campaign against corruption in January 2001 suggests that he has tightened his grip on power since the summer.

The new president does not yet have the absolute authority enjoyed by his father and must balance the views of the different interest groups when considering decisions. He must steer a careful course between the old guard in the army, party and bureaucracy produced by 30 years of authoritarian, Arab-nationalist and socialist-style rule and the new wave represented by intellectuals, businessmen and a younger generation who expect him to deliver on modernisation. The president will need to look constantly over his shoulder. Coups were endemic in Syria in the early 1950s: his father seized power from a comrade of 20 years, Salih Jadid, in 1970. In 1983, the new president's paternal uncle Rifaat al-Assad was involved in a coup attempt.

Even if he were able to, it is doubtful that Bashar al-Assad would want to push through revolutionary change. Although he has been presented as representative of a new generation and as a progressive reformer, he is a product of the system. His approach of continuity with change was signalled by his actions as head of the Syrian Computer Society, a post he held before becoming president: he introduced the Internet to the country, but made sure that access was controlled and limited.

Reforming the economy is the most pressing problem on the new president's agenda. There is an enormous need to create jobs and to develop services and institutions in a country with an antiquated and crumbling infrastructure. The public sector is bloated and inefficient, and agriculture, the source of livelihood for 25% of Syrians, is heavily subsidised. In 2000, unemployment was conservatively (and unofficially) estimated at 20% and in recent years, growth has varied from 1 to 2% per annum. Population growth is still 3.3% per annum and almost 50% of the population is under 15 years of age. The banking system is virtually non-existent and commercial and customs regulations are often contradictory. Syria does have some oil of its own, but reserves are declining while internal demand is rising. Production in 2000 declined from 550,000 to 530,000 barrels per day.

The Syrian regime has recognised the need for economic reform for at least a decade. A 1991 law provided some incentives for private investment but the process petered out with the former president's single-minded concentration on the Arab–Israeli peace process, which began that year in Madrid. Under Bashar al-Assad, the reform process has been cautiously revived. Serious privatisation of the loss-making public sector has been ruled out for the moment as too threatening to the *wasta* public patronage system that has helped keep the regime in power, but the private sector is being encouraged. In December 2000, in what was hailed as the most important decision taken by the new regime to that time, the ruling *Ba'ath* Party sanctioned the establishment of private banks, a stock market and the liberalisation of foreign-exchange transactions. However, delays and restrictions on application are anticipated given the lack of a regulatory framework and the weakness of the Central Bank.

The beginnings of economic reform have been accompanied by limited political change. At his inauguration in July, Bashar al-Assad waved the banner of reform and made clear his respect for 'other opinions'. In line with this view, 600 dissidents were released from prison in mid-November 2000. Towards the end of the year, Vice-President Abdul Halim Khaddam announced that the government would soon make laws allowing the formation of parties outside the Popular National Front, the coalition of parties in government with the *Ba'ath* Party. Regime newspapers like *Al-Thaura* and *Tishrin* have been the focus for lively debates, which have often involved the views of former political prisoners. By early 2001, the anti-corruption campaign had begun again, with the investigation of three *Ba'ath* Party members of parliament on corruption charges. Three provincial governors were removed from office on similar charges on 3 February, including one in Damascus who was replaced by a Bashar al-Assad loyalist.

Encouraged by the freer atmosphere, Syrians have been discussing politics more openly in the street and in salons and coffee shops. In September, 99 Syrian intellectuals signed a charter calling for the lifting of martial law, the release of 1,500 political prisoners and a free press. In late January 2001, 1,000 prominent figures signed a manifesto with similar themes. In a sign of the times, the minister of information, Adnan Omran, seemed to respond a few days later by claiming that martial law had effectively been frozen, even if it was still on the books. Arbitrary arrests, authorised under martial law, had been stopped in April 2000, he claimed.

Various political groups have emerged, like the Movement for Civil Society, made up mostly of intellectuals, and the Committee for the Defence of Human Rights, involving an unaffiliated group of lawyers dedicated to raising awareness of human-rights issues. In January 2001, Riyadh Seif, an outspoken independent politician, said he was setting up his own political party. And Syria's first independent magazine in 38 years, called *al-Domari* (*The Lamplighter*) and devoted to political satire and caricature, sold out within hours of its initial 50,000-copy release in March. Ali Farzat, the magazine's owner and publisher, is a well-known, often-censored cartoonist who has enjoyed the support of the new president. There were also reports that intellectuals within the Movement for Civil Society were working towards producing their own publication.

Middle East

The new regime may embark on a programme of privatisation and there may be attempts to streamline the bureaucracy. Comprehensive reform of the country's financial system is likely to proceed, albeit slowly and cautiously. Loans and remittances will be used to expand the business sector and to develop the country's infrastructure.

But, despite these promising signs on the economic and political fronts, caution is in order. The new regime is unlikely to hit the bloated public sector in the near future because of the vested interests involved and the threat of social unrest at a transitional time. Political reform will be even lower-key. Despite recent moves, press or party freedom is not likely for some time. And until the opposition is given legal standing, its position will be very precarious. Dissidents remember that Assad senior occasionally gave them room for manoeuvre, only to clamp down later when circumstances changed.

In the longer term, Syria may take the Egyptian route, characterised by authoritarian rule, some legal safeguards for citizens and considerable room for relatively open political debate. But there are a number of threats along the way. Economic hardship could lead to social unrest. Political Islam remains a potent rallying cry for the discontented, and economic change could increase political factionalisation in identity politics in Syria and heighten Sunni–Alawite sectarian antagonism. Lebanon could be a source of tension, and there is always the threat of Israel and its ally Turkey to the north. Competitors for power will be carefully watching how Bashar al-Assad handles these and other problems. Syrians, however remember the vicious clampdown in Hama in 1982, for which his eldest brother was responsible. In that instance, the army moved against the Muslim Brothers, resulting in an estimated 20,000 deaths. The Syrian people have no desire to return to those dark days. For this and other reasons it is likely that, for the moment, most Syrians will support the new president in his efforts to secure change with continuity.

The Syrian–Israeli Peace Process

When Bashar al-Assad came to power, it appeared that the peace process with Israel was dead. The new regime nevertheless reiterated the assurance, given by al-Assad senior to US President Bill Clinton in Geneva in 1994, that Syria had made a 'strategic choice' for peace. Hopes of movement in the near future were made highly unlikely, however, when Ariel Sharon emerged victorious in the Israeli elections of 6 February 2001. Instead, there may be increased tension between the two countries.

Only a few months before Bashar came to power, it had seemed as if peace between Israel and Syria was imminent. Negotiations had begun again in the US (in Shepherdstown, West Virginia) at the end of December 1999, after a standstill during the three years that Binyamin Netanyahu headed a *Likud* government in Israel. The primary reasons for expecting rapid progress were Hafez al-Assad's declining health and his desire to smooth the way for his son's succession. On the Israeli side, former Prime Minister Ehud Barak had promised to withdraw from South Lebanon, where Israel was suffering unacceptable losses at the hands of *Hizbollah*, within a year of his election victory.

The talks foundered after only a short period, however, partly because of different interpretations of proposals put forward by former Israeli Prime Minister Yitzhak Rabin in 1994 and reiterated by Prime Minister Shimon Peres in 1995. The Syrians insisted that these proposals promised full withdrawal from the Golan Heights to the pre-1967 war lines. Hafez al-Assad had been insisting on this since the Madrid conference of 1991. Above all he wanted to avoid the ambiguity of the Israeli–Palestinian agreement, which Syrians saw as a disaster for the Palestinians. In this context he made it clear that he would settle for no less than what former Egyptian President Anwar Sadat had gained at Camp David in 1979: full Israeli withdrawal. The Israeli side, however, insisted that Rabin and Peres had only put forward hypothetical proposals intended to advance talks rather than firm promises.

The US invitation to the Shepherdstown talks finessed this point, allowing for different interpretations. It seems likely that the Syrians believed that Barak had accepted their position but could not say so publicly. Four joint committees were set up to discuss security arrangements, normalisation, water and the demarcation of borders. In January, however, the Israelis failed to attend the border and water committees and focused instead on determining what concessions the Syrians would make on security and normalisation. This led to Syrian fears that Barak would offer less than full withdrawal.

Shortly after the Shepherdstown talks recessed, Israel leaked a document laying out the US understanding of what had been achieved. The document suggested that the Syrians had made unprecedented concessions on security, normalisation and, above all, on withdrawal. According to the document, the Syrians had agreed to monitoring devices on Mount Hermon, staffed by international and US personnel and to full normalisation between the two countries. Most surprising of all, the Syrians seemed to have agreed to these concessions without receiving Israeli assurances about full withdrawal from the Golan Heights. The received Israeli position was that, while there would be redeployment of Israeli forces in the Golan, Israel would maintain a military presence there based on security and legal considerations.

When details of this US understanding became public, Syria refused to return to the talks, which had been scheduled to restart on 20 January 2000, and made their resumption conditional on a written Israeli guarantee that it would fully withdraw from the Golan Heights. This was the background to the Geneva talks between presidents Clinton and Assad on 26 March 2000. Amid widespread expectations that Clinton would bring an assurance that Barak was ready to recognise pre-1967 war lines, in return for which Assad would give assurances about other subjects in dispute, there were high hopes that the peace process would take off once more. Instead, the Syrians were shocked when the US relayed Barak's requirements, which included Israeli retention of land along the Sea of Galilee, thus effectively blocking Syrian access. But in the court of Israeli public opinion, Syrian behaviour at Shepherdstown, where Assad had refused to meet Barak, and Syrian Foreign Minister Farouk ash Sharaa had refused to shake his hand, had politically precluded a softer line. The summit failed.

Press reports that the only remaining dispute was over less than 200 metres of the northern shoreline appeared to be an oversimplification. While the gap between Syria and Israel had narrowed, there remained a number of unresolved issues in addition to the extent of the land involved, such as the timetable of a prospective withdrawal and subsequent security arrangements. But Hafiz al-Assad had made it clear that he would accept no less than full withdrawal to the lines of 4 June 1967. And while the Syrian leader was keen to secure an agreement that would enable his son's smooth succession, he was not willing to accept an agreement that would place Bashar's future in jeopardy. At the same time, Assad's health was deteriorating and he may have felt that it was better to concentrate on domestic affairs with a view to securing his son's succession.

While Bashar al-Assad represents the new generation and is less bound by the enmities of the past, the prospects for Syrian–Israeli peace are slim, at least in the short term. The new president is focusing on consolidating his position in power and is unlikely to take unnecessary risks. He has harshly criticised Israel's response to the Palestinian *intifada* that broke out in autumn 2000, and it is likely that he will keep the old guard onside by following its line on this issue, with a view to pursuing an agenda of continuity and change at home. With Ariel Sharon in power in Israel, the immediate future is fraught with uncertainty. The Israeli leader would be very unlikely to accept Syria's longstanding demand for full withdrawal from the Golan Heights. Politically cautious, Bashar al-Assad is unlikely to enter into serious dialogue with an Israeli leader so disposed. That said, the Syria–Israel border should remain stable, as it has for 25 years. But in light of *Hizbollah's* support for the *intifada* and its occasional provocations in the disputed Shebaa farms, tensions between Israel and Syria in Lebanon may escalate.

Lebanon

While the new Syrian president has worked on improving relations with Iraq and Turkey, Lebanon has been the main focus of his energies outside

Syria, particularly in the wake of Lebanese calls for Syrian withdrawal following Israel's pullout in May 2000. These calls began with an article published on 9 June by Jibran Tueni, editor of the influential *al-Nahar* newspaper, arguing that it was now time for Syria to withdraw in line with the 1989 Taif agreement that had brought the Lebanese civil war to an end. The calls were taken up by Maronite Catholic Patriarch Nasrallah Boutros Sfeir and his bishops and by Druze leader Walid Jumblatt. The defeat of Syrian-backed candidates in Lebanon's August 2000 general election and in particular the victory of Rafiq al-Hariri over incumbent Prime Minister Selim al-Hoss were seen by some as a defeat for Damascus and a sign that Syrian influence in Lebanon was waning.

There has been widespread Lebanese resentment of the Syrian presence in Lebanon, which in the early 1990s included up to 40,000 soldiers and up to a million labourers working in agriculture and construction. Lebanese businessmen spoke of Syrian-controlled corruption involving kickbacks and the imposition of Syrian partners. They said that Lebanon was flooded with Syrian agricultural and other products, threatening the livelihood of Lebanese producers, while Lebanese businessmen and goods did not have access to Syria. There were also complaints that Syrian workers were undercutting their Lebanese counterparts in the labour market. These views were manifest in widespread jokes about Syrians, who are generally presented as authoritarian and backward.

Yet most Lebanese recognised that the Syrians were in Lebanon to stay for some time. They pointed out that the Maronites have a long-held position of calling for a Syrian pullout and cynics said that Druze and other politicians were supportive because they wanted Maronite votes in the August elections. Most Lebanese also recognised Syrian power and knew that Rafiq al-Hariri could not have become prime minister without toeing the Syrian line. Nevertheless, there was widespread support for change in the relationship, particularly in Lebanon's influential business community.

The new Syrian president has shown some willingness to respond to these calls for change. He has forged a direct link with Lebanese President Emile Lahoud and taken steps to reduce the power of General Kanaan, the Syrian intelligence chief in Lebanon and the man most often cited in corruption allegations. Troops have been withdrawn from the cities and the number of Syrian soldiers in Lebanon has been reduced to about 20,000 in the last two years. Fifty-four Lebanese and Palestinian political prisoners in Syrian jails were released on 11 December 2000, with the promise of more to come. The new Syrian president has also sought to signal that Lebanon will have a special and potentially lucrative role in Syrian economic reform. In August, three Lebanese banks were allowed to open branches in Syrian free-trade zones. There has been talk of lifting some customs restrictions on Lebanese goods entering Syria and plans for a Syrian–Lebanese free-trade zone in 2005.

President Assad's watchword of continuity and change holds true for the relationship with Lebanon, as do the considerations underlying it. He will seek to lighten Lebanon's burden in the Syrian–Israeli conflict, but not to the point of endangering Syrian interests. The bottom line is that Syrian withdrawal from Lebanon is very unlikely prior to a comprehensive peace between Syria and Israel, and even then economic and political links may be too strong to permit separation. In the meantime, Ariel Sharon's election victory in Israel in February 2001 and disputes over the border between Lebanon and Israel in the Shebaa farms area suggests that there may be an escalation in tension between Syria and Lebanon on the one hand, and between Syria and Israel on the other, in the second half of 2001.

Iraq Sanctions: Towards a New Policy

In the ten years since the end of the Gulf War, the coalition which drove Saddam Hussein out of Kuwait has followed a policy of containing him. Despite much comment to the contrary, that policy has been largely effective. The serial aggressor who until 1991 had invaded and fought with immediate neighbours for all but two of his years as leader has since been unable to attack anyone. His armed forces, once one of the largest in the world, are severely constrained by shortages of equipment and spare parts. His weapons of mass destruction (WMD) programme has been exposed and reduced. Where ten years ago Saddam was on the verge of a nuclear capability, that prospect has been indefinitely postponed.

Nevertheless, criticism of containment is mounting, and containment itself leaks badly. As reaction to their airstrikes in February 2001 underlined, the US and UK can no longer count on overt support for the use of force to safeguard the No-Fly Zones. Saddam has exploited the suffering of his own people and the breakdown in the peace process to turn regional and wider popular opinion against sanctions. Inspections are on hold. And both sanctions evasion and sanctions breaches are increasing. Last year, many companies attended the Baghdad Trade Fair, while some countries (including three permanent members of the UN Security Council) have permitted flights to Baghdad. Oil smuggling, principally via Jordan, Iran and Turkey, is estimated at nearly $1 billion a year. And Syria has now agreed to take large quantities of Iraqi oil through a reopened cross-border pipeline.

Is Containment Finished?

Those who see in these developments the collapse of containment are overstating the case. Containment remains the only viable option if Saddam can not be removed and can not be rehabilitated. Removal looks unlikely – Saddam is as strong internally as he has ever been. Rehabilitation is unacceptable if it means a Saddam free to develop his weapons of mass destruction and rebuild his armed forces. Yet, containment will increasingly become less effective unless it commands approval as well as authority. To achieve that, it is increasingly clear that the current instruments of containment need to be recalibrated.

In considering changes to the existing sanctions regime, the US, UK and France (the three Western members of the Security Council or P-3) should keep three objectives in focus:

- Depriving Saddam Hussein of the military capabilities he needs to launch aggression against his neighbours;

- impeding, if not completely eliminating, his ability to produce medium- and long-range ballistic missiles and weapons of mass destruction; and

- preserving, as much as possible, regional support for these objectives.

A continued, robust, sanctions regime that keeps military components, offensive technology and WMD precursors out of Iraq, and money out of the hands of regime members, is essential to the first two objectives. A sanctions regime that enables the majority of Iraqi citizens to get on with their lives, reduces their isolation and fosters a reconstitution of the Iraqi middle class is the key to the third objective.

With these objectives in mind, the US, UK and France should explore the following options:

Eliminate sanctions on commercial goods Nearly 85% of contracts submitted to the UN Iraq Sanctions Committee for civilian, commercial goods are already approved automatically. Sanctions on civilian goods, where they are applied, spur the local black market, which increases the price of commodities to the further detriment of an already impoverished middle class. They also contribute to perceptions that the Iraqi people are the real targets of sanctions. Perhaps just as important, increased civilian cross-border commercial activity would provide a badly needed boost for the Jordanian and Turkish economies. It is true that some money will pay for cigars and champagne for Saddam and his cronies. But this is a trivial reason to maintain a sanctions policy that undermines the regional public support required to sustain long-term containment of Iraq's revanchist ambitions.

Middle East

Refine the use of force As long as Saddam is in power, the US and UK – at a minimum – must be prepared to use force to prevent reconstitution of his WMD programme, deter him from suppressing Iraq's minorities and pre-empt aggression against his neighbours. Yet, as the Russian, French and Egyptian reactions to the US/UK airstrikes against air defence command-and-control assets north of the thirty-third parallel showed, tolerance for the use of force is rapidly shrinking. It is essential that the US and UK preserve the international political leeway for using force when it is absolutely essential, even if this means forgoing attacks like that in February 2001 and having to use force much more intensively when it finally becomes unavoidable. In practical terms, this means suspending *Operation Southern Watch*, while maintaining the aircraft and crews in place – as France has done – against the day when they must resume operations for the reasons stated above.

Although frequent combat air patrols are the best way to ensure that Iraqi aggression is countered before it develops fully, the proximity of standby, high-readiness *Southern Watch* aircraft to their patrol areas over southern Iraq and proper intelligence support should ensure a rapid reaction to Iraqi air or ground incursions. The suspension of flight operations, however, should be predicated on French, and perhaps Russian, willingness to state publicly that there are scenarios in which concerned states would have no choice but to use force. These scenarios would include Iraqi troop concentrations south of the thirty-third parallel that indicate offensive intentions toward Kuwait or Saudi Arabia, or massacres of Shi'a living in southern Iraq. Thus, a suspension should be undertaken only with the express caveat that flight operations can be resumed at any time without notice should it be judged necessary to fulfilling UN-supported coalition objectives. *Operation Northern Watch*, or *Provide Comfort*, should not be suspended because the proximity of Iraqi heavy armour and the less favourable conditions for coalition flight operations already deprive the coalition of the time it needs effectively to pre-empt a determined Iraqi incursion.

Unleash investment in Iraq's oil infrastructure Iraq's infrastructure is deteriorating, which in turn endangers the structural integrity and long-term viability of the oil fields themselves. Although the UN has allowed some work to go forward, and Security Council Resolution 1284 authorises the UN Secretary-General to permit additional investment, much more needs to be done. At the same time, significant commercial energy interests are driving some governments to push for the elimination of the entire sanctions regime. As long as UN control over Iraqi oil revenues is maintained, there is no reason why foreign companies should be prevented from repairing Iraq's infrastructure, especially if the opportunity to do so reduces the pressure on their governments to undermine the sanctions regime. Thus, a new Security Council resolution should eliminate all restrictions on investment in Iraq's energy sector.

Eliminate civil flight restrictions Flights into and out of Iraq have become the lowest-risk way for third countries to show Iraq that they care. Such flights are also very difficult, indeed impossible, to prevent. The result is that sanctions violations that are meaningless in practical terms have been transformed into tangible evidence that the entire sanctions regime is collapsing. Since some members of the coalition have long argued, with some justification, that isolation of the Iraqi people is not in the long-term interest of the West, it would make sense to drop this particular sanction. This reasoning also applies to civilian flights that transit the no-fly zones within Iraq, which the regime occasionally violates to claim a propaganda coup. Ending this prohibition under the rubric of giving Iraq back to its people would make political sense. From a military perspective, where such aircraft would have to be distinguished in combat conditions should coalition aircraft have to enter Iraqi airspace, it makes less sense. Indeed, by introducing the risk that the coalition might shoot down a civilian aircraft, it creates the potential for a major propaganda victory for Saddam as well as a human tragedy.

Tighten controls on a narrower range of dual-use items Suppliers now notify the sanctions committee of their intent to export items listed in the annex of Security Council Resolution 1051 (1996); Iraq also informs the committee of its intent to import items on the list. These contract requests are reviewed on a case-by-case basis. Since the range of items is so wide – virtually everything is potentially dual-use – some contract applications are turned down even though the items are destined for civilian use. Power generation, telecommunications, sewage treatment and water purification have deteriorated as a result.

'Presumption to deny', the standard applied by some countries on the sanctions committee, is still warranted, as Iraqis showed by using imported fibre-optics to enhance their ability to destroy coalition aircraft. Nevertheless, for purposes of public diplomacy and avoiding embarrassing instances of blocked contracts for items that have plausible civilian use, the sanctions committee could declare a shift to 'presumption to permit' and allow export of a greater range of 'dual-use' commodities. Intelligence agencies, the UN Monitoring, Inspection and Verification Commission (UNMOVIC) and the International Atomic Energy Administration should be pressed to create a list of truly dangerous dual-use items. At the same time, the Security Council must insist that supplier countries tighten enforcement of their own export control laws as they apply to items destined for Iraq. The US and UK, in particular, are capable of monitoring illegal transfers to Iraq, much as they did with respect to Iran,

Middle East

during the Iran–Iraq war, and to Libya, for nearly a decade. During these periods, the US and UK were assiduous in using this information to ensure that governments knew what offending national firms were doing, and to press them to take appropriate action.

Block the assets of regime members. While many Iraqis go without basics, the regime élites have fortunes stashed away in foreign banks. Although there are a large number of regulatory barriers to blocking and seizing these assets, the effort to get at them would force account holders to move their assets, while demonstrating – in combination with elimination of civilian trade sanctions – that the UN was sanctioning the regime, not the Iraqi people.

Make a serious effort to reduce oil smuggling The regime lines its pockets with about $2 million per day in revenue from oil piped to and swapped with Syria, shipped through the strait in Iranian waters, or trucked out through other transit points. Not all of this can be stopped. If, however, the US chooses to relax unilateral sanctions on Iran after the end of the Iran–Libya Sanctions Act mandate in August 2001, it could – with strong UK and French support – insist upon an end to Iranian collaboration with Iraqi smuggling as a pre-condition to ending economic sanctions. At the same time, coordinated diplomatic pressure should be brought to bear on Syria to close the pipeline. This will serve the coalition's broader purpose of putting as much money as possible into the hands of Iraq's people, while taking as much as possible away from the regime.

Put controls on the ground to keep contraband out of Iraq The UN will have to make a stronger effort to ensure that neither military nor especially dangerous dual-use items reach the regime. This is expensive and difficult to arrange, but it is well within the realm of possibility. All flights destined for Iraqi ports of entry should be inspected. Truck traffic at the existing four land entry points should be checked, not just vehicles transporting items purchased under the oil-for-food programme. The more thoroughly these checks are done, the less important is Iraqi cooperation at ports of entry. Verifying end-use would obviously be desirable, but the more the UN relies upon Iraqi cooperation, the more leverage Iraq will enjoy. These quarantine measures could easily be paid for out of Iraqi oil revenues. To the extent that on-the-ground-controls were coordinated with intelligence information provided by UN member countries, the more efficient, or 'smart', these inspections will be.

Sharply limit contact with senior Iraqi regime members In contrast to removal of restrictions on the ability of most Iraqis to travel, restrictions on the ability of regime members to move around the world should be sharply reduced. Governments should not issue visas to those on an agreed list of regime figures, except for certain necessary exceptions, e.g., travel of senior Iraqi officials to New York or Geneva for UN-related business. Governments should make it known that they would not stand in the way of local Iraqi opposition expatriates and local law enforcement agencies seeking to prosecute regime officials for criminal acts within Iraq.

Insist on tough UNMOVIC inspection guidelines The P-3 and UN Secretary-General should press UNMOVIC Executive Chairman Hans Blix not to accept Iraqi restrictions on inspections to be carried out under Security Council Resolution 1284. Ersatz inspections will lead to an undeserved bill of health for Saddam Hussein and inundate him with the cash to turn his revanchist fantasies into reality. No inspections are better than phoney ones.

UNMOVIC: Making it Effective

UNMOVIC was created by Resolution 1284 in December 1999 as the successor to the UN Special Commission (UNSCOM). According to Resolution 1284, if Blix reports to the Security Council after four months of UNMOVIC operations that Iraq has 'fulfilled the work program in all its aspects,' then the Council can suspend sanctions against Iraq for 120 days. Suspension would be renewable if Blix continued to certify Iraqi coopera-tion. If, on the other hand, Iraq ceases to cooperate, sanctions would be re-imposed within five days. The resolution is ambiguous as to which sanctions are to be suspended and on the nature of UNMOVIC ground-rules for operating within Iraq.

During his trip to the Middle East in late February 2001, US Secretary of State Colin Powell indicated that sanctions could become 'smarter' to encourage Baghdad to compromise. But in meetings in New York immediately thereafter, on 26 and 27 February, Iraqi and UN officials failed to make headway on resolving the ambiguities. Iraqi Deputy Prime Minister Tariq Aziz did not attend these meetings, which some construed as an indication that Baghdad did not take them seriously and con-templated no compromise. Nevertheless, before an effective new policy can be implemented, it is essential that UNMOVIC be empowered to conduct probing and meaningful inspections rather than merely cosmetic ones. In particular, the commission would have to be accorded complete freedom of movement and the right to stage no-notice inspections, and could not be subject to any limits on the intrusiveness of inspections. The US and the UK, for their part, would have to be clear at the outset of the new policy initiative that any interference with UNMOVIC inspectors would make it impossible for them to endorse an otherwise favourable

Blix report or to go forward with suspension of residual sanctions and foreign direct investment.

If American and British diplomacy brings about the adoption of a new Security Council resolution along the lines described here, Iraq should have enough incentive to cooperate. But even if Iraq fails to cooperate, it will remain contained. In either event, the use of force should be reserved for purposes that are clear and for which it is well suited. These include:

- pre-empting or countering Iraqi aggression against its neighbours;

- preventing or disrupting large-scale suppression of minority populations within Iraq; and

- eliminating Iraqi attempts to reconstitute their programmes relating to development, production and stockpiling of WMD.

Rolling Out the Policy

As a grand bargain between those governments working to contain Iraq and others with more urgent concerns about the effect of economic sanctions and loss of commercial opportunities, the impact and perceived legitimacy of this approach will depend on how it is launched. It must be announced jointly and in public at the ministerial level and explicitly backed by the UN Secretary-General. The US, the UK and France would be essential participants; Russian cooperation would be highly desirable. A thorough but careful diplomatic campaign should aim to elicit timely public statements of support in Cairo and Gulf Cooperation Council capitals.

In addition to showcasing the end to economic sanctions, the joint statement would have to include the following elements:

- If UNMOVIC goes into Iraq, it will go in to conduct real inspections. No inspectors are better than hamstrung inspectors.

- Suspension of *Southern Watch* is an indication of coalition restraint, not a sign of weakness. Reconstitution of WMD, suppression of minorities, or aggression by Saddam against his neighbours will warrant the use of force.

- The UN Security Council will view blatant violations of the new, streamlined sanctions regime with the utmost seriousness; the P-3, in particular, will press violators hard to comply with sanctions.

Can the Coalition be Reinvigorated?

On 27 March 2001, at the Arab League summit in Amman, Iraqi Deputy Prime Minister Aziz reiterated Iraq's rejection of sanctions of any kind – smart or otherwise. A draft resolution released at the end of the summit called for Iraq to comply with UN Security Council resolutions passed since the end of the Gulf War, for the UN to lift sanctions and for the US and Britain to cease patrolling the no-fly zones. The draft resolution stopped short of endorsing Iraq's request for a unilateral lifting of sanctions by Arab states. Iraqi Foreign Minister Mohammad Said al-Sahhaf labelled the summit 'a failure'. The Arab states are plainly uncomfortable with the existing containment policy. But their continued support for UN resolutions and refusal to step outside the UN regime suggests that they would support smarter sanctions, more selective air operations and a strengthened mandate for UNMOVIC.

The more critical and less predictable factor is transatlantic relations. A successful new policy will require substantial agreement on three main pillars: sanctions, regime change in Iraq and arms control (via UNMOVIC inspections). US Vice-President Dick Cheney and Secretary of Defense Donald Rumsfeld are open to smartening sanctions. France supports such a shift. In late March 2001, the Bush administration was reviewing its missions in the No-Fly Zones and floating proposals for sanctions reforms to moderate Arab states and European coalition partners, in hopes of arriving at a consensus on a new sanctions package in June. US Deputy Secretary of Defense Paul Wolfowitz – the chief American advocate of more active efforts to overthrow Saddam Hussein – has softened his views on that score, questioning whether it is possible. The narrowing of differences on sanctions and regime change, however, may still be hard to translate into an overall policy consensus. There are disagreements within the Bush administration that are likely to continue. Moreover, the US opposes UNMOVIC inspections under the restrictive conditions on which Baghdad currently insists, while France supports them.

Despite these remaining differences within the US administration and between the US and Europe, the Bush administration does not appear to be seriously entertaining a unilateral alternative. At the same time, moderate Arab countries are apprehensive about both Saddam Hussein's regime and the existing sanctions regime. Thus, there are strong reasons for coalition partners to seek a less divisive alternative under which international control over Saddam is preserved. Such an effort requires earnest and sustained transatlantic consultation.

Middle East

Asia

Asia faced another fitful year in 2000. The major regional powers confronted a security environment rendered more uncertain by the change in the US administration. After eight years of a Clinton administration that embraced China as a 'strategic partner', Beijing faces increased tension with a new administration that considers it a 'strategic competitor' and that is more disposed to arm Taiwan. Japan managed its bilateral regional relationships adequately, but has hard choices to make about whether to complement the United States' more aggressive strategic posture by expanding its own regional security role. In North-east Asia, the US change of administration has cramped South Korea's diplomatic style: where the former president, Bill Clinton was inclined to support Seoul's enthusiastic attempt to engage North Korea, President George W. Bush showed deeper scepticism of Pyongyang's motives and stepped back. The one area in which the US election made little impact was South Asia, but that has meant only continued stasis: India and Pakistan have stabilised their postures on nuclear deterrence and the crisis in Kashmir has reached a plateau.

In South-east Asia, the disruptive stimuli have tended to be home-grown. Indonesia's government confronts several separatist movements – notably in Aceh and Irian Jaya (West Papua) – and has shown few signs of opting for mediation over force. Adding to this instability, President Abdurrahman Wahid has continued to be an erratic and inept leader, and may well be impeached and forced from office. Filipino President Joseph Estrada was, in fact, driven out as popular anger over corruption and mismanagement erupted, leaving his successor a debt-burdened economy on the decline. Border tensions between Thailand and Myanmar have grown, as Myanmar instigated ethnic fighting and indulged in cross-border drug trafficking. As for regional diplomacy, Vietnam, and Thailand's new nationalistic *Thai-Rak-Thai* government have both reinforced the principle of non-interference in an increasingly ineffectual Association of South East Asian Nations (ASEAN).

On the economic front, ambiguity reigns. The benefits of China's impending membership of the World Trade Organisation (WTO) are likely to be countered by unfamiliar competitive pressure that will produce an element of domestic instability and make continued high growth critical. Japan's economy has shown little sign of breaking out of its decade-long slump, which a panoply of monetary and fiscal measures have not

Map 4 Asia

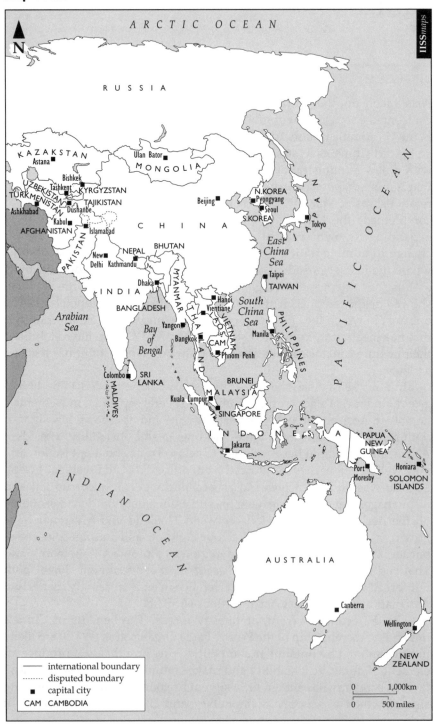

reversed. South Korea has weathered the storm better. It has maintained its recovery from the 1997–98 financial crisis, although large-scale job losses have produced widespread dissatisfaction. In addition, both the resources and the patience of its *chaebols* have been stretched thin by President Kim Dae Jung's 'sunshine policy' of economic engagement with North Korea. Thailand too managed the financial crisis reasonably well, but the new government's protectionist outlook has introduced uncertainty into the country's economic future. Pakistan and Indonesia remain economic basket-cases in need of help from the International Monetary Fund; help that the fund often finds difficult to offer because of the conduct of their regimes.

Amid the domestic and regional tumult in Asia, the clearest positive chord in 2000 was North Korea's apparent interest in diplomatic engagement. But North Korean President Kim Jong Il remains an unpredictable and equivocal interlocutor. In addition, the possibility of a Korean rapprochement and a consequent US withdrawal from South Korea has raised worries in China about a strengthened US–Japan alliance. Thus, on top of its ongoing strategic priorities in the Taiwan Strait and South Asia, the US will be paying close attention to Beijing's and Tokyo's concerns in steering developments on the Korean Peninsula.

China: Struggling with Change

The biggest challenge for China's leadership in 2000 was coping with disorienting changes in the country's strategic environment and the impact of wrenching social and economic dislocation at home. Abroad, unexpected developments on the Korean Peninsula and in Taiwan raised new uncertainties – the possibility of a realignment of power in North-east Asia should a Korean rapprochement lead to a US withdrawal, and the possibility of an accelerating drift by Taiwan towards independence. Within China, high-level corruption, impending leadership changes and frequent, if mostly small-scale, protests by disaffected citizens presented growing political difficulties.

Beijing is now bracing itself for renewed turbulence in its relations with the United States, with President George W. Bush likely to decide in favour of deploying a national missile defence (NMD) system that could render China's small strategic nuclear arsenal even less effective as a deterrent than hitherto. China also fears that Bush might be less cautious than his predecessor Bill Clinton when it comes to deciding what weapons to sell to Taiwan.

By the autumn, China is almost certain to succeed at last in its 14-year quest to join the international body that sets the rules for global economic activity. Membership of the World Trade Organisation (WTO) will help to boost exports and foreign investment, but it will also pose new challenges: factory closures, growing unemployment in some sectors and acceptance that other countries will effectively gain a say in the setting of China's own economic policies. WTO membership will help to draw China closer to Taiwan, but it will by no means end trade disputes with China's biggest export market, the United States. Indeed, Washington is likely to be particularly sensitive to any perceived violations by China of its WTO commitments, given the enormous trade gap in China's favour and the passionate political debate that the question of China's WTO accession generated in the US in 1999 and 2000.

Compromise with Taiwan

The election of Chen Shui-bian as Taiwan's president in March 2000, if only by a very narrow margin, startled China's leadership. Beijing had clearly hoped that its menacing rhetoric in the build-up to the election would prompt voters to back candidates more clearly committed to Taiwan's eventual reunification with the mainland. Chen's Democratic Progressive Party (DPP) had long supported the idea of Taiwan's formal independence. His victory marked an historic transformation of Taiwan's political scene after more than 50 years of rule by presidents from the pro-reunification Nationalist Party (*Kuomintang* or KMT). But China's response was relatively muted. Beijing said only that it would watch Chen's 'words and deeds'. It toned down the sense of urgency that it had communicated just before the elections when it warned in a White Paper that continued stalling by Taiwan on reunification could prompt a military attack by the mainland.

Beijing's restrained response suggested that pragmatic forces in the Chinese leadership remained in control of external policy despite the increasingly public expression of virulent nationalism in China. Such nationalism has been particularly evident in mainland publications advocating tough policies towards Taiwan and the United States as well as in the outpouring of anti-Western sentiment after the May 1999 bombing of the Chinese Embassy in Belgrade. In the build-up to the annual informal conclave of China's leaders in the seaside resort of Beidaihe in August 2000, President Jiang Zemin worked hard to persuade his colleagues that it would be best to continue with a wait-and-see approach towards Taiwan. He advocated building up economic contacts in order to exert influence over Taiwan's business community, while avoiding contacts with the DPP-led administration. Low-level dialogue between the mainland and Taiwan, suspended by Beijing since 1999, was to remain on hold until Chen publicly acknowledged that there was only 'one China'.

Chen sought to reduce tensions by talking of eventual 'political integration' with the mainland and by indicating that the 'one China' concept was already implicit in Taiwan's own constitution. He also, from January 2001, opened the 'mini three links' between the small outlying islands of Kinmen and Matsu and the mainland – thus ending the 50-year ban on direct communications, transportation and trade. Jiang clearly did not regard these cautious moves as anything more than a smokescreen for attempts by Chen to consolidate the status quo. But Chen's gestures at least enabled Jiang to fend off criticisms from hardliners within the Communist Party and military that he was not exerting sufficient pressure on Taiwan. With mounting problems to deal with at home, Jiang did not want to have to deal with an escalation of tension with Taiwan – and by extension the US – as well.

The Taiwan–mainland relationship will still be fraught with difficulties in the months ahead. Beijing will respond angrily if the US decides to sell more sophisticated military technology to Taiwan – particularly if this includes *Arleigh-Burke*-class destroyers equipped with the *Aegis* combat system that would considerably improve Taiwan's capabilities in anti-air, anti-surface and anti-submarine warfare.

As Taiwan prepares for parliamentary elections in December, Beijing will attempt as usual to deter voters from voting for pro-independence candidates. This may take the form of the ritual strident warnings that a move towards independence could lead to war, and it could additionally involve military manoeuvres. But it appears unlikely, in any event, that the DPP will win a majority of the parliamentary seats. Chen will continue having to make compromises with the KMT in order to secure parliamentary approval for his policies, as he did in February 2001 when, under pressure from the KMT and the smaller New Party, he retreated from an earlier decision to halt construction of the island's fourth nuclear power plant.

Any overt support by Chen for Taiwan's formal independence would be political suicide. The president's decision in October 2000 to replace the prime minister he had appointed from the KMT, Tang Fei, with a member of his own party, Chang Chun-hsiung, has so far done little if anything to bolster Chen's position. While it may have helped to facilitate policy-making coordination between the cabinet and the DPP, it has complicated relations between the cabinet and the KMT-dominated legislature.

Asia

Restraint in US–China Relations

The same desire to secure a stable external environment that has restrained Jiang from a knee-jerk response to developments in Taiwan has also encouraged him to mend fences with the United States. On 7 May 2000, China marked the anniversary of the Belgrade Embassy bombing with a renewed demand that the US issue a fuller explanation of the attack, but it also issued secret orders to university campuses to deter students from staging anti-US protests. Beijing clearly worried that a repeat of the outpouring of anti-US sentiment a year earlier would seriously undermine relations with Washington. It also knew that protests staged in the name of patriotism have a history in China of turning against the government itself. In June, then US Secretary of State Madeleine Albright visited Beijing and said the subject of the Belgrade bombing did not even come up in her talks with Chinese leaders. In July, then US Defense Secretary William Cohen also paid a visit, setting the seal on the restoration of top-level military contacts after the Belgrade incident.

China made a symbolic gesture of concern about US domination of the post-Cold War order by pursuing close ties with Russia's newly elected president, Vladimir Putin. But the Sino-Russian relationship remained based more on rhetoric than substance. Putin paid a brief visit to Beijing in July 2000 on his way to the summit of the G-8 group of leading industrial countries in Okinawa; China had refused Japan's invitation to attend as an observer. The two sides issued a joint declaration of their opposition to the US deploying a national missile defence system. They also reaffirmed their 'strategic partnership'. But despite their shared sense of frustration with the supremacy of US power, there was no sign of readiness to develop a coordinated strategy to counterbalance American influence. And brisk sales of Russian arms to China notwithstanding, economic ties between the two countries remained weak, with miniscule bilateral trade compared with that between China and the United States. China remains distrustful of Russia's stance on missile defence – it was clearly taken by surprise when Putin suggested Russian cooperation with NATO on developing a European theatre missile defence (TMD) system. It worries about the potential impact of Russian nationalism on the relationship and the growing misgivings in the Russian Far East about the influx of Chinese migrants.

China kept up its harsh rhetoric against NMD, accusing the US of harbouring secret intentions to render China's small arsenal of strategic nuclear weapons useless by deploying the system. Bush's victory in the US elections led to renewed anxiety in Beijing that Washington would proceed with deployment on a grander scale than envisaged by Clinton. Yet hints began to emerge from Beijing that even on this issue China might be flexible. Some scholars in state-controlled think-tanks in Beijing began to suggest that if the US were to take China's views on this issue seriously and recognise the validity of China's desire for a credible nuclear deterrent, there might be room for compromise. China wants to ensure that Bush accepts the need for continued engagement with China, despite his administration's view that the two countries are 'competitors' rather than the 'strategic partners' Clinton hoped they would become.

Top-level dialogue between the two countries leading to a clear-cut commitment by the US on the limits of its NMD deployment might allow China to proceed with its nuclear-modernisation programme in a more open manner. This would reduce the risk of alarming China's neighbours, particularly Japan and India. The use of precision guided weapons by Western powers in the 1991 Gulf War and the 1999 Kosovo conflict has convinced China's leadership that modernisation is urgently needed in order to ensure that the Chinese strategic nuclear arsenal could survive a conventional attack.

China's agreement with the US in November 2000 on the export of nuclear-capable missiles and their technologies was a sign that Beijing was still committed to non-proliferation dialogue with the US despite its concerns about NMD and US weapon sales to Taiwan. The deal was significant because for the first time China agreed to ban the export of not only nuclear-capable missiles, but also of their technologies. In return, Washington agreed to resume processing the licences necessary for US companies to launch commercial satellites in China. Beijing's acceptance of this agreement may have been intended partly to show its gratitude to Clinton for his announcement in September that he would leave a decision on NMD deployment to his successor. But with US–Japan research on TMD systems still under way, and the Pentagon having recently announced plans to sell 200 AIM-120C Advanced Medium Range Air-to-Air Missiles (AMRAAM) to Taiwan, the accord on Chinese missile exports showed that Beijing could still cooperate on international arms-control issues despite serious disagreements with Washington.

Relations between China and the US gained a major boost with the US Senate's vote on 19 September 2000 to extend permanent normal trade relations (PNTR) status to China. This was essential if the US was to enjoy the same right of access to China's markets as other WTO members after China's accession to the body. The vote removed the need for Congress to vote each year on whether to renew China's normal trade-relations (previously known as most-favoured nation) status. This procedure had been a major irritant in Sino-US relations since the crushing of the Tiananmen Square protests in 1989 because of the annual debate that it provoked in the US about human rights in China.

Hardliners in the Chinese leadership are still deeply sceptical about the value of WTO membership. They see it as limiting China's economic-policy options at a time when it needs flexibility in order to cope with a possible public backlash against factory closures and layoffs. They also see it as undermining China's rights as a sovereign nation. If social unrest grows following WTO accession, there is a risk that the hardline camp – led by the National People's Congress (NPC) Chairman Li Peng – will gain ammunition in their campaign to slow down economic reforms and roll back some of the commitments made to the WTO. A retreat by China from its WTO pledges would exacerbate tensions with the US, where one of the key arguments made in favour of admitting China to the body was that it would boost the reformist cause.

Strategic Uncertainties in North-east Asia

In the run-up to the June 2000 Korean summit, China indirectly signalled to the US that it would play a crucial role in developments on the peninsula. The surprise visit to Beijing by the North Korean leader, Kim Jong Il, in May was of considerable symbolic importance. It suggested that Kim – whose visit to Beijing was his first public trip abroad since he succeeded his father in 1994 – regarded the Chinese leadership as important advisors on how to handle ties with Washington and possibly also on how to reform a Stalinist economic system. Kim's follow-up visit to Shanghai in January 2001 was clearly aimed at studying China's experience of economic reform.

Beijing gave Kim considerable encouragement. It welcomed the de-escalation of tension on the peninsula and the improvement of North Korea's ties with the US and other major powers. It probably felt that a Pyongyang–Washington rapprochement would have the side effect of undermining the case for NMD. An improvement in North Korea's ties with Japan would similarly undermine one of the main arguments in Japan in favour of boosting defence spending and revising the constitution to give Tokyo greater flexibility in its defence policy. But China must also have worried about the longer-term implications of change. The possibility of an eventual withdrawal of US forces from the peninsula raised the question of how Japan would then justify a continued close defence relationship with the US. The unwinding of the Cold War on the peninsula risked stoking a new cold war between China on the one hand and Japan and the US on the other. No less worrying from Beijing's perspective was the possibility in the longer term of a US withdrawal from Japan as well. This could lead to more direct confrontation between China and Japan, fuelled by rising nationalist sentiment in both countries.

Perhaps mindful of such longer-term uncertainties, China tried in 2000 to present a different face to Japan. During a trip to Tokyo in October, Prime Minister Zhu Rongji avoided the usual lecturing on Japan's wartime atrocities in China and expressed gratitude for Japan's economic aid. He also sought to soothe Japan's misgivings over an increase in the number of Chinese survey vessels detected near the Japanese coast. But such diplomatic blandishments were unlikely to reduce profound uncertainties in Japan about China's strategic intentions.

China's publication of its latest Defence White Paper during Zhu's visit was clearly aimed at reducing these uncertainties. It was only the second such White Paper ever published by Beijing – the first appeared in 1998 – and thus marked another small step towards greater openness by China's intensely secretive military. But while stressing China's commitment to peace and stability in the region, the document attacked the US–Japan defence relationship and warned of a possible regional arms race triggered by TMD cooperation between Washington and Tokyo. It also failed to mention anything about the reasons for its deployments of intermediate-range ballistic missiles capable of hitting Japan; nor for that matter did it say anything about Chinese missile deployments on the coast facing Taiwan. China's missile deployments had been specifically mentioned in Japan's own White Paper on defence earlier in the year.

Rising Social Tensions

China's wait-and-see policy following Chen Shui-bian's victory in the March presidential elections in Taiwan was further evidence of the continuing strength of pragmatic forces in Chinese external policy-making. Despite widespread speculation that China might adopt a tougher approach after the Beidaihe conclave in August, the gathering endorsed the idea of seeking closer economic ties with the island while keeping its leadership at arm's length. To President Jiang and his colleagues, political, economic and social challenges at home were matters of more pressing urgency.

The crackdown during 2000 on the quasi-religious sect *Falun Gong* was clearly failing. Despite the arrests of thousands of followers and the sentencing of several leaders to lengthy jail terms, small but highly visible protests by *Falun Gong* adherents were still frequent on Tiananmen Square. These protests usually lasted no more than a few minutes before participants were hauled off by the police. They did not represent a direct challenge to the Communist Party's rule and had no apparent political motive beyond a desire for party recognition of the sect. But the fact they occurred at all was deeply worrying to the leadership, given that they highlighted the party's increasing inability to ensure public obedience. Part of the leadership's problem was likely to have been lingering sympathy for the protesters among party members and members of the security services. The ability of several hundred *Falun Gong* followers to gather at the same time and stage a brief protest on Tiananmen Square during China's 1

October 2001 national day celebrations, despite seemingly elaborate security measures, suggested a significant failing on the part of law and order officials.

In January 2001, the self-immolation on Tiananmen Square of five people said by the authorities to be *Falun Gong* followers was exploited by the government to step up its propaganda against the sect. The official media highlighted the involvement of a mother and her 12-year-old daughter in the incident. The mother died and the daughter suffered serious burns. Government propaganda aimed to persuade the public that *Falun Gong* had actively encouraged suicides, although the sect's leaders denied this. It is unlikely, however, that the media campaign against *Falun Gong* will diminish the determination of followers to stage protests. There are signs, meanwhile, that the leadership is divided over whether to maintain such a hardline approach, particularly given that a continuing crackdown could undermine China's vigorous bid to host the Olympic Games in 2008. The International Olympic Committee is due to decide on the winning city in July 2001.

China is also looking forward to the biggest-ever gathering of foreign leaders on its soil, namely an informal summit of the Asia-Pacific Economic Cooperation (APEC) Forum in Shanghai in October. This event is likely to be attended by US President Bush, whose administration has criticised China's treatment of *Falun Gong* followers. But President Jiang, despite implicit reservations among some of his colleagues about the severity of the crackdown, is determined to vigorously suppress what remains of the *Falun Gong* organisation within China. The official media have described the campaign against the movement as a major 'political struggle' – implying that the prestige of the party leadership could be undermined if the struggle fails.

The party, however, will be unable to crush sects such as *Falun Gong* to the extent that it was able to suppress organised political dissent after the Tiananmen Square protests of 1989. The authorities find it easier to monitor and control political activists because they tend to belong to easily identifiable groups – mostly urban intellectuals with a long record of anti-government behaviour, or workers in state enterprises. But *Falun Gong*'s adherents represent a broader spectrum – from urban party members and entrepreneurs to the unemployed and peasants. Most of them were probably supporters of the political status quo before the crackdown began. Even if the movement itself is suppressed, similar sects are sure to emerge. *Falun Gong*, after all, is deeply rooted in traditional Chinese healing practices and spiritual beliefs. Jiang's confrontational approach risks creating a large new body of disaffected citizens. This could undermine his efforts to ensure that the party's crucial Sixteenth Congress in 2002 projects an image of a China that is stable and confident.

Pressures on Hong Kong

China's determination to eradicate *Falun Gong* imposed new stresses on the Special Administrative Region of Hong Kong and the 'high degree of autonomy' promised in its post-colonial constitution. Although *Falun Gong* has only a few hundred active supporters in the territory, their status as a legally registered group and their freedom to speak openly about their beliefs and the crackdown in China has embarrassed and angered the Chinese leadership. Through its close allies in Hong Kong the communist authorities have made it clear that the sect should be treated as a subversive organisation, just as it is on the mainland. Pro-Beijing figures in the territory have called for the swift enactment of a law against subversion that would enable the Hong Kong government to outlaw the movement. Hong Kong's constitution requires that such a law be adopted, but since Britain's 1997 handover of the territory to China, the Hong Kong government has delayed taking action in order to avoid fuelling fears that China's sweeping definition of subversion might be used to suppress what is now regarded in Hong Kong as normal political debate.

Hong Kong's Chief Executive Tung Chee-hwa has so far resisted pressures to introduce a subversion bill, but in early 2001 he supported the referral of a key immigration lawsuit to Beijing – thus raising further questions about the territory's legal autonomy. Tung's usually placatory approach towards Beijing is widely believed to be one factor that led to the resignation of the head of the civil service, Anson Chan, in January 2001. Chan said she was stepping down 'for personal reasons' and that she wanted to spend more time with her family, but it was well known that she disliked Tung's autocratic style and his failure to speak out more vigorously in defence of Hong Kong's freedoms. In September 2000, Beijing delivered a public rebuke to Chan by urging her to give more support to Tung. Days after Chan announced her departure, *Falun Gong* held an international meeting of its followers in Hong Kong's town hall – triggering a furious response from Beijing. Tung later told the legislature that he regarded *Falun Gong* as an 'evil cult' and that the group's activities in Hong Kong would be closely monitored. Chan, however, conspicuously avoided echoing such views.

The choice of Donald Tsang as Chan's successor suggests that Tung is eager to project an image of continuity in his administration. Tsang served as financial secretary in the colonial administration and continued to do so until his latest appointment. He has not been as outspoken an upholder of civil liberties as Chan, but neither is he closely associated with the pro-Beijing camp.

Asia

Political Struggle

Preparations for major leadership changes at the Sixteenth Congress and the following year's annual session of the NPC, China's legislature, will be an increasing preoccupation of the Chinese leadership in the months ahead. Already there are signs that Jiang will not be able to impose his will without a struggle. At a central committee meeting held in October 2000, he failed to secure the promotion of his protégé, Zeng Qinghong, to full membership of the Politburo. Zeng is the chief of the party's Organisation Department and an alternate member of the Politburo. Many senior party officials resent his power because he belongs to a coterie of Jiang's former colleagues in Shanghai who have enjoyed rapid promotion since Jiang began consolidating his power in the mid-1990s. Jiang is widely believed to want a leader whom he can fully trust to counterbalance the power of Hu Jintao, who is all but certain to be appointed as president in 2003, and quite likely to become party leader in 2002. Although Hu shows no open sign of opposition to Jiang, he owes his power and position as heir apparent to his links with the late paramount leader Deng Xiaoping rather than to Jiang himself.

Jiang wants to retain a role beyond the Sixteenth Congress similar to that enjoyed by Deng in the late 1980s and early 1990s: as a semi-retired elder statesman who continues to play a decisive role in any critical issue facing the party. This would mean giving up all his posts except the chairmanship of the Central Military Commission (CMC). But he has powerful rivals, mostly notably Li Peng, the leader of a more conservative grouping within the leadership. If Jiang forces Li's retirement from chairmanship of the NPC in 2003 on the grounds of age – he will be 74 – Li is likely to resent Jiang, who is two years older, playing a continued role in the CMC. There are signs that the intensifying campaign against corruption is being used to undercut Li's position. In September 2000, one of his deputies in the NPC, Cheng Kejie, was executed for corruption. The highest-ranking official to receive such punishment since the communist takeover in 1949, Cheng had been promoted by Li himself. In January 2001, details emerged of the arrest of two senior officials from the State Power Corporation, also on corruption charges. These officials had close ties with Li's children who work for subsidiaries of the corporation. Although no one has suggested that Li himself may be corrupt, the actions against those closely associated with him send a clear message in China's political culture.

The Cancer of Corruption

Jiang has often described rampant corruption in China as a major threat to party rule. In 2000, the authorities gave details of the biggest corruption scandal since 1949 – a $6 billion-smuggling case in the port city of Xiamen involving more than 200 middle-ranking and senior local party and police officials as well as a deputy minister of public security in Beijing. Press reports in Hong Kong also linked the case with the wife of a Politburo member (who has denied involvement) and a former senior military commander. In November, 14 officials were sentenced to death for their part in the smuggling ring. In the north-eastern city of Shenyang, the authorities are investigating collusion between top officials and the local mafia. The case caused the resignation of the city's mayor in December and has involved the arrest of a deputy mayor and as many as 300 local officials. In Guangdong Province, a tax fraud case now under investigation could eclipse in scale even the Xiamen case.

Jiang will want to declare success in his campaign against corruption at the Sixteenth Congress, but it is likely that the problem will if anything worsen by then, as officials take advantage of economic changes necessitated by WTO membership and ongoing reforms to line their pockets. A number of incidents of social unrest during 2000 were triggered by official wrongdoing. In February in Yangjiazhanzi, a town in north-east China, some 20,000 workers from a bankrupt mine battled with the police in a protest over severance payments. The protesters accused their employers of pocketing funds, leaving them with derisory pay-outs. In August, thousands of farmers in the southern province of Jiangxi staged violent protests against excessive taxes imposed illegally by local officials.

These protests were among the largest reported in China in recent years, but they were by no means unique. Corruption, combined with hardships caused by economic change, has fuelled growing unrest in rural and urban China, with tens of thousands of sit-ins, strikes and demonstrations now taking place annually. The protests have so far been isolated and easily contained by the authorities, but they are a potential cause of more critical instability should political unity break down as it did during the 1989 unrest.

Economic Growth Crucial

Whether China can maintain social and political stability despite the enormous stresses that it will have to endure in the coming two to three years – from WTO accession to leadership succession – will substantially depend on the country's ability to maintain a high economic growth rate. In 2000, China's economy grew by around 8%, somewhat faster than expected, thanks not least to massive government spending programmes. Although most economists expect growth in 2001 to be somewhat lower, at 7–8%, mainly as a result of the US slowdown, this would be sufficient to ensure that many urban residents, at least, continue to feel the benefits of economic change.

Asia

Growth on its own will not be a sufficient guarantee of stability. The rapidly widening gap between rich and poor, between urban and rural areas and between the relatively prosperous east and underdeveloped west of the country will exacerbate social tensions. The government's new campaign launched in 1999 to promote investment in western areas – often known as the 'Go West' initiative – is unlikely to narrow significantly the huge disparities in wealth. Nor in the foreseeable future will it stem the flow of migrant labour from impoverished areas to the cities, which is fuelling crime, spreading diseases such as tuberculosis and AIDS, and putting enormous stresses on public services such as transportation and healthcare.

China's major problems are still domestic, including the fragility of its political structure and its uneven economic development. Insofar as they can, its leaders will try to avoid foreign problems while they sort out the country's domestic difficulties, making carefully modulated adjustments in China's relations with the US and other powers to avoid unnecessary confrontations. Those powers, while refusing to accept Beijing's occasional aggressive behaviour, must continue to show understanding of China's difficulties, as part of their efforts to nudge it into a deeper and more comfortable relationship with the outside world.

Japan 2000: No New Dawn Yet

Unlike most Western media, the Japanese press and many Japanese, emphasised that January 2001 was the start of the new millennium. Given the economic and political difficulties that had continued to plague the country during 2000, it was probably very sensible to consign that year to the dustbin of the 'lost decade' of the 1990s and hope for better things ahead.

Sluggish consumer spending and corporate mismanagement hampered the economy's gathering recovery. The rosy light visible at the end of the tunnel in the summer had faded by the end of the year as the economy once again showed signs of stalling. The combined stresses of trying to find ways to get the economy back on track and of struggling with troublesome political allies within the coalition government laid Prime Minister Keizo Obuchi low. His incapacitation and subsequent death thrust high office into the hands of Yoshiro Mori, who singularly failed to inspire confidence either at home or abroad and provided plenty of verbal gaffes for the ever-expectant media and opposition to exploit. Somehow he survived politically through the rest of the year, but at the beginning of 2001 the question that was being asked was when, not if, he would be pushed out of office.

For most of the year, therefore, Japan's political leaders found themselves preoccupied with domestic matters that were stuck in a familiar and dismal groove. At the same time, the Group of Eight (G-8) summit in Okinawa and slight improvements in relationships with China, North Korea and Russia could be counted on the positive side. And while Japan remains a country struggling to pull its weight in international affairs, the new defence programme indicates that Tokyo is preparing to contribute substantially more to regional security.

Regional Fears

US President Bill Clinton attended Obuchi's funeral and commercial disputes between the US and Japan were comparatively subdued during the year, but the Japanese could not rid themselves of the suspicion that the Clinton administration was bypassing them in favour of China as the Asian power with which US engagement was most important. Although a new US administration means new uncertainties, many Japanese policy-makers feel that they can build stronger ties with a Republican-led US administration. Japanese defence analysts consider Taiwan an essential bulwark against Chinese hegemony, and favour preserving the status quo on Taiwan–China relations. They were uneasy with Clinton's 'China first' policy, and more broadly fear that a rapprochement on the Korean Peninsula could precipitate a withdrawal of US forward deployments in Asia that would leave Japan unprotected. From a strategic point of view, therefore, the more cautious approach to China of President George W. Bush (in particular, his disavowal of the US–China 'strategic partnership' mooted by Clinton) and his emphasis on regional security and declared interest in working with allies would appeal to Tokyo.

Greater US interest in Japan, however, could also produce some dilemmas for Japan. Locally, the need to settle the long-running dispute over the relocation site for the US base in Futenma, Okinawa, will be politically complicated owing to public opinion in Okinawa that strongly favours time limits to the US deployment. In the regional context, while developments on the Korean Peninsula may partially undermine the rationale for developing a theatre missile defence (TMD) system with the United States, the incoming Bush team's enthusiasm for missile-defence systems will inspire Japan to move ahead anyway. This might inordinately antagonise Beijing. China remains Japan's second-largest trading partner (after the US), and Japan cannot afford to treat the relationship cavalierly.

Asia

There were signs of activity in Japan's bilateral relations with regional powers other than China but little real advancement. While Japanese policy-makers and public alike welcomed the apparent easing of tension on the Korean Peninsula, they remained cautious about the lessons to be drawn and reluctant to move as fast or as far as South Korea's President Kim Dae Jung had hoped. Formal negotiations with Pyongyang did take place in April, August and October 2000 after an eight-year suspension, but no real progress was achieved. Some food aid was supplied, and Japan's substantial economic assistance through the Korean Peninsula Energy Development Organisation (KEDO) continued. But negotiations on more substantial matters foundered over the problems generated by the alleged kidnap of Japanese citizens by the North, compensation for Japanese colonial and wartime activities in Korea and North Korean missiles. Similarly, there were more frequent meetings during 2000 between Japanese and Russian leaders and negotiators over the disputed Northern Territories. But despite Russian President Vladimir Putin's confirmation of the validity of the 1956 Joint Declaration (which the Japanese interpret as allowing the return of two of the four territories when a peace treaty is concluded), the gap remains significant. The pledge of the 1997 Krasnoyarsk Russo-Japanese summit to conclude a peace treaty by the end of the year 2000 went unfulfilled.

A potentially significant development emerged from Prime Minister Mori's August 2000 visit to Delhi, when India and Japan agreed to form a 'global partnership'. Though at odds over nuclear issues, the two countries now recognise a coalescence of their security interests and a need for a geopolitical relationship. Both see China as a threat that neither country can counter on its own; both depend on energy imports from the Persian Gulf. Tokyo and Delhi's increasing diplomatic closeness may, therefore, precede some mutual accord for ensuring safety in sea lanes between the Indian Ocean and the Malacca Strait and heightened naval cooperation as each country enhances its projection capabilities.

Japan's relations with China remained cool during the first half of the year. The Japanese warned Beijing against its repeated (and increasing) maritime incursions in the disputed Senkaku/Diaoyu Islands area and in the straits near Japan. In turn, the Chinese criticised the Japanese involvement in the TMD programme. China declined Japan's invitation to the July 2000 G-8 summit in Okinawa, and Japanese politicians – particularly those in opposition – began to press for curtailing overseas development assistance (ODA) to China. After an incursion by a Chinese intelligence ship on 23 May 2000 – for the apparent purpose of mapping the seabed for submarine operations – the Diet delayed a $158 million loan and resumed payment only after China agreed to a mutual notification system for 'research' in Japanese waters. The message to Beijing was that

ODA from Japan – which has so far totalled over $60 billion – was no longer unconditional.

Subsequently, the Chinese decided to adopt a softer line. On a visit to Japan in October 2000, Chinese Premier Zhu Rongji took a noticeably more relaxed approach than President Jiang Zemin had done during his disastrous visit two years earlier, concentrating on media-friendly public appearances and on economic issues important to Japanese companies preparing themselves for China's entry into the World Trade Organisation. Another hopeful sign for future bilateral relations was the cooperation in September 2000 of Japanese technical experts and Chinese army personnel in removing chemical-weapon shells abandoned by the Japanese military in China at the end of the Second World War. The two-week operation was the culmination of a diplomatic process that began in 1991.

Japan's Defence White Paper, released in July 2000, reflected increased concern about China's growing military power in general and naval expansion in particular. According to opinion polls, more than 60% of the Japanese public favours changing Article IX of the 'Peace Constitution', which inhibits Japan from using force, and in February 2000 the Diet opened formal debate on the matter. Some 55% of Japanese view China negatively, and 90% support strong Japanese responses to regional and even extra-regional security crises. And indeed, China ranks Japan alongside the United States as a potential enemy and is raising defence expenditures faster than any other country, reflecting the limits of both American and Japanese economic diplomacy.

Several other harsh security realities also face Japan: China's naval expansion; North Korea's *Taepo-dong* missile launch in 1998; the incursion of North Korean spy ships into Japanese territorial waters in April 1999; rising threats of piracy to maritime interests, particularly in oil lanes; the need for more direct involvement in regional peacekeeping prompted by the East Timor crisis; and uncertainty about the long-term future of the US regional security umbrella. In addition, many Japanese have grown weary of apologising for Japan's bellicose past. These factors produced the most significant development of the year: the completion of the government's deliberations on the medium-term defence programme. Spurred by the heightened level of alliance commitments to the US under the 1997 defence-cooperation guidelines, the cabinet approved in mid-December a ¥25 trillion ($220bn) five-year plan, starting in fiscal 2001, that reflects a significant enlargement of the roles that the Self-Defence Forces (SDF) will be expected to play.

The new defence dispensation emphasises 'diverse missions', which means that the SDF should be able not only to support the US military under the terms of the 1997 guidelines but also to cope with various types of emergencies, including attacks by armed guerrillas, weapons of mass destruction, natural disasters and cyber-terrorism. The approved requests for equipment reflected these needs: new large-size helicopter-carrying destroyers (which have been criticised as being surrogate aircraft carriers), air-refuelling tanker aircraft, additional *Aegis*-equipped destroyers and new information technology for patrol aircraft and tanks. Dismissed by critics as merely a shopping list with no vision, these purchases were, however, justified by the enhanced awareness that the SDF should be better prepared to deal with disaster-relief activities, transporting Japanese in the case of overseas emergencies and UN-led peacekeeping operations. The planned acquisitions will inevitably extend the boundaries of Japan's 'preventive defence' posture, and may improve its case for permanent membership on the UN Security Council.

With the new five-year plan, momentum towards eventual deployment of a TMD system that would strengthen regional alliances has continued to build in Japan. First, during the 1990s, Japan dramatically improved its early-warning capabilities, which are essential to TMD. It plans to field its own fleet of reconnaissance satellites by 2002, and now has airborne signals intelligence (SIGINT) capabilities second only to the United States' in the Asia-Pacific theatre. Key SIGINT features include Airborne Early Warning and Control (AWACS) and 13 US-built E2-C early-warning aircraft equipped to detect and portray targets, tracks and trajectories, as well as signal emissions. Upgrades are budgeted for 2001–05. Second, Japan has deployed some 120 *Patriot* Advanced Capability (PAC)-2 land-based missiles and is installing the more sophisticated PAC-3 version. For sea-based missile defence, the two upgraded *Kongou*-class destroyers outfitted with the US-built *Aegis* interception system, slated for purchase in 2001–05, will increase Japan's *Aegis*-equipped fleet to six.

Finally, since 1999 Japan and the United States have been co-developing TMD technologies – concentrating on missile identification and tracking sensors, warhead protectors, rocket-propulsion systems and warheads – for use with advanced 'upper-tier' missile-defence systems. Of primary interest to Japan is the seaborne US Navy Theater-Wide (NTW) system, which could be deployed on the destroyers, though the technologies in theory could also fit the land-based US Army Theater High-Altitude Area Defense (THAAD) system. While neither NTW nor THAAD is likely to be deployable until 2008 at the earliest, and Japan has not firmly committed to deployment, Japan's 2000 budgetary allocation for research and development on TMD was $17m.

Several Asian neighbours, led most vocally by China and North Korea, continued to criticise Japan's involvement in the TMD research programme, while the new defence programme received comparatively little attention. At the same time, regional powers responded quite positively to an earlier Japanese proposal for ships from Japan's coast guard (the Maritime Safety Agency) to join with Asian states' forces in joint patrols against pirates in the Strait of Malacca and other seaways in South-east Asia. Small, low-key but nonetheless creative steps such as this are likely to enable Japan to play a more constructive and politically acceptable role in regional security. Also promising was the three-way summit meeting of Mori, Kim and Jiang in November in Singapore. While this may not presage the start of a new North-east Asian forum, it does at least provide the basis for what will probably become regular dialogues in the margins of the new 'ASEAN+3' format, which will most likely be instituted on an annual basis.

Despite fraught relations with other regional powers, at the end of 2000 Japan looked poised at last to punch its weight in regional and international affairs. Indeed, in early 2000, a high-profile panel of experts presented to Obuchi a lengthy report setting out a vision for the nation's future. They prescribed a Japan that is more open to the world (for instance, using English as a second official language), with a greater stress on individualism and a 'bottom-up' model of governance. The report ends with the caveat that the Japanese should be prepared to devote 'three generations' to creating a new Japan. But it does at least indicate that calls for positive change are coming from within Japan, not just from outside. The key inhibitors of such change are economic stasis and political paralysis.

More Economic Blues

Following a modest two-year rally, Japan's economic troubles revived in 2000. Mergers between big banks in 1999 had suggested that weaknesses in the banking system were being mended, and fresh business investment added encouragement. Negative growth had slowed from -2.6% in 1998 to -1.4% in 1999, and 2.4% growth in the first quarter of 2000 raised hopes for the long-awaited recovery. The benchmark Nikkei 225 index peaked at 20,883.21 on 12 April. These early signs of revival spurred the Bank of Japan to abolish its zero interest rate policy in August 2000. The first rate rise in a decade, it was opposed by Obuchi's Liberal Democratic Party (LDP) and the Ministry of Finance.

In retrospect, the timing was poor. In the second quarter, the stock-exchange boom in Internet stocks was deflating. Although corporate profits did begin to stabilise and even rise, corporate bankruptcies (including household names such as the department store Sogo and the Kyoei insurance company) also accelerated. As a result, the consolidated banks were still saddled with non-performing loans. These signals were too mixed to inspire consumer demand. Consumer spending remained weak, as reflected by the proliferation of '100 yen shops', where all goods were priced at less than one US dollar. By the end of the year, the economy was again stalling: 2000 ended with the Nikkei 225 down 27% on the year

Asia

at 13,785.69, having fallen to its lowest level in more than two years. On 13 March 2001, the index hit a 16-year low. Politicians were once again back to the routine of considering pump-priming supplementary budgets.

Erratic economic policies – Japan has tried everything from stimulus packages to bank bail-outs – have failed to rescue the Japanese economy from its despondency. The boom-and-bust nature of the technology-based 'new economy' also is not conducive to steady recovery. In any case, Japan's adjustment to the new economy has proceeded fitfully: the heavily regulated and subsidised 'old economy' still accounts for about 85% of gross domestic product and 90% of Japan's jobs. In addition, the trauma caused by sweeping anti-protectionist financial reforms undertaken in 1996 has lingered. Though necessary medicine, the so-called 'Big Bang' produced a wave of financial collapses in 1997 and 1998, making it more difficult for deregulation and foreign investment to revive Japan's already depressed economy. One hopeful possibility is that Tokyo's further easing of foreign investment restrictions and trade liberalisation may soon start to pay off in improved economic performance. Foreign direct investment reached a record of $21bn for the year ended March 2000 and is expected to surpass that amount in 2001. The spectre of a US recession and Japan's domestic political uncertainty, however, make this a highly uncertain stimulus to recovery.

Coalition Capers

The economic situation has not been helped by the fractious state of Japanese politics. The coalition that Obuchi had put together in autumn 1999, covering his own LDP, the smaller Liberal Party (LP) led by the maverick Ichiro Ozawa and the revamped *Komeito* party, proved pettily argumentative and wearing. Public support for the partnership steadily declined. Once the budget was passed in mid-March, differing views within the coalition intensified. In particular, the LP favoured calling Lower House elections (which had to be held by mid-October) sooner rather than later; the LDP, hoping for better evidence of an economic recovery, sought delay. Finally, on 1 April, Obuchi lost patience with Ozawa and his LP and decided to throw them out of the coalition. Within a few hours, however, he had collapsed and fallen into a coma from which he was never to recover. The most prominent victim yet of the 'Japanese disease' of overwork, Obuchi died 43 days later.

Subsequently, following backroom negotiations, Yoshiro Mori, then LDP secretary-general, was made Obuchi's successor. Mori headed the third-largest faction and had been a loyal lieutenant of Obuchi, but had very little experience in either economic policy or foreign affairs. With an election due soon he seemed the best short-term solution. His fortunes were boosted by a split within the wayward LP, which led to a number of that party defecting to form a new Conservative Party, which then went back into coalition with the LDP and the *Komeito*. To establish his mandate and capitalise on public sympathy for Obuchi, Mori chose to hold elections on the relatively early date of 25 June – Obuchi's birthday. He proved a less than visionary candidate. On the eve of the election campaign, he asserted that Japan was still 'a divine country', which to many within Japan smacked of the pre-war nationalist rhetoric about the emperor being a god.

More generally, the public was unsure about the state of the economy and Mori's abilities. The election was an anti-climax for all concerned. The LDP took barely 28% of the popular vote and lost 38 seats but nonetheless remained the largest party with 233 seats. Its two allies, the *Komeito* and the Conservative parties, also lost ground to the opposition Democratic Party (DP), the LP and the Social Democratic Party, but combined the three still had sufficient seats for a parliamentary majority. The 62.5% voter turnout – barely above the all-time low of 1996 – suggested that none of the parties provided particularly inspiring images or policies. Political loyalties followed depressingly traditional lines, split between the urban areas that voted for the opposition and the *Komeito* and the rural areas which retained their customary loyalty to the LDP.

In autumn 2000, with the economy still weak and scandals emerging within the cabinet, one of the aspiring LDP leaders waiting in the wings, Koichi Kato, decided to mount a serious challenge to Mori's leadership. Taking advantage of the opposition's intention to force a no-confidence motion against the prime minister in mid-November, Kato went public with his criticism by calling for reform and threatening to vote against Mori. Perhaps recalling Ozawa's abortive and politically costly challenge of the LDP president and prime minister, Kiichi Miyazawa in 1993, around half of Kato's faction and another smaller faction in alliance with him balked at the prospect of voting against the party once they were warned that such action would result in automatic expulsion. Kato lost his nerve and at the last moment announced, tearfully, that he had no option but to reverse course and abstain; the opposition motion was defeated in a raucous, all-night session. But Mori's public-support levels showed barely any improvement, and Kato had lost the confidence of reformists within the LDP and of the public because he had failed to carry through on his promises and his own faction was split. When the cabinet was reshuffled in December 2000, Mori took his revenge by ensuring that neither Kato nor any of those who had abstained in the no-confidence vote obtained posts. While the LDP mainstream had proven sufficiently savvy to fight off the reformists, they had failed to forge any new policies that might appeal to the public in the Upper House election that would have to be held in July 2001. Although he survived a March 2001 no-confidence vote, 138 to 105, Mori's public approval rating was less than 10%.

Asia

Japan's Medium-term Challenge

Mori limped on as prime minister and looked for support where he could get it. In the reshuffled cabinet, he retained the aged Miyazawa as finance minister, despite the economy's lacklustre performance. He also felt it necessary to bring in from the cold another former prime minister, Ryutaro Hashimoto, giving him responsibility for the new administrative-reform portfolio as well as Okinawan affairs. Backroom discussions among LDP leaders and factions intensified over whether to dump Mori or keep him on as the scapegoat for the expected July 2001 electoral setbacks. As a replacement, though political precedent is against the return of former prime ministers, Hashimoto's name was mentioned – perhaps because he stood out as the one dynamic force in Japanese government in the 1990s. He has emerged as leader of the largest LDP faction.

Hashimoto, when prime minister from 1996 to 1998, had introduced proposals for government streamlining and reorganisation, which he finally implemented himself, in his new role, at the beginning of January 2001. They constituted the largest government reorganisation in Japan's post-war history. The number of ministries and agencies were reduced by amalgamation from 23 to 12 plus a new Cabinet Office. Traditional names disappeared. Most importantly, after 130 years, the Finance Ministry changed its Japanese name (although the English translation remained the same). It also, theoretically at least, lost its influence over budget allocation to a new entity known as the Council of Economic and Fiscal Policy, which combined ministers with private sector experts. The intention behind the reforms is to wrest power over devising and implementing government policies from bureaucrats and make politicians more proactive and responsible. In practice, the administrative success or failure of the overhaul will depend on whether barriers between bureaucrats from the former ministries and agencies are broken down in the new mega-ministries and whether politicians competent enough to seize the new opportunities presented by the reforms come to the fore.

Japan remains the world's second-largest economy, a very high defence spender and a major sea power. A post-Cold War domestic consensus appears to be emerging that Japan should aggressively address a more volatile regional balance of power. But the key variable in Japan's immediate strategic future is the precise way in which the Japanese leadership formulates its strategic challenge. Just how extroverted does Japan want to be? It remains important for the country to advance regional diplomacy *vis-à-vis* China and North Korea. To do so, Japan will have to impose limits on the degree to which it supports US policies. Those limits have not been articulated.

There are, however, clear indications that Tokyo intends to capitalise on the Bush administration's rejection of China as a strategic partner by fortifying the US–Japan alliance. In spite of Japan's messy domestic situation and economic woes, Japanese Foreign Minister Yohei Kono moved quickly to establish close diplomatic links with the new American administration, meeting with US Secretary of State Colin Powell less than a week after he took office. Japan has not publicly opposed American plans for national missile defence and has shown resilient interest in TMD, both of which Beijing considers highly provocative. But Japan's present alliance commitments to the United States remain largely logistical, and becoming part of an American TMD net would represent a sea-change in its defence posture. As the time for decision on whether to deploy TMD draws nearer, Tokyo will have to consider more carefully and systematically not only wrenching domestic constitutional questions, but also how far it can accept deteriorating relations with Beijing as the cost of decreasing its vulnerability and reasserting itself militarily.

Ebbing Tensions on the Korean Peninsula

In the worst winter in 50 years, the streets of Pyongyang remain dark at nights, and while starvation may no longer stalk the land as it did five years ago, people still go hungry in some parts of the country. The North Korean economy remains in a parlous state. At the same time, North Korea maintains massive conventional forces and is widely seen as a probable supplier of missiles and weapons of mass destruction to a number of volatile regions around the world.

In South Korea, while the economic recovery after the 1997 crash has continued, the cost has been high. Militant strikers have confronted riot police in protest over massive job losses as a result of forced downsizing and compulsory mergers. Despite the real hardship faced by many in South Korea, there remains a widespread international belief that economic reform in the country has not gone very deep, and that serious problems remain untouched. In addition, while President Kim Dae Jung remains popular abroad, at home there is much criticism of his failure to tackle urgent domestic issues, of his apparent aloofness, and of his alleged softness towards North Korea. For much of the year, normal political

Asia

processes have been paralysed, as the main opposition party, still dominant in the National Assembly after the April 2000 elections, refused to cooperate with the government.

All this has been overshadowed by the summit meeting in June 2000 between Kim Dae Jung and the North Korean leader, Kim Jong Il. A world that had been led to believe that Kim Jong Il was a virtual recluse, watched in amazement as the younger Kim was shown arriving at Pyongyang airport to greet his South Korean guest. He appeared clearly in command, sure of himself, and yet sufficiently deferent towards Kim Dae Jung to show that he was a true Korean, who understood the respect due to age and seniority. There was some amusement at his hairstyle, his clothes and his Cuban heels, but it was obvious that much of the previous speculation about him and his abilities had been wrong. For a brief moment, even the South Korean opposition fell silent, as the two leaders held a series of wide-ranging talks and reached agreements that held out much hope for a reduction of tension on the peninsula. And even if the high hopes of June had not been entirely fulfilled by the end of 2000, there was sufficient progress to indicate that North Korea's new-found openness was not suddenly going to disappear. Whether it signified a deeper commitment to change was another matter.

Heralding a Sea Change

In 2000, the North–South relationship underwent an extraordinary shift and caught the world's attention. There had been little hint of this at the start of the year. Although Kim Dae Jung's government had continually pledged to maintain its 'sunshine' or 'engagement' policy during the previous period, it had come in for much domestic criticism as a result, especially following the naval clashes in the Yellow Sea in 1999. While aid flowed to the North, and there was some trade, no spectacular breakthrough seemed likely. Then in March 2000, Kim Dae Jung made a speech in Berlin that offered assistance to the North, together with a pledge that the South's policy was not aimed at the overthrow of the Northern regime. There was no immediate response from the North, but in April, it emerged that the two sides had almost immediately begun talking, despite continuing public hard-line rhetoric. What was more, they had agreed that the leaders of the two Koreas would meet in the North's capital, Pyongyang, in June.

Such a summit was not in itself a new idea. There had been many proposals in the past for just such a meeting; and as recently as 1994, a summit had been planned between Kim Il Sung and the then South Korean president, Kim Young Sam. Kim Il Sung died before the summit could be held, however, and the two sides relapsed into their customary hostile mode. There was thus understandable scepticism about this latest proposal. Planning continued, nevertheless, and, despite an unexplained one-day postponement just before the planned meeting, on 13 June, Kim Dae Jung flew North in the first direct civil flight between North and South since 1948, to become the first South Korean president to visit North Korea.

From the start, it was Kim Jong Il who dominated the summit. Unannounced, he appeared at the airport to greet his guest, according the older man all the deference Koreans would expect, and over the next few days, he became the unlikely star of the media coverage of the visit. Although the formal talks were conducted on the North Korean side by the nearest equivalent to a head of state, Chairman of the Supreme People's Assembly Kim Yong Nam, Kim Jong Il appeared at several informal sessions. Instead of the unattractive recluse so often depicted in the South Korean and Western media, he proved an accomplished showman, well able to play to the gallery, and aware of what others had said about him.

After two days of talks, both sides pledged in a joint declaration to work for national unification, accepted that there were common elements in each side's proposals about some form of federated state, agreed to work together for a balanced national economy, promised to promote exchanges and cooperation and agreed to work towards further humanitarian exchanges by 15 August, the anniversary of Korea's liberation from Japan in 1945.

All this went further than anybody had expected. The North reported events in a low-key manner, not revealing the more human side of Kim Jong Il. South Korea, which did see this, experienced a brief wave of Kim Jong Il euphoria, especially among the young. This worried many conservatives and the opposition began what was to become an extensive and long-running attack on Kim Dae Jung's policies towards the North. Meanwhile, implementation of the summit agreements began. Red Cross discussions led to two rounds of meetings between separated families. These were stilted affairs, with the North's choice of participants carefully chosen from among the most loyal groups. Attempts to agree on more regular exchanges, with a permanent meeting place, reached an impasse early in 2001; the South wanted the venue to be Panmunjom, while the North held out for the more remote Kumgang mountains.

The June declaration remains in place and both sides remain pledged to fulfil it. Inevitably, however, the pace has been slower than many hoped, and in the South, there is a widespread belief that the North has thus far gained more than the South. Not only has there been continued aid and economic assistance to the North, but the South also agreed to release and repatriate to the North a number of long-term unconverted prisoners. Despite claims to the contrary, the North denied that it held any similar prisoners. In other areas too, the North appeared to be moving more slowly than the South. Work to reconnect the Seoul–Pyongyang railway

Asia

began on the southern side of the Demilitarised Zone, but there was no corresponding work on the northern side. In particular, the North did not begin extracting landmines in the railway corridor on the scheduled date. Talks between military leaders of both sides were held, but again, the South felt that these lacked substance, and in particular, failed to begin the implementation of confidence-building measures that would reduce the military stand-off on the peninsula.

Change Is Slow, but Change There Is

North Korea began 2000 still regarded internationally as a failed state. Although there had been signs from 1998 onwards that the state–party system was beginning to function more normally, most outsiders could detect little indication of fundamental change. The economy continued to decline. Planning, or even an understanding of what was needed, seemed generally absent. The party and state media pumped out praise for Kim Jong Il, and announced the end of a six-year long 'arduous march' since the death of Kim Il Sung in 1994, with huge successes in all areas. It was claimed that these included many new power stations, a new super-highway between the capital Pyongyang and the west-coast port of Nampo, as well as new agricultural ventures.

The reality was a non-functioning industrial base and widespread semi-starvation. The by-now familiar mixture of the long-term consequences of over-intensive farming and bad weather conditions seems to have produced yet another grain shortfall. International agencies felt it necessary to continue to supply food, with the World Food Programme (WFP) still appealing for international aid to help the most vulnerable groups, especially children and pregnant women. After many years of deprivation, North Korean officials now admit that the country's children are well below the body weight of their contemporaries in the South, and probably well below that of their parents and even their grandparents at the same age. Electricity supplies remained precarious, with frequent power reductions even in Pyongyang, and severe deprivation elsewhere. Lack of power not only affects industrial output, but it also means that everything that depends on electricity, from streetcars to clean water supplies and sanitation, functions less efficiently. A bad winter has placed even more demands than usual on a power grid that is badly in need of replacement.

There were few signs that the leadership in the North fully understood how deep the crisis was and at first, little to indicate that they were willing to follow other East Asian socialist countries into market reforms. Even so, the severe economic difficulties were clearly introducing some changes. There were reports of widespread use of the US dollar, and many more *ad hoc* markets seemed to function than had been the case in the past; few foreigners got anywhere near these, however. A campaign to diversify crops to avoid over-dependence on rice was endorsed by Kim Jong Il. This was important, especially as he was making a minor break with his father's policies by encouraging the growth of potatoes. Some of the new farming methods, such as wide-scale levelling of the land to produce bigger and more machine-workable fields, could have a major negative impact on the environment in due course, even if they produce some improvement in the short term.

The rising trend in inter-Korean trade noted in 1999 continued, although the figures were perhaps inflated by counting aid as trade in some cases. According to South Korean government sources, 52% of North Korea's aid in 2000 came from the South, and amounted to $113.76 million, more than double the 1999 figure. A growing number of South Korean companies operated in one way or another in the North, in areas such as garment manufacturing and food production. South Korea's Hyundai Corporation remained the biggest investor in the North, as its founder Chung Ju Yung poured money into the Mount Kumgang tourist venture, and began pushing for the development of a special economic zone, along Chinese lines, at Kaesong, near the Demilitarised Zone.

But even Hyundai was finding it hard to sustain its involvement with the North, as the expected numbers of visitors to the Kumgang mountains failed to materialise. By January 2001, the company was desperately seeking a reduction in the monthly fees it was expected to pay to the North. When the North did not respond, Hyundai unilaterally decided to pay only $6m instead of the agreed $12m for that month's fee. At the same time, Hyundai hoped that its proposed Kaesong development would take off in 2001.

Visits by Kim Jong Il to China in June 2000 and January 2001 seemed to mark a more positive development. On both occasions, his main focus was on technological development and economic experiments. On the second visit, he even went to the Shanghai Stock Exchange, as well as a number of factories, including joint ventures. Initially, the North Korean media only showed Kim meeting Chinese leaders, but they then began to cover the other visits in some detail, thus apparently endorsing the idea that these were good developments, perhaps worthy of imitation. Meanwhile, Chinese aid to North Korea appears to have continued at a high, though undisclosed, level. There were reports that the relative improvement in energy supplies in Pyongyang during winter 2000–01 were the result of Chinese generosity.

The 1994 Agreed Framework between the United States and North Korea, under which the latter agreed to cease its nuclear weapons programme in return for the construction of two light-water reactors, has remained in place, although the date for the completion of the reactors appears to be steadily slipping from 2003 to 2008, or even later. They are

Asia

being built by the Korean Peninsula Energy Development Organisation (KEDO), a consortium led by Japan, the United States, South Korea and the European Atomic Energy Community (EAEC). The North has expressed concern over the delays, and has occasionally said that it may have to restart its own nuclear programme if the terms of the Agreed Framework are not met. The allegations of KEDO's non-compliance are insupportable: as of January 2001, 27 countries had contributed $675m to the project and KEDO had furnished North Korea with $187m worth of heavy fuel oil. International concern about North Korea as a possible missile supplier to volatile areas such as the Middle East remained high and featured in many of the year's diplomatic dialogues. While insisting that they had the right to make and sell rockets – which is technically correct – Pyongyang held to the moratorium agreement made with the Americans in Berlin in September 1999, following the North Koreans' 1998 'satellite launch', that they would not test any further missiles while negotiations were in progress. They appeared, however, to continue exporting missile technology.

Although no comprehensive agreement was reached, the improved atmosphere in the wake of the June summit, plus a throwaway remark by Kim Jong Il to Russia's President Vladimir Putin about his willingness to give up missile development in return for help with space launches, led to unprecedented exchanges with the United States. These included a meeting between the North Korean Foreign Minister Paek Nam Sun and the then US Secretary of State, Madeleine Albright, in Bangkok in October 2000. North Korea sent a leading military figure, Vice-Marshal Jo Myong Nok to the United States from 9–12 October, to be followed, even more astonishingly, by Albright visiting Pyongyang late the same month. The prospect emerged in autumn 2000 of a visit by then US President Bill Clinton to strike a deal, whereby North Korea would agree not to develop, produce or test long-range missiles and to stop exporting all missile technology. The White House, however, judged Pyongyang's ostensible enthusiasm to be a ploy for gaining further international kudos, and a missile deal to be unlikely. Clinton, also distracted by post-election turmoil, stayed home.

With the advent of an administration under President George W. Bush that is far more suspicious of North Korean motives than Clinton, any such deal is likely to be on hold for a considerable time. Indeed, in February 2001 Pyongyang threatened to resume the testing of long-range missiles unless the US engaged in negotiations on a missile agreement and expedited KEDO's construction of the nuclear plants. Moreover, when Kim Dae Jung met Bush in the United States on 7 March 2001, Bush voiced scepticism about North Korea's good faith, based on its refusal to permit on-site verification inspections, to destroy long-range missiles or to provide an inventory of its existing arsenal. Bush therefore indicated that, while Washington continued to embrace Kim Dae Jung's 'vision of peace on the Korean Peninsula', it would not immediately renew discussions with Pyongyang on a missile agreement.

Despite this slight downturn in relations with the US, in other ways 2000 was a good year internationally for the North. It began with the opening of diplomatic relations with Italy, the first G-7 country to make such a move. Soon others were beating a track to Pyongyang. Australia restored relations, broken since 1975, and the Australian Foreign Minister Alexander Downer visited Pyongyang. The Philippines followed, and this seems to have led to a North Korean decision to join the Association of South East Asian Nations (ASEAN) Regional Forum (ARF). Previously, Pyongyang had refused to join, arguing that it wanted to establish or restore relations with all the ASEAN countries before joining the ARF. Myanmar, scene of a 1983 bomb attack on South Korean officials, refused to institute diplomatic relations because the North Koreans had refused to admit responsibility and apologise. In the end, North Korea joined the ARF anyway, ignoring its own precondition.

In December 2000, in a move which caught many by surprise, the UK established diplomatic relations, appointing a *chargé d'affaires* resident in Seoul as a temporary measure. Several other European countries announced that they would follow suit, some accrediting their ambassadors in Seoul to Pyongyang. Such moves reflected South Korean encouragement of greater international engagement with North Korea as much as any new assessment of the North, but it was a remarkable achievement for a previously ostracised state. Kim Jong Il's visits to China and Russian President Putin's visit to North Korea in July 2000 showed that North Korea was also keen to maintain and develop links with older allies. The Russians, for their part, while unable to match Chinese aid generosity, have indicated that they would like to play some role on the peninsula.

Foreign Firsts, Domestic Difficulties

South Korea's recovery from the 1997 Asian financial crisis continued, but Seoul still faced major economic problems. Daewoo Motors went bankrupt in November 2000, the latest in a long line of once-proud companies to be forced to the wall. The remaining industrial conglomerates, the *chaebols*, for years the symbol of the country's economic development, resisted restructuring and modernisation, despite government pressure. The difficulties of the government's position were reflected in its relationship with Hyundai. Whatever the importance of reforming that group, it paled beside the need to keep its North Korean ventures in play, and so pressure to reform was never very strong. Even so, by the beginning of 2001, the high cost of doing business in North Korea was souring Hyundai on the venture.

Politically, Kim Dae Jung's government was in a state of perpetual crisis. Despite a long-standing commitment, Kim failed to begin a proper examination of the National Security Law. The ruling New Millennium Democratic Party did not win an overall majority in the April 2000 National Assembly elections. Eventually, it overcame its difficulties by the somewhat-unorthodox transfer of some of its members to its former coalition partner, the United Liberal Democrats, so that the latter could function as a party in the National Assembly, and thus join with the ruling party to form a majority coalition.

While Kim Dae Jung remained popular abroad and won the Nobel Peace Prize for his efforts to bring peace to the Korean Peninsula, at home he faced mounting criticism from conservatives that he was giving too much away to the North, at vast cost to the South. The reality was that the opposition had no viable alternative policy to offer, but this mattered little in a society where personal loyalty to leaders is more important than principles. Bush's election victory in the United States increased South Korean opposition pressure on Kim Dae Jung.

A Rosier Glow in the East

The South Korean euphoria that surrounded the June 2000 summit has inevitably evaporated as progress on a range of issues has failed to keep pace with the high hopes of the summer. For all his unexpected social and political capabilities, Kim Jong Il remains unpredictable and manipulative. There is room for doubt about how much he has really changed.

Domestic attacks on Kim Dae Jung are bound to intensify as South Korea gears up for a presidential election at the end of 2001. Where South Koreans once feared the cost of a North Korean collapse or of possible reunification, they now equally fear the costs of providing an economic prop to the North. The sunshine policy is imposing heavy costs on South Korea's *chaebols* and their capacity to absorb them is limited. During the run-up to the election, the opposition is likely to press the question of what material dividends the policy has paid. While tearful reunions and the initiation of bilateral relations are appreciable historic gains, the debate may yield a more discriminating cost-benefit approach to South Korea's engagement with North Korea. Washington's support for the sunshine policy could be vital to its survival. Bush may also pressure Seoul to use sticks as well as carrots and impose more stringent conditions on its largesse.

Yet despite all the caveats, the outlook for the Korean Peninsula is better than it has been for many years. The North's economic difficulties continue, but the economic situation has eased. The South still has its own economic problems and a downturn in the international economy would undoubtedly deepen them. Yet South Korea's recovery from the 1997 crash has been remarkable. While the pace of reform in the North may be slow, there are hopeful signs, including Kim Jong Il's apparent new enthusiasm for the Chinese reform model and the prospects for a Kaesong Special Economic Zone. Similarly, the importance of Kim Jong Il's personal involvement in the June 2000 summit should not be underestimated. Problems there may be, but his behaviour in the summer, and his public endorsement of the benefits of outside interest in North Korea and its problems, have put the North Korean leader's personal stamp on the process, which will make it difficult for his lieutenants to step back. Even in the South, the opposition, while protesting at the apparent string of South Korean concessions to the North, has so far failed to provide any real alternative to the process of engagement. Thus, despite being an election year in South Korea, 2001 might see far more progress than could have been predicted a year ago.

Institutional Torpor and Political Debility in South-east Asia

When the nations that founded the Association of South East Asian Nations (ASEAN) agreed in the closing years of the twentieth century to include all South-east Asian nations in their grouping, they hoped that this would aid the development of a coherent regional identity and role. That hope has not been realised. Instead, the enlargement has resulted in institutional paralysis that was particularly noticeable when ASEAN was unable to provide either leadership or aid as East Timor staggered towards independence from Indonesia. To be sure, the devastating economic crisis that swept the area at about the same time as the enlargement was part of the reason, but even the measure of economic recovery that has since occurred has done little to reinvigorate ASEAN. The greater diversity of identities and interests now included in ASEAN and its unwillingness to bend its cardinal rule of non-interference in domestic affairs has left the association unable to address its structural weaknesses. It is now, to an even greater extent than before, tied to the lowest common denominator in managing consensus. In addition, the authority vacuum in Indonesia in the face of its continuing troubles has deprived ASEAN of a locus of leadership and has diminished its international standing.

Asia

Indonesia is hardly alone among South-east Asian countries to have been both hit by economic crisis and to have subsequently demonstrated significant political weaknesses. In the Philippines, misrule by President Joseph Estrada led to his removal from office in January 2001, and in Malaysia, the long-entrenched autocratic government under Prime Minister Mahathir Mohammed was rocked by election losses in January 2001 and has demonstrated shaky underpinnings and a weakening ability to contain ethnic strife. Along with the other difficulties, an upsurge in Islamic militancy in Indonesia, the Philippines and, to an extent, Malaysia, has reinforced the appearance of instability in these countries.

Indonesia: A Vacuum of Authority

President Abdurrahman Wahid took office in October 1999 as the leader of a minority parliamentary party in a climate of promise that has since turned sour. Although admired at first for his shrewd political insights and manoeuvring ability, he has disappointed expectations that he would act as a bridge between the contending Islamic and secular-nationalist traditions. Moreover, political opponents who have links to the regime of former President Suharto and are intent on flouting presidential authority have deliberately fomented sectarian violence. Those bent on discrediting the Jakarta government have made use of Islamic militia known as *laskars* (warriors), who have been engaged in anti-Christian violence, particularly in the Moluccas where some 4,000 deaths have been officially recorded since 1999. Such violence has also spread to Lombok, Sulawesi and Sumbawa. The government's authority, as well as that of the UN, has been flouted in West Timor where three United Nations officials working in refugee camps were murdered in September 2000, while criminal militia gangs have been allowed free rein by the local armed forces. On Christmas Eve 2000, a series of coordinated bomb attacks was launched against churches in 38 locations in Sumatra, Java, Batam and Lombok without any group claiming responsibility.

The distinguishing feature of Wahid's first year or so as president has been his failure to fill the authority vacuum that Suharto left as his political legacy. Wahid's erratic and inconsequential style of government, as well as his greater interest in international travel than in tackling domestic problems, has attracted criticism at home and abroad. Trying to deal with endemic corruption and restoring the rule of law have been beyond the competence of a government that began as a diverse coalition, but was then reshuffled into a more pliable instrument in August 2000, at the cost of alienating the major parliamentary parties. Attempts to bring Suharto to trial and to imprison his youngest son Tommy, who has been convicted of corruption, have degenerated into farce at the expense of the government's credibility, already dented by its inability to identify the source of a series of bombings in Jakarta, especially the September stock-exchange blast that left 15 dead.

In its first few months, Wahid's government appeared to be successfully bringing the armed forces under civilian control. The initial success could not be sustained; a series of senior appointments within the armed forces without the president's sanction reflected rising recalcitrance in the military hierarchy. Wahid had managed in February 2000 to remove from office former armed forces commander and coordinating minister for politics and security, General Wiranto, and had simultaneously arranged the appointment of a reformist general, Agus Wirahadikusumah, as head of *Kostrad*, the army's strategic-reserve command. In July, however, Wirahadikusumah was replaced by General Ryamizard Ryacudu without reference to Wahid or to civilian defence minister, Juwono Sudarsono. The latter was removed from office in August and replaced by Mohamed Mahfud, a relatively unknown constitutional-law professor considered to be controlled by the military élite.

How the wind was blowing could be seen by the actions of Vice-President Megawati Sukarnoputri, who was given responsibility for day-to-day governmental duties in August. Since then she has entered into an alignment with the military establishment as part of a declared bid to replace the beleaguered president, albeit by constitutional means. She could succeed through Wahid's death or incapacity, and either prospect is fairly likely, for he is nearly blind and suffers from a number of debilitating illnesses. Unwilling to wait, some of his opponents raised the prospect of impeachment in August at the annual session of the People's Consultative Assembly to which Wahid is accountable. The effort failed because his opponents were unable to agree on an acceptable replacement, but in February 2001, the assembly censured Wahid over two financial scandals. He was given until May to vindicate himself; if the assembly remains unsatisfied, he is afforded another month to produce a better explanation.

Against a background of political stalemate in Jakarta, the running sore of separatism has continued to test the integrity of the republic, but only at the outer margins of the archipelago. In the two critical cases of Aceh and Irian Jaya (West Papua), the government has only been prepared to offer a form of autonomy sweetened by the offer of a greater share of revenues from the exploitation of natural resources and, in the special case of Aceh, the introduction of the Islamic *Sharia* law. Aceh differs from West Papua by the unity and Islamic identity of its insurgent independence movement. The Indonesian Army has deployed superior force against it, but despite an unrelenting and vicious campaign has been unable to squash the rebels. A truce, described as a humanitarian pause, was concluded in May 2000. It was extended in August and then again in January 2001, but the violence has continued throughout. Negotiations in Geneva have failed to develop any basis for compromise.

In Irian Jaya, where there are significant tribal divisions, opposition to Jakarta has been expressed primarily through political protest centred on raising the banned *Morning Star* independence flag. The security forces have reacted with extreme violence to these manifestations of independent political thinking. In early June, a Papuan People's Congress meeting in Jayapura adopted a resolution reinstating a declaration of independence proclaimed in 1961, while the territory was still subject to Dutch administration.

The independence movement in Irian Jaya celebrated the fortieth anniversary of its formation on 1 December 2000; three days later its counterpart in Aceh was 25 years old. Both movements marked the events with major demonstrations in provincial capitals. Their political alienation persists but without, so far, either movement demonstrating an ability to repudiate the writ of the central government, which is committed to an integral republic. At issue is not the imminent break-up of Indonesia but the prospect of eventual separatist success should central government break down. In spring 2001, the administration in Jakarta was tottering in the face of continuing economic difficulties, further violence in other parts of its widespread dominion and Wahid's entanglement in corruption charges.

The weakness of the central government was shown when tribal antagonisms flared into brutal violence in Borneo in February 2001. The indigenous Dayak tribe, former headhunters and cannibals, turned on Madurese immigrants, intent on driving them out of Central Kalimantan Province. Their victims had been brought to Kalimantan by the government from the Madura Islands of Indonesia, both to relieve the population strain there and to provide labourers for business projects in Borneo that have benefited the armed forces. The Dayaks had never accepted the Madurese, who had been relocated against the wishes of the local population. The ensuing violence claimed over 400 lives; police and military alike were unable to prevent the killing, but tried to gather the Madurese under some protection while preparing to move them back to the Madura Islands. Further violence here and throughout Indonesia can be expected until large-scale political and economic reform is carried out, and this is beyond the capacity of the present government.

The burning national question for the near term is not whether Wahid will go, but when and how. Possibilities include his stepping down voluntarily on the pretext of ill health or his being overthrown by popular demand as Estrada was in the Philippines. A more likely scenario is that political alignments in the People's Consultative Assembly will remain materially unchanged from those prevailing in February 2001 when the convoluted impeachment process was triggered, and that, after rejecting Wahid's justifications in May and June, the assembly would call a special session sometime in the summer to complete the impeachment. Megawati would then take over. A secularist like Wahid, she would face many of the same political and religious pressures, and would probably be even more reluctant to restructure the military. It is also hard to discern palpable differences between Megawati and Wahid on economic policy, though some of her advisers are resolute reformers. And she is likely to be less inclined to negotiate with separatists in Aceh, Irian Jaya and elsewhere. Inevitably, Megawati would be more attentive, more efficient bureaucratically, more responsive to parliament and more competent in diplomacy than her predecessor, but it is difficult to see how her promotion to the presidency would translate into quick improvements in Indonesia's stability.

The Philippines: Impeachment, Kidnapping and Bombings

The Philippines was beset by political crisis in November 2000 when Joseph Estrada became the first president to be impeached by the House of Representatives. He was charged with bribery, betrayal of public trust and violating the constitution for having received income from illegal gambling and provincial tobacco taxes. The 22-member Senate began his trial on 7 December with a two-thirds vote required to remove him from office. Ranged publicly against Estrada was the coalition that toppled the late President Ferdinand Marcos, including former president, Corazon Aquino and Cardinal Jaime Sin.

Estrada was speedily deserted by close congressional allies as well as by Vice-President Gloria Macapagal Arroyo, elected on a different party ticket, who resigned from the cabinet to play a leading role in calling on the president to step down. He denied the charges and tried desperately to hold on to office in the face of compelling evidence of guilt, while uncertainty over the outcome of the protracted constitutional process played havoc with the peso and the stock market, and undermined investor confidence. The denouement came in January 2001 when Estrada's supporters in the Senate managed to gather enough votes to block the examination of bank records, which his opponents insisted would make clear that he had illegally amassed millions of dollars while in office. Estrada's senatorial accusers then stormed out of the impeachment proceedings, the streets of Manila were once again filled with protestors, and leaders of the army transferred their loyalty to Arroyo. With the loss of the military leaders' support, Estrada was finally forced to recognise that he could no longer cling to power.

The impeachment resulted from a conspicuous abrogation of good governance by a president who had returned the Philippines to the base practices of economic cronyism. Paradoxically, Estrada's popularity in the country did not decline dramatically in line with congressional disapproval. His support, based on an appeal to popular grievance at economic inequity, which won over evangelical Christians among others, held up to a point. His political detractors, who have tended to look down on him as a coarse parvenu, have come primarily from the traditional ruling class.

Estrada came into politics after a career as a swashbuckling hero in local films. He revived that role in confronting Muslim insurgency in the south of the country where the separatist Moro Islamic Liberation Front (MILF) had long resisted the writ of the government in Manila. Negotiations and armed confrontation proceeded concurrently until the end of June 2000 when Philippine forces embarked on a major assault on Camp Abubakar, the MILF's military headquarters in Mindanao, which was overrun in early July with heavy casualties on both sides. A second base, Camp Salahuddin, was captured in the middle of the month. Peace talks began, but were suspended in August after the government offered bounties for the detention of the MILF's three most senior leaders.

A more dramatic expression of Islamic militancy was registered by the *Abu Sayyaf* (Father of the Sword) faction, which claims links with co-religionists in Afghanistan and has combined criminal enterprise with a veneer of religious rectitude. In March 2000, the militants kidnapped 51 people in a raid on a school in Basilan Province, releasing 18 of them before ransom negotiations began. The ostensible demand was for the release of three Islamic terrorists detained in American prisons after conviction for their role in the 1993 bombing of the World Trade Centre in New York. The army launched an attack on *Abu Sayyaf*'s base in April and overran it by the end of the month, but without rescuing the bulk of the hostages. A number were rescued in May, while others were exchanged in June for relatives of a rebel leader.

Abu Sayyaf attracted international attention in April 2000, when a Jolo-based group abducted 21 people, including ten foreign tourists from Sipidan, a Malaysian resort-island off the coast of Sabah. The militants combined a public demand for an Islamic state in the south of the Philippines with private insistence on ransom of $1 million per hostage. Unofficial Malaysian intercession did little but provoke tension between Manila and Kuala Lumpur; later a piecemeal process of ransoming the hostages was negotiated with Libya mediating and supplying the ransom money. Having collected the ransoms, *Abu Sayyaf* promptly abducted three more Malaysian hostages in early September from the island of Pandanan off the Sabah coast. This prompted a Philippine military assault in mid-September against the faction's Jolo base, which resulted in a temporary rise in Estrada's national standing. The government's authority had been challenged in May by two bombings in Manila shopping malls attributed to Islamic separatists. At the end of December, a series of five almost simultaneous explosions occurred in Manila, killing 13 and leaving nearly 100 people wounded. The blasts took place just over a week after two *Abu Sayyaf* leaders had been arrested in the capital, including Hector Janjalani, the brother of the late leader of the movement. Government claims in both Manila and Jakarta of an Afghan connection with the coordinated bombings were greeted with scepticism.

New President Arroyo was thus faced with a rumbling rebel insurgency along with the many other serious problems that Estrada had failed to solve. His removal from power gave a welcome boost to the stock market and the peso, both of which had fallen to very low levels in the last days of his rule, but there was still a long way to go to recovery. Arroyo, an American-trained economist with many years of government service behind her, will need all her skill to overcome a budget deficit in 2000 of more than $2.8 billion, more than twice the budget target, a slowing economy and concern that agriculture is facing a bad year. Perhaps the most pressing, and most difficult task will be to tackle corruption and to pass on any improved economic prospects to the poor, who still support the disgraced Estrada. Without some amelioration of their misery, the glow of this latest Philippine 'people's revolution' will soon fade.

Malaysia: Islamic Challenge to the Mould of Politics?

In July 2000, members of the previously unknown *Al-Ma'unah* (Brotherhood of Inner Power) raided two military arms depots in the state of Perak and seized a large quantity of heavy weapons. The episode came to a bloody end when anti-terrorist commandos overran the sect's jungle camp. The bare-faced challenge to the authority of the inter-racial *Barisan Nasional* (National Front) coalition government was quickly quashed and the sect's members were arraigned on charges of treason. While the episode ended speedily, and unquestionably in the government's favour, other problems were less tractable.

A far more significant challenge to the United Malays National Organisation (UMNO), the dominant party in the ruling coalition, has been posed by the Islamic-based opposition *Parti Islam*, which made major inroads into UMNO's Malay constituency in federal and state elections in November 1999, although not enough to displace the government in Kuala Lumpur. A decisive factor in Malay political alienation, especially among the younger voters, has been the seemingly cruel treatment by Mahathir of his former deputy, Anwar Ibrahim, who was convicted and imprisoned for six years in April 1999 on charges of corruption. In August 2000, Anwar was convicted on an additional charge of sodomy and sentenced to a further nine years.

Although *Parti Islam* is committed to an Islamic state, it joined the *Barisan Alternatif* (Alternative Front), the new inter-racial party alignment within the Federal Parliament, mirroring the National Front, which includes the Chinese-based Democratic Action Party. Concerned that his once-unassailable position in Malaysia was under threat, Mahathir spent part of the year consolidating his position within UMNO. His success was demonstrated in May 2000 at the party's General Assembly, where he was re-elected unopposed as president of the party, with his chosen successor, Deputy Prime Minister Abdullah Ahmad Badawi, also elected unopposed as the party's deputy president. After his federal electoral victory in November 1999, Mahathir had indicated that he would not seek a further term of office. In October 2000, however, he announced that he would retire when UMNO was able to place some younger supporters within the ruling inter-racial coalition. Ostensibly to that end, a special General Assembly was convened in November, but a proposal to change the voting system increasing the number of delegates eligible to vote for senior offices within the party was not adopted. Mahathir's attempt to extend the interval between party elections from three to five years also failed.

At the end of October, in a by-election for the Kedah state legislature, a Malay nominee from the opposition National Justice Party (NJP) overcame the National Front's Indian candidate, who had been considered the front runner. There were two significant aspects to this development: the seat had been held by the National Front for the past 40 years, while the NJP had only been formed in April 1999 as a vehicle for campaigning on behalf of the incarcerated Anwar. The predominantly Malay-based NJP had also joined the opposition *Barisan Alternatif*. A major question is whether this looser inter-racial coalition is capable of decisive electoral challenge to the National Front. And if so, whether its dominant Malay party will sustain a long-standing pattern of inter-racial political consensus or press ahead with a theocratic agenda. Mahathir turned 75 in December 2000, still in control, but subject to a growing view within UMNO that he has become a political liability.

Thailand: Elections and Political Disarray?

General elections were held in Thailand on 6 January 2001 under a new constitution intended to eradicate money politics and to stabilise coalition government. The outcome of the polls had been thrown into temporary confusion when the leading prime-ministerial candidate, Thaksin Shinawatra, was found guilty by the National Counter Corruption Commission in late December 2000 of failing to disclose financial assets while deputy prime minister in 1997. The verdict carries a penalty of disbarment from public office for five years. In the event, Thaksin's *Thai-Rak-Thai* (Thai-Love-Thai) Party secured an unprecedented overall majority in the lower house of 500 seats. Appealing to nationalist and populist sentiments during the election campaign, the party railed against economic reforms imposed by the International Monetary fund (IMF), promised to defend debt-laden Thai companies from foreign takeovers, pledged $23,800 to each of Thailand's 70,000 villages and vowed to suspend interest payments on farm indebtedness for three years.

Despite his majority, Thaksin announced his intention of forming a coalition government with two smaller parties. At the same time, he announced that he would not challenge the decision of the Constitutional Court, which reviews the verdicts of the National Counter Corruption Commission. If it upheld the guilty charge, he promised to step down as prime minister and appoint a replacement from the senior ranks of his party. Meanwhile, the Electoral Commission indicated that it intended to investigate up to 100 cases of alleged fraud. This, combined with the possibility that a confirmed guilty verdict on Thaksin would remove a prime minister who had created the majority party in the legislature as a personal political following, has cast a pall of uncertainty over Thai politics. An element of potential instability was added in March 2001, when the prime minister's plane was blown up at Bangkok's Don Muang International Airport, in a possible assassination attempt.

Ongoing border tensions between the armed forces of Thailand and Myanmar remain a dangerous potential source of more intense conflict. Myanmar's forces have instigated ethnic fighting and actively participate in the cross-border narcotics trade. Bangkok is considering the direct use of force against the troops, and may have difficulty avoiding such action if refugee pressures and narcotics flows persist. In February 2001, conflict appeared close to breaking out when the Myanmar seized territory and shelled targets on Thai soil. Thai military observers reported that 10,000 Myanmarese troops were massing across the border to face fewer but better-equipped Thai Border Patrol Police. Both sides mobilised artillery, and the Thais moved in several tanks. Newly appointed Thai Foreign Minister Surakiart Sathianthai indicated firmly that Thai armed forces would protect Thais against hostile Myanmar actions. He also indicated, however, that the new government would seek bilateral negotiations with Yangon, aimed at increasing mutual trust through personal diplomacy, and would try to reopen trade. Thaksin also stated his intention to visit Myanmar, which his predecessor, Chuan Leekpai had not done during three years in office. Thus, there appears to be some scope for improved Thai–Myanmar relations, but it is hard to be too optimistic.

More broadly, Surakiart announced that Thai foreign policy would be conducted in an 'Asian way', whereby Bangkok would adopt a non-confrontational regional focus, rather than the previous administration's unrealistic global approach cued by the US. An important emerging pillar of the new policy appears to be closer relations with China. The new government has three particular goals:

• lowering trade barriers between the two countries;

Asia

- developing a transport network linking northern Thailand and southern China; and
- exploring trilateral cooperation between China, Thailand and Myanmar in areas including drug interdiction and roads.

Unsurprisingly, the Thai government will continue its 'one China' position.

Institutional Torpor

Fortunately, ASEAN's lack of drive has not been tested by any crisis in intra-regional relations. There are some bilateral tensions among a number of member governments, in particular along the border between Thailand and Myanmar, but the region is no longer threatened by a central conflict that might develop into a major clash of arms or attract competing intervention from external powers. Nevertheless, issues of regional concern illustrate the chronic political barriers to regional cooperation. Piracy in the Strait of Malacca, the South China Sea, the Indonesian archipelago and around the Philippines is posing a growing threat to shipping lanes for oil and other vital imports. Japan has called for combined action by Asian coast guards. While regional powers recognised the desirability of cooperation at a meeting of maritime and law-enforcement officials in April 2000 in Singapore, and ASEAN has taken up the issue, sovereignty disputes and China's opposition to offshore Japanese enforcement operations limit the scope for concerted action.

Contending claims to jurisdiction over islets in the South China Sea remain a potential source of confrontation both within ASEAN and between ASEAN states and China and Taiwan. Yet, during 2000, no country tried to occupy any unoccupied parcels, which has been the method countries intent on expansion have used since the late 1980s. In the meantime, interested parties continue to indulge in protracted negotiations over a code of conduct in this area, which is not intended to address the intractable issue of sovereignty but is thought of as a means of confidence-building.

Singapore Foreign Minister Professor S. Jayakumar sought to instil some sense of urgency when he warned the July 2000 annual meeting of ASEAN foreign ministers in Bangkok of the widespread perception that the association is an ineffective 'sunset' organisation, but this had little impact. In the event, the joint communiqué that emerged from the meeting was a diplomatic masterpiece, totally lacking political substance. It was notable only for the collective expression of support for the territorial integrity of Indonesia. ASEAN's ambitious aim to be 'a concert of South-east Asian nations' was not advanced beyond once again approving a formula for preventive diplomacy that had conspicuously failed in the case of Cambodia after the coup of July 1997.

Following an initiative among heads of government at an informal ASEAN summit in Manila in November 1999, a meeting took place in Bangkok of ASEAN foreign ministers with counterparts from China, Japan and South Korea in an extension of the ASEAN+3 formula. At the annual ministerial meeting of the ASEAN Regional Forum (ARF), also held in Bangkok in July, North Korea participated for the first time. The ASEAN+3 constellation was a response to economic crisis and the failings of Asia-Pacific Economic Cooperation (APEC). The cooperation has been functional and of an incremental kind; it has been sustained mostly by rhetoric about closer political and economic ties between South-east and North-east Asia, with China's Prime Minister Zhu Rongji even raising the prospect of an East Asian Forum. Underlying the trend towards a new alignment is a concern among South-east Asian governments that the economic centre of gravity, as reflected in the pattern of foreign investments, has shifted to North-east Asia.

Singapore provided the most vocal concern at the direction things were moving. Prime Minister Goh Chok Tong pointed to the danger of ASEAN being eclipsed by the proposed wider East Asia grouping, while Senior Minister Lee Kuan Yew made a characteristic call for the United States to sustain its crucial role as the counterweight to China's prospective formidable economic power in order to ensure that other Asian economies had scope for growth. One example of that balancing role was the historic visit by former US President Bill Clinton to Vietnam in November. His ecstatic reception by younger Vietnamese, in particular, gave the ageing leadership of the country's conservative Communist Party serious cause for political concern.

Indonesian President Wahid's criticism that Singapore only wanted to develop relations with China appeared incongruous in context. His remarks almost certainly reflected Indonesia's resentment at its diminished international standing, as well as Wahid's personal pique at a wholly unsubstantiated report that Lee Kuan Yew had commented on the likelihood of the Indonesian president's tenure being limited. Wahid's initiative in November to establish a West Pacific Forum comprising Indonesia, Papua New Guinea, Australia, New Zealand, East Timor and the Philippines, ostensibly to counter separatism, suggested an ill-considered attempt to raise Indonesia's diplomatic profile. The Australian government, in particular, was not in a position to demur at the initiative given its priority in the wake of its East Timor intervention of restoring a working relationship with Jakarta. Nonetheless, the undertaking has the potential to weaken further the cohesion of both ASEAN and the Pacific Islands Forum.

Despite its weaknesses, ASEAN is expected to expand further to bring all South-east Asian states under its wing. Jose Ramos-Horta, the minister for foreign affairs in the East Timor Transitional Authority, has indicated a strong interest in the embryo state joining the association when the United Nations tutelage ends in September 2001. Although accepting East Timor as a member would unify all South-east Asia within ASEAN, it has become a unity that lacks political substance, and the grouping is decreasingly able to speak credibly with one voice. The continuing role of the Asia-Pacific-wide ARF in security matters and the development of the ASEAN+3 arrangement for economic cooperation, together with the greater diversity of interests that have been absorbed with ASEAN's enlargement, mean that South-east Asia's relevance as a strategic entity has been seriously reduced.

South Asia: Activity Without Progress

Though rocked by a devastating earthquake in February 2001, the domestic scene in India has been relatively stable in 2000–01. Economic performance, while short of expectations, has not been disastrous. Indian Prime Minister Atal Behari Vajpayee, to be sure, faces ongoing political challenges in controlling the 23 parties of his ruling coalition, in mollifying the Hindu-nationalist ideologues in his own *Bharatiya Janata* Party (BJP) and generally in balancing secular against religious interests. Nevertheless, he has been able to meet these challenges effectively. State elections, which are due in 2001, could test the BJP in various places – particularly in Uttar Pradesh, where Vajpayee raised ethnic tensions in December 2000 by endorsing the building of a Hindu temple on a site where Hindu zealots had earlier destroyed a mosque. This apparent tilt toward religious intolerance concerned his secular allies. But while the BJP may be susceptible to splits, most of its competitors in India's fractious polity are equally vulnerable.

In March 2001, journalists from the Internet magazine *tehelka.com* released videotapes obtained in their own sting operation of Indian bureaucrats, politicians and generals taking cash bribes in exchange for favourable defence-procurement decisions. BJP party president Bangaru Laxman was filmed accepting the rupee equivalent of $2,175. Laxman, Defence Minister George Fernandes, and *Samata* Party president, Jaya Jaitley all resigned. The scandal was particularly egregious, as indicated by the resignation of Fernandes, until then one of the most powerful figures in government. Some opposition politicians hailed the revelation as the beginning of the end for the BJP's coalition. But government corruption is common in India and the public is so accustomed to it that tainted politicians often win elections. Indeed, some observers merely wondered why Laxman had accepted such a small bribe. As the government vowed to investigate and impose severe discipline on anyone determined to have behaved improperly, the coalition appeared to hold. On balance, it remains unlikely that India will encounter any serious disruptions to its basic democratic stability in the medium term.

Pakistan, under military rule since General Pervez Musharraf ousted Nawaz Sharif in October 1999, is by far the more precarious state. While the failure of Sharif's corrupt civilian government and its predecessors to run the country effectively laid the groundwork for Pakistan's present political predicament, Musharraf has not been an improvement. He has not produced the economic reforms that would permit the International Monetary Fund (IMF) to guarantee robust or uninterrupted support, notwithstanding approval of a $596 million 10-month stand-by loan in November 2000. The budget deficit for fiscal year 1999–2000 was 6.4% of gross domestic product and debt service constituted more than 50% of the budget. Furthermore, Pakistan's economic problems are deeply structural: an inefficient tax system and narrow tax base, undiversified exports, massive public and private debt and low human capital. To take just one example, collected taxes fell eight billion rupees ($154m) short of the budgetary target in 1999–2000; traditionally less than 1% of people actually pay tax. Though Musharraf is trying to downsize government and improve tax enforcement, at least in the short and even the medium term such problems are substantially irremediable.

Pakistan's political prospects are also fraught. In 2000, over a dozen civilians resigned or were dismissed from national or provincial cabinets; hundreds more of Musharraf's political opponents have been imprisoned or otherwise marginalised under the government's 'accountability' law. Islamic extremists have become more sceptical about the government's piety. At the end of 2000, Islamabad did launch a tightly controlled democratic experiment, consisting of 'non party' local-government elections in 18 of Pakistan's 106 districts, to be followed by staggered elections elsewhere over the subsequent six months, provincial elections in summer 2002, and federal elections before the end of October 2002. This programme raised suspicions that Musharraf was more interested in maintaining a firm grip on who was elected than in establishing democracy. The six-day delay in announcing results added fears of outright vote-rigging.

Finally, Musharraf has to contend with internecine difficulties. Like Pakistan itself, the Pakistani military is becoming increasingly polarised between secular and Islamist groups. Musharraf is thus forced to straddle the two camps. While he and his inner circle are secularists, he is politically unable to flout the will of the Islamist forces within the military. Thus, Pakistan's succour to the *Taleban* regime in Afghanistan increased in 2000. On balance, Musharraf has been unable to do much to dispel the impression that Pakistan is close to being a nuclear-armed 'failed state' run by an ever more insular yet disempowered cohort of generals.

Is Nuclear Deterrence Stabilising?

India's and Pakistan's domestic situations have produced neither wonderful news nor great shocks. But their troubled bilateral relationship continues to be a rapidly evolving test-bed for nuclear deterrence theory. Immediately after the May 1998 nuclear tests by India and Pakistan, officials in both countries expressed optimism that stability and rationality would soon emerge from their nuclear stand off. Affirming these intentions, Vajpayee made a bold visit to Pakistan in February 1999. At the symbolic venue of the Minar-i-Pakistan in Lahore, the site where Pakistan's founding father declared the need for a separate homeland for the subcontinent's Muslims, Vajpayee penned the following lines into the distinguished visitors' guest-book:

> I wish to assure the people of Pakistan of My Country's deep desire for lasting peace and friendship. I have said this before, and I will say it again: A stable, secure and prosperous Pakistan is in India's interest. Let no one in Pakistan be in doubt about this. India sincerely wishes the people of Pakistan well.

With the Lahore summit, the argument that some, like neo-realist Kenneth Waltz, have advanced that offsetting nuclear-weapon capabilities are conducive to stability and peace seemed applicable to the subcontinent. Appearances, however, can be deceptive. While Vajpayee was writing the above lines, two brigades of the Pakistani Army were preparing to scale the heights above Kargil in a daring effort to seize territory on India's side of the Line of Control dividing Kashmir. Sharif's government claimed that the aggressors were Kashmiri 'freedom fighters' acting on their own initiative, but voiced support for their efforts. India, which ordinarily patrolled the rugged area only in warmer months, was taken by surprise. In any event, the subsequent high-altitude eight-week war in the summer of 1999 was a potent reminder that the threat of massive retaliation is insufficient to prevent – and might even encourage – violence at lower levels.

The Kargil War, like the 1990 crisis in Indo-Pakistan relations, included threats of escalation and increased readiness rates for Indian and Pakistani nuclear forces. Both sides have often claimed the ability to monitor accurately the status of nuclear forces in crises, but such claims leave much room for doubt. Moreover, the failure of Indian intelligence to anticipate Pakistan's breach of the Line of Control has negative implications for crisis stability in a potential nuclear confrontation, as does the Pakistani military's apparent circumvention of civilian authority in planning the operation. To the extent that monitoring exists, it is based primarily on human intelligence sources, which can be unreliable. Moreover, the record of high-level crisis communications between Indian and Pakistani political and military leaders is far from reassuring.

Throughout 2000, India and Pakistan continued to be pulled between the two poles of Lahore and Kargil. For most of the year, firing across the Line of Control reached intense levels, a ritualistic signalling of vigilance in the aftermath of the Kargil campaign. During June and July, however, Pakistan initiated an unpublicised cessation of artillery fire, seeking to resume the bilateral talks suspended after Kargil. Then, starting in November, India and Pakistan publicly traded cease-fire and troop pullback announcements. Political leaders once again made favourable references to the composite peacemaking approach spelled out in Lahore. These oscillations provided both supporters and sceptics of the stabilising properties of nuclear deterrence with plenty of supporting evidence to assert their claims.

Priorities, Opportunities and the CTBT

The nuclear balance of forces and capabilities on the subcontinent is opaque, as expected for nuclear-weapon states early in the development and acquisition cycles. By the end of 1999, the most detailed non-governmental assessment of fissile material stockpiles in South Asia credited India with the means to make 65 nuclear weapons and Pakistan to make 39. Word has leaked out, however, that India used reactor-grade plutonium for one of its detonations, suggesting that its nuclear potential – as well as that of any other similarly inclined state with a civilian nuclear power industry – is greater than anticipated. The relative balance in nuclear capabilities on the subcontinent was further clouded by press reports in June 2000 asserting Pakistani advantages in missiles, nuclear weaponisation for missiles, and command-and-control arrangements.

While Pakistani officials assert that they do not intend to compete with India in nuclear weapons, they have certainly invested heavily in doing so. Pakistan's military oversees duplicate nuclear and missile laboratories. Moreover, Pakistani officials have defined minimal nuclear deterrence in relative, not absolute, terms: if India increases its nuclear and missile capabilities, Pakistan's requirements would be adjusted accordingly.

Pakistan does not seek to maintain nuclear parity with India and probably could not do so. Instead, it wants to establish a credible operational capability that India must take seriously. This Islamabad can most likely accomplish. Although India's nuclear infrastructure and financial means are far greater, Pakistan's military programmes, especially the nuclear and missile ones, have first call on available resources. Islamabad's ability to compete with New Delhi is constrained less by finances than by difficulties with supply and production lines. India's more complex political and military circumstances (and ambitions) pose a more demanding problem. In particular, New Delhi will establish requirements against Beijing's strategic modernisation programmes as well as against Islamabad's.

US dealings with Beijing and Pyongyang in 2000 have affected Pakistan's external sources of supply. North Korea, one previous source, is engaged in talks with the United States for meaningful stakes; these talks could be short-circuited by new proliferation-related transactions with Islamabad. China – another past supplier – has repeatedly promised not to continue to be one. These promises could be broken, however, especially if an old friend once again asks Beijing for help with production problems.

During the past twelve months, both India and Pakistan have maintained a moratorium on nuclear testing. In January 2000, Pakistan's foreign minister, Abdul Sattar, promoted the idea of Pakistan signing the Comprehensive Test Ban Treaty (CTBT) before India, perhaps to repair his military government's relations with Washington and to constrain New Delhi's options for future testing. But this initiative was dropped after receiving no public support from Chief Executive Musharraf and intense opposition from religious parties.

Throughout 2000, the Vajpayee government in India professed a sincere interest in seeking a domestic consensus to sign the CTBT on the grounds that no new tests were needed. These efforts appeared less than purposeful, however, and never came to fruition in the *Lok Sabha*, the Indian parliament. The rejection of the CTBT by US Senate Republicans in 1999 drained the US leverage on this issue. At the same time, a small but influential lobby within India began to beat the drums for at least one more test, expressing scepticism about the government's claims of a successful thermonuclear explosion. If the Indian government equates thermonuclear weapons with deterrence of China, domestic gain and international status, there is a small chance that nuclear testing could be renewed during the US administration of George W. Bush.

Nuclear Doctrine: Still Vague on Both Fronts

As Indian and Pakistani missile programmes moved forward, the year was punctuated by missile flight tests. In September, Pakistan announced serial production of the *Shaheen* 1 with an advertised, and perhaps exaggerated, range of 750 kilometres. An extended-range version is expected in due course. In January 2001, as China's second-ranking leader, Li Peng, was concluding his visit to New Delhi, India flight-tested an 'operational configuration' of the *Agni* 1 medium-range ballistic missile. The *Agni* 2's range places within reach the southern Chinese cities of Chengdu and Kunming. The *Agni* 2 also puts fixed targets throughout Pakistan at risk. A longer-range variant of the *Agni*, capable of reaching Beijing, is expected. No warhead has yet been developed, however.

Pakistan's leaders express confidence in the survivability of their nuclear deterrent, while making the non-deployment of nuclear forces a central component of their proposed strategic restraint regime. Pakistan's airfields, missile-production facilities and bases are limited in number and their geographical coordinates are generally known. The extent to which critical targets on the subcontinent (and elsewhere) have become visible was amply demonstrated in 2000, when the Federation of American Scientists published over the Internet commercial-satellite images of missile garrisons near Sargoda, Pakistan and Sikanderabad, India.

Pakistan publicised in general terms its command-and-control organisational arrangements in February 2000, but neither Islamabad nor New Delhi provided greater clarity with regard to nuclear doctrine and force requirements. Pakistan's military leaders are said to have formulated a doctrine, but have chosen not to publicise it in 2000. The Vajpayee government has been content to leave in the public domain a draft nuclear doctrine developed by an eclectic group of government-appointed advisors, while noting that their report had no official sanction. India's strategic depth provides many advantages, including an assured second-strike capability. Throughout 2000, Pakistani officials steadfastly rejected India's 'No First Use' declaratory posture. On several occasions during the year, high-ranking Indian officials – but not the prime minister – publicly distanced government policy from the advisory group's endorsement of prompt retaliatory capabilities and high launch-readiness.

India, Pakistan and China have officially declared fealty to the concept of minimal nuclear deterrence, while noting that its implementation would depend on the actions of others. New Delhi, Islamabad and Beijing have formidable challenges ahead, seeking three-cornered stability in a region where missile and nuclear programmes serve weighty symbolic and political purposes. An arms race is unlikely, but an arms competition appears unavoidable as long as all three countries determine nuclear force requirements in relative rather than absolute terms. To complicate matters further, the prospective deployment of a national missile defence system by the United States may prompt increases in Chinese strategic nuclear forces beyond those already planned under Beijing's modernisation programme. Such a development could have knock-on effects on India and Pakistan.

Asia

Diplomacy: Regional Stasis, Global Progress

The search for stability, reassurance and nuclear risk-reduction between India and Pakistan was stymied by the absence of official talks during 2000. After Kargil, New Delhi froze relations with Pakistan, seeking to isolate the Musharraf government and to highlight Pakistan's support for militant groups operating from its soil. Indeed, at the beginning of 2000, New Delhi pursued a campaign to label Pakistan a terrorist state. New Delhi has linked the resumption of dialogue on nuclear issues to significant and demonstrable changes in Pakistan's support for militancy. India also announced a defence-budget increase of 13.8% on 28 February 2001. Both are clear indications of the Vajpayee government's priorities.

Nuclear risk-reduction and stability talks between India and China were frozen during 2000 for different reasons: officially, Beijing refuses to compromise on the subject of India's nuclear tests and is unwilling to talk to India about them in any way that might suggest equality. Beijing has agreed, however, to undertake a wide-ranging strategic dialogue with New Delhi, and Indian officials hope that nuclear issues will be included. Talks to demarcate the least-contentious sector of the border between India and China have made progress, with an exchange of maps in November 2000. Officials from the Indian Ministry of External Affairs are upbeat on this front, an outlook not shared by the Minister of Defence and army leaders.

The central diplomatic developments during 2000 were former US President Bill Clinton's trip to the region in March, visits to New York by Vajpayee and Musharraf to attend the United Nations Millennial Summit in September, and Vajpayee's subsequent state visit to Washington. Clinton's visit to the region, the first by a sitting president in 22 years, provided unmistakable evidence of Washington's India-centric approach to the region. The first Clinton term had followed a 'Pakistan first' approach that alienated India without changing Pakistan's policies. At the outset of the second term, Clinton shifted to an 'India first' posture, which was chilled by New Delhi's surprise tests of nuclear devices.

The freeze in Indo-US relations following the 1998 nuclear tests was thawed by an extended dialogue between Deputy Secretary of State Strobe Talbott and Minister of External Affairs Jaswant Singh. The net result of this dialogue was considerable movement by the United States while India kept its options open. President Clinton's long-sought visit – ironically, prompted by a pledge given to then Pakistani Prime Minister Sharif in return for the army's climb-down from Kargil – was a striking success in India and a humbling experience for Pakistan. Clinton struck grace notes and played down nuclear issues in India. In sharp contrast, he spoke in blunt terms during his brief visit to Islamabad. In Clinton's national television address in Pakistan, he said that 'democracy cannot develop if it is constantly uprooted before it has a chance to firmly take hold'. Alluding to Pakistan's heavy political and military support of the *Taleban* in Afghanistan and for Kashmiri terrorists, he also asked 'Pakistan to intensify its efforts to defeat those who inflict terror'.

The decision on whether to visit Islamabad and its military leader was played out in extended, semi-public fashion, centring around security concerns for the presidential party. Clinton's decision to make only a brief stopover and the extraordinary safety precautions taken were bitter pills to swallow for an old ally on the frontlines of the Cold War. For Pakistan's leaders, however, this was still better than no stopover at all. The Millennial Summit in New York provided further evidence of the widening gulf between India and Pakistan in terms of international status. Vajpayee's trip, shortened by ill health, was a triumphant recognition of India's new status in the United States, culminating in a huge state dinner attended by distinguished representatives of the politically active Indian-American community. Musharraf, who also participated in the Millennial Summit, did not receive an invitation to visit Washington, and his plane trip home was diverted back to the United States because of a bomb threat.

To the consternation of Russia and Iran as well as of the US, Pakistan is the sole state supporter of the *Taleban* in Afghanistan, who host the international terrorist Osama bin Laden. That support aims to promote a sympathetic *Pushtun*-dominated government in Kabul, which would afford Pakistan strategic depth *vis-à-vis* India and ensure trade and pipeline access to Central Asia. In December 2000, the UN Security Council passed Resolution 1333, which imposes strict UN arms and anti-drug sanctions against the *Taleban*. The resolution, which became effective on 19 January 2001, is likely to force some tough decisions in Islamabad. While Washington may be apprehensive that an isolated Pakistan would be more inclined sell its nuclear technology, the Bush administration is still likely to insist that Islamabad enforce the sanctions. Yet Pakistani champions of the *Taleban*'s *jihad* have become increasingly vociferous. Thus, Musharraf will have to balance key elements of Pakistan's regional security policy as well as domestic political realities against the need to secure the American diplomatic favour that is essential to its economic survival. Musharraf could encourage the *Taleban* to compromise and form a coalition government, but moderates within the *Taleban* are unlikely to hold sway.

The Extended Tragedy of Kashmir

Indo-US relations travelled a considerable distance from the nuclear detonations in May 1998 to the toasts exchanged by Clinton and Vajpayee on the White House lawn in September 2000. One consequence of this journey was New Delhi's willing acceptance of a US role in 'facilitating' a resolution of the Kashmir dispute.

Prior to the summer of 2000, it was dangerous for any Kashmiri leader to even suggest the possibility of a cease-fire; by the autumn, it was quite acceptable to support such initiatives. This breakthrough was largely due to a short-lived July 2000 cease-fire announced by Abdul Majid Dar, the *Hizbul Mujahedeen*'s top commander based in Kashmir. Dar's announcement of the unconditional, three-month long cease-fire was reportedly preceded by private discussions with Indian government officials. There has been much speculation about Dar's motivations. When interviewed in December, he explained his reasoning as being: 'The militancy cannot throw out the army and the army cannot eradicate the militancy. Because of this, there has to be a political solution'.

Whatever his reasons, Dar's audacious and popular initiative caused consternation in Pakistan and in Kashmir. The *Hizbul Mujahedeen* is Kashmir's largest and most indigenous militant group. Its readiness to accept an unconditional cease-fire undercuts the position of 'guest' militants and their Pakistani hosts. Indeed, if the *Hizbul Mujahedeen* were prepared to suspend *jihad*, and if it were in tune with public sentiment, then on whose behalf would militancy continue to be waged? Leaders of the All Parties *Hurriyat* Conference (APHC) – political dissidents receiving strong backing from Pakistan – were now suddenly stuck with an outdated stance. Dar's initiative also caught Kashmiri Chief Minister Farooq Abdullah in an awkward position. His theatrical initiative in June to pass a bill calling for Kashmiri autonomy – and its subsequent, summary dismissal by the Indian cabinet – were now overtaken by events.

No one reacted with distinction to Dar's initiative. The Indian government called for a suspension of military activities against the *Hizbul Mujahedeen* but not other militant groups, an impossible operational plan for the security forces to execute. The *Hurriyat* Conference initially responded that the cease-fire was decided 'in desperate haste' and that there should have been more groundwork before such a consequential act. After extensive consultations, the APHC leadership offered qualified endorsement of the initiative while rejecting any effort to marginalise its role.

The Pakistani government chose not to respond publicly to Dar's cease-fire, saying only that it was a Kashmiri matter. Nor did it publicise its own cease-fire initiative along the Line of Control. In the days after Dar's announcement, the *Hizbul Mujahedeen*'s Supreme Commander based in Pakistan, Syed Salahuddin, became the object of considerable attention. Pakistan-based militant groups repudiated the cease-fire and expelled the *Hizbul Mujahedeen* from the United *Jihad* Council, which Salahuddin chaired. The *Jammat-i-Islami*, Pakistan's largest religious party and the *Hizbul Mujahedeen*'s parent political organisation, severed ties with its wayward progeny.

Salahuddin emerged in Islamabad 11 days after Dar's announcement, calling for tripartite talks to resolve the Kashmir dispute. Two days later, *Hizbul Mujahedeen* representatives met with Indian officials in Kashmir, laying down a twelve-point agenda, including the withdrawal of security forces and release of political prisoners. Then on 8 August, 15 days after Dar's announcement, Salahuddin reappeared in Islamabad to announce the withdrawal of the cease-fire offer. This could be reconsidered, he said, if New Delhi would agree to tripartite talks with Pakistani officials and Kashmiris or would consent to conducting a UN-sponsored plebiscite. With the unravelling of Dar's initiative, artillery shelling resumed with a vengeance along the Line of Control.

In retrospect, the summer's abortive cease-fire proved to be a useful trial run. On 17 November, the *imam* of Old Delhi's Jama Masjid, the largest mosque in India, publicly called for India and Pakistan to observe a cease-fire during the holy month of *Ramadan*. On 19 November, the Indian government followed up with precisely this initiative, applicable now to all militant groups. Pakistani authorities wrestled with this move, then responded positively on 2 December, announcing a cease-fire along the entire Line of Control. They also dropped their initial insistence on three-party talks. On 20 December, and again on 23 January and 22 February 2001, the Indian government extended the cease-fire for month-long periods. The APHC was now more supportive of a suspension of violence, offering to visit Pakistan to convey indigenous views to Pakistani and militant leaders.

Attacks over the winter by 'guest' militant groups based in Pakistan continued in spectacular fashion, however. The aim of suicidal acts of violence, such as the *Lashkar-e-Taib* group's assault on Srinagar airport in January 2001, was clearly to disrupt further steps in a peace process. The rhythms of violence in Kashmir, as in other places long afflicted by the politics of the gun, are predictable: good news on the political front generates bad news for local hospitals. In this sense, dramatic acts of violence by largely non-indigenous groups constitute a perverse sign of progress in the normalisation of Kashmiri political life.

The extent to which positive developments will gain traction against continued attempts to disrupt peacemaking depends largely on domestic and bureaucratic politics in India and on calculations of national interest among Pakistan's military leadership. An Indian government led by Vajpayee is both well-positioned to pursue bold initiatives and susceptible to pressure from Hindu chauvinists opposed to compromise. In year-end reflections, Vajpayee again appeared to be tacking towards diplomacy: 'A self confident and resilient nation does not postpone the inconvenient issues of yesterday to a distant tomorrow'. On Kashmir, Vajpayee wrote that, 'both in its external and internal dimensions, we shall not traverse solely on the beaten track of the past. Rather, we shall be bold and innovative designers of a future architecture of peace'. These are remarkable words, coming less than one year after travelling to the Minar-i-Pakistan and then being singed at Kargil. They come with a catch: Pakistan must back away from supporting militancy.

Is the Pakistani army leadership capable of reassessing a Kashmir policy that is now doing severe economic, social, political and diplomatic damage to the nation? The military's principal means of leverage over its Indian counterparts and on diplomatic outcomes – support for militancy – has backfired. Every violent act by groups that operate freely in Pakistan places its army and the entire country in a terrible light – especially in the context of cease-fire initiatives by the Indian government. Acts of violence by militant groups are also increasingly contrary to Kashmiri sentiment.

The wellbeing of Pakistan now requires a fundamental reassessment of its Kashmir policy. Islamabad's unconditional support for a cessation of violence along the Line of Control and other moves over the winter could be explained either as tactical manoeuvres or as the opening gambits of a new policy. Disruptive acts of violence by militants who have crossed the Line of Control before the cease-fires came into effect provide insufficient insight into the thinking of Pakistani army leadership. The extent of infiltration and level of violence in the spring and summer of 2001 will clarify matters. The army has no public mandate to shut down the religious schools, or *madrassas*; but it could stop facilitating infiltration and it could shut down the *jihad* training camps.

While India and Pakistan have made surprising progress in moving from Kargil back to Lahore over the winter months, political backsliding and tragic interventions are staples of this dispute. Kashmir provides few clear storylines beyond the extended tragedy of the past 11 years. Many important developments are shrouded in mystery, including acts of bloodshed, shady economic transactions tied to militancy and counter-militancy, and abrupt changes in political stances.

Under these circumstances, it is far easier to identify key indicators of the future course of events in Kashmir than to predict outcomes. Those indicators include the level of firing and the extent of infiltration across the Line of Control; the level of violence in Kashmir carried out by militant groups based in Pakistan; and the willingness of the Indian government to allow further normalisation in Kashmiri politics, such as permitting dissident leaders to travel and to conduct public rallies. New state-wide elections will be held in late 2001 or 2002. If New Delhi takes steps to encourage dissidents to compete in elections, such as by accepting outside election monitors, an internal Kashmiri peace process will continue. If, however, the Pakistani army leadership still believes that militancy provides leverage, an external peace process will not fare very well in 2001.

A Coming Year of Uncertainty

At least publicly Bush appears inclined to follow Clinton's lead in South Asia. The new administration did, however, tone down its anti-proliferation position with respect to both countries, courting India diplomatically and focusing its harshest criticism on Pakistan for its support of Islamic extremists in Afghanistan and Kashmir. The Bush administration may capitalise on the warming of US–Indian relations by lifting economic sanctions imposed on India in 1998. Of the two countries, India has been the coolest towards the possibility of international mediation on the Kashmir issue and has arguably shown the least transparency on nuclear policy. Lifting sanctions may position Washington to exercise greater influence over both Kashmir and the broader problem of stabilising nuclear deterrence in South Asia.

Owing to Pakistan's dicey political and economic state, Washington is likely to continue to hedge its interest in Pakistan with a more enthusiastic engagement of India, as it did during the Clinton administration. Washington opposes Islamabad's support for the *Taleban* for a variety of reasons – the group's massive human-rights violations, its support for Islamic terrorists, its anti-Semitic position – and is therefore likely to pressure Islamabad to enforce UN sanctions against the *Taleban*. Pakistan remains a traditional ally of sporadic strategic importance to the US. Moreover, it is a nuclear power whose further economic and political instability would increase risks to regional security. Thus, Washington will generally support bilateral and multilateral assistance to Pakistan, encourage Musharraf to democratise more aggressively and urge Islamabad to lower tensions and prevent provocations in Kashmir.

Unfortunately, 2001 promises to be a year of great uncertainty. Long-frozen positions have begun to thaw, creating opportunities as well as dangers. Amid such unusual fluidity, quite different alternative futures could begin to play out. A process of reconciliation in Kashmir could be fostered, or there could be new cycles of violence, despair and cynicism. Relations between India and Pakistan could warm further, or there could be renewed exchanges across the Line of Control between the Indian and Pakistani armies. Alternatively, the storyline unfolding in 2001 could include all of these chapters in search of an ending.

Asia

Africa

The new millennium has not blessed Africa. A destructive mix of natural and man-made disasters made 2000 a negative year for most of the continent. To create sustainable growth and enable Africa to escape from poverty, it needs at least a 6% aggregate growth rate for a period of ten years. In 1999, Africa's growth dropped below the 3% of the previous two years and in 2000 it may have fallen even lower. The HIV/AIDS pandemic is as bad as the predictions. According to a United Nations study issued in July 2000, 25.3 million Africans are infected with HIV/AIDS, almost three-quarters of the worldwide total. The UN reported a slight decline in new infections in 2000, but estimated that the worst-hit countries will suffer a 15–20% decline in national wealth as a result of AIDS. Of the 100,000 people killed as a direct result of armed conflict during the year to August 2000, over 60% were sub-Saharan Africans. According to the UN High Commissioner for Refugees (UNHCR), there were roughly 4.2m refugees and internally displaced people in Africa at the end of 1999. Natural disasters also took their toll in 2000. In Mozambique, floods destroyed villages and crops and swept away roads and other infrastructure. In the Horn of Africa and Kenya, drought killed livestock and devastated agriculture.

The hoped-for leadership of sub-Saharan Africa by the heavyweight countries – South Africa and Nigeria – has disappointed. President Thabo Mbeki of South Africa, trying to spearhead a revival of the continent through promoting a concept of an African renaissance, lost credibility by suggesting that AIDS was not caused by HIV, an impression he later corrected. He lost more credibility by taking a private, and apparently soft, line in registering concern with President Robert Mugabe of Zimbabwe over his policy of seizing white farmland by force. It failed to have any effect. There may be more problems ahead for South Africa since its economy, though stable, is not growing at a rate sufficient to fulfil the expectations created by the ending of apartheid. One manifestation of this frustration is the prevalence of violent crime, which tarnishes the country's image and further undermines confidence.

Nigeria is still too embroiled in its own problems to help others. It remains entangled in corruption and vicious crime. The politicians of the northern, mainly Muslim, states have tried to impose Islamic law. This has led to riots in northern cities and reciprocal violence in the south, particularly in the south-west, where a Yoruba nationalist movement is now actively promoting secession. Hundreds, possibly thousands, died in

Map 5 Africa

these riots in 2000. In the south-east, resentment against oil companies, which are reaping huge profits in an impoverished region, has resulted in the periodic shutdown of oil wells and the kidnapping of oil workers, though oil has continued to flow. The most that can be said of President Olusegun Obasanjo, the first civilian president of Nigeria for 16 years, is that he has survived. But he has not yet established a working relationship with the legislature, which would enable him to take the necessary measures to turn the economy and the country around and realise Nigeria's huge potential.

The world economy has not been kind to non-oil producing African countries. Medium-sized states such as Ghana and Uganda, which have opened up their economies, were badly hit by high oil prices and the collapse of world prices for their commodities. Two of them, Zimbabwe and Côte d'Ivoire, which had been doing reasonably well, also fell victim to the short-term ambitions of individual politicians. In Zimbabwe, President Mugabe's party won an election in June 2000 by violence and intimidation. In Côte d'Ivoire, General Robert Guei lost power through a popular uprising when he tried to steal an election in October 2000. The winner, Laurent Gbagbo, continued General Guei's disastrous policy of excluding his northern rival, Alassane Outtara, by stirring up xenophobia. Both countries will register negative growth rates this year but, more importantly, their social and political fabric has been badly torn, making recovery difficult in the short term.

There were moments in 2000 when the whole of West Africa appeared to be falling victim to the violence that had begun in Liberia in 1989 and engulfed Sierra Leone in the 1990s. In 2000 it spread to Guinea. While the proximate trigger for this violence was the political and military failure of UN peacekeeping, it was also an expression of a deeper social breakdown that manifested itself in armed gangs of young men with no particular political direction, looting, raping and living off the land. Worryingly, the social conditions that allowed this to happen are prevalent in most other West African countries.

With the exception of Botswana, all the countries that have been held up by Western politicians and technocrats in recent years as political and economic models for the rest of the continent to follow now have serious problems. Even Tanzania, which has been politically stable and has been slowly turning its economy around, got ugly in January 2001 when troops and police attacked opposition rallies in Zanzibar, killing at least 30 people. Tanzania also stands accused of helping Hutu militias in Burundi.

The news was not all bad, however. While President Laurent Kabila of the Democratic Republic of Congo was assassinated, the succession of his apparently more flexible son, Joseph, re-opened the possibility of peace through negotiation in Congo and the withdrawal of soldiers from neighbouring countries that have been drawn into the conflict. The two-year war between Eritrea and Ethiopia ended in June 2000 as a result of Ethiopian military superiority and international mediation. It remains to be seen if there will be a sustainable settlement of the border issue that triggered the war. Re-establishing trust in other areas, such as economic cooperation and access to the sea for Ethiopia, will be even more difficult. A four-month meeting of representatives of all the Somali clans reached an agreement in Djibouti in August and produced a parliament and an elected president. The rest of the world welcomed the new government after a decade of national breakdown, but the two areas of Somalia that have their own administrations, Somaliland and Puntland, rejected it. So did groups in the south-west of the country that were supported by Ethiopian troops. There were also elections in Senegal and Ghana in which the elected incumbents lost and accepted defeat gracefully. That has rarely happened before in Africa.

These brighter spots apart, Africa's unstable politics, economic failure, declining infrastructure and the collapse of education and health services, bode ill for the future. How will the rest of the world, in particular the new administration in Washington, respond to the prospect of a long campaign to help Africa find its feet? The danger for Western governments, for which Africa is a low priority, is that they will respond to television images of disaster and suffering by seeking a 'quick fix'. No short-term solutions by outsiders have been found to any of Africa's problems so far; they require long-term solutions. Developed nations have maintained a modest commitment to Africa through bilateral development aid and through the Bretton Woods institutions. While the record has been mixed, at best, the application of aid conditionality is becoming more consistent and better aimed at encouraging indigenous participation and reform. Given that Western nations are likely to remain reluctant to intervene militarily in African conflicts for some time, enhanced and refined economic engagement appears to be the most realistic and promising way forward.

Meanwhile, matters are likely to worsen. African leaders may resort to the poisonous politics of blaming aliens or outsiders. Mugabe's campaign against whites or the government campaign against 'foreigners' in Côte d'Ivoire – where immigrant workers constitute 40% of the population – may prompt others to try to divert attention from their failure by encouraging violence against scapegoats. As new generations of Africans grow up to a prospect of poverty and oppression, they will try to emigrate to America or Europe in greater numbers or may turn to violent movements, such as Sierra Leone's Revolutionary United Front or even to cults such as The Movement for the Restoration of the Ten Commandments in Uganda, which murdered over 1,000 of its members last year. Neither direction bodes well for Africa's future.

Congo: Less Fighting, but No Peace

By the end of 2000, the two-year-old war in the Democratic Republic of Congo had reached an unstable equilibrium. The government of President Laurent Kabila and his allies, Angola, Zimbabwe and Namibia, were unable to defeat the invaders or suppress the rebel movements they had set up. The invaders, Uganda, Rwanda and Burundi, and the rebel movements had lost momentum and credibility. They occupied, but did not control, the north and east of the country while the government and its allies held towns and strong points in the west, south and south-east. All sides said they wanted an end to the war and in July and August 1999, most participants had signed a peace agreement in Lusaka. It was never implemented because none of the participants trusted each other.

The murder of President Laurent Kabila on 16 January 2001 and the succession of his son, Joseph, at first seemed to change nothing. Kabila was reported to have been murdered by an aide or bodyguard, but since there was no immediate change of government, either the killer must have been acting alone or it was coup by the government itself against Kabila. Kabila was regarded by both his enemies and allies as an obstacle to peace and his removal may make new negotiations possible. His son promptly made overtures to Western countries shunned by his father and seemed more amenable to peace talks.

Shortly after being sworn in, Joseph Kabila flew to Paris to meet President Jacques Chirac and then to America, where he met members of the new Bush administration, the UN Secretary-General Kofi Annan and, most significantly, President Paul Kagame of Rwanda. In public he made no new commitments, but his tone was positive. He said that the UN should be deployed and an internal political dialogue should begin. These were all measures that his father had agreed to but had blocked. At the same time, however, he reiterated his father's insistence that the Lusaka peace accord should be renegotiated and that the invaders must leave Congo unconditionally.

The Dimensions of the War

A vast disparate country with decades of ineffective venal government, Congo's very weakness has sucked in its neighbours. In the early stages of the war, at least eight countries sent their troops to fight there. Rebels from some of these same countries are also in Congo, so the Congolese civil war is complicated by the civil wars of Angola, Rwanda, Uganda and Burundi also being fought on Congolese territory. In eastern Congo, the intervention has sparked off several local wars. And, in the chaos, several armed groups have tried to carve out an area of control or simply to live off the land by pillaging.

Africa

These wars affect all of Congo's eight bordering neighbours. In some cases, such as Angola and Rwanda, the war in Congo is linked to their own wars; others are affected by an influx of refugees or interrupted trade routes. At a regional level, it has divided and almost wrecked the Southern African Development Community, the regional cooperation body. At an international level, the war in Congo involves the US and Europe, in particular France, which have oil interests in the region. They also exercise considerable influence over the United Nations' political, military and humanitarian response to the crisis.

Despite the large potential wealth of Congo and Laurent Kabila's paranoid belief that the West wanted to recolonise the country, there is no evidence of heavyweight companies trying to exploit the war in Congo. They do, however, keep a close watch on it in the hope that one day the country will be safe for investment. Small mining companies fish around for deals and diamond dealers hang around trying to pick up what they can, but no big players are fuelling the war. Arms suppliers purchasing cheap stocks of weapons and planes from the former Soviet Union are making fortunes, though, contrary to expectation, there are very few foreign mercenaries involved.

Madeleine Albright, the former US Secretary of State, described Congo as Africa's First World War. That creates an image of vast armies and trench warfare. Congo, an area the size of Western Europe, is nothing like that. The total number of fighters is less than 200,000. Large parts of the country have no military presence at all. Congo itself has about 55,000 soldiers. Until the death of Kabila, Rwanda had up to 20,000 troops in Congo, Uganda 10,000, Angola 2,500, Zimbabwe 11,000 and Namibia up to 2,000. The rebel movements between them field about 30,000, the *Mouvement pour la libération du Congo* (MLC) about 3,000 and the two wings of the *Rassemblement congolais pour la démocratie* (RCD) between them about 22,000. There are also about 35,000 Rwandan Hutu fighters and 16,000 Burundians fighting on the side of the government.

Fighting may be sporadic and limited, but its effects on the local population are catastrophic. The UN has estimated that some two million Congolese have fled their homes and are without access to regular food or medicine. Tens of thousands may have been killed directly by fighting but hundreds of thousands in Congo and its neighbouring countries may have died indirectly through hunger and disease.

Who's In It For What

When the war began in 1998, all sides expected a quick victory. Each had different and complex motives for entering the war, which have changed since they first became involved. Politically the origins of the war lie in the unstable relationship between Hutu and Tutsi in eastern Congo, south-west Uganda, Rwanda and Burundi. Though different tribes with a history of mutual repression, these two groups cohabit the same territory as one society, sharing a single culture, religion and language. Despite inter-marriage between the groups, society and politics were ruled by a caste system that was strengthened and exploited by colonial rulers and politicians after independence.

After the genocide of Tutsis in 1994, the remnants of the Rwandan Hutu army and militias fled to Congo (then known as Zaire) and began to launch raids back across the border, assisted by the government of then Zairean President Mobutu Sese Seko. In 1995, Rwanda and its ally Uganda launched a cross-border attack on the Hutu refugee camps that housed both civilians and soldiers. At the same time, they launched a Congo rebel movement led by Laurent Kabila. It was intended to set up a buffer zone in eastern Congo, but it proved extraordinarily successful and in May 1997, the rebels, directed by Rwanda and Uganda, marched into Kinshasa and made Kabila president.

Kabila promptly fell out with his allies and began to support their enemies, the Hutu militias in eastern Congo. In August 1998, Rwanda and Uganda tried to overthrow him in a daring cross-continental airborne attack but Zimbabwe, Angola, Namibia and other countries came to Kabila's rescue and drove them out of western Congo. Rwanda and Uganda continued to fight in the east, setting up the RCD rebel movement and beginning a long march across the continent as they had in 1996. This time, however, they were stopped by Kabila's allies. They also found they were not as popular as they had been in 1996 when they were marching to overthrow Mobutu. When the rebellion failed, in May 1999, Uganda and Rwanda fell out.

Uganda, which regarded Rwanda as its baby brother, prefers a political approach to guerrilla war, working with local people. Rwanda takes a more military approach and resents Ugandan patronage. Their rift caused the RCD to split. The movement's leader, Professor Ernest Wamba dia Wamba, was ousted but refused to resign and set up a new movement, *Rassemblement congolais pour la democratie – mouvement de libération* (RCD–ML), with its base in Kisangani, backed by Uganda. The Rwandans also tried to keep a foothold in Kisangani, a strategic town, and after two skirmishes in May 2000, serious fighting erupted. The two armies fought a pitched battle in the centre of Kisangani, killing more than 600 civilians and some 150 of each other's soldiers. Uganda lost and the centre of the town was destroyed.

Uganda also set up another rebel movement, the MLC, led by Jean-Pierre Bemba, a former Mobutuist, which rapidly captured Mobutu's home province of Equateur. By the end of 2000, however, it was clear that Rwanda and Uganda could not overthrow Kabila as they had Mobutu. Not only were they up against proper armies, but their intervention was

Africa

unpopular. Donor-dependent, they were also under pressure to settle, though it is clear that they are continuing to receive outside military assistance, probably from the United States. Rwanda insists that it will not leave Congo until it has destroyed the Rwandan Hutu militias, now a formal rebel movement known as the *Armée de libération du Rwanda*. Kabila integrated it into the Congolese armed forces and it provides some of its best fighters.

Uganda is in Congo to hunt down Ugandan rebels based there and because President Yoweri Museveni wishes to project himself as a regional leader, bringing stability and prosperity to eastern Congo under Ugandan hegemony. But he and Paul Kagame, once close allies, are now rivals for this position. Museveni's intervention is unpopular at home; his fight with Rwanda has cost him much-needed debt relief and he faces an election in 2001.

Burundi, also Tutsi-ruled, has troops in eastern Congo to hunt down a 16,000-strong Hutu militia, the *Forces de la défense de la démocratie* (FDD). It has no further ambitions there and its profile is low. Kabila, however, enmeshed the Burundian civil war in Congo's by furnishing Burundian forces with a base in Lubumbashi.

On the other side, the pro-Kabila alliance claimed they were acting on principle, defending the territorial integrity of a fellow African state from invasion. They also had their own political motives. Zimbabwe sent troops to Congo because President Robert Mugabe wants to establish himself as a powerful regional military leader. He resented what he perceived as Rwandan and Ugandan adventurism. He also believed, wrongly, that the war in Congo would pay for itself through deals that gave Zimbabwe a share in Congo's copper and cobalt mines and other projects. Unfortunately for Zimbabwe, all these projects required capital and technical expertise, neither of which Zimbabwe had. The cost of the Congo involvement is now contributing to Zimbabwe's own economic catastrophe, but politically Mugabe cannot admit defeat and pull out.

Angola, the most militarily and economically powerful player, joined the war to enable it to attack the bases of the Angolan rebel movement, National Union for the Total Independence of Angola (UNITA), inside Congo and to prevent UNITA trading diamonds for arms and fuel in Congo. Angola may have been spurred into action because it was convinced that Rwanda and Uganda were already colluding with UNITA. True or not, once the Angolan government weighed in against Uganda and Rwanda, they did cooperate with UNITA. The Angolan rebels helped the defeated Rwandan and Ugandan troops escape from western Congo in September 1998. Angola also hopes to benefit commercially from the venture in Congo. It has gained control of Congo's oil refining and distribution and is involved in oil exploration in Congolese territorial waters. With American and French backing, Angola is emerging as the regional policeman for their oil interests in the region.

Other minor players have included Sudan and Chad, which sent troops to help Kabila early in the war but have since withdrawn. Sudan, already embroiled in a proxy war with Uganda in southern Sudan, wanted to open another front against its enemy. There are also several hundred North Korean military advisers and trainers in Congo who are also manufacturing ammunition for the government. In return, they obtain cheap Congolese cobalt and, they hope, uranium. Mining the latter has proved difficult, however.

The Course of the Fighting

The strategic aim of all sides is to control towns and airstrips. Roads are almost non-existent in Congo. The government and its allies defend towns and use aircraft to move troops and supplies and to bomb rebel positions. In the east, the aircraft are needed to supply local militias. The Rwandan and Ugandan invaders and their rebel movements use forest paths and rivers to infiltrate areas, but rely on air supply for ammunition and fuel. Their tactics are to probe, seek weakness and attack when they are confident of success.

In February 2000, government forces tried to mount an offensive in northern Katanga, but the Rwandans launched a counter-attack that culminated in the capture of the strategic town of Pweto, on Lake Mweru, in December 2000, sending hundreds of government and Zimbabwean troops and thousands of refugees fleeing into Zambia. In the north-west, the Ugandans, supporting the MLC rebel movement, captured Dongo on the Ubangi river in July and also destroyed a ferry barge with up to 1,000 troops and heavy weapons on board. That brought the MLC to Mbandaka, a few days by river from the capital. Angola, which has troops in Mbandaka, and Washington warned Museveni and Bemba not to attack Mbandaka. So far they have not.

As the war has progressed the participants' motives have changed. Senior army officers from all the armies found a wealth of loot in Congo. Several of them, and their political cronies back home, have become millionaires. The Ugandan army, in particular, has been deeply corrupted by its involvement in Congo. Traders buying timber, diamonds, gold and other precious metals exported from eastern Congo by officers and politicians have invaded Kampala and Kigali. Little of this loot is funding the treasuries of the intervening countries, with the possible exception of Rwanda. Instead, the war is ruining their fragile economies. This creates a dilemma for the presidents. On the one hand, the political cost of admitting defeat and pulling out could be fatal. They also depend on the support of their senior army officers, who are enriching themselves. On the other hand, they can see that continued involvement will end in economic and, possibly, political catastrophe.

It has also meant that the war has become less a struggle for control of the whole country and more about grabbing and controlling mining areas and trade routes. The entrance to the Kilo Moto gold mine in eastern Congo, for example, is guarded by Ugandan troops who tax local people to mine there. There are frequent reports of Rwandan and Ugandan officers diverting their troops to provide protection for their mining and timber companies.

The intervention of foreign armies has also upset delicate local ethnic and economic balances. This is especially true in crowded eastern Congo where, ironically, the Rwandan attempt to create security by destroying militant Hutu forces in Congo has created more regional insecurity and even more anti-Tutsi feelings among local people. Several small local wars have broken out there. In South Kivu, the alliance between Rwanda and the local Tutsis, known as *Banyamulenge*, has created a strong and widespread anti-Tutsi feeling. In North Kivu, the Ugandans have had the same problem with the Hema, another group related to the Tutsis. Some Ugandan officers have business deals with Hema leaders while other Ugandan units support their rivals, the Lendu. That war exploded in January 2001 with an estimated 7,000 killed.

Throughout Kivu a patchwork of local self-defence units, known as *Mai Mai*, have emerged to protect their own areas. Some are allied to Kinshasa, which sends them weapons and ammunition, while others simply became mercenaries for whichever side pays them or resorted to killing, looting and raping.

Trying to Make Peace

Laurent Kabila was unable to take advantage of the rift between Rwanda and Uganda, and his supporters grew exasperated with his duplicity and stubbornness. Yet Congo seemed unable to produce an alternative leader capable of uniting the country. Kabila meanwhile destroyed any hope of decent government and economic revival in Congo and undermined efforts to make peace. Perhaps his position did depend on war. A would-be dictator, Kabila tried to imitate Mobutu by running Congo as a personal fiefdom, but he lacked Mobutu's political skills. His energies were directed solely to staying in power, regardless of the cost to Congo. He was a man without vision, stuck in the political thinking of the Cold War period of the early 1960s. His attempts to control the economy caused a flight of capital and created terrible hardship for ordinary people. He had almost no enemies when he came to power and the world was ready to help rebuild Congo, but Kabila was paranoid and mistrusted the rest of the world.

For this reason he was one of the main obstacles to peace, but not the only one. As the war has progressed, all sides have met, talked and declared their desire for peace but their attitude seems to be to sign up to any agreement and meanwhile to keep shooting until the other side stops. Increasingly the meetings have been bilateral, which suggests their purpose is to contain the war, not to stop it, and to carve up Congo by agreement rather than by force. The Lusaka peace agreement remains the only agreed basis for peace but, even apart from the lack of trust between the signatories, it has serious flaws. It stipulated that all sides should disengage and a Joint Military Commission (JMC), made up of all parties should monitor a cease-fire and the permanent withdrawal of troops. It called on the UN to provide an observer mission to monitor and help supervise this process and then provide a Chapter VII peacekeeping force to disarm the militias from Rwanda and Burundi and the *Mai Mai* self defence forces. It also provided for a Congolese national political dialogue leading to a transitional government.

It was left to the signatories to fulfil the agreement but, although they continued to meet, no one was prepared to take the first step. President Frederick Chiluba of Zambia was first delegated to keep the process going, and later President Joaquim Chissano of Mozambique took up the challenge. Each time, agreements were reaffirmed but fighting continued. General Rachid Lallali, an Algerian, appointed as neutral chairman of the JMC by the Organisation of African Unity, resigned because of lack of cooperation by the participants. Ketumile Masire, the former president of Botswana appointed to oversee the internal dialogue, was persistently thwarted and even abused by Kabila. He closed his office in Kinshasa in June 2000.

The UN, faced with the daunting task of peacekeeping in such a vast area with little infrastructure, was unsurprisingly hesitant about providing troops. The United States, keen on the idea of African solutions to African problems, would not send its own troops and wanted to keep UN involvement to a minimum. A small mission of just over 200 (of 5,537 authorised) was sent, but they never got near the front lines and remained dependent on the belligerents. They were frustrated by all sides but especially by the government, which consistently blocked their attempts to travel, saying that the mission was an infringement of Congolese national sovereignty. Through March 2001, the UN's only palpable achievement was brokering a cease-fire between Uganda and Rwanda at Kisangani. The UN's humanitarian mission has been unable to reach the civilian victims of the war, and an appeal for $38m for Congo raised barely a quarter of that.

On 22 February 2001, the UN Security Council unanimously passed Resolution 1341 approving plans for all parties to the conflict to withdraw. The programme emerged from two days of consultations in New York among representatives of the parties to the Lusaka accord, as well as

Masire. Under the plans, these groups were to start to pull back 15 kilometres from the front lines by 15 March 2001, creating an 30km-wide buffer zone stretching from south-east to northeast Congo. The withdrawals were to be monitored by 500 UN observers, supported by 2,500 troops. Once the pullback is complete, the combatants would have until 15 May 2001 to arrive at an agreement for the complete withdrawal of all foreign forces from Congolese territory. On 28 February 2001, the Rwandan government, the most aggressive in the region, unilaterally began to pull its troops back 200km from frontline points in Pweto – ten times the distance stipulated in the Lusaka agreement – on condition that UN forces and not the Congolese government would, as agreed in New York, fill the vacuum. Uganda announced its intention to do the same, and Namibia was to follow suit.

The Security Council's February 2001 allotment of 3,000 'bluehelmets', however, is substantially fewer than the 5,537 authorised in 2000. They may prove inadequate to police the withdrawal and subsequently a sustained cease-fire, particularly if the political process becomes fraught as it has in the past. Indeed, within a week of Rwanda's audacious move, the Congolese government accused Rwanda of pulling back only 10km rather than the promised 200 and leaving RCD soldiers in Pweto under Rwandan command, and impugned UN 'lethargy'. Moreover, neither the Lusaka agreement nor the February 2001 resolution dealt with the rebel armies from Angola, Rwanda, Burundi and Uganda on Congolese territory. It simply referred to them as 'negative forces' and they were not signatories to the Lusaka peace agreement. It is not credible that these groups, some of whom were instrumental in the 1994 genocide in Rwanda, will calmly line up to be disarmed by a force of peacekeepers.

Looking Ahead

The prospects for peace in Congo are still opaque. Joseph Kabila seems more open to dialogue than his father, but talking has never been a Congolese problem. Lacking experience, knowledge of Congolese politics and even a working knowledge of its main languages, French and Lingala, he seems an unlikely candidate to unite the country. Nor is there any sign of real leadership among the rebel movements. There have been recent attempts to reunite them, but it is unlikely that they will unite behind a single programme and a single leader. Bemba is effective and popular in his own area, but this was Mobutu's area and Bemba's popularity there guarantees his unpopularity in other areas.

Throughout the war, the belligerents have met amicably and talked and even agreed, only to return to their positions afterwards. It is clear none of them, except Rwanda, has the stomach for a fight, but none have the courage to admit the game is pointless and withdraw. Inside Congo, the wars sparked by the intervention will take longer to solve than the intervention itself; many could disintegrate into the sort of warlordism and banditry that are devastating Sierra Leone and Liberia.

Even with a national peace agreement, it will take years for a government in Kinshasa to extend its writ throughout the country, let alone rebuild infrastructure and provide services. The chances of that government being democratic and inclusive are remote. Congo has not been a nation-state in practice for decades and may formally break up, though at present there is no serious movement demanding secession. Despite all their suffering and a history of war, exploitation, and separatism, most Congolese still seem wedded to the concept of Congo.

Creating a viable Congo is not a realistic short-term goal, particularly in light of the West's reluctance to contribute large peacekeeping contingents. Joseph Kabila's relative openness to international mediation, however, does present clearer possibilities. Continued pressure from bilateral donors – such as the United States, the United Kingdom, France and Belgium – on Uganda and Rwanda to show military restraint could make cease-fire enforcement by the UN force feasible and keep the revived peace talks on track. Kabila's southern allies – especially Zimbabwe – may be less amenable to influence by external actors. Nevertheless, the International Monetary Fund (IMF) and the World Bank's hard line, coupled with Mugabe's mounting domestic problems, could have a positive effect. Moreover, even should the peace process yield greater stability, in the short and even the medium term, a war-ravaged Congo will not be able to sustain itself economically. Bilateral and multilateral aid providers will need to focus early and deeply on the vexing question of how to nurture political viability with appropriate economic planning and support.

Africa

Sierra Leone:
The Collapse of Regional Stability

The effort to resolve the nine-year conflict in Sierra Leone stalled in late 2000 as a result of the May 2000 collapse of the Lomé peace accord, signed in July 1999, and the glaring inadequacies of the UN Mission in Sierra Leone (UNAMSIL). Insecurity has spread throughout the region and now affects neighbouring Liberia and Guinea. In Sierra Leone, the rebel Revolutionary United Front (RUF) and government forces are tenuously observing a cease-fire declared in November 2000, but the threat of the conflict's regional expansion makes bringing about stability in Sierra Leone all the more crucial. Sierra Leone remains the leading test case for UN peace operations: a test that the UN is in grave danger of failing.

The Unravelling of the Lomé Accord

In July 1999, the government of Ahmed Tejan Kabbah was in a position of grave weakness. The brutal attack on Freetown by the RUF in January 1999 had left some 6,000 people dead and had shown that neither the international community nor the government-affiliated civil defence forces were able to defend the capital from an increasingly well-armed and well-organised rebel coalition. The government was also under pressure to come to an agreement from the United States, the United Kingdom and the Nigerian government, which was eager to bring home its Economic Community of West African States Cease-fire Monitoring Group (ECOMOG) peacekeepers. In these less-than-favourable circumstances, the Lomé accord was signed. Under the agreement, the RUF was given amnesty and a share in political power in exchange for a pledge to disarm.

The Lomé accord soon began to unravel. Despite the accord's concession of political power to RUF leader Foday Sankoh, widespread civilian revulsion at the atrocities carried out by the RUF – which include hacking off limbs as well as the mass killing of unarmed civilians – made Sankoh's chances of prospering in any subsequent elections very slim. Sankoh calculated that the demobilisation of the RUF would remove his claim to power and any insurance against prosecution, and so he prevented combatants from joining the Lomé-prescribed disarmament, demobilisation and reintegration (DDR) programme. As of March 2000, the UN had registered and disarmed only about 4,000 of 15,000 RUF combatants. Sankoh maintained military control of the key diamond-mining area of Kono, which yielded both personal riches and funds for rearming and sustaining combatants.

In addition, international support for the DDR programme was weak, resulting in a $19 million shortfall in funding by mid-2000. The proliferation of factions and the splintering of RUF lines of command in Sierra Leone had raised the possibility of luring rank-and-file fighters and relative 'moderates' into the peace process and of marginalising the more bellicose elements in the war. Such a strategy was unlikely to work, however, without a sufficiently funded DDR programme to reward and support fighters for relinquishing their arms. In the event, demobilisation centres were slow to be established and too few; payments were delayed;

dependants were not provided for; and little attention was paid to reintegrating fighters back into the economy and into their communities.

A third reason for the failure of Lomé was the weakness of the UN peacekeeping force. It was not until 22 October 1999 that the Security Council adopted a resolution establishing UNAMSIL and authorising a force of 6,000 (including 260 military observers) 'to monitor adherence to the cease-fire'. It took four months for the troops to arrive. In February, the UN agreed to an increase in strength to 11,100 and UNAMSIL was authorised 'to take the necessary action to ensure the freedom of movement and security of its personnel and, within its capabilities and areas of deployment, to afford protection to civilians under imminent threat of physical violence, taking into account the responsibilities of the Government of Sierra Leone'. By the end of April 2000, the number of UN soldiers had still reached only 8,700. Even at full strength, the UN force was a motley multinational force that included soldiers of 27 different nationalities, none of whom spoke the local language. The peacekeepers were also under-funded, lacking in equipment necessary for force protection, generally inexperienced, and unfamiliar with Sierra Leone's terrain.

These underlying vulnerabilities led UNAMSIL to fail its first military test. At the end of April, the Nigerian-led ECOMOG force passed its mantle to UNAMSIL. Some 4,000 Nigerian troops 'switched hats' and became a part of the UNAMSIL force. UNAMSIL commander Major-General Vijay Jetley then declared that his forces would begin in June to disarm RUF forces in the diamond fields. These appear to have been the twin triggers for RUF military action in May. On 1 May, the RUF began detaining Zambian and Kenyan forces between Makeni and Kono. Within a week, close to 500 peacekeepers had been taken hostage by the RUF, including an entire Zambian battalion. The RUF also managed to capture 13 UN armoured vehicles and some 1,000 UN-issue small arms, as well as seizing most of the 5,000 small arms they had surrendered to the UN since the Lomé peace agreement was signed.

UNAMSIL was paralysed. Angered by this state of affairs, a crowd of around 5,000 marched on Foday Sankoh's house in Freetown, overwhelmed a handful of UNAMSIL guards and began throwing stones and bricks at the house. Sankoh's bodyguards opened fire on the crowd, killing at least 19. The British government then announced it was sending five warships and more than 1,000 troops to assist UNAMSIL and to safeguard the evacuation of British nationals. The troops were also intended to help with a British-run training programme for the new Sierra Leonean Army and, implicitly, to deter an RUF attack on Freetown. The British soldiers proved effective, enabling Sierra Leonean government troops to round up RUF leaders in Freetown – including Mike Lamin, Eldred Collins and

Idrissa Kamara – on 9 May and take them to the Pademba Road prison. Much of the core RUF leadership was scheduled to stand trial.

On 17 May, when Sankoh returned to his house to recover some items, a passer-by spotted him and alerted government troops who attempted to arrest Sankoh, shooting him in the thigh. Civilians then grabbed Sankoh, beat him up, stripped him naked and paraded him along the streets. Sankoh was handed over to the government police and, after being briefly under British protection, was transferred to Pademba Road prison. Acting as a broker, Liberian President Charles Taylor helped to secure the release by the RUF of all the abducted UN peacekeepers.

By autumn 2000, UNAMSIL had fallen into internal wrangling. UNAMSIL commander Major-General Jetley, an Indian, attached great importance to patrolling the border with Liberia. Because he suspected that the Nigerians were engaged in illicit diamond mining and were taking large sums of money from the RUF in return for letting the rebels continue their operations, he preferred to use Indian troops for the task. Unfortunately, these suspicions were leaked, and Nigeria rebutted the allegations in the strongest terms. For political reasons, Jetley was removed from command and replaced by the Kenyan Lieutenant-General Daniel Opande. Thereupon, in September 2000, India pulled its 3,161 troops from Sierra Leone; in October 2000, Jordan announced that its 1,831-strong contingent would also be withdrawn.

A cease-fire was agreed in November 2000 in Abuja, and has generally held. But the Jordanian and Indian troops were gone by February 2001, leaving an aggregate force of under 10,500. This is too small to be effectively deployed in RUF-controlled territory, which constitutes a large swath running from the Liberian border in the east through the diamond region to the Guinean border in the north-west. There is rebel activity in over half the country. UN Secretary-General Kofi Annan, however, was pushing for a UNAMSIL peacekeeping force of 20,500 and a budget of $782m. In December 2000, UNAMSIL's mandate was extended until 31 March 2001. But the conflict is now regional, and a new peacekeeping framework and mandate may be required. British contingency support for UNAMSIL and training for the Sierra Leonean Army can stabilise a precarious situation for a few weeks or months, but cannot redress the deeper challenges now posed in Sierra Leone and neighbouring states.

The Liberian Connection

President Charles Taylor of Liberia has supported and provided arms to the RUF in exchange for diamonds, which are extracted from fields in RUF territory. Thus, the success of the Lomé peace agreement depended a great deal on the willingness and ability of Taylor to persuade the RUF to disarm. But Taylor continued – as he had in his pre-presidential incarnation as a rebel – to provide assistance to the RUF. Detailed evidence of this was plentiful: with British troops at risk in Sierra Leone, Britain stepped up its efforts to track the RUF and its allies. British diplomatic officials estimated that 60% of Sierra Leone's diamonds from RUF-held territory were smuggled through Liberia and 40% through Burkina Faso. They also traced several RUF arms shipments to Liberia. Burkina Faso has bartered weapons for diamonds with the RUF.

Taylor and Burkina Faso President Blaise Compaore were also believed to be directing strategy meetings with RUF commanders, including Issa Sesay, Gibril Massaquei, Morris Kallon and Augustin Gbow (all based in Sierra Leone), Sam Bockarie and Edward Kanneh (based in Liberia) and Ibrahim Bah (based in Burkina Faso). Taylor appears to fear that if Sierra Leonean forces or Nigerian troops took control of eastern Sierra Leone, they would allow Liberian dissidents to attack across the border, just as Taylor himself did at the outset of the Liberian civil war. Further, many Liberians have joined RUF field commander Sam Bockarie's forces, at odds with Sankoh's group and operating in the south of Sierra Leone. Discontented demobilised soldiers within Liberia were already a threat to Taylor's government, and this threat would have increased with any demobilisation of Liberians fighting with the RUF.

In addition to managing internal and regional power struggles, diamonds have been Taylor's other main motivation. According to figures from DeBeers, the world's largest diamond producer and seller, in 2000 Sierra Leone's total diamond production was valued at $70m and Liberia's at $10m; yet Sierra Leone exported $12.5m worth of rough diamonds, while the value of Liberia's diamond exports was $68m. Even allowing for restrictions on Sierra Leone's diamond exports, these figures indicate that an overwhelming proportion of Liberia's diamond exports are produced elsewhere and suggest that many of those originate in Sierra Leone.

Taylor has been supplying arms and materiel to Bockarie's wing of the RUF as well as to Sankoh's wing, probably to ensure leverage over the diamond trade. With Sankoh increasingly looking to shift diamond exports to middlemen other than Taylor, the Liberian president has been able to use his ties to Bockarie (forced out of Sierra Leone and into Liberia by Sankoh in December 1999) to consolidate his hold on the Sierra Leonean diamond industry. On 13 June 2000, British Foreign Secretary Robin Cook made public an intelligence dossier detailing Taylor's military support for the RUF and the flow of diamonds from RUF-controlled areas to Liberia. European Union ministers were persuaded to agree to freeze a two-year $47m development aid programme for Liberia.

On 7 March 2001, prompted by a US motion, the UN Security Council passed a resolution imposing sanctions on the Liberian government for its support of the RUF and for rebel groups in Guinea. Effective 7 May 2001, these sanctions included a ban on Liberian diamond and timber exports, the grounding of Liberian-registered aircraft and a ban on travel by senior Liberian officials. The resolution also imposed a strengthened arms embargo, effective immediately. Liberia has clearly been alarmed by the US initiative and has been trying to distance itself from Bockarie and, more generally, from the accusation of fuelling war in Sierra Leone. Sierra Leone has requested his extradition, and Liberia was reported to be looking for a third country willing to accept him. Shortly before the resolution was passed, the Liberian government announced it was banning diamond imports and, to deter smuggling, grounding Liberian-registered planes for 120 days. Monrovia also stated that it would set up a certificate-of-origin scheme similiar to the one in place in Sierra Leone.

Controlling the Diamond Trade

Less than 4% of the diamonds sold internationally are illicit 'conflict diamonds'. Nevertheless, they have helped sustain conflicts in Sierra Leone, Angola and, to an extent, the Democratic Republic of Congo. In June 2000, the UN passed a resolution demanding that all states take measures to prohibit the direct or indirect import of rough diamonds from Sierra Leone, and requiring the government of Sierra Leone to implement a certificate-of-origin system for diamond exports. Official diamond exports from Sierra Leone were suspended while a certification scheme was put in place. They resumed on 12 October. The certification scheme has been combined with diplomatic pressure on Liberia to stop its dealings with the RUF. To an extent, these measures have worked. Since they were put in place, selling diamonds through Liberia has been much more difficult and less profitable for the RUF. Discouraged from dealing with Monrovia, the RUF is forced to sell through Freetown.

Significant loopholes remain, however. Many diamonds continue to leave via Guinea and Liberia, and many still end up in the Middle East and South Asia. Elements of the Antwerp market remain hard to regulate, including unregistered but legitimate diamond dealers and illicit buyers of smuggled stones. Tel Aviv's market is even less regulated than Antwerp's. The RUF has also apparently found ways to sell to traders who have access to certificates issued by the Sierra Leone government. Diamond traders in Kenema were reported to be buying from the rebels. Ascertaining the origin of the stones and isolating illicit buyers continues to be difficult. Nevertheless, moral pressure from the UN and the Group of 8 (G-8) leading industrial nations, efforts on the part of diamond merchants (led by De Beers) and certification schemes appear to have depressed the price of conflict diamonds. Consequently, they have provided attenuated support to the Sierra Leone peace process.

Political Economy: Problems Beyond the RUF

The Sierra Leone government's attempted fight-back after the RUF's May 2000 'uprising' was impeded by divisions within the pro-government forces. Accusations of human rights abuses by the civil defence forces have become increasingly common, and there was serious friction between them and former enemies from the old Sierra Leonean Army (SLA). Many of the latter had abused civilians under the National Provisional Military Council (NPRC) government of 1992–96 and had subsequently joined with the RUF in the May 1997 military coup that replaced Kabbah with the Armed Forces Revolutionary Council (AFRC). After Lomé, the post-AFRC democratic government made concessions to the council's leader Johnny Paul Koroma, including provisions for incorporating many old SLA soldiers into the new Sierra Leonean Army. Koroma subsequently abided by the Lomé agreement, apparently hoping to rebuild his political credibility.

Many other former SLA soldiers, however, were not integrated into the new SLA, and they were unhappy that past salaries were not being paid. Among these, the West Side Boys militia, centred in the Occra Hills north-east of Freetown, were particularly restive. On 25 August 2000, the West Side Boys captured 11 British soldiers from the Royal Irish Regiment, who had been detailed to take part in the training of the new Sierra Leonean Army. In exchange for the British soldiers' release, they demanded supplies, reinstatement in the national army and the release of one of their leaders, 'Brigadier' Bomb Blast, from prison. Five of the soldiers were freed, but negotiations for the release of the remainder broke down. On 7 September, about 150 British commandos attacked two villages controlled by the West Side Boys. The attack left 25 Sierra Leoneans and one Briton dead. The six remaining hostages were airlifted to safety. After this mission, several hundred West Side Boys fighters and camp followers reported for demobilisation. Koroma claimed the AFRC was also a thing of the past, and he and some 90 followers handed over weapons and equipment to UNAMSIL in a symbolic ceremony.

While the weakening of the AFRC rump is a positive development, it has probably only been possible because the new SLA has absorbed large numbers of AFRC personnel with highly dubious histories of human-rights abuses. It remains doubtful whether such an army can be transformed into a disciplined force. Both Amnesty International and Human Rights Watch argue that not only RUF fighters but many in Kabbah's forces should be brought to justice for human-rights abuses. In response, in August 2000 the UN Security Council authorised the creation of a joint international and Sierra Leonean court to investigate atrocities.

The credibility of the Kabbah government also suffers from Sierra Leone's dismal record of government corruption. Past governments have

Africa

trampled on human rights, drained away Sierra Leone's valuable natural resources and shrunk educational and employment opportunities. Although attempts to restrict diamond flows from RUF areas are promising, much of the shortfall between Sierra Leonean diamond production and government revenue has arisen from illegal mining by forces associated with the present Kabbah government. These include the *kamajors* – traditional tribal hunters loosely configured as a roughly 10,000-strong armed militia known as the Forces of Civil Defence – and elements of the Sierra Leone People's Party (SLPP) political élite. Some elements of the new SLA still force child soldiers into service. According to the United Nations Children's Fund (UNICEF), Sierra Leone's infant mortality is the highest in the world, with under-five mortality at 316 children per 1,000. Thus, the RUF – though profoundly brutal and unpopular in their own right – has fed off a widespread and justified disillusionment (particularly among young Sierra Leoneans) with the government.

Unless some of the deeper grievances in Sierra Leone are addressed, even a defeated RUF might quickly be replaced by 'another RUF'. Moreover, any new government-affiliated occupants of Kono can themselves be expected to try to profit from its diamond mines. In any case, since the RUF is still having no difficulty trading diamonds for arms with Liberia and Burkina Faso, a military victory will not be easy. If Kono were retaken by government forces, the RUF could retreat to the fertile agricultural areas of Kailahun, as it has in the past when under pressure in Kono.

Potential Expansion of the Conflict

In the absence of a military or political solution, humanitarian problems will persist and threaten to widen the conflict. In October 2000, the UN estimated there were some 486,000 internally displaced persons within Sierra Leone, of whom some 338,000 were new cases, mainly in Northern Province. It appears that the principal cause of displacement of civilians around Makeni – one of the main conflict areas, in the centre of the country – has not been rebel attacks but government helicopter gunships. Civilians fleeing these attacks have generally refused to go south, probably out of fear of the *kamajors*. As of January 2001, the UNHCR also estimated there were 328,100 Sierra Leonean and 122,300 Liberian refugees in Guinea. Guinea has bombarded villages on both sides of the Sierra Leonean border, believing them to be bases used by RUF fighters allied with Guinean dissidents. Guinea has accused Liberia of backing incursions into its territory by the RUF and Guinean insurgents, and Liberia has accused Guinea of backing Liberian insurgents.

Guinean fears that refugees will harbour dissident elements, commit crimes, facilitate drug and arms smuggling and spread AIDS has produced growing hostility to refugees both on the part of the Guinean government and many local residents. Fleeing insecurity in both Guinea and Sierra Leone, some 180,000 Sierra Leonean and Liberian refugees and 70,000 displaced Guineans have been stranded in the volatile 'parrot's peak' region along the Guinean border with Sierra Leone and deprived of food and medicine. These refugees are also at risk due to fighting between the Guinean Army, rebel forces and various militia groups. The Guinean government remains reluctant to permit the UN High Commissioner for Refugees (UNHCR) to move the refugees from the border area. In December 2000, however, the Economic Community of West African States (ECOWAS) approved the deployment of 1,676 soldiers (half from Nigeria and the rest from Mali, Niger and Senegal) on the Guinean border. Although the deployment was scheduled for no later than 15 February 2001, the ECOWAS governments have been reluctant to act . The principal reasons appear to be failure of the UN Security Council, Liberia or Guinea to endorse the ECOWAS mandate, and inadequate force protection.

On 15 February, Taylor – under threat of the additional UN arms, export and travel sanctions proposed by the US – pledged to open a humanitarian corridor to allow the UN access to the refugees. He also endorsed deployment of the ECOWAS contingent to ensure the safety of refugees, UN personnel and other aid workers. A day later, Washington and London, at the request of West African foreign ministers backed by France, tentatively agreed to delay for two months the imposition of some of the new sanctions to give Taylor an opportunity to break his connections with Guinean rebels. In March 2001, the UN Security Council unanimously voted for sanctions, but with the two-month delay.

Another Testing Year for UNAMSIL

Cathartic political change within Sierra Leone is not on the horizon. Although the cease-fire appears to be holding, there has been no effective political negotiation since the Lomé accord broke down in May 2000. A committee of West African rulers set up to help resolve the conflict has moved glacially and is politically hobbled by the presence of Liberian President Charles Taylor. President Kabbah asked his parliament to delay by six months the presidential and parliamentary elections scheduled respectively for February and March 2001, citing the war, the large numbers of displaced people and lack of funds for preparing and holding the election. (The last elections cost some $25m and were largely funded by the United Kingdom.) While some have argued for a government of national unity in the interim, the failure of the Lomé accord to tame the RUF by giving it a role in government makes the success of such a measure remote.

Nevertheless, there are a few encouraging signs. International efforts to tighten the noose on the RUF's illicit diamond trade show tentative signs of working. In August 2000, the US committed $50m and 200 military advisers to equip and train five Nigerian battalions, one Ghanaian battalion and one Senegalese battalion for eventual deployment as peacekeepers, while in November 2000 the UK sent 600 soldiers (including 350 Gurkhas) mainly to train and rehabilitate the Sierra Leonean Army. Though not a short-term solution to the peacekeeping problem – British officers say the SLA will not be a fully competent fighting force for several years – regional and national security-sector reform is essential to longer-term stability in West Africa. On the ground, the southern part of Sierra Leone is mostly resettled and calm, and in some diamond fields *kamajors* have been seen fraternising with RUF fighters. With much of the RUF leadership in jail, Issa Sesay has emerged as interim leader. Many observers feel he wants to limit abuses and to present the RUF as a valid political movement. At the same time, RUF harassment has increased around Makeni, where Sesay appears to be headquartered.

It is doubtful that the military capability of UNAMSIL will improve in the near future, since first-rank military powers are unlikely to consider substantial sustained contributions. The United Kingdom, the only one of the five permanent members of the UN Security Council to have troops in Sierra Leone, has pledged to keep its 600 military advisers in-country until the end of 2001 and perhaps augment that force. It also plans to keep an 'over-the-horizon' contingent of 5,000 available for rapid deployment in an emergency. London, however, has been unwilling to place British troops under UN command and is reluctant to maintain a lengthy combat presence. The UK considered the UN commander incompetent and the UN's rules of engagement insufficiently aggressive. London is also uncomfortable with the UN's view, in keeping with the spirit of the Lomé accord, that the RUF should have a stake in government. But Britain's attitude also more broadly reflects the West's unwillingness to become deeply involved in African conflicts, despite rhetoric that is generally supportive of peacekeeping and international involvement in conflict-resolution.

These constraining realities make non-military measures paramount. There is little doubt that Taylor is the region's principal 'spoiler'. Thus, continuing economic pressure on his government – in the form of threatened or actual sanctions and commercial controls on diamonds – will be vital. This pressure will have to come from an array of external actors – including international players like the US, the UK and France, and regional players like Nigeria and Ghana – for UNAMSIL to have a reasonable prospect of success. Even then the overall outlook for Sierra Leone's short-term prospects is fairly grim. The increasing spillover of conflict into Liberia and Guinea indicates that only a regional approach to peacekeeping in West Africa is likely to be effective. This demands still more troops in the daunting context of major powers' steady disinclination to provide them.

South Africa and Zimbabwe: Failures of Leadership

Prospects for effective regional leadership in southern Africa were hindered over the past year. The primary problems were Zimbabwean President Robert Mugabe's coercive approach to land reform, and South African President Thabo Mbeki's reticence in responding to Mugabe's policies and his shaky stewardship of South Africa itself. Mugabe's excesses, however, have diminished his prestige as a regional player. In the resulting leadership vacuum, Mbeki may have an opportunity to entrench South Africa's political influence in southern Africa, and align it more closely with his nation's regional economic and military rank.

Mbeki's challenges begin at home. As the nation that overcame apartheid, South Africa is the most internationally respected country in sub-Saharan Africa. But the South African president's tepid diplomatic reaction to Mugabe's land seizures obliquely reflects Mbeki's inclination to curry favour with his predominantly black constituency by pitting blacks against whites to secure elections and by implementing racially divisive programmes. Practices like these have resulted in capital flight from South Africa, inhibited economic liberalisation, discomforted international donors and lenders, and jeopardised the economy's long-term capacity to accommodate the country's growing population.

Zimbabwe's Land Reform Crisis

In 2000–01, Zimbabwe's international reputation and domestic fortunes were seriously damaged by Robert Mugabe's disruptive land-reform policy. This policy has become a major threat to regional stability.

Mugabe has not always been so reckless. Following a successful revolt against white minority rule culminating in independent black rule in 1980, he allowed white Zimbabweans to keep most of their land. At present, 4,500 white farmers hold about a third of Zimbabwe's farmland. To foster

Africa

more equitable landholding, in the late 1980s and early 1990s the government bought substantial farmland from whites by eminent domain. Redistribution, however, has not been well executed. The government has tended to shift land to already well-off friends of Mugabe's, who have failed to put the land to comparably productive use. The few poor black farmers who have been given government leases have not been provided with loan support, so their plots have continued to be cultivated at subsistence level or have been abandoned altogether. Consequently, Mugabe faced growing pressure from constituents agitating for their own land.

In early 2000, Mugabe proposed constitutional amendments that would have permitted him to order the seizure of white-owned farms without government compensation and installed him as president for another ten years. In a national referendum in February 2000, Zimbabweans voted, by a decisive 55% to 45%, against the proposed amendments. This result indicated that Mugabe would need to make special efforts to secure sufficient votes for his ruling Zanu-PF party to defeat the opposition Movement for Democratic Change (MDC) party and retain control of the government in the upcoming June 2000 parliamentary elections. Mugabe's response was to rely on emotive populism buttressed by illegal action. Less than two weeks after the referendum, ignoring both the voters' will and a High Court ruling establishing the illegality of the seizures, he encouraged black squatters forcibly to occupy land owned by white farmers. Although Zanu-PF characterised the squatters as veterans of the civil war 20 years earlier, only a fraction were in fact war veterans.

Within the year, about 1,700 white-owned farms had been occupied and Mugabe had announced plans to increase the total number of farms seized to 3,000. Eight white farmers and over 30 members of the MDC were killed by squatters between March 2000 and March 2001. In allowing squatters to terrorise white farmers and his political opponents in the MDC – which most white farmers support – and promising quick and massive white-to-black land redistribution, Mugabe was in fact able to secure votes for Zanu-PF in the June 2000 parliamentary elections that the party might otherwise have lost due to economic mismanagement.

Any domestic political gains for Zanu-PF were more than offset by international economic ostracism. The British government had pledged to help finance redistribution at the inception of independence in 1979 under the Lancaster House Agreement and had in fact done so. In 1998, London had earmarked some £40 million to support a new government land-distribution policy. But throughout 2000, Mugabe jingoistically accused London of racism and, even more bizarrely, cast Tony Blair's government as part of a gay conspiracy against him. The United Kingdom held up the dispensation of the funds pending the cessation of the illegal occupations. Mugabe also alienated the International Monetary Fund (IMF) and the World Bank. The IMF suspended its Zimbabwe programmes in late 1999 on account of Harare's misappropriation of IMF funds for military adventurism in the Democratic Republic of Congo (DROC) despite massive external debt; the World Bank suspended aid in May 2000 due to arrears. Although Belgian officials and French President Jacques Chirac controversially met Mugabe in March 2001 – only two days after the murder of a 68-year old white woman farmer – later that month the European Parliament formally regretted the meetings and called for European Union aid through Harare to be halted. In October 2000, the United States denied Zimbabwe improved trade access to the American market, and in September 2000, the Senate passed the Zimbabwe Democracy Bill, which would have placed firm 'good governance' conditions on further aid. In March 2001, a more stringent version, which would ban aid until democracy and the rule of law were restored, was presented to Congress and seemed likely to be passed.

Unsurprisingly, Zimbabwe developed severe food and fuel shortages in 2000–01. As of January 2001, inflation stood at 70%, unemployment at 50%. Zimbabwe's debt requires 30% of its gross domestic product (GDP) to service. The economy, which grew at a rate of 1.2% in 1999, contracted by over 5% in 2000 according to an IMF estimate, making Zimbabwe's the world's fastest-shrinking economy. Agricultural disruptions and general insecurity owing to the squatters' violent activities caused revenues from tobacco farming and tourism – the country's prime sources of hard currency – to suffer double-digit percentage declines in 2000, with larger decreases expected for 2001. Harare is unable to pay the roughly $30m it owes to Eskom – South Africa's electric company, which supplies 20% of Zimbabwe's power. The collapse of the economy and uncertainty about the integrity of property rights has prompted international companies and private investors to flee Zimbabwe *en masse*.

Despite such evidence of government incompetence, as a result of systematic and frequently lethal voter intimidation, probable election fraud, and the 20 unelected seats where Mugabe is constitutionally entitled to appoint the incumbents, Mugabe's Zanu-PF party narrowly retained control of the government in Zimbabwe's June 2000 parliamentary elections. But the quick and courageous electoral success (gaining 48% of the popularly elected seats) of the MDC – whose singing supporters gathered on the streets of Harare and comfortably outnumbered their clenched-fisted Zanu-PF counterparts as the new parliament opened on 20 July 2000 – has considerably weakened Mugabe.

During the MDC's election campaign, party leader Morgan Tsvangirai pledged that if the party gained control of the government it would follow

Africa

IMF and World Bank macroeconomic guidelines, and thus induce the Bretton Woods institutions to resume much-needed lending programmes in Zimbabwe. He also promised to end the deployment of the 11,000 Zimbabwean troops in Congo, where they have been supporting Congolese President Laurent Kabila, who was assassinated in January 2001. According to leaked government documents this engagement costs over $25m per month; it is considered the principal cause of Zimbabwe's critical hard-currency shortage. In exchange for military assistance, Kabila had granted diamond, gold and timber concessions to companies in which Zimbabwean politicians and military officers have interests, but these concessions are difficult to exploit and no portion of any possible profits appears to have ended up in Zimbabwe's treasury. After the election, Mugabe showed little inclination to clean up his act.

Troops remain deployed in Congo and the Zimbabwean military's business interests there have expanded. Within Zimbabwe, Mugabe has encouraged more land confiscations and hinted at the nationalisation of factories and mines – retrograde moves towards a command economy, likely to hasten economic collapse and further dismay investors. In November 2000, the new parliament passed the Land Acquisition Act, outlining orderly judicial procedures for redistributing land. Mugabe has completely ignored it, authorising more 'fast track' land seizures, proclaiming the land programme 'irreversible', and threatening 'even more angry' seizures if white farmers attempt to seek redress through the courts. Mugabe has also become more broadly autocratic, withholding Zimbabwean passports from citizens of British descent and refusing to allow state funding for the MDC, despite judicial rulings holding these actions illegal. In early 2001, the government's crackdown on political dissent and free speech intensified.

As long as Mugabe remains in power, there is little chance that Zimbabwe will extricate itself from economic and political disarray. Although the MDC has nominal strength in parliament, in early 2001 Mugabe moved to suppress opposition in anticipation of the presidential election in 2002. He stepped up his attacks on pro-MDC journalists and judges, and Mugabe supporters bombed a newspaper sympathetic to the MDC and threatened to burn down churches having pro-MDC congregations. While Zimbabwe needs outside aid to restart its economy, the IMF and the World Bank as well as bilateral donors will be reluctant to resume assistance in the violent political environment that Mugabe has created and nurtured. The best prospect for the country is that voters in 2002 will be even braver than they were in 2000 and vote Mugabe out of office. Should they do so, external actors would probably move swiftly to support the MDC on the strength of its democratic mandate – financially, diplomatically and perhaps even militarily – and help ensure Mugabe's removal from power. Until then, outside powers can do little more than what they have been doing: withholding aid and diplomatically isolating Mugabe.

South Africa's Post-Mandela Blues

When Thabo Mbeki became president of South Africa in June 1999, there were considerable doubts about whether he could fill the shoes of Nelson Mandela as a politician, let alone as a statesman. His reluctance to confront regional problems head-on and his inflammatory approach to balancing domestic political interests have lent credence to those doubts.

South Africa's most pressing regional challenge has been its neighbour to the north, Zimbabwe. As Mugabe has fallen from grace, Mbeki has been slow to condemn his support for lawlessness and has procrastinated about when the squatters should have to desist. His private negotiations with Mugabe in April 2000, though initially salutary, were followed by more squatter attacks and more xenophobic, anti-white rhetoric from the Zanu-PF party. Mbeki failed to respond decisively. It was not until November 2000 that Mbeki, visiting Harare with Nigerian President Olusegun Obasanjo as part of multilateral efforts to resolve Zimbabwe's land problem, indicated publicly that respect for the rule of law must take precedence over land redistribution. This gesture was muted, however, expressed only by Mbeki's nodding acknowledgement of assertions that Obasanjo made in a speech.

A stance roundly and unequivocally condemning Mugabe would pose domestic political risks to Mbeki. Land reform in South Africa has been slow: as of May 2000, only 6% of land claims there had been settled. Redistribution is also a politically charged issue: according to a mid-2000 poll, 54% of South Africans supported the Zimbabwean squatters. South Africa's first outright seizure of a white farmer's land, after failed price negotiations, was scheduled to occur in March 2001. Mbeki does not wish to appear to his own constituents a defender of residual white colonial interests. Yet similar interests in South Africa control a disproportionate share of its wealth and financial resources. A majority of the nation's private companies are still white-owned. The reality is that commercial confidence in national and regional stability is essential if South Africa is to avoid capital flight and attract further investment.

That confidence is waning. In 2000, South African companies increasingly shifted their listings from the Johannesburg Stock Exchange (JSE) to overseas boards. During the calendar year, the JSE's benchmark All Share Index dropped by around 16% while the South African rand lost 18% of its value against the dollar. The prospective purchase of DeBeers – the JSE's largest listed company – by a private consortium would further devastate the South African equity market and bleed the country of hard currency. In December 2000, the South African

Consumer Confidence Index reached seven-year lows for both blacks and whites.

While the post-apartheid honeymoon is plainly over, South Africa is not yet in a state of crisis. The domestic landscape has some positive features. The country's second all-race local elections in December 2000 proceeded smoothly, and democracy appears entrenched. During its six years in power, the ruling African National Congress (ANC) has forged some degree of economic stability, improved housing, provided basic services like water and electricity to many who had lived without them, and widened the social safety net by increasing pensions. Inflation in 1999 was only 5.1%. The government's deficit is shrinking, and trade is being liberalised faster than the World Trade Organisation requires.

Nevertheless, South Africa's domestic situation is unstable. Unemployment, predominantly among blacks, has skyrocketed to more than 30%. South Africa is home to more HIV-positive people than any other country in the world, with an estimated 4.2m – roughly a tenth of the population – afflicted. At the same time, economists estimate that current annual population growth of 1.3% requires GDP growth of 6–8% to reduce unemployment. The economy's 1.2% growth rate in 1999 thus was insufficient to make headway in eradicating poverty: average incomes remained roughly the same between 1994 and 1999, though forecast growth of 3% in 2000 signalled improvement. Labour strikes are an endemic problem. And South Africa's notorious crime rate – among the highest in the world for murder and rape – continues to rise.

These problems have amplified racial polarisation, which is growing in domestic politics. Although the ANC ostensibly advocates racial neutrality, it is supported mainly by blacks. Conversely, while the main opposition party, the Democratic Alliance (DA) – formed from the liberal Democratic Party and the remnants of the old white-dominated ruling party, the National Party – is also rhetorically multiracial, in fact it is supported primarily by whites, 'coloureds' and Indians, who together constitute 25% of the population. Taking their cue from Mbeki, ANC political leaders have used these alignments to garner short-term support and distract voters from bread-and-butter issues such as poverty, crime and AIDS, as well as widespread ANC corruption. In the December 2000 elections, Mbeki proclaimed that the DA would inevitably favour non-blacks. The normally restrained Mandela chimed in that 'no white party can run this country. No matter how they cover up by getting a few black stooges, they remain a white party'. The ANC also distributed pamphlets in the Western Cape depicting the opposition as Nazi-saluting white supremacists. The DA, for its part, blamed regional disinvestment on Mbeki's failure to condemn Mugabe's land policy.

While the DA did win the mayoral election in Cape Town and precluded an ANC majority in Durban, the ANC's negative campaigning may have kept the lid on DA support. But it also helped reduce voter turnout in the December elections to below 50% compared to 89% in the June 1999 national election, and diminished ANC support to 60% from 66.4%. These figures seem to reflect growing scepticism about the capacity of government to bring about meaningful change, and the voters' insistence that the ANC – while historically esteemed as the party of liberation – must deliver politically and economically to maintain support. This is no easy task. Mbeki must both keep the economy on course through conservative fiscal and monetary policies and cater to his constituency's broadly socialist inclinations.

Mbeki's approach to governance is to micromanage and concentrate on minutiae at the expense of broader long-term vision with respect to national policy. His preferred device for harmonising the divergent requirements of economic vitality and the public's socialist bent is an aggressively Africanist employment policy, including rigid statutory requirements of 'positive discrimination' applicable to all companies with 50 or more employees. Insofar as Mbeki may want to preserve maximum control over government jobs, this policy seems to have slowed privatisation and foreign investment, thus delaying the market efficiencies and government savings that they would generate.

Unquestionably the policy has produced 'white flight', which is also economically disadvantageous, without appreciably helping the most under-privileged blacks, who do not compete with whites for jobs anyway. Moreover, according to a September 2000 survey, only 19% of young, educated blacks believe that a black should automatically be hired over an equally qualified white. The figure was 27% in 1996. More broadly, a slight 51% majority of blacks – up from 41% in 1996 – are now against positive discrimination. This shift in black public opinion suggests that black South Africans may be amenable to less positive discrimination.

So far, Mbeki has not been up to the challenge of resolving South Africa's intricate dilemmas. His idiosyncratic and scientifically dubious personal stance on AIDS – that poverty rather than the HIV virus causes the disease, and that claims to the contrary are part of a conspiracy among Western pharmaceutical companies – has not helped his credibility. Both the ANC leadership and Mandela disavowed this position.

In January and February 2001, Mbeki further undermined public confidence by blocking an investigation into charges that ANC members of parliament took bribes in awarding £4 billion in arms contracts, baselessly labelling a white judge 'out of control'. Should Mbeki continue to cater to race-sensitive emotions for short-term political gain and to balk at supporting the rule of law in Zimbabwe, he may ultimately weaken his capacity to maintain economic and political stability in South Africa. This would make it difficult for him to consolidate South Africa's putative position as a 'middle power', able to exert regional and global influence particularly at the multilateral level.

The Regional Leadership Vacuum

South Africa, with a GDP of $128bn in 1999, is by far southern Africa's largest economy; Zimbabwe, which had only $6.8bn GDP in 1999, is a distant second. With appreciable air power and active armed forces that include almost 65,000 troops, South Africa is also the region's ranking military power (though indiscipline, racism, morale and AIDS remain major problems). South Africa, then, is the natural regional power, and indisputably a pivotal country. Indeed, President Mbeki's expressed aim is to spearhead an 'African renaissance', whereby African nations enjoy a degree of stability that enables them to compete in the global marketplace and affords them a greater voice in world affairs.

In May 2000, Mbeki opened the Zimbabwe Trade Fair by announcing that regional economic and political integration should be expedited through the 14-member Southern African Development Community (SADC). The signing on 1 September 2000 of a free-trade agreement by 11 smaller SADC members, with provisions coordinating these economies with dominant South Africa, advances the economic part of this agenda. So far, however, Pretoria's efforts to marshal its latent political power have been disappointing.

First, South Africa's most conspicuous displays of multilateral leadership (such as its key role as a broker at the 1995 Non-Proliferation Treaty Review and Extension Conference) or moral criticism (like its condemnation of Nigeria's government over the execution of dissident journalist Ken Saro-Wiwa in November 1995) occurred during Nelson Mandela's presidency. By contrast, Mbeki has shown little interest in foreign policy or regional affairs. Whereas some African leaders accused South Africa of being a 'lackey of the West' under Mandela, its disengagement under Mbeki has equally damaged its credibility as a regional actor.

Second, the ongoing turmoil in Congo has contributed to paralysis in the development of a coherent regional intervention policy for the SADC – in particular its Organ on Politics, Defence and Security (OPDS), which was conceived in 1996 and has since been chaired by Mugabe. Whereas Zimbabwe has favoured the use of force for resolving the Congo crisis, South Africa has advocated diplomatic negotiation. Contradicting this apparent reluctance to resort to force, South Africa's violent and politically disastrous 600-troop intervention in Lesotho in September 1998 under a slender SADC mandate – purportedly to quell election-related anti-government unrest – further obscured what conditions would justify SADC military action.

Third, African capitals have tended to interpret Pretoria's reluctance to commit armed forces to African crises, such as the conflict in Congo, as indicating lack of political will. Though willing to use some of its regionally superior military capabilities for disaster relief in Mozambique, South Africa has not shown the enthusiasm for regional peacekeeping of, for example, Nigeria – in terms of overall military power, its chief sub-Saharan rival. On the other hand, Mugabe's personal desire for Zimbabwe to be a regional power – reflected in his aggressive support for the late Laurent Kabila in Congo and his recruitment of other SADC nations including Angola and Namibia to that cause – has accorded Zimbabwe weight well beyond what it deserves.

Mbeki's timid stand on Mugabe's domestic policies has only weakened South Africa's claim to regional leadership. But Zimbabwe's economic troubles and internal security crisis over the past year have severely compromised Mugabe's regional position and set clear prospective limits on his capacity to dominate the region. In November 2000, defence ministers of SADC nations meeting in Harare criticised Mugabe's aggressiveness in Congo and moved to curtail his power as chair of the OPDS. The leadership vacuum that these circumstances have created give Mbeki an opportunity to enhance South Africa's status as regional leader in spite of the aforementioned barriers. Other regional factors could sweeten this opportunity. Laurent Kabila has been replaced by his son Joseph, who appears more open to international mediation. Mugabe has admitted that he is 'looking for middle ground' in Congo. Were Zimbabwe to relinquish its leadership of Congo's three SADC allies by scaling back its involvement there, Angola and Namibia are likely to follow, leaving a period of SADC military inactivity more conducive to calmly formulating an OPDS mandate.

To capitalise on this broadened scope for increasing South Africa's regional prestige, Mbeki's first priority must be to ensure his own country's economic growth and keep investors confident in South Africa and in southern Africa as a whole. The prospects for his doing so remain somewhat remote. Nevertheless, in opening parliament on 9 February 2001, he urged racial unity in reinvigorating the economy and eradicating poverty and pointedly praised forward-looking whites for their contributions to the new South Africa. This was, at least, a hopeful sign that he is aware that significant changes in government policy are needed. On the regional level, other than Mbeki himself, the chief leader is Mugabe, who has lost the necessary standing to influence other leaders. Under President George W. Bush, American engagement in sub-Saharan Africa – despite his appointment of blacks to the two top US foreign-policy posts and new rhetoric about Africa's importance – is likely to remain marginal.

Given that the economy's travails have heightened South Africa's need for hard currency and development aid, however, the Bretton Woods

Africa

institutions are a possible source of influence over South African domestic policies. South Africa has no outstanding indebtedness to the IMF, so there is nothing to impede an IMF initiative. Although Mbeki would resist overt attempts to intrude on his sovereign authority, carefully framed lending conditions could encourage him to rejuvenate bipartisan politics and perhaps to take a more assertive stand against Mugabe's land policy. Any resulting improvement in South Africa's economic performance would sound a reassuring note to wary donors and investors, and help avert the economic contagion triggered by Zimbabwe's woes. Such a development, in turn, might free Mbeki to attend more seriously to foreign policy and regional matters. But this is a chain of contingencies that will be difficult to start, let alone sustain.

Up and Down on the Horn

Although the Horn of Africa generally generates only gloomy news, in 2000 there was a little good news as well. The 30-month war between Eritrea and Ethiopia, which had threatened to spin out of control in mid-2000, was brought to an end and UN cease-fire monitors were deployed. Effective international pressure and domestic political and economic realities forced the two sides to return to the negotiating table, with positive results. Somalia, which has gone without an effective government since the early 1990s, announced a 'transitional' government in August 2000, but this was an administration that had very little hope or means of fulfilling its responsibilities because of endemic instability throughout the country. In Sudan, riven by more than 17 years of civil war, longstanding political differences between the Muslim, Arabic-speaking northerners and the predominantly Christian southerners were still strong in 2000. However, Sudan held presidential and parliamentary elections in December 2000. While an Islamic-based military government remained in place, it showed signs of becoming more tolerant and more open to reconciliation.

Sudan: Oil, War and Islam

Three familiar interconnected issues characterised developments in Sudan in 2000: war, oil and dictatorship. The continuing war in the south between the Khartoum government and the south Sudanese guerrilla forces is in its eighteenth year. The main guerrilla movement in the south, the Sudan People's Liberation Army (SPLA), led by John Garang, made no significant military or political gains over the year. Its political wing, the Sudan People's Liberation Movement (SPLM), already weakened in the past few years by its loss of support from Eritrea, Ethiopia and Uganda, was further damaged by new splits within the ranks of southern Sudanese. For example, a new group, the South Sudan Liberation Movement (SSLM), was formed in Upper Nile in January 2000. These fissures have given Sudanese President Omar Bashir considerable room to play one southern group against another; as a result, he saw no reason during 2000 to negotiate seriously to bring the war to an end.

As they had in previous years, Sudanese government representatives and liberation fighters held desultory peace talks on several occasions in 2000, but these talks again came to nought. Years of negotiations have failed to narrow the gap between the two sides. The southerners still resent the political and economic domination of the northerners. The Intergovernmental Authority on Development (IGAD), which has been negotiating peace in Sudan, was until recently debilitated by the fighting between two of its members, Eritrea and Ethiopia. It had launched an initiative for a referendum on the future of the south more than two years ago, but this initiative did not move forward during 2000. Gabriel Roric Jur, a junior minister in the Khartoum government, said in January 2001 that President Bashir had accepted the idea of a referendum on self-determination whatever the outcome, but there was no indication that his government had reached an understanding with the SPLM over the issue. Both sides continued to express willingness to reach a settlement, but neither was ready to make the compromises that would be necessary to achieve it.

The Khartoum government's refusal to negotiate seriously has been very costly to the people of southern Sudan. As of 2000, some 52,000 had been killed as a direct result of military action; more than two million southern lives had been lost since 1983 through drought and famine whose consequences have been exacerbated by the war. Others have been maimed, raped or subjected to other atrocities. It is estimated that more than 4.5m southern Sudanese have been displaced – the largest group of displaced persons anywhere in the world. In recent years, UN agencies and non-governmental organisations (NGOs) have highlighted the social, economic, psychological and humanitarian impacts of the civil war on the people of southern Sudan, but the international community has yet to treat this situation with the seriousness it deserves.

According to Sudanese government officials, the war has made it difficult for Sudan to drill and export oil, which is produced in the south. Indeed, some of the causes of the war itself hinge on that oil. Khartoum has been trying to assure its right to exploit southern oil deposits, while one of the southerners' main grievances since 1983 involves the distribution of income from the production of oil in their region. Despite obvious security problems, foreign petroleum companies have been keen to exploit the oil. The Canadian oil company, Talisman Energy, owns 25% of an operating $1.2 billion, 1,600-kilometre pipeline from southern Sudan to Port Sudan on the Red Sea. A consortium including Petronas, a Malaysian corporation; Lundin Oil AB, a Swedish outfit; OMV (Sudan) Exploration GmbH of Austria; and Sudan's own Sudapet Ltd have an exploration site in southern Sudan, and struck oil in March 2001. In late 2000, it was reported that the French oil company, Total, had also signed an exploration agreement with the Sudanese government. China National Petroleum Corporation is involved in the financing of the pipeline, and, with Petronas, Talisman and Sudapet, is part of another consortium, the Greater Nile Petroleum Operating Company, which is producing oil. Rolls-Royce of the UK has provided diesel engines for the pipeline and the Glasgow-based Weir Group has contracted to furnish the pumping stations.

In 2000, representatives of the southern Sudanese people repeatedly accused Talisman Energy of financing the war against them. Some village chiefs said that systematic government bombing and ground attacks began in March 2000. In January 2001, the SPLA reported that it had attacked several production sites in the Bantiyu region, killing 'dozens' of government soldiers and destroying three wells. The government denied these claims. Specific allegations have also surfaced – some from Amnesty International and Christian Aid – that the government has forcibly depopulated drilling areas in order to facilitate exploration and attract further investment, and that the oil companies therefore are indirectly buttressing the extreme Islamic government. In March 2001, Lundin responded on CNN to one such claim by stating that its programme entailed the enhancement of the Sudanese people's quality of life and economic and social development, and that the company would not tolerate human-rights violations. Lundin promised to investigate the claims. NGOs and the media – including the *New York Times*, the *Washington Post* and *The Guardian* – have implored Western governments to impose capital-markets sanctions against the oil companies themselves or moral pressure on shareholders to discourage the companies from doing business in Sudan. The Lundin drama, however, suggests that public disclosures could also motivate foreign oil companies to exert positive pressure on the Sudanese government by continuing rather than suspending in-country operations.

President Bashir, for his part, seems determined to change Sudan's image. In an effort to lend legitimacy to his regime, he organised presidential and parliamentary elections in December 2000. There were four other candidates for the presidency, including former President Jaafar

Nimeiri, who had introduced Islamic law (*Sharia*) in 1983. These men were political novices, however, and the result was foreordained. Because 90 of the 360 parliamentary seats were nominated by the president, several political parties, including the Democratic Unionist Party (DUP), the National Democratic Alliance (NDA) and the SPLM, boycotted the elections. Hassan al-Turabi, the architect of Bashir's dictatorship who had fallen out with him in December 1999 and formed the opposition People's National Congress, described the Bashir government in December 2000 as presiding over a police state. Another leader whose intimate dealings with Bashir would give him keen insight into the government's methods of operation is the Umma Party leader and former prime minister, Saddiq al-Mahdi. He emphasised to journalists in January 2001 that notwithstanding the elections, Bashir's government was still unmistakably totalitarian.

Bashir's showdown with Turabi in late 1999 and early 2000 helped him to improve his relations with other countries in the region, as Eritrea and Ethiopia shifted their support to him. However, in the mainstream of world opinion Sudan was still regarded as a pariah state with unacceptable policies, including the sponsorship of terrorism. For this reason, Sudan's bid to join the UN Security Council was thwarted by the international community in October 2000. Sudan, geographically the largest African state, lost out to the tiny island nation of Mauritius.

Nevertheless, there are grounds for modest optimism. In August 2000, the International Monetary Fund (IMF) lifted its suspension of Sudan's voting and related rights, suggesting that the United States perceived or anticipated a shift in Sudanese policies worth encouraging. And Bashir has tried to shed some Islamic extremist baggage since his split with Turabi. The Sudanese economy is also doing well, with gross domestic product growing by over 6% in 2000 due to increased agricultural output, particularly cotton andlivestock, as well as oil production. While this relative prosperity serves to bolster Bashir's regime, he has endeavoured to gain more international respectability – for example, by joining the Chemical Weapons Convention and by limiting relations with other countries suspected of sponsoring terrorism, such as Iran. These ostensibly positive departures, however, may be driven by internal and regional power struggles or the prospect of short-term political gain internationally, and therefore could be subject to reversal.

Somalia: Factions and a Virtual Government

In 2000 the world was reminded of the major contradiction that exists in Somalia's political situation. Although government and public institutions had disintegrated in the early 1990s, the anarchy that resulted was not total because the traditional clan networks in the country, which is 98% Muslim, remained virtually intact. The warlords, who have ruled their individual fiefdoms since the overthrow of former dictator Mohammed Siad Barre in 1991, are still heavily armed and have a great deal to lose should order return to the country. At the same time, the Somali clan elders and religious leaders represent a form of governance that was not completely overwhelmed by the gun-wielding militias in the 1990s.

In an effort to recreate a national government, more than 2,000 Somali clan elders, religious leaders, business people and peace activists met in relatively peaceful Djibouti in August 2000 under the aegis of the Intergovernmental Authority on Development (IGAD), the Horn of Africa's principal regional organisation, and formed a transitional government for Somalia. Neither it nor the new 245-member parliament chosen by the elders perform the normal functions of administering the country, however, because of insecurity in Mogadishu. The transitional government has been unable to establish public institutions or to start collecting taxes with which it can perform governmental functions. The prime minister and his ministers have small offices in a three-story building in Mogadishu, but they have little furniture and no phones or other basic office equipment.

The initiative for a Somali government in exile came from Djibouti's President Ismael Omar Guelleh. Unlike the UN in the early 1990s, which relied on armed militias to try to form a government of national unity, the Djibouti initiative relied on religious leaders, traditional elders and other members of civil society. The newly appointed Somali transitional president, Abdiqassim Salad Hassan, was an interior minister in Siad Barre's government. The transitional government includes Ali Mahdi Mohammed, the nemesis of the late Mohamed Farah Aideed, who gave the UN peacekeeping force such a rough time in the early 1990s. As expected, Aideed's son, Hussein Mohamed Aideed, who now leads his father's faction, the Somali National Alliance, dismissed the transitional government as a cynical move by outsiders.

Indeed, the creation of Somalia's government in neighbouring Djibouti raised several questions. From where does it derive its legitimacy? What are its chances of success without the backing of the armed factions? And how does it relate to the breakaway regions of Somaliland and Puntland? Besides the opposition of Aideed, five Mogadishu-based faction leaders sent a letter in early 2001 to the UN Secretary-General Kofi Annan objecting to a UN proposal for a peace-building mission to assist the transitional government, arguing that there was no legitimate authority in the country. There is no doubt that the transitional government's legitimacy will remain tenuous and that it constitutes an administration only in name. However, its supporters argue that the legitimacy of any

Somali government rests with the people of Somalia, and that the elders who met in Djibouti do indeed represent the people.

An immediate challenge that the transitional government faces is the splintering of the country into so-called autonomous states. Two parts of Somalia have declared themselves independent. The north-western 'state' of Somaliland, which declared itself independent in 1991, does not recognise the transitional government. Somaliland has its own government, legislature, police force and currency, and has gained a measure of economic viability via trading with its Gulf neighbours across the Red Sea. Its leader, Mohammed Ibrahim Egal, was prime minister of Somalia until Barre overthrew him in 1969. In a letter to the UN Security Council in January 2001, Egal called on the UN to accord Somaliland a special status like that of East Timor and Kosovo. This would give Somaliland the recognition it needs to deal with donors and international financial institutions. Crucially, he declared that Somaliland was not a part of Somalia.

In the north-east, the mini-state of Puntland, which declared its 'independence' a few years ago, also refuses to recognise the authority of the transitional government of Somalia. Furthermore, in January 2001 several groups met in the southern town of El Berde, Bakool Region, to establish an autonomous regional state in southern and south-western Somalia along the lines of Puntland. Ironically, they also proposed the establishment of a National Restoration Council that would seek to bring all Somali factions together. Omar Haji Masale of the Somali National Front (SNF), Mohammed Said Hersi 'Morgan' (the son-in-law of Siad Barre), and Hassan Mohammed Nur of the Rahanwein Resistance Army (RRA) are among the major supporters of efforts to establish an autonomous state, 'Jubaland', in southern Somalia. The other factions that backed the initiative were the Somali Patriotic Movement (SPM) and Southern Somali National Movement (SSNM). Abdullahi Yusuf Ahmad, leader of Puntland, also attended the El Berde meeting, but it ended inconclusively.

The initiative to form an autonomous state in southern Somalia was clearly designed to undermine the authority of the transitional government from within. It appeared to have the tacit backing of two of Somalia's neighbours, Ethiopia and Kenya. They may have strategic reasons for discouraging a unitary Somali state or mercenary motivations for backing dissident factions. Thus, while Djibouti supports the transitional government, other bigger and strategically more important neighbours appear to be moving in the opposite direction. Meanwhile, Somalia continues to accuse Ethiopia of illegally occupying parts of Somalia, particularly the Bulo Hawa, Luq and Dolo districts in the south-western Gedo region. The Ethiopian government consistently denies such activity.

Africa

In early 2001, however, the transitional government of Somalia claimed that Ethiopian troops killed several civilians when they staged pro-Somalia demonstrations. The UN Secretary-General's special representative to Somalia also expressed concern about Ethiopia's interference in its neighbour's affairs.

For a new Somali government to succeed, it would need considerable support from at least three sources: the Somali people both within and outside the country; the neighbouring states, especially Djibouti, Ethiopia and Kenya; and the international community, especially Western donors, the UN and international financial institutions. However, by early 2001 serious support from these sources had not materialised. In any case, the durability of the transitional government remains doubtful. It may be more realistic for the UN and outside donors to support the smaller political subdivisions in the hope of nurturing, from the 'bottom up', an emerging political order that could eventually render Somalia politically and economically viable. Though the US reportedly endorses limited recognition of Somaliland, the UN has declined to deem any of the self-proclaimed Somali statelets a legal political entity, rendering them ineligible for IMF and World Bank membership and hence, funding. The former Somalia is also roughly $600m in arrears to these institutions, which also makes them reluctant to lend for economic reasons. Meanwhile, without a government infrastructure, most Somalis remain highly vulnerable to floods, droughts and disease. The UN Food and Agriculture Organisation rates Somalis the hungriest people in the world, with 27% failing to get their minimum daily nutritional requirement. As of autumn 2000, severe food shortages and a cholera epidemic put 1.2m Somalis at direct risk.

Ethiopia–Eritrea: Fighting Ends

After more than two years of fighting, Ethiopia and Eritrea signed an agreement to end their war in December 2000. The war, which was fought over a barren patch of land near the two countries' common border, had caused tens of thousands of deaths, with several thousand more maimed and in excess of a million civilians displaced. In addition, famine, exacerbated by drought and war, jeopardised hundreds of thousands of people. As they had been in 1999, the Organisation of African Unity (OAU) and the UN were deeply involved in negotiating an end to the Eritrea–Ethiopian war. In early May 2000, a seven-member special mission of the UN Security Council, headed by US ambassador to the UN Richard Holbrooke, visited the two countries and discussed with their leaders how to end the conflict and avoid a renewal of hostilities. Within less than a week of their visit, however, Ethiopia opened a new offensive. UN Security

Council Resolution 1297 of 12 May 2000 strongly condemned the renewed fighting and demanded that both parties 'immediately cease all military action'. Less than a week later, UNSC Resolution 1298 imposed further sanctions on Eritrea and Ethiopia and demanded that OAU peace talks convene without preconditions.

Intense fighting in mid-May 2000 was decidedly one-sided. Ethiopia, whose population is 60m, launched a swift military offensive against Eritrea, whose population numbers about 4m. After several weeks of bombardment and more destruction, Ethiopia declared the war over, and in June the two countries signed a cease-fire agreement. It then took many months of negotiations by the OAU and relentless pressure from the US and the UN before Ethiopian Prime Minister Meles Zenawi and Eritrean President Issaias Afwerki swallowed their pride and signed the peace agreement in December 2000.

The OAU drafted a six-article peace agreement which commits both countries to a permanent cessation of military activities along the border. It also calls for the establishment of a neutral, five-member commission based in Geneva to demarcate the border between Eritrea and Ethiopia, using colonial treaties. This commission is expected to complete its work within three years. The treaty states that after the demarcation, 'each party shall respect the border so determined, as well as the territorial integrity and sovereignty of the other party'. Under the agreement, the UN cartographer is expected to serve as secretary to the boundary commission. The peace agreement also sets up commissions to swap prisoners of war, return displaced persons and hear claims for compensation for war damage.

While the peace agreement had considerable international support, it is not likely to satisfy powerful constituencies in the two countries, especially those in Ethiopia. This is because the war was driven by many factors that had very little to do with the border *per se*. Rather, it turned on unresolved problems between Eritrea and Ethiopia concerning sovereignty, legitimacy and the nature of political institutions. Other factors included economic development, national currencies, trade and Ethiopia's lack of direct access to the sea. Since most of these long-term problems were not addressed by the peace agreement, it was not surprising that in early 2001 eight Ethiopian opposition parties demonstrated in Addis Ababa, claiming that the peace agreement had left Ethiopia without unhindered access to the sea and that it was based on nineteenth-century colonial treaties between Ethiopia and Italy that were not binding.

The UN is doing what it can to prevent a new outbreak of fighting. Security Council Resolution 1320 of 15 September 2000 called on both countries 'to fulfil all their obligations under international law, including the agreement on cessation of hostilities'. It also authorised the deployment of 4,200 troops, 'including up to 220 military observers, until 15 March 2001'. The peacekeeping component of the UN mission to Ethiopia and Eritrea (UNMEE), headed by the Dutch Major-General Patrick Cammaert, began its deployment in December 2000. It has a wide mandate that includes chairing a military coordination commission 'to be established by the United Nations and the Organisation of African Unity in accordance with the agreement on the cessation of hostilities'. Resolution 1320 urged both sides 'to proceed immediately with de-mining, in order to ensure safe access' of UN and associated personnel to the areas being monitored. By mid-January 2001, Kofi Annan reported that the military component of UNMEE stood at 3,432 military personnel from 35 countries and 153 military observers. The Netherlands has contributed the largest contingent of 1,104 troops, followed by Jordan with 956, Canada with 550, Denmark with 331, Slovakia with 157 and Italy with 124. Although several African countries sent in a handful of military observers, none of them contributed troops to UNMEE. While efforts to enforce a buffer zone encountered some difficulties in March 2001, UNMEE's mission was extended to 15 September 2001.

The international community has moved swiftly to promise support for Eritrea and Ethiopia. Having put pressure on both sides to reach an agreement, former US Secretary of State Madeleine Albright pledged in December 2000 that the US would help with mine clearance and provide development assistance to the two countries. The World Bank also committed itself to raising assistance worth about $270m in emergency reconstruction. Of this, the World Bank itself and the European Union initially pledged $90m, while Italy and other Western countries are expected to make up the balance.

What's Down the Road?

The Horn of Africa continues to be an unstable region. On balance, however, it has not been a bad year. Having signed a peace agreement, the Ethiopian and Eritrean governments have a chance to pay more attention to their development problems. Because the peace agreement addressed only some of the differences between the two sides, however, tensions are still high, and it would not take a large spark to ignite a war yet again – especially given the small size and limited capability of the UN force. Somalia's transitional government has no public institutions at its disposal and no money with which to create them. Thus, clan militias and self-proclaimed political entities are likely to offer more security and sustenance to the Somali people in the medium term, and will probably prevail over the new government. These entities could serve as building blocks for a new dispensation. While a full conversion of Sudan to the secular political mainstream is unlikely, Bashir's downplaying of extreme Islamism and his cautious inching of Sudan away from 'rogue' status suggests that he may be hoping to attract more Western support and may become more amenable to negotiating seriously for peace with the southern rebels.

Prospectives

Although 2000–01 was distinguished by multiple transitions, the consequences of the American election loom largest for international affairs in the coming year. Rhetorically at least, in President George W. Bush's administration the big picture trumps smaller issues. His team has presented a classical geopolitical worldview, the principal foci of which are the balance of power and alliance-building, and seems to be sending clearer signals to allies and rivals alike. There is also a perception that 'the pros' who steered the American resurgence in international affairs culminating in the Gulf War triumph are finally back in the driver's seat.

But no matter how astute the US administration might be in implementing its policies, developments beyond Washington's control will have a major impact on security in the coming year. These will include not only international frictions in the Middle East and the Gulf but also domestic political and economic changes in Asia – particularly China and Indonesia. Even Russia, downgraded in priority by the US administration, will doubtless force its way to the top end of international policy concerns. And non-governmental actions – by groups ranging from humanitarian non-governmental organisations to terrorists – will also influence the policy environment.

The Bush team's champions believe it has a clearer picture of the world it wishes to shape and a more 'strategic' and less *ad hoc* approach to foreign policy, and that it will be able to field these challenges adroitly. But they call for the sustained and simultaneous management of alliances, rivalries and global economic issues, many of which may arrive at critical junctures in 2001–02.

Europe and Asia

A key unknown is how Washington will handle alliances and rivalries in Europe and Asia. In Europe, worries about maintaining a smooth relationship with Russia, the decoupling of American and European defence and marginalisation of deterrence as a thematic basis of global security will continue to make European capitals cool toward national missile defence (NMD) – a pillar of Bush policy. It has, of course, customarily taken time to build consensus for major shifts in frameworks for maintaining nuclear stability. The ratification of the Anti-Ballistic Missile (ABM) Treaty to preserve 'mutual assured destruction' was as hotly debated in 1972 as its relaxation or abrogation is now being debated as a means of eliminating vulnerability as the linchpin of deterrence. Indeed, the Clinton administration's deferral of and the Bush administration's greater enthusiasm for NMD have created time and space for easing differences: longer-term prospects and plans for a thicker shield have pushed full deployment back.

In this less-urgent atmosphere, over the course of late 2000 and early 2001, NMD became a less divisive issue. Russia is engaging and being engaged with respect to the ABM Treaty. A new *modus vivendi* between Russia and the US may even emerge on the balance between offensive and defensive forces, and a codicil defining the new dispensation could replace the treaty altogether. China remains extremely concerned about US plans for theatre missile defence that may include Japan and Taiwan. But Washington is paying marginally more attention to China's concerns about the degradation of its nuclear deterrent, and the removal of stringent deadlines for deployment of a limited system have relaxed Beijing. European capitals, notably London and Berlin, seem to be slowly acquiescing to American determination. In light of that resoluteness, however, it will be essential for the United States' European allies to take the initiative in engaging Washington if they are to stand a chance of shaping NMD policy. Further, this move should be made early in the Bush administration to ensure that a satisfactory transatlantic political accommodation is reached before the US decides to disregard external input. Success will require more earnest transatlantic consultation, and probably less public posturing, on Russian and Chinese threat perceptions, the ABM Treaty and missile-defence coverage for Europe.

Also important is a better mutual understanding between the US and European Union (EU) member states on the role of the proposed 60,000-strong EU rapid-reaction force, initiated by France and the United Kingdom at St Malo in 1998. Because European defence budgets and military capabilities fall short of what is required to meet the headline goals for the force, as put forth at the 1999 EU summit in Helsinki, the force remains more aspirational than real. At the December 2000 EU summit in Nice, though, France made it clear that it expected the EU force to have access to NATO assets while retaining operational autonomy. However remote the prospect of the force's actual deployment, the French view appears to depart from Britain's stance that the EU force should not impinge on NATO's readiness to act or its actual operations. It also remains unclear precisely what the force's primary mission will be.

Thus, Britain and France will have to iron out their misunderstandings before transatlantic anxieties can be fully assuaged. Insofar as the UK remains Washington's first point of contact on European matters and France is uncomfortable with what it considers American *hyperpuissance*, London may have to take the lead on building an EU consensus on the rapid-reaction force's operating parameters and its mission. The Bush administration, for its part, may have to accept a standing peacekeeping role for NATO in order to help sell to France the idea of keeping the European force secondary to NATO.

The Bush administration has made clear its intention to focus more on Asia than did the Clinton administration. Nevertheless, Asian powers fear that the Bush team's geopolitical approach and its more confrontational view of China as a 'strategic competitor' will dictate a return to bilateral diplomacy, relegating the strategic roles of the Association of South East Asian Nations (ASEAN) Regional Forum, ASEAN and APEC. Beyond that, re-orienting US engagement with China could require extra effort on the part of the Bush team. That alliances not suffer, however, is crucial. South Korea will need Washington's close attention if North Korea's opening up is to be accorded the best chance to bear fruit. Likewise, while Bush may court Japan as a stronger ally as part of his China policy, he must also be sensitive to the domestic challenges Tokyo would face in raising its military profile and the regional challenges it would encounter from China if the US diminished its forward presence. The US relationship with Taiwan will call for delicate balancing, with Washington demonstrating clear support for Taipei without provoking China.

The onus, then, is on Washington to develop a clear and comprehensive Asia policy that embraces the full array of regional ramifications. Bush's team may discover that maintaining the American role as the bulwark of Asian regional stability, and moving in ways that might change the regional military balance, will not be an easy trick. Washington might be wise, in particular, to consider the importance of pursuing policies that help preserve the prevalence of pragmatists over hawks in Beijing.

The Middle East and the Gulf

In the wake of Clinton's failures in Geneva and Camp David and subsequent frustrations, the Bush administration has made plain its aversion to final-status peace agreements in favour of *ad hoc* agreements and *modi vivendi*, and suggested that it would stand back from actively mediating a peace process. This policy position may not be sustainable. When the newly elected Israeli Prime Minister Ariel Sharon visited the White House in March 2001, Bush disappointed Arabs by strongly supporting Sharon's condition that Palestinian violence cease before further negotiations could commence and extolling his leadership. But particularly if tensions continue to be high on the West Bank and Gaza, Bush will come under pressure from moderate Arab states to make the territories more liveable for Palestinians. Doing so will probably require Washington to re-immerse itself in trying to broker a deal between Israel and the Palestinian Authority. In addition, to support the continued containment policy against Iraq, some coalition partners may insist that the United States try to alleviate tensions in the territories.

Vice-President Dick Cheney and Secretary of Defense Donald Rumsfeld, of course, have advocated adopting an even harder line on Iraq. But given the hostility of coalition partners (in particular, France) and UN Security Council members (notably, France and Russia) to continuing the existing sanctions regime and the policing of the No-Fly Zones, a tougher policy would be politically difficult to implement. Moreover, the Iraq issue has the potential to poison transatlantic relations. To avoid this, the best approach is to rebuild the coalition with 'smarter' sanctions while reserving the option of using force. Whatever policy is adopted, of course, the objective should be not merely to expedite a short-term transatlantic consensus but also to enhance regional security.

On his visit to the Middle East in February 2001, Secretary of State Colin Powell supported the relaxation of civilian sanctions. Cheney and Rumsfeld appear open to this option. France is enthusiastic about it. The Bush administration, however, may find it difficult to build on this nascent convergence. The next logical phase of policy development is arms control. The US opposes UN Monitoring, Verification and Inspection Commission (UNMOVIC) inspections under the restrictive conditions on which Baghdad currently insists, while France favours them. Despite the improvement in the transatlantic climate as to Iraq policy, the Bush team needs to avoid the trap of accepting cosmetic UNMOVIC inspections that would give Saddam Hussein a falsely clean bill of health. Washington, with London, should be prepared to argue in the Security Council for a strengthened mandate for UNMOVIC, whereby the body can conduct probing and meaningful inspections. This time around, loosened civilian sanctions combined with a credible threat to use force should give Saddam a stronger incentive to comply.

Trade: a Transatlantic Bone of Contention and More

Annual trade between the US and the EU is approaching half a trillion dollars, and two-way investment (almost equally divided) exceeds $700 billion. Three million Americans are employed by European subsidiaries, the same number by American subsidiaries. Yet the two blocs have serious differences over trade. Brussels is resistant to ending its farm subsidy programme, has restricted American banana and beef imports, and also props up European aircraft and services industries, in apparent contravention of World Trade Organisation (WTO) rulings and rules. Several key EU members – notably France – want the WTO's open trading rules to include environmental and labour standards, to the consternation of developing nations whose chief assets are light regulation and cheap labour. The Bush administration advocates trade agreements without environmental or labour conditions.

How the EU–US trade dispute plays out goes to the very heart of the north–south relationship between developed and developing nations. While north–south inequalities diminished in the 1990s after 30 years of divergence, per-capita income in Africa remains lower now than it was a generation ago. Building the right global consensus on trade is paramount if the gap between northern priorities and southern needs is to be further bridged. The futility of UN peacekeeping and the difficulties involved in major-power military intervention in the wars of Africa are leaving the burden of nation building, in the broad sense, to globalisation-driven development. But the spotty record of structural adjustment policies and the reluctance of private concerns to invest in risky economies demonstrate that the Bretton Woods institutions and private capital alone cannot propel third-world economies into the twenty-first century. Thus, the complement of free trade is essential. The US should press EU members and other states to reject the message of anti-globalisation protesters who disrupted the WTO summit in Seattle in December 1999, and take on board the fact that restrictive labour and environmental riders to trade pacts will only impede the flow of capital from north to south and delay economic advancement. Dismantling trade barriers may also hasten economic recovery from the looming global downturn.

In the wake of the disappointment of Seattle, launching an inclusive new round in which the outstanding issues are confronted forthrightly, on a multilateral basis, appears crucial. US Trade Representative Robert Zoellick, in seeking 'fast track' negotiating authority from Congress for the president to close trade deals, has shown his commitment to free trade and to solving bilateral issues so as to pave the way for a new world trade round. But European insularity and Asia's regional preoccupations threaten to thwart such a development. Bush's concentration on the Western Hemisphere and congressional delays on fast-track authority could also sideline a new round. The best engine of progress would be a strong and unified American voice on the need for a new global agreement on trade. But the Bush administration must first tackle a difficult political task: building a domestic consensus in favour of globalisation and free trade among sceptical Americans.

The 'New Security Agenda'

Reflecting globalisation as well, the 'new security agenda' encompasses an array of post-modern concerns – transnational terrorism, ethnic strife, environmental degradation, food and energy scarcities, drug trafficking, unchecked population growth, rampant migration, organised crime, cyber-attacks – that call for multilateral redress. If the question of the 1990s was what shape the world would take after the Cold War, the question for the coming decade may be how political structures that are still driven by Westphalian states can manage a world that has become logistically and commercially global. Certainly multinational organisations – such as the UN, the EU, the Group of Eight and the Bretton Woods institutions – have key parts to play in facilitating consensus and softening sovereign divisions. But both national policies and national approaches to multilateral activities should complement their efforts.

Under the Bush administration's new national military policy, the Pentagon intends to 'skip a generation' in military technology to allow for streamlined, more agile and less vulnerable US power-projection capabilities, and for better repelling 'asymmetrical' attacks. This makes sense from the standpoint of the US, which has greater responsibility for international security than does Europe and faces some unique threats. Given the disinclination of EU capitals to raise defence budgets in real terms, however, accelerated US modernisation could widen the capability gap between the US and Europe revealed by the Kosovo campaign and hamper interoperability in joint operations on a broader scale. Europeans have a different security agenda from Washington, embracing primarily regional stability but in political and economic as well as military terms. Despite this divergence, Washington's extraordinary strategic responsibilities require it to maintain a healthy transatlantic security relationship.

Thus, the Bush team should consider how to enable both the EU and NATO Europe to close the gap without unduly compromising American or European priorities. Helpful measures could include lowering trade barriers that discourage European defence firms from competing with US outfits, and vice-versa; sharing American technology, especially with countries (like France and the UK) that are serious about modernising their own forces; cooperating with Europeans on peacekeeping; and improving coalition planning. European governments, for their part, need to moderate their fears – evidenced by their equity ownership of defence companies – that transatlantic commercial collaboration will undermine the viability of European defence industries. More generally, the EU and European capitals need to harmonise better their political priorities with their military limitations – for instance, by providing technical and financial support for threat reduction rather than maintaining a pretence to a major military capability.

The US also needs to think and act more multilaterally. The Bush administration has been aptly likened to a dominant corporation, angling for a greater share of the world power market. As such, it has manifested a tendency to treat foreign affairs as a set of bilateral transactions, sub-ordinating multilateral interaction. But the latter, in one way or the other, is required to address new security issues. In March 2001, for instance, Washington strained transatlantic relations by unceremoniously rejecting the Kyoto accord on greenhouse gas emissions. Yet European cooperation with the US on environmental issues affecting multilateral trade agreements might require more delicate handling of an international environmental pact that, while of dubious effectiveness, is politically important to Europeans. As of April 2001, the Bush administration had managed to aggravate both Russia and China by treating them as hostile strategic competitors. While confrontation may serve the American strategic agenda, if too blunt it can also limit Washington's options for securing the cooperation of those capitals in reducing security threats like organised crime, drug trafficking and terrorism that transcend national boundaries.

The EU membership's myopic preoccupation with its own supra-national institutional arrangements has permitted only sporadic and unpredictable political posturing in the diplomatic arena. It seems that EU representatives are in Skopje one day and Pyongyang the next, usually devoid of a clear plan. Over the past year, the EU has weighed in on the Middle East peace process merely to act as a counterweight to US support for Israel; criticised the US–UK sanctions policy on Iraq without articulating a better way to suppress the production of weapons of mass destruction; and hurriedly interposed itself between North and South Korea merely to fill a vacuum created by US disengagement, with no hint of an endgame in mind. Brussels appears to react to what it perceives as negative American signals rather than to act on its own. This reflexive mode of operation does not materially contribute to the resolution of diplomatic differences, and frequently widens them. Further, it crowds out transatlantic cooperation as a foreign-policy tool. The EU needs to develop an approach that is more affirmative and considered than the 'protest foreign policy' it now employs. Given the difficulty of generating consensus among 15 member states, however, it may not be possible for the EU to produce collective diplomatic clout commensurate with its economic power. Brussels would be wise to adopt more modest foreign-policy aims.

While superficially 'geopolitical' and purportedly 'realist', the Bush administration's initial manner of doing business has not fully exploited alliances or engaged non-allies in an optimally constructive way. Nor, for different reasons, has the EU done so. What specific new policies emerge on either side of the Atlantic remains to be seen. But it is clear that neither Bush's geopolitical mindset nor Europe's alternately insular and reactive approach is, by itself, enough to meet today's security requirements.

IISS*maps*

Strategic Geography 2000/2001

Europe

EU: Schengen agreements and asylum seekers II
EU: Security and defence III
Violence spreads into Macedonia IV

Middle East

Iraq no-fly zones V
West Bank and Gaza: renewed violence and proposals for peace VI

Asia

Russia's new federal districts VIII
Korean Peninsula: the changing relationship X

Central Asia

Drug trafficking in the Fergana Valley XII

Latin America

Mercosur's external trade XIII

Africa

Implementing peace: Ethiopia and Eritrea XIV
Conflict and refugees on Guinea's border XVI
Sierra Leone: the continuing conflict XVIII

Global Trends

The impact of global warming XX
Piracy hot-spots XXII
Worldwide internet usage XXIV
International terrorism XXVI
The spread of infectious diseases XXVIII
The global oil economy XXX
Oil chokepoints XXXII

——————	international boundaries	🌟 🌟	attack(s)/incident(s) and skirmishes
— · — · —	province or state boundaries		
— — — —	disputed and other boundaries	*Dar El Beida* ⊕	international airport/airfield
════════	roads	*Al Kharj* ⊕	air base
┄┄┄┄	railways		
LOFA	province or state	∿	rivers
◆	built-up areas	∿⋅⋅	seasonal or intermittent rivers
▣	capital cities	⬭	lakes
●	cities/towns	▲	mountain peaks (height in metres)

Europe EU: Schengen agreements and asylum seekers

The Schengen Agreements, signed since 1985, are integrated into the structures of the EU. The Contracting States have abolished checks on individuals at their common borders and harmonised control at their external borders. To accommodate greater freedom of movement, Schengen States have reinforced cooperation among authorities responsible for internal security matters.

Asylum applications to EU member states have risen from 387,000 in 1999 to almost 390,000 in 2000. The UK received the largest number of asylum applications (22% of the applications). Significant decreases were reported in applications from the Federal Republic of Yugoslavia, while applications from Iran nearly doubled.

IISS*maps*

BiH BOSNIA-HERZEGOVINA
FRY FEDERAL REPUBLIC OF YUGOSLAVIA
FYROM FORMER YUGOSLAV REPUBLIC OF MACEDONIA
L LIECHTENSTEIN
SL SLOVENIA
SWITZ SWITZERLAND
R RUSSIA

Greece participates in Euro from 1 January 2001

| SPAIN | EU member, March 2001 | EU member participating in the Euro since 1 January 1999 | EU member under the Schengen Convention |

Number of asylum seekers, 1999–2000

UK
Germany
Netherlands
Belgium
France

1999
2000

0 20 40 60 80 100
thousands

Nationality of asylum seekers, 1999–2000

FRY
Iraq
Afghanistan
Turkey
Iran

1999
2000

0 20 40 60 80 100 120
thousands

Europe EU: Security and defence

The European Union (EU) formally launched its enlargement process in March 1998. There are currently 13 applicant countries. If enlargement is carried out in full, the EU's area will increase by 34%, and its population by 105 million.

The decision to create a European Rapid Reaction Force (ERRF) was made during the Euro-Summit in Helsinki, December 2000. The ERRF was stated to comprise 60,000 troops but current pledged contributions are at 84,600. The force's primary mission and its relationship with NATO have not been fully clarified. National governments are to retain the authority to decide in which operations their forces will take part.

BiH	BOSNIA-HERZEGOVINA
CR	CROATIA
FRY	FEDERAL REPUBLIC OF YUGOSLAVIA
FYROM	FORMER YUGOSLAV REPUBLIC OF MACEDONIA
L	LIECHTENSTEIN
SWITZ	SWITZERLAND
R	RUSSIA

SPAIN — EU member, March 2001

MALTA — applicants for EU enlargement

■ NATO members

European Rapid Reaction Force as proposed December 2000

Europe Violence spreads into Macedonia

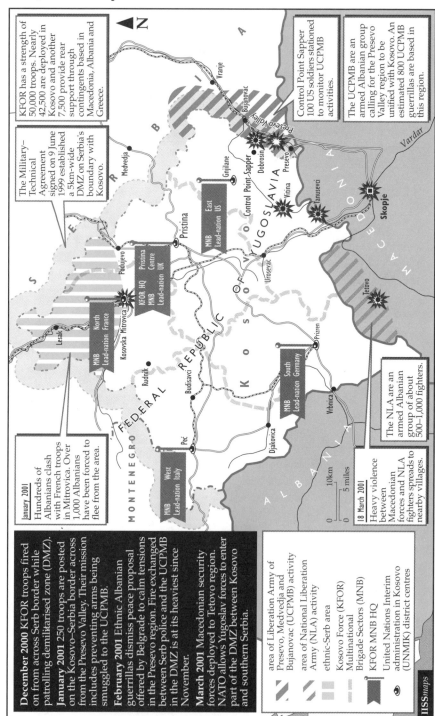

KFOR has a strength of 50,000 troops. Nearly 42,500 are deployed in Kosovo and another 7,500 provide rear support through contingents based in Macedonia, Albania and Greece.

The Military–Technical Agreement signed on 9 June 1999 established a 5km-wide DMZ on Serbia's boundary with Kosovo.

Control Point Sapper 100 US soldiers stationed to monitor UCPMB activities.

The UCPMB are an armed Albanian group calling for the Presevo Valley region to be unified with Kosovo. An estimated 800 UCPMB guerrillas are based in this region.

January 2001
Hundreds of Albanians clash with French troops in Mitrovica. Over 1,000 Albanians have been forced to flee from the area.

December 2000 KFOR troops fired on from across Serb border while patrolling demilitarised zone (DMZ).

January 2001 250 troops are posted on the Kosovo–Serbia border across from the Presevo Valley. Their mission includes preventing arms being smuggled to the UCPMB.

February 2001 Ethnic Albanian guerrillas dismiss peace proposal offered by Belgrade to calm tensions in the Presevo region. Fire exchanged between Serb police and the UCPMB in the DMZ is at its heaviest since November.

March 2001 Macedonian security forces deployed to Tetovo region. NATO allows Yugoslav forces to enter part of the DMZ between Kosovo and southern Serbia.

18 March 2001
Heavy violence between Macedonian forces and NLA fighters spreads to nearby villages.

The NLA are an armed Albanian group of about 500–1,000 fighters.

area of Liberation Army of Presevo, Medvedja and Bujanovac (UCPMB) activity

area of National Liberation Army (NLA) activity

ethnic-Serb area

Kosovo Force (KFOR) Multinational Brigade Sectors (MNB)

KFOR MNB HQ

United Nations Interim administration in Kosovo (UNMIK) district centres

IISS*maps*

Middle East Iraq no-fly zones

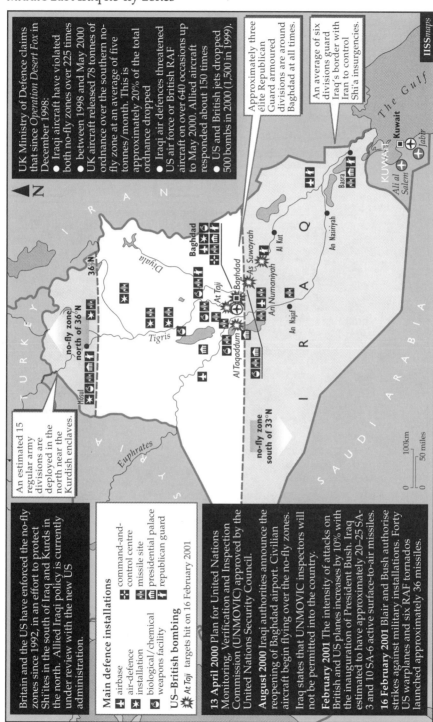

Britain and the US have enforced the no-fly zones since 1992, in an effort to protect Shi'ites in the south of Iraq and Kurds in the north. Allied Iraqi policy is currently under review with the new US administration.

An estimated 15 regular army divisions are deployed in the north near the Kurdish enclaves.

Main defence installations

- ✈ airbase
- ★ air-defence installation
- ◆ biological/chemical weapons facility
- ✚ command-and-control centre
- ⚑ missile site
- ⛫ presidential palace
- ✝ republican guard

US–British bombing

✹ *At Taji* targets hit on 16 February 2001

13 April 2000 Plan for United Nations Monitoring, Verification and Inspection Commission (UNMOVIC) approved by the United Nations Security Council.

August 2000 Iraqi authorities announce the reopening of Baghdad airport. Civilian aircraft begin flying over the no-fly zones. Iraq states that UNMOVIC inspectors will not be permitted into the country.

February 2001 The intensity of attacks on British and US planes increases by 10% with the inauguration of President Bush. Iraq estimated to have approximately 20–25 SA-3 and 10 SA-6 active surface-to-air missiles.

16 February 2001 Blair and Bush authorise strikes against military installations. Forty US warplanes and six RAF tornados launched approximately 36 missiles.

UK Ministry of Defence claims that since *Operation Desert Fox* in December 1998:

- Iraqi aircraft have violated both no-fly zones over 225 times between 1998 and May 2000
- UK aircraft released 78 tonnes of ordnance over the southern no-fly zone at an average of five tonnes/month. This is approximately 20% of the total ordnance dropped
- Iraqi air defences threatened US air force or British RAF aircraft on over 640 occasions up to May 2000. Allied aircraft responded about 150 times
- US and British jets dropped 500 bombs in 2000 (1,500 in 1999).

Approximately three élite Republican Guard armoured divisions are around Baghdad at all times.

An average of six divisions guard Iraq's border with Iran to control Shi'a insurgencies.

IISSmaps

Middle East West Bank and Gaza: renewed violence and proposals for peace

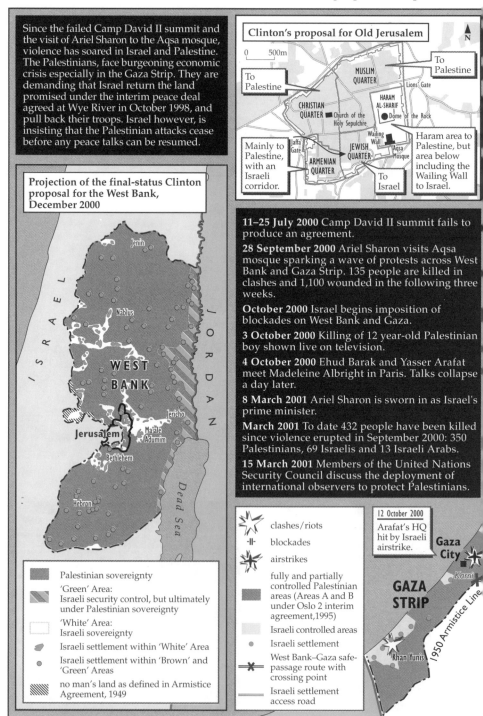

Since the failed Camp David II summit and the visit of Ariel Sharon to the Aqsa mosque, violence has soared in Israel and Palestine. The Palestinians, face burgeoning economic crisis especially in the Gaza Strip. They are demanding that Israel return the land promised under the interim peace deal agreed at Wye River in October 1998, and pull back their troops. Israel however, is insisting that the Palestinian attacks cease before any peace talks can be resumed.

Clinton's proposal for Old Jerusalem

0   500m

To Palestine

To Palestine

MUSLIM QUARTER

Lions' Gate

HARAM AL-SHARIF

CHRISTIAN QUARTER ■ Church of the Holy Sepulchre

● Dome of the Rock

Wailing Wall

Haram area to Palestine, but area below including the Wailing Wall to Israel.

Mainly to Palestine, with an Israeli corridor.

Jaffa Gate

JEWISH QUARTER

ARMENIAN QUARTER

Aqsa Mosque

To Israel

Projection of the final-status Clinton proposal for the West Bank, December 2000

Jenin

ISRAEL

Nablus

WEST BANK

JORDAN

Jericho

Jerusalem

Ma'ale Adumim

Bethlehem

Dead Sea

Hebron

11–25 July 2000 Camp David II summit fails to produce an agreement.

28 September 2000 Ariel Sharon visits Aqsa mosque sparking a wave of protests across West Bank and Gaza Strip. 135 people are killed in clashes and 1,100 wounded in the following three weeks.

October 2000 Israel begins imposition of blockades on West Bank and Gaza.

3 October 2000 Killing of 12 year-old Palestinian boy shown live on television.

4 October 2000 Ehud Barak and Yasser Arafat meet Madeleine Albright in Paris. Talks collapse a day later.

8 March 2001 Ariel Sharon is sworn in as Israel's prime minister.

March 2001 To date 432 people have been killed since violence erupted in September 2000: 350 Palestinians, 69 Israelis and 13 Israeli Arabs.

15 March 2001 Members of the United Nations Security Council discuss the deployment of international observers to protect Palestinians.

clashes/riots

blockades

airstrikes

12 October 2000 Arafat's HQ hit by Israeli airstrike.

Gaza City

Karni

GAZA STRIP

1950 Armistice Line

Khan Yunis

fully and partially controlled Palestinian areas (Areas A and B under Oslo 2 interim agreement,1995)

Israeli controlled areas

Israeli settlement

West Bank–Gaza safe-passage route with crossing point

Israeli settlement access road

Palestinian sovereignty

'Green' Area: Israeli security control, but ultimately under Palestinian sovereignty

'White' Area: Israeli sovereignty

Israeli settlement within 'White' Area

Israeli settlement within 'Brown' and 'Green' Areas

no man's land as defined in Armistice Agreement, 1949

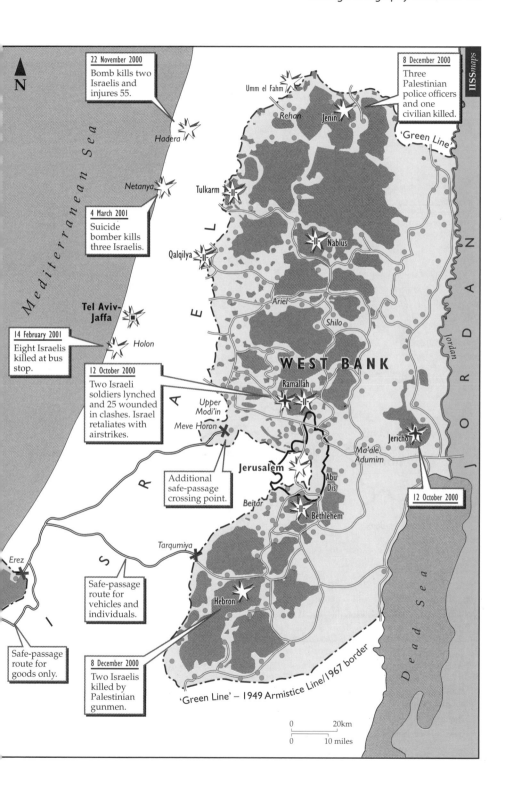

N

22 November 2000
Bomb kills two
Israelis and
injures 55.

Umm el Fahm

Rehan

Jenin

8 December 2000
Three
Palestinian
police officers
and one
civilian killed.

'Green Line'

M e d i t e r r a n e a n   S e a

Hadera

Netanya

Tulkarm

4 March 2001
Suicide
bomber kills
three Israelis.

Qalqilya

Nablus

Ariel

Shilo

Jordan

JORDAN

Tel Aviv-Jaffa

Holon

14 February 2001
Eight Israelis
killed at bus
stop.

WEST BANK

12 October 2000
Two Israeli
soldiers lynched
and 25 wounded
in clashes. Israel
retaliates with
airstrikes.

Ramallah

Upper
Modi'in

Meve Horon

Additional
safe-passage
crossing point.

Jerusalem

Abu
Dis

Ma'ale
Adumim

Jericho

12 October 2000

Beitar

Bethlehem

Tarqumiya

Erez

Safe-passage
route for
vehicles and
individuals.

Hebron

Safe-passage
route for
goods only.

8 December 2000
Two Israelis
killed by
Palestinian
gunmen.

'Green Line' – 1949 Armistice Line/1967 border

D e a d   S e a

ISRAEL

IISSmaps

0   20km
0   10 miles

Asia Russia's new federal districts

Central Federal District
The Federal District includes 17 regions
of the Russian Federation

Plenipotentiary Representative
of Russian President   Georgy S. Poltavchenko

Population   37,489,000

Centre of Federal District: Moscow

North-Western Federal District
The Federal District includes 11 regions
of the Russian Federation

Plenipotentiary Representative
of Russian President   Viktor V. Cherkesov

Population   14,848,000

Centre of Federal District: St Petersburg

NORWAY

SWEDEN

Baltic Sea

FINLAND

ESTONIA

LITHUANIA

LATVIA

R

BELARUS

UKRAINE

St Petersburg

North-Western Federal District

Moscow

Central Federal District

Nizhni Novgorod

Volga Federal District

Ural Federal District

Yekaterinburg

Rostov-on-Don

Southern Federal District

Novosibirsk

GEORGIA

ARMENIA

Caspian Sea

KAZAKSTAN

Aral

CHINA

Southern Federal District
The Federal District includes 13 regions
of the Russian Federation

Plenipotentiary Representative
of Russian President   Viktor G. Kazantsev

Population   21,790,000

Centre of Federal District: Rostov-on-Don

Volga Federal District
The Federal District includes 15 regions
of the Russian Federation

Plenipotentiary Representative
of Russian President   Sergei V. Kiriyenko

Population   32,443,000

Centre of Federal District   Nizhni Novgorod

Far Eastern Federal District
The Federal District includes 10 regions
of the Russian Federation

Plenipotentiary Representative
of Russian President   Konstantin B. Pulikovsky

Population   7,538,000

Centre of Federal District   Khabarovsk

In May 2000 President Putin issued a decree dividing the
country into seven federal districts, each with an appointed
presidential representative. These appointees' main source
of power is patronage, and they control appointments in
the local branches of federal agencies. The purpose of this
and other reforms is to strengthen the president's
constitutional powers in practice, and to exert more control
over the work of federal bodies and regional leaders.

Far Eastern
Federal
District

Siberian
Federal
District

Khabarovsk

CHINA

Lake
Baikal

JAPAN

NORTH
KOREA

SOUTH
KOREA

Ural Federal District
The Federal District includes 6 regions
of the Russian Federation

Plenipotentiary Representative
of Russian President   Pyotr M. Latyshev

Population   14,476,000

Centre of Federal District   Yekaterinburg

Siberian Federal District
The Federal District includes 16 regions
of the Russian Federation

Plenipotentiary Representative
of Russian President   Leonid V. Drachevsky

Population   21,391,000

Centre of Federal District   Novosibirsk

IISSmaps

Asia Korean Peninsula: the changing relationship

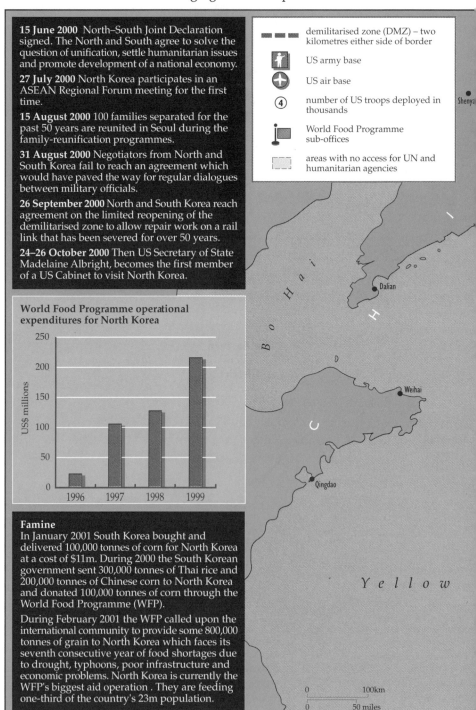

15 June 2000 North–South Joint Declaration signed. The North and South agree to solve the question of unification, settle humanitarian issues and promote development of a national economy.

27 July 2000 North Korea participates in an ASEAN Regional Forum meeting for the first time.

15 August 2000 100 families separated for the past 50 years are reunited in Seoul during the family-reunification programmes.

31 August 2000 Negotiators from North and South Korea fail to reach an agreement which would have paved the way for regular dialogues between military officials.

26 September 2000 North and South Korea reach agreement on the limited reopening of the demilitarised zone to allow repair work on a rail link that has been severed for over 50 years.

24–26 October 2000 Then US Secretary of State Madelaine Albright, becomes the first member of a US Cabinet to visit North Korea.

- - - - demilitarised zone (DMZ) – two kilometres either side of border

US army base

US air base

④ number of US troops deployed in thousands

World Food Programme sub-offices

areas with no access for UN and humanitarian agencies

World Food Programme operational expenditures for North Korea

US$ millions (y-axis: 0, 50, 100, 150, 200, 250)

x-axis: 1996, 1997, 1998, 1999

Famine
In January 2001 South Korea bought and delivered 100,000 tonnes of corn for North Korea at a cost of $11m. During 2000 the South Korean government sent 300,000 tonnes of Thai rice and 200,000 tonnes of Chinese corn to North Korea and donated 100,000 tonnes of corn through the World Food Programme (WFP).

During February 2001 the WFP called upon the international community to provide some 800,000 tonnes of grain to North Korea which faces its seventh consecutive year of food shortages due to drought, typhoons, poor infrastructure and economic problems. North Korea is currently the WFP's biggest aid operation . They are feeding one-third of the country's 23m population.

Shenya

Dalian

Bo Hai

Weihai

Qingdao

Yellow

0   100km
0   50 miles

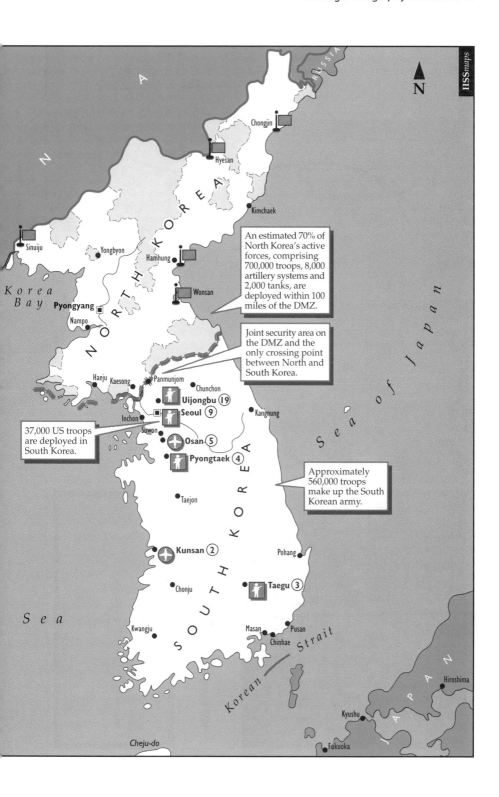

An estimated 70% of
North Korea's active
forces, comprising
700,000 troops, 8,000
artillery systems and
2,000 tanks, are
deployed within 100
miles of the DMZ.

Joint security area on
the DMZ and the
only crossing point
between North and
South Korea.

37,000 US troops
are deployed in
South Korea.

Approximately
560,000 troops
make up the South
Korean army.

Central Asia Drug trafficking in the Fergana Valley

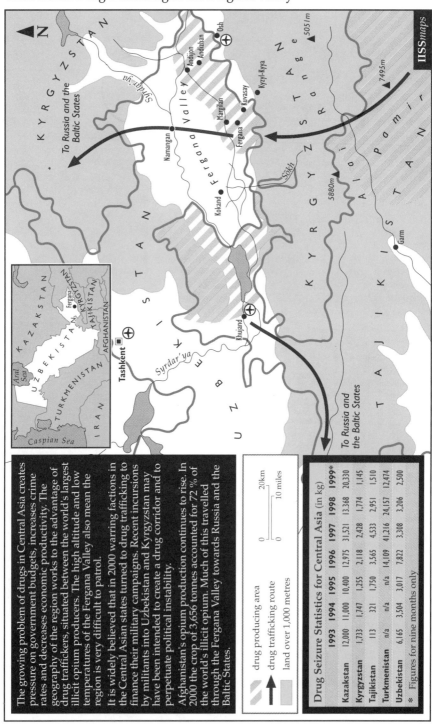

The growing problem of drugs in Central Asia creates pressure on government budgets, increases crime rates and decreases economic productivity. The geography of the region works to the advantage of drug traffickers, situated between the world's largest illicit opium producers. The high altitude and low temperatures of the Fergana Valley also mean the region is very difficult to patrol.

It is widely believed that in 2000 warring factions in the Central Asian states turned to drug trafficking to finance their military campaigns. Recent incursions by militants into Uzbekistan and Kyrgyzstan may have been intended to create a drug corridor and to perpetuate political instability.

Afghanistan's opium production continues to rise. In 2000 the crop of 3,656 tonnes accounted for 72% of the world's illicit opium. Much of this travelled through the Fergana Valley towards Russia and the Baltic States.

drug producing area

drug trafficking route

land over 1,000 metres

0   20km
0   10 miles

Drug Seizure Statistics for Central Asia (in kg)

	1993	1994	1995	1996	1997	1998	1999*
Kazakstan	12,000	11,000	10,400	12,975	31,521	13,368	20,330
Kyrgyzstan	1,733	1,747	1,255	2,118	2,428	1,774	1,145
Tajikistan	113	321	1,750	3,565	4,533	2,951	1,510
Turkmenistan	n/a	n/a	n/a	14,109	41,216	24,157	12,474
Uzbekistan	6,165	3,504	3,017	7,822	3,308	3,206	2,500

* Figures for nine months only

Latin America Mercosur's external trade

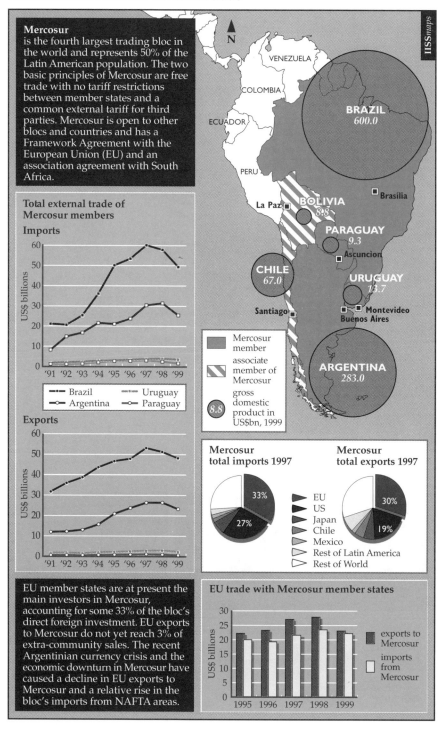

Mercosur
is the fourth largest trading bloc in the world and represents 50% of the Latin American population. The two basic principles of Mercosur are free trade with no tariff restrictions between member states and a common external tariff for third parties. Mercosur is open to other blocs and countries and has a Framework Agreement with the European Union (EU) and an association agreement with South Africa.

Total external trade of Mercosur members

Imports

Exports

- Brazil
- Argentina
- Uruguay
- Paraguay

Mercosur total imports 1997

Mercosur total exports 1997

- EU
- US
- Japan
- Chile
- Mexico
- Rest of Latin America
- Rest of World

EU member states are at present the main investors in Mercosur, accounting for some 33% of the bloc's direct foreign investment. EU exports to Mercosur do not yet reach 3% of extra-community sales. The recent Argentinian currency crisis and the economic downturn in Mercosur have caused a decline in EU exports to Mercosur and a relative rise in the bloc's imports from NAFTA areas.

EU trade with Mercosur member states

- exports to Mercosur
- imports from Mercosur

Africa Implementing peace: Ethiopia and Eritrea

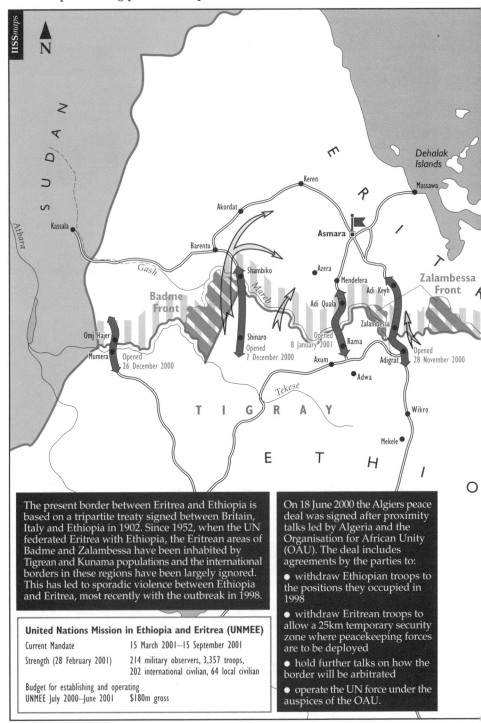

The present border between Eritrea and Ethiopia is based on a tripartite treaty signed between Britain, Italy and Ethiopia in 1902. Since 1952, when the UN federated Eritrea with Ethiopia, the Eritrean areas of Badme and Zalambessa have been inhabited by Tigrean and Kunama populations and the international borders in these regions have been largely ignored. This has led to sporadic violence between Ethiopia and Eritrea, most recently with the outbreak in 1998.

United Nations Mission in Ethiopia and Eritrea (UNMEE)

Current Mandate	15 March 2001–15 September 2001
Strength (28 February 2001)	214 military observers, 3,357 troops, 202 international civilian, 64 local civilian
Budget for establishing and operating UNMEE July 2000–June 2001	$180m gross

On 18 June 2000 the Algiers peace deal was signed after proximity talks led by Algeria and the Organisation for African Unity (OAU). The deal includes agreements by the parties to:

● withdraw Ethiopian troops to the positions they occupied in 1998

● withdraw Eritrean troops to allow a 25km temporary security zone where peacekeeping forces are to be deployed

● hold further talks on how the border will be arbitrated

● operate the UN force under the auspices of the OAU.

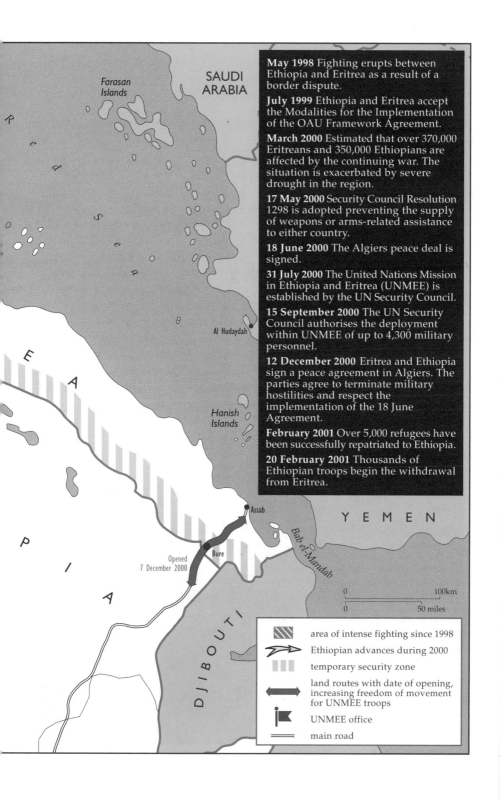

May 1998 Fighting erupts between Ethiopia and Eritrea as a result of a border dispute.

July 1999 Ethiopia and Eritrea accept the Modalities for the Implementation of the OAU Framework Agreement.

March 2000 Estimated that over 370,000 Eritreans and 350,000 Ethiopians are affected by the continuing war. The situation is exacerbated by severe drought in the region.

17 May 2000 Security Council Resolution 1298 is adopted preventing the supply of weapons or arms-related assistance to either country.

18 June 2000 The Algiers peace deal is signed.

31 July 2000 The United Nations Mission in Ethiopia and Eritrea (UNMEE) is established by the UN Security Council.

15 September 2000 The UN Security Council authorises the deployment within UNMEE of up to 4,300 military personnel.

12 December 2000 Eritrea and Ethiopia sign a peace agreement in Algiers. The parties agree to terminate military hostilities and respect the implementation of the 18 June Agreement.

February 2001 Over 5,000 refugees have been successfully repatriated to Ethiopia.

20 February 2001 Thousands of Ethiopian troops begin the withdrawal from Eritrea.

SAUDI ARABIA

Farasan Islands

Red Sea

Al Hudaydah

Hanish Islands

Assab

Bure

Opened 7 December 2000

YEMEN

Bab el-Mandab

DJIBOUTI

ERITREA

ETHIOPIA

0   100km
0   50 miles

area of intense fighting since 1998

Ethiopian advances during 2000

temporary security zone

land routes with date of opening, increasing freedom of movement for UNMEE troops

UNMEE office

main road

Africa Conflict and refugees on Guinea's border

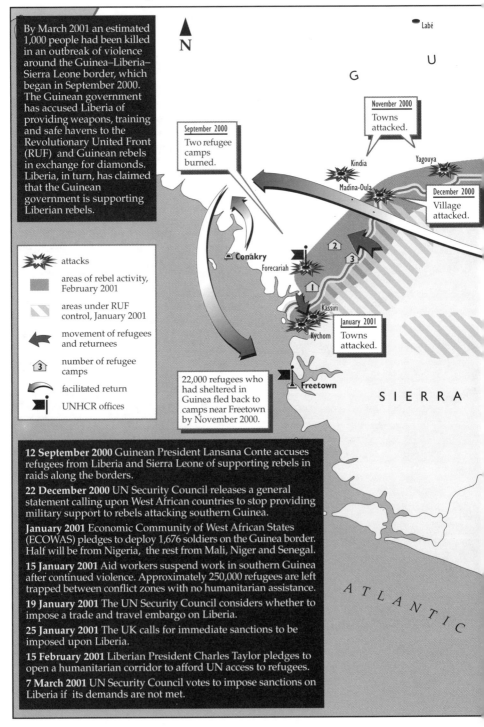

By March 2001 an estimated 1,000 people had been killed in an outbreak of violence around the Guinea–Liberia–Sierra Leone border, which began in September 2000. The Guinean government has accused Liberia of providing weapons, training and safe havens to the Revolutionary United Front (RUF) and Guinean rebels in exchange for diamonds. Liberia, in turn, has claimed that the Guinean government is supporting Liberian rebels.

September 2000
Two refugee camps burned.

November 2000
Towns attacked.

December 2000
Village attacked.

January 2001
Towns attacked.

22,000 refugees who had sheltered in Guinea fled back to camps near Freetown by November 2000.

Labé

U

G

Kindia

Yagouya

Madina-Oula

Conakry

Forecariah

Kassiri

Kychom

Freetown

SIERRA

ATLANTIC

attacks

areas of rebel activity, February 2001

areas under RUF control, January 2001

movement of refugees and returnees

number of refugee camps

facilitated return

UNHCR offices

12 September 2000 Guinean President Lansana Conte accuses refugees from Liberia and Sierra Leone of supporting rebels in raids along the borders.

22 December 2000 UN Security Council releases a general statement calling upon West African countries to stop providing military support to rebels attacking southern Guinea.

January 2001 Economic Community of West African States (ECOWAS) pledges to deploy 1,676 soldiers on the Guinea border. Half will be from Nigeria, the rest from Mali, Niger and Senegal.

15 January 2001 Aid workers suspend work in southern Guinea after continued violence. Approximately 250,000 refugees are left trapped between conflict zones with no humanitarian assistance.

19 January 2001 The UN Security Council considers whether to impose a trade and travel embargo on Liberia.

25 January 2001 The UK calls for immediate sanctions to be imposed upon Liberia.

15 February 2001 Liberian President Charles Taylor pledges to open a humanitarian corridor to afford UN access to refugees.

7 March 2001 UN Security Council votes to impose sanctions on Liberia if its demands are not met.

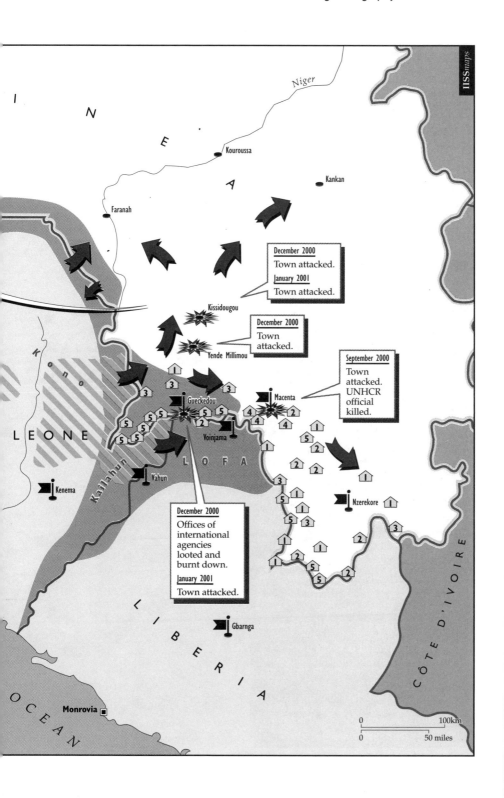

Africa Sierra Leone: the continuing conflict

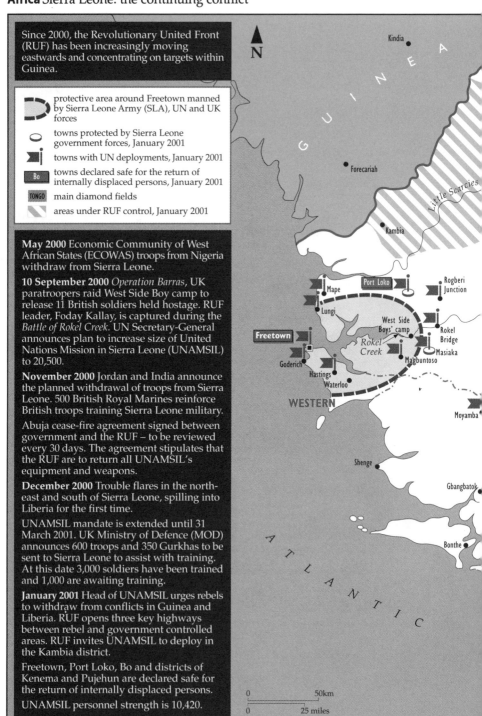

Since 2000, the Revolutionary United Front (RUF) has been increasingly moving eastwards and concentrating on targets within Guinea.

protective area around Freetown manned by Sierra Leone Army (SLA), UN and UK forces

towns protected by Sierra Leone government forces, January 2001

towns with UN deployments, January 2001

Bo towns declared safe for the return of internally displaced persons, January 2001

TONGO main diamond fields

areas under RUF control, January 2001

May 2000 Economic Community of West African States (ECOWAS) troops from Nigeria withdraw from Sierra Leone.

10 September 2000 *Operation Barras*, UK paratroopers raid West Side Boy camp to release 11 British soldiers held hostage. RUF leader, Foday Kallay, is captured during the *Battle of Rokel Creek*. UN Secretary-General announces plan to increase size of United Nations Mission in Sierra Leone (UNAMSIL) to 20,500.

November 2000 Jordan and India announce the planned withdrawal of troops from Sierra Leone. 500 British Royal Marines reinforce British troops training Sierra Leone military.

Abuja cease-fire agreement signed between government and the RUF – to be reviewed every 30 days. The agreement stipulates that the RUF are to return all UNAMSIL's equipment and weapons.

December 2000 Trouble flares in the north-east and south of Sierra Leone, spilling into Liberia for the first time.

UNAMSIL mandate is extended until 31 March 2001. UK Ministry of Defence (MOD) announces 600 troops and 350 Gurkhas to be sent to Sierra Leone to assist with training. At this date 3,000 soldiers have been trained and 1,000 are awaiting training.

January 2001 Head of UNAMSIL urges rebels to withdraw from conflicts in Guinea and Liberia. RUF opens three key highways between rebel and government controlled areas. RUF invites UNAMSIL to deploy in the Kambia district.

Freetown, Port Loko, Bo and districts of Kenema and Pujehun are declared safe for the return of internally displaced persons.

UNAMSIL personnel strength is 10,420.

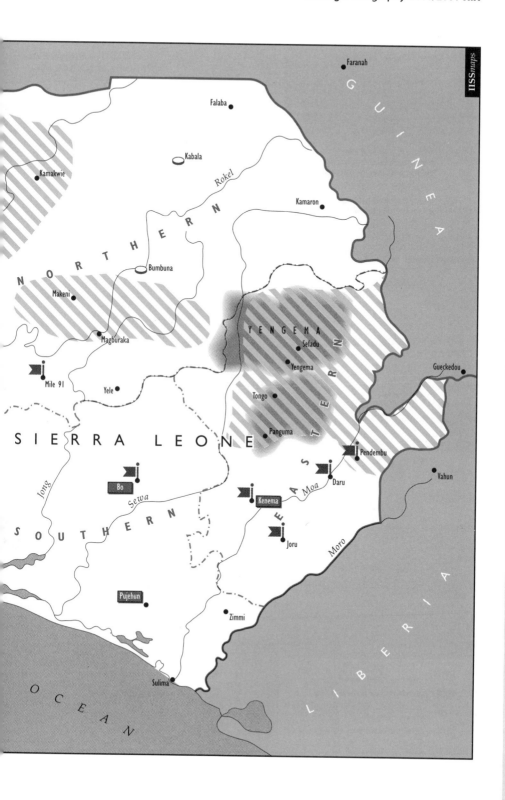

Faranah

Falaba

Kabala

Kamakwie

Rokel

N O R T H E R N

Kamaron

G U I N E A

Bumbuna

Makeni

Magburaka

Y E N G E M A

Sefadu

Yengema

Gueckedou

Mile 91

Yele

Tongo

S I E R R A   L E O N E

Panguma

E A S T E R N

Pendembu

Bo

Sewa

Jong

Moa

Daru

Vahun

Kenema

S O U T H E R N

Joru

Moro

Pujehun

L I B E R I A

Zimmi

Sulima

O C E A N

IISS*maps*

Global Trends The impact of global warming

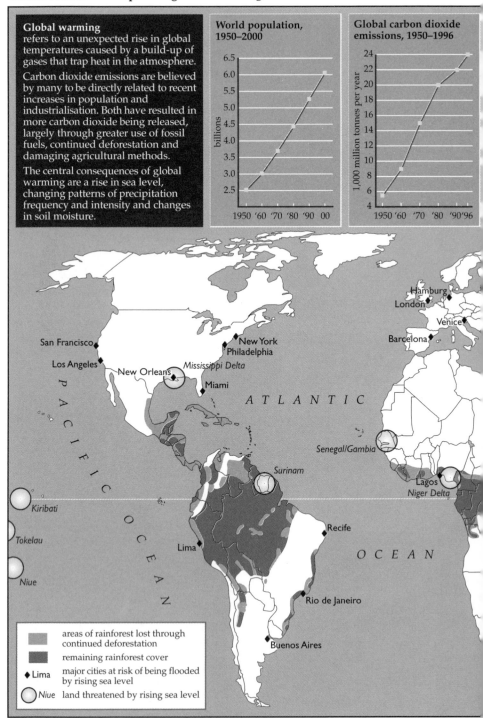

Global warming
refers to an unexpected rise in global temperatures caused by a build-up of gases that trap heat in the atmosphere.

Carbon dioxide emissions are believed by many to be directly related to recent increases in population and industrialisation. Both have resulted in more carbon dioxide being released, largely through greater use of fossil fuels, continued deforestation and damaging agricultural methods.

The central consequences of global warming are a rise in sea level, changing patterns of precipitation frequency and intensity and changes in soil moisture.

World population, 1950–2000

billions

6.5
6.0
5.5
5.0
4.5
4.0
3.5
3.0
2.5

1950 '60 '70 '80 '90 00

Global carbon dioxide emissions, 1950–1996

1,000 million tonnes per year

24
22
20
18
16
14
12
10
8
6
4

1950 '60 '70 '80 '90'96

San Francisco
Los Angeles
New Orleans
Mississippi Delta
Miami

New York
Philadelphia

ATLANTIC

Hamburg
London
Venice
Barcelona

Senegal/Gambia

Surinam

Lagos
Niger Delta

Kiribati

Tokelau
Lima

Niue

Recife

OCEAN

Rio de Janeiro

Buenos Aires

PACIFIC OCEAN

Legend

- areas of rainforest lost through continued deforestation
- remaining rainforest cover
- ◆Lima major cities at risk of being flooded by rising sea level
- ◯Niue land threatened by rising sea level

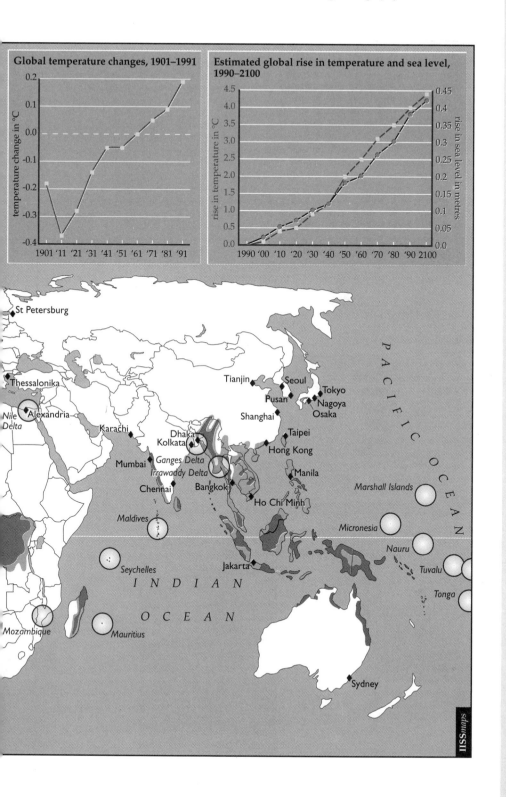

Global temperature changes, 1901–1991

temperature change in °C

1901 '11 '21 '31 '41 '51 '61 '71 '81 '91

Estimated global rise in temperature and sea level, 1990–2100

rise in temperature in °C

rise in sea level in metres

1990 '00 '10 '20 '30 '40 '50 '60 '70 '80 '90 2100

St Petersburg

Thessalonika

Nile Delta

Alexandria

Karachi

Tianjin

Seoul

Pusan

Tokyo

Nagoya

Osaka

Shanghai

Dhaka

Kolkata

Taipei

Hong Kong

Mumbai

Ganges Delta

Irrawaddy Delta

Manila

Chennai

Bangkok

Marshall Islands

Ho Chi Minh

Maldives

Micronesia

Nauru

Seychelles

Jakarta

Tuvalu

Tonga

Mozambique

Mauritius

Sydney

P A C I F I C   O C E A N

I N D I A N   O C E A N

IISS*maps*

Global Trends Piracy hot-spots

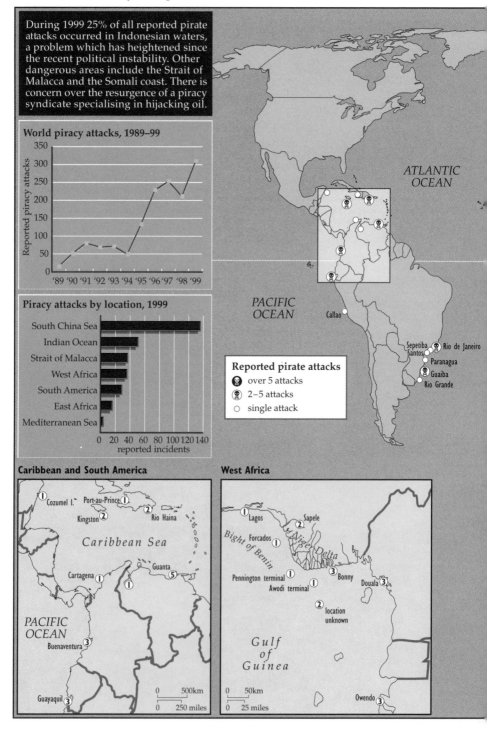

During 1999 25% of all reported pirate attacks occurred in Indonesian waters, a problem which has heightened since the recent political instability. Other dangerous areas include the Strait of Malacca and the Somali coast. There is concern over the resurgence of a piracy syndicate specialising in hijacking oil.

World piracy attacks, 1989–99

Reported piracy attacks

350
300
250
200
150
100
50
0

'89 '90 '91 '92 '93 '94 '95 '96 '97 '98 '99

Piracy attacks by location, 1999

South China Sea
Indian Ocean
Strait of Malacca
West Africa
South America
East Africa
Mediterranean Sea

0 20 40 60 80 100 120 140
reported incidents

ATLANTIC
OCEAN

PACIFIC
OCEAN

Callao

Sepetiba · Rio de Janeiro
Santos
Paranagua
Guaiba
Rio Grande

Reported pirate attacks
- over 5 attacks
- 2–5 attacks
- single attack

Caribbean and South America

Cozumel I.   Port-au-Prince
Kingston   Rio Haina
Caribbean Sea
Cartagena   Guanta
PACIFIC
OCEAN
Buenaventura

Guayaquil

0   500km
0   250 miles

West Africa

Lagos   Sapele
Bight of Benin Forcados   *Niger Delta*
Pennington terminal   Bonny   Douala
Awodi terminal
location
unknown
*Gulf
of
Guinea*
Owendo

0   50km
0   25 miles

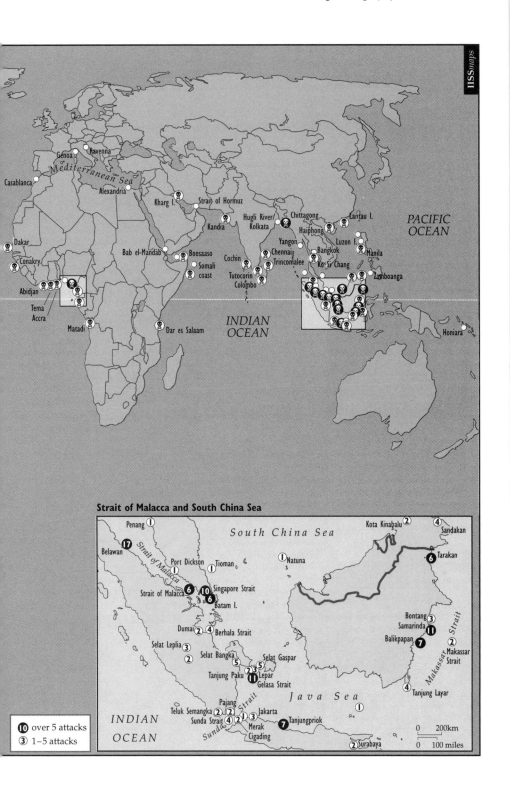

IISS*maps*

Genoa · Ravenna
Mediterranean Sea
Casablanca
Alexandria
Kharg I. · Strait of Hormuz
Kandia · Hugli River/Kolkata · Chittagong · Lantau I.
Dakar · Haiphong
Conakry · Bab el-Mandab · Boosaaso · Cochin · Yangon · Chennai · Bangkok · Luzon I. · Manila
Somali coast · Trincomalee · Ko Si Chang · Zamboanga
Abidjan · Tutocorin · Colombo
Tema · Accra
Matadi · Dar es Salaam
INDIAN OCEAN
PACIFIC OCEAN
Honiara

Strait of Malacca and South China Sea

Penang ①
South China Sea
Kota Kinabalu ② ④ Sandakan
Belawan ⑰
Strait of Malacca
Port Dickson ① Tioman ①
① Natuna
⑥ Tarakan
Strait of Malacca ⑥ ⑩ Singapore Strait
⑥ Batam I.
Bontang ③
Samarinda ⑪
Balikpapan ⑦
② *Makassar Strait*
Dumai ② ④ Berhala Strait
Selat Leplia ③
②
Selat Bangka ⑤
Selat Gaspar ⑤
Tanjung Paku ② ③ Lepar ⑪
Gelasa Strait
④ Tanjung Layar
Java Sea
Pajang
Teluk Semangka ② ② ② ① ③ Jakarta
Sunda Strait ④ ②
Merak ⑦ Tanjungpriok
Cigading
①
② Surabaya

INDIAN OCEAN

⑩ over 5 attacks
③ 1–5 attacks

0   200km
0   100 miles

Global Trends Worldwide internet usage

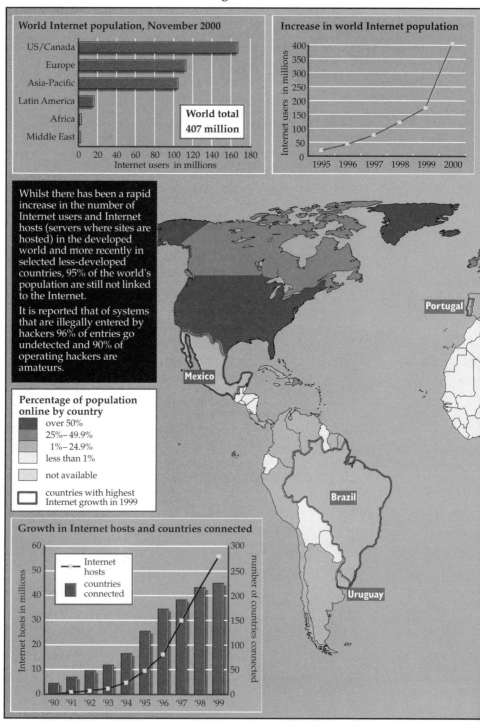

World Internet population, November 2000

US/Canada	
Europe	
Asia-Pacific	
Latin America	
Africa	
Middle East	

0 20 40 60 80 100 120 140 160 180
Internet users in millions

**World total
407 million**

Increase in world Internet population

Internet users in millions

400
350
300
250
200
150
100
50
0

1995 1996 1997 1998 1999 2000

Whilst there has been a rapid increase in the number of Internet users and Internet hosts (servers where sites are hosted) in the developed world and more recently in selected less-developed countries, 95% of the world's population are still not linked to the Internet.

It is reported that of systems that are illegally entered by hackers 96% of entries go undetected and 90% of operating hackers are amateurs.

**Percentage of population
online by country**

- over 50%
- 25%–49.9%
- 1%–24.9%
- less than 1%
- not available
- countries with highest Internet growth in 1999

Portugal

Mexico

Brazil

Uruguay

Growth in Internet hosts and countries connected

Internet hosts in millions

60
50
40
30
20
10
0

300
250
200
150
100
50
0

number of countries connected

— Internet hosts
■ countries connected

'90 '91 '92 '93 '94 '95 '96 '97 '98 '99

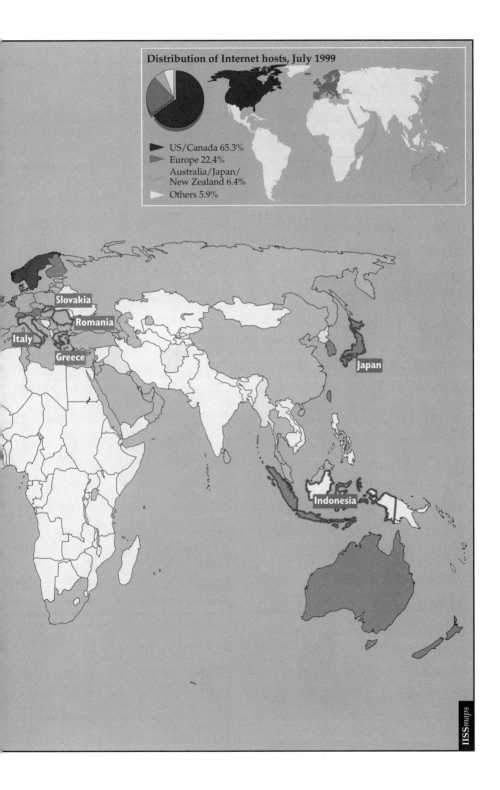

Distribution of Internet hosts, July 1999

- US/Canada 65.3%
- Europe 22.4%
- Australia/Japan/ New Zealand 6.4%
- Others 5.9%

Global Trends International terrorism

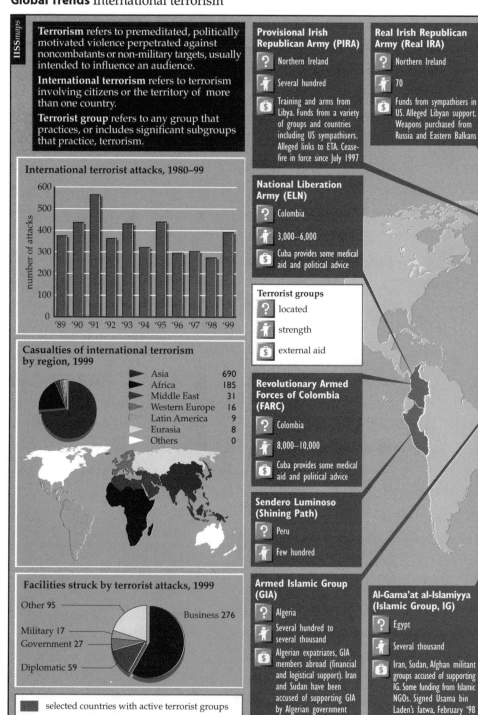

Terrorism refers to premeditated, politically motivated violence perpetrated against noncombatants or non-military targets, usually intended to influence an audience.

International terrorism refers to terrorism involving citizens or the territory of more than one country.

Terrorist group refers to any group that practices, or includes significant subgroups that practice, terrorism.

International terrorist attacks, 1980–99

number of attacks

'89 '90 '91 '92 '93 '94 '95 '96 '97 '98 '99

Casualties of international terrorism by region, 1999

Asia	690
Africa	185
Middle East	31
Western Europe	16
Latin America	9
Eurasia	8
Others	0

Facilities struck by terrorist attacks, 1999

Other 95
Business 276
Military 17
Government 27
Diplomatic 59

selected countries with active terrorist groups

Provisional Irish Republican Army (PIRA)

? Northern Ireland

👤 Several hundred

$ Training and arms from Libya. Funds from a variety of groups and countries including US sympathisers. Alleged links to ETA. Cease-fire in force since July 1997

Real Irish Republican Army (Real IRA)

? Northern Ireland

👤 70

$ Funds from sympathisers in US. Alleged Libyan support. Weapons purchased from Russia and Eastern Balkans

National Liberation Army (ELN)

? Colombia

👤 3,000–6,000

$ Cuba provides some medical aid and political advice

Terrorist groups

? located

👤 strength

$ external aid

Revolutionary Armed Forces of Colombia (FARC)

? Colombia

👤 8,000–10,000

$ Cuba provides some medical aid and political advice

Sendero Luminoso (Shining Path)

? Peru

👤 Few hundred

Armed Islamic Group (GIA)

? Algeria

👤 Several hundred to several thousand

$ Algerian expatriates, GIA members abroad (financial and logistical support). Iran and Sudan have been accused of supporting GIA by Algerian government

Al-Gama'at al-Islamiyya (Islamic Group, IG)

? Egypt

👤 Several thousand

$ Iran, Sudan, Afghan militant groups accused of supporting IG. Some funding from Islamic NGOs. Signed Usama bin Laden's fatwa, February '98

Basque Fatherland and Liberty (ETA)

? Spain

👤 Hundreds

💲 Training in Libya, Lebanon, Nicaragua. Some members receive sanctuary in Cuba. Alleged ties with the IRA

Kurdistan Workers' Party (PKK)

? Turkey

👤 10,000–15,000

💲 Aid from Syria, Iraq and Iran

Islamic Movement of Uzbekistan (IMU)

? Uzbekistan

👤 In thousands

💲 Support from other extremist Islamic groups in Central Asia

al-Qaida

? Afghanistan

👤 Several hundred to several thousand

💲 Maintains moneymaking businesses, collects donations. Sudan acts as meeting-place and safehaven

Harakat ul-Mujahidin (HIM)

? Pakistan (Kashmir)

👤 Several thousand armed supporters

💲 Donations from Saudi Arabia, other Gulf and Islamic states, Pakistanis and Kashmiris. Signed Usama bin Laden's fatwa February 1998

Abu Sayyaf Group (ASG)

? Philippines

👤 Est. 200 fighters

💲 Islamic extremists in Middle East and South Asia. Has been tied to the Mujaheddin

Liberation Tigers of Tamil Eelam (LTTE)

? Sri Lanka

👤 8,000–10,000

💲 Tamil communities in North America, Europe and Asia donate funds and supplies

al-Jihad

? Egypt (networks in Sudan, Afghanistan, Pakistan, UK)

👤 Several thousand

💲 Support from Iran, Sudan, militant Afghani Islamic groups according to government. Some funding through Islamic NGOs

Islamic Resistance Movement (HAMAS)

? Israel

👤 Unknown; tens of thousands of supporters

💲 Funding from Palestinian ex-patriates, Iran and private benefactors (Saudi Arabia, other moderate Arab states)

Hizbollah

? Lebanon

👤 Several thousand

💲 Substantial aid from Syria and Sudan. Sudan also acts as a safehaven and meeting-place

Mujaheddin-e Khalq Organisation (MEK/MKO)

? Iraq

👤 Several thousand

💲 Support from Iraq. Contributions from expatriate Iranian communities

Global Trends The spread of infectious diseases

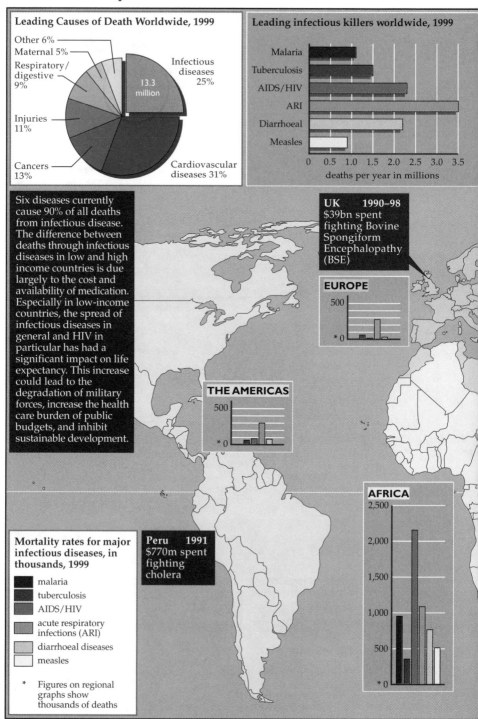

Leading Causes of Death Worldwide, 1999

Other 6%
Maternal 5%
Respiratory/digestive 9%
Injuries 11%
Cancers 13%
Infectious diseases 25%
13.3 million
Cardiovascular diseases 31%

Leading infectious killers worldwide, 1999

Malaria
Tuberculosis
AIDS/HIV
ARI
Diarrhoeal
Measles

0   0.5   1.0   1.5   2.0   2.5   3.0   3.5
deaths per year in millions

Six diseases currently cause 90% of all deaths from infectious disease. The difference between deaths through infectious diseases in low and high income countries is due largely to the cost and availability of medication. Especially in low-income countries, the spread of infectious diseases in general and HIV in particular has had a significant impact on life expectancy. This increase could lead to the degradation of military forces, increase the health care burden of public budgets, and inhibit sustainable development.

UK   1990–98
$39bn spent fighting Bovine Spongiform Encephalopathy (BSE)

EUROPE
500
*0

THE AMERICAS
500
*0

AFRICA
2,500
2,000
1,500
1,000
500
*0

Mortality rates for major infectious diseases, in thousands, 1999

- malaria
- tuberculosis
- AIDS/HIV
- acute respiratory infections (ARI)
- diarrhoeal diseases
- measles

*   Figures on regional graphs show thousands of deaths

Peru   1991
$770m spent fighting cholera

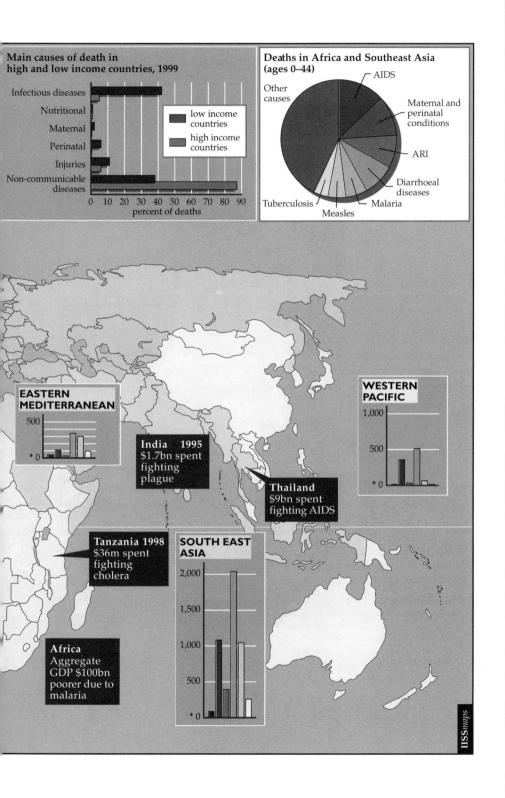

**Main causes of death in
high and low income countries, 1999**

Infectious diseases
Nutritional
Maternal
Perinatal
Injuries
Non-communicable
diseases

low income
countries

high income
countries

0 10 20 30 40 50 60 70 80 90
percent of deaths

**Deaths in Africa and Southeast Asia
(ages 0–44)**

Other
causes

AIDS

Maternal and
perinatal
conditions

ARI

Diarrhoeal
diseases

Tuberculosis

Measles

Malaria

**EASTERN
MEDITERRANEAN**

500

* 0

**WESTERN
PACIFIC**

1,000

500

* 0

India   1995
$1.7bn spent
fighting
plague

Thailand
$9bn spent
fighting AIDS

Tanzania 1998
$36m spent
fighting
cholera

**SOUTH EAST
ASIA**

2,000

1,500

1,000

500

* 0

Africa
Aggregate
GDP $100bn
poorer due to
malaria

IISS*maps*

Global Trends The global oil economy

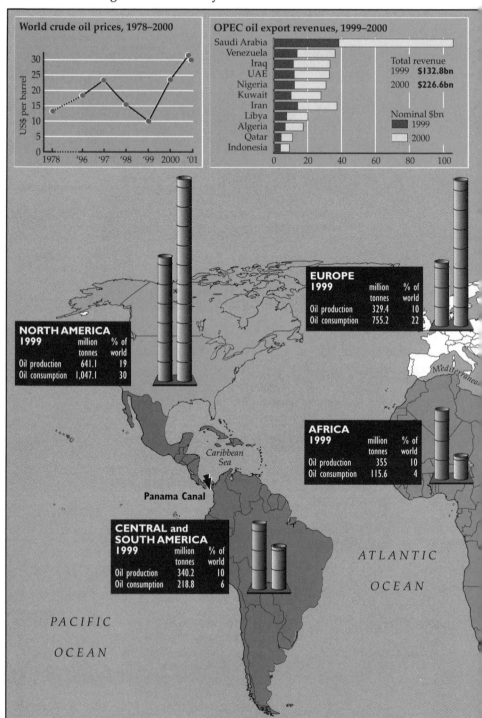

World crude oil prices, 1978–2000

US$ per barrel (y-axis: 0 to 30)
Years: 1978, '96, '97, '98, '99, 2000, '01

OPEC oil export revenues, 1999–2000

Saudi Arabia
Venezuela
Iraq
UAE
Nigeria
Kuwait
Iran
Libya
Algeria
Qatar
Indonesia

(x-axis: 0, 20, 40, 60, 80, 100)

Total revenue
1999 $132.8bn
2000 $226.6bn

Nominal $bn
1999
2000

EUROPE 1999

	million tonnes	% of world
Oil production	329.4	10
Oil consumption	755.2	22

NORTH AMERICA 1999

	million tonnes	% of world
Oil production	641.1	19
Oil consumption	1,047.1	30

AFRICA 1999

	million tonnes	% of world
Oil production	355	10
Oil consumption	115.6	4

Caribbean Sea

Panama Canal

CENTRAL and SOUTH AMERICA 1999

	million tonnes	% of world
Oil production	340.2	10
Oil consumption	218.8	6

Mediterranean

ATLANTIC OCEAN

PACIFIC OCEAN

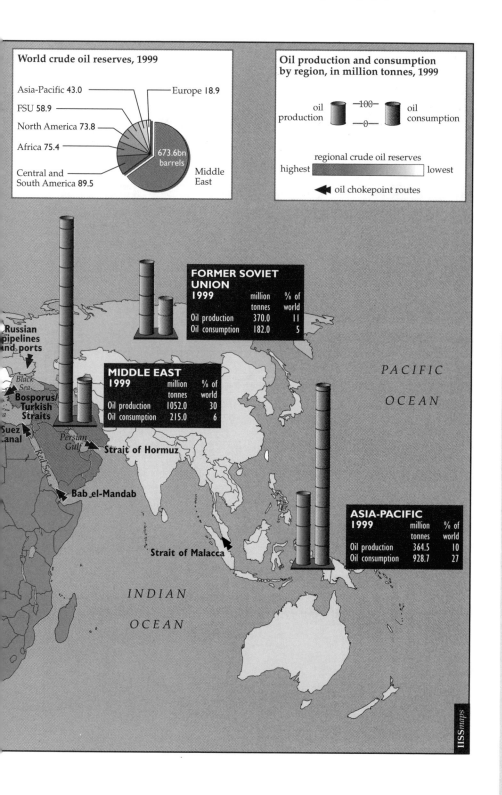

World crude oil reserves, 1999

Asia-Pacific 43.0 — — Europe 18.9
FSU 58.9 —
North America 73.8 —
Africa 75.4 —
673.6bn barrels
Central and — Middle
South America 89.5 East

Oil production and consumption by region, in million tonnes, 1999

oil production —100— oil consumption
—0—

regional crude oil reserves
highest | | lowest

◄ oil chokepoint routes

FORMER SOVIET UNION 1999

	million tonnes	% of world
Oil production	370.0	11
Oil consumption	182.0	5

MIDDLE EAST 1999

	million tonnes	% of world
Oil production	1052.0	30
Oil consumption	215.0	6

ASIA-PACIFIC 1999

	million tonnes	% of world
Oil production	364.5	10
Oil consumption	928.7	27

Russian pipelines and ports

Black Sea
Bosporus/ Turkish Straits
Suez Canal
Red Sea
Persian Gulf ◄ Strait of Hormuz
◄ Bab el-Mandab

Strait of Malacca ◄

PACIFIC OCEAN

INDIAN OCEAN

IISS*maps*

Global Trends Oil chokepoints

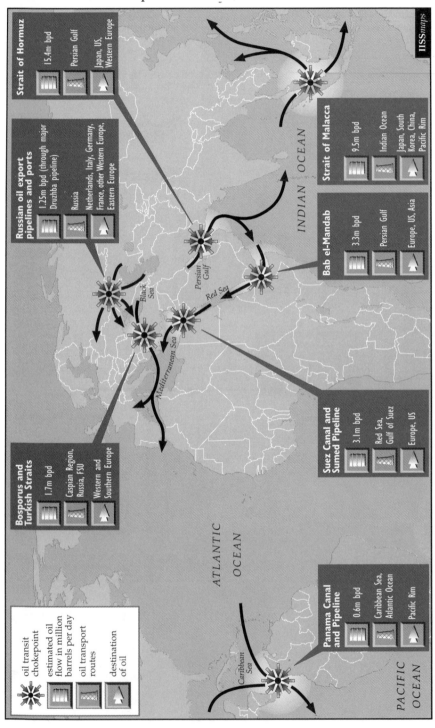

IISS*maps*

Strait of Hormuz
15.4m bpd
Persian Gulf
Japan, US, Western Europe

Russian oil export pipelines and ports
1.25m bpd (through major Druzhba pipeline)
Russia
Netherlands, Italy, Germany, France, other Western Europe, Eastern Europe

Strait of Malacca
9.5m bpd
Indian Ocean
Japan, South Korea, China, Pacific Rim

Bab el-Mandab
3.3m bpd
Persian Gulf
Europe, US, Asia

Bosporus and Turkish Straits
1.7m bpd
Caspian Region, Russia, FSU
Western and Southern Europe

Suez Canal and Sumed Pipeline
3.1m bpd
Red Sea, Gulf of Suez
Europe, US

Panama Canal and Pipeline
0.6m bpd
Caribbean Sea, Atlantic Ocean
Pacific Rim

INDIAN OCEAN

Persian Gulf

Red Sea

Black Sea

Mediterranean Sea

ATLANTIC OCEAN

PACIFIC OCEAN

Caribbean Sea

oil transit chokepoint
estimated oil flow in million barrels per day
oil transport routes
destination of oil